W9-AOG-402

WITHDRAWN

WITHDRAWN

Contemporary Portugal

António Costa Pinto
Edited by

Contemporary Portugal

politics,
society
and culture

SOCIAL SCIENCE MONOGRAPHS, BOULDER
DISTRIBUTED BY COLUMBIA UNIVERSITY PRESS, NEW YORK
2003

Published with the support of the

LUSO-AMERICAN
FOUNDATION

Copyright by António Costa Pinto
ISBN 0-88033-996-9
Library of Congress Catalog Card Number 2003110838
Printed in the United States of America

Contents

List of Tables and Figures   ix

Preface and acknowledgements   xi

1. Twentieth Century Portugal: An Introduction   I
   António Costa Pinto

2. Cultural Myths and Portuguese National Identity   47
   Nuno G. Monteiro and António Costa Pinto

3. The Colonial Empire   63
   Valentim Alexandre

4. Between Africa and Europe: Portuguese Foreign
   Policy, 1890-2000   85
   Nuno Severiano Teixeira

5. The Portuguese Economy in the Twentieth Century:
   Growth and Structural Change   119
   Pedro Lains

6. Portuguese Emigration After World War II   139
   Maria Ioannis B. Baganha

7. Social Change in Portugal: 1960-2000   159
   António Barreto

8. Elections, Parties, and Policy-Making Institutions in
   Democratic Portugal   183
   Pedro C. Magalhães

9. Legitimizing the EU? Elections to the European
   Parliament in Portugal, 1987-1999   203
   Marina Costa Lobo

10. Contemporary Portuguese Literature   227
    João Camilo dos Santos

11. Portuguese Art in the Twentieth Century   265
    João Pinharanda

Notes   297

Contributors   325

Index   329

List of Tables and Figures

TABLES

1.1 Ratio of Eligible to Actual Voters, 1911-1925   5

1.2 Distribution of Parties in Parliament, 1910-1917   6

1.3 Distribution of Parties in Parliament, 1919-1926   16

5.1 Growth of Real Income per capita in Portugal and
    Europe, 1910-1990   123

5.2 Growth of Real Income per capita in the European
    Periphery, 1913-1998   125

5.3 Convergence of Real Incomes per capita in the
    European Periphery, 1913-1998   126

5.4 Growth of Factors and GDP, 1910-1990   128

5.5 Growth Accounting for Portugal: Sources of Growth
    and Output Growth, 1910-1990   130

5.6 Sectoral Output and Productivity Growth, 1950-1990   134

6.1 Principal Destinations of Portuguese Legal Emigration,
    1950-1988   143

6.2 Principal Destinations of Portuguese Emigration,
    1950-1988   144

6.3 Percentage of Portuguese Emigration by District,
    1950-1988   147

6.4 Characteristics of Legal Migrants, 1955-1988 149

6.5 Demographic Evolution, 1951-1981 152

6.6 Portuguese Emigration by Destination, 1950-1988 156

8.1 Total and Interbloc Volatility in Portuguese Elections 190

8.2 Distribution of Seats and Votes in Legislative Elections 191

8.3 Portuguese Cabinets since 1976 195

8.4 Presidents and Cabinets, 1981-2002 198

9.1 Interest in European Election Campaign and Media
 Exposure to it 212

9.2 European Parliament Elections Results, 1987-1999 213

9.3 Participation in European Parliament Elections in
 EU Member States 217

9.4 Measuring the Individual Level Effects on Turnout at
 European Parliamentary Elections 218

9.5 Party Share of the Vote in National and European
 Parliamentary Elections 221

9.6 Number of Effective Parliamentary Parties in National
 and European Parliamentary Elections in Portugal
 and the EU, 1976-1999 223

FIGURES

5.1 Growth of Income per capita: Portugal and Average 9,
 1910-1998 123

6.1 Portuguese Emigration by Destination 145

8.1 Operational Properties of the Electoral System and Party
 System Fragmentation, 1975-2002 189

Preface and Acknowledgements

Portugal has undergone a significant process of change during the last 30 years. It has seen political transformation, marked by the end of 48 years of dictatorial rule and the consolidation of democracy. Economic and social change has taken place, with Portugal, once a backward and socially underdeveloped country becoming a developed nation. The aim of this book is to present an introduction to that process of change and to examine it as part of the evolution of Portuguese politics and society since the beginning of the twentieth century.

Written by historians, sociologists, political scientists and specialists in literature and art, this book seeks to provide specialists, students and general readers a global view of contemporary Portugal. Essays written by Portuguese academics explore a broad spectrum of topics: the colonial empire, international relations, economic development, patterns of emigration, social change, democratic consolidation, Portugal and the European Union, issues of national identity and characteristics of Portuguese contemporary literature and art.

There is a small history to this project of publishing new books on contemporary Portugal in English. It was during my stay as a Visiting Professor at Stanford University during 1992-1993, that I accepted the challenge of Peter Stansky, who was at that time a Professor in the Department of History, to produce the first such book, *Modern Portugal* (Palo Alto, 1998). This work was integrated into a

series of books on recent developments in various European countries. Given the lack of books in English on contemporary Portugal,
however, I felt it would be important to include an analysis of the
twentieth century as a whole, rather than limiting the book to only
the most recent developments in the country. I must confess that
when I embarked on this project, I did not imagine that the book
would be so successful, having been adopted as required reading in
various university courses, ranging from comparative politics
through European history to literature, and having been translated
into both Spanish and Portuguese.

This second book was conceived and planned during my time at
the University of California-Berkeley, where I was Luso-American
Foundation Visiting Fellow during the first semester of 2000-2001.
Some of the authors of chapters included in this book also participated in a conference that Beverly Crawford and I organized, and
which took place at the Institute of European Studies in November
2002 as part of the Institute's Portuguese Studies Program.

This new book incorporates some of the suggestions that were
made in many of the reviews of *Modern Portugal*; limitations of space
have prevented me from developing all of the themes that I would
have liked to, however. Nevertheless, I hope that the topics covered
in these chapters will provide a good basis for further study by a
wider English-language readership in the various fields and disciplines of the social sciences and humanities.

Publication of this book would not have been possible had it not
been for the support of the Luso-American Foundation for Development (FLAD) and its president, Rui Machete, whose efficiency
and lack of bureaucratic delay is a rare thing in Portugal.

The establishment of FLAD, a foundation created to foster scientific and cultural relations between Portugal and the United States,
has strengthened the field. Contracts and agreements with North
American universities and research centers have increased notably.
Further evidence of a rapidly developing field of study is provided
by the creation of Visiting Professorships at Brown, Georgetown,
Chicago, Massachusetts-Dartmouth and the University of Califor-

nia-Berkeley; of Visiting Fellowships at Princeton and Stanford Universities; and by the consolidation of a network of contacts with Portuguese universities and cultural institutions, such as the programs for research missions at both the Portuguese National Library and the National Archives (ANTT).

I would also like to acknowledge the support of Lisbon University's Social Science Institute and give thanks to Stewart Lloyd-Jones of the CPHRC for his invaluable assistance in translating several chapters and editing the book within the very tight deadlines. Last, but not least, I would like to thank Gerald Feldman, Director of the Institute of European Studies of UC-Berkeley, and Shawn Parkhurst, formerly responsible for the Portuguese Studies Program, for the excellent working conditions and stimulating intellectual environment at the IES, where I completed this project.

António Costa Pinto

I Twentieth-Century Portugal: An Introduction

António Costa Pinto

The "age of the masses" was inaugurated in Portugal without the upheavals affecting parallel processes of democratic regime crisis and overthrow in inter-war Europe. On the eve of the twentieth century, Portugal, an old nation-state with political frontiers unchanged since the late middle ages, was the "ideal" state envisioned by liberal nationalists. State and nation coincided in conditions of cultural homogeneity. There were no national or ethno-cultural minorities in Portugal, or Portuguese populations in neighboring countries; similarly, Portugal had no religious or ethno-linguistic minorities. Dialects were rare, found only in some areas near the Spanish border. Portugal had no territorial claims in Europe, thus the historical and cultural variables so markedly present in other cases were either negligible or absent in the case of Portugal.[1]

Portugal's imperial and colonial past, however, is vital to understanding the country's history. From the seventeenth century on, Portugal was both an imperial power and a political and economic dependency of Britain; indeed, Britain protected the country's vast colonial empire. Africa had been the stronghold of Portuguese colonialism since Brazilian independence in 1822, but at the end of the nineteenth century, Portugal's "historical rights" in Africa were threatened by other European powers.

Tensions with Britain increased dramatically in the 1880s, culminating in the Ultimatum of 1890, which foiled Portuguese aspira-

tions to what is now Zimbabwe. Britain forced Portugal to abandon
its project to unify Angola and Mozambique by threatening to
invade the country. This episode gave rise to modern Portuguese
nationalism; it provoked the first wave of anti-British sentiment,
cementing what was to become the mainstay of Portuguese foreign
policy until the 1970s: the defense of the colonial empire.[2] Indeed,
"the identification of the colonial empire with nationalism in Portugal is a functional equivalent of [the] divisive nation-state issues"
that plagued other contemporary European societies.[3]

Portugal stood on the periphery of the world economy.[4] Its own
economy was backward, with a weak and sparse industrial base.[5] In
1911, Portugal had about 5.5 million inhabitants. The economically
active population stood at 2,545,000. Of these, 58 per cent worked
in agriculture, 25 per cent in industry, and 17 per cent in the tertiary sector. By 1930, the active population in agriculture had
decreased by three per cent, the tertiary sector had increased by three
per cent, and the secondary sector had remained stable.[6]

Levels of urbanization were also low. Between 1900 and 1930,
the number of people living in cities or towns with more than
20,000 inhabitants increased from 10.5 per cent to 13.9 per cent. Of
these, eight per cent lived in Lisbon. The second largest city, Oporto, trailed far behind. These were the only centers of "urban political culture" in Portugal. Few of the country's cities were more than
towns or large villages. Even considering concentrations of 10,000
as urban, the numbers do not differ significantly. The rural and village world dominated Portuguese society, accounting for more than
80 per cent of the population in 1930. After the 1920s, urban growth
was extremely slow and modestly paced. It was only in the 1960s
that the growth rate picked up. Even so, in 1960, only 23 per cent
of the population was urban, and 77 per cent was still rural.

Late nineteenth-century Portugal was a non-industrialized country governed by a stable, "oligarchic parliamentarism".[7] The dynamic of social and economic change was similar to that of other peripheral countries, which, according to Nicos Mouzelis, experienced
"early parliamentarism and late industrialization."[8] At the turn of the

century, however, Portugal's oligarchic and "clientelistic" liberalism—based on the exploitation of the African colonies and on a timid import-substituting industrialization—began to come apart. The republican movement, which mobilized large sections of the previously "politically excluded" urban middle- and lower middle-class, heralded the regime crisis.

From the beginning of the twentieth century, the republicans managed to erode the "clientelist" system, based on monarchical "rotativism," through a strategy of populist electoral and social mobilization. The Republican Party's program was very flexible: it made successful use of nationalist, anticlerical themes, as well as advocating political participation and the right to strike—one demand of the feeble labor movement. On the eve of the 1910 Revolution, the republicans were a mixed political group. At one extreme stood the moderate electoral faction, at the other, the authoritarian Jacobins. The coalition included secret groups of radical republicans, such as the *Carbonária,* and anarchists which had a strong popular base in Lisbon, and which worked within local party committees.[9]

Although most armed forces units remained neutral during the October 1910 overthrow of the constitutional monarchy, the coup was led by republican military officers, aided and abetted by civilians, as well as by members of the *Carbonária* (mostly sergeants and corporals). Portugal thereby became one of Europe's first republics, and republican elites undertook a timid "mass nationalization," always conscious of the social and political hold that the rural areas still exerted on Portuguese society.

The First Republic: Dominant Party Parliamentarism

When the republicans overthrew the constitutional monarchy and began to implement their political program, Portuguese society did not entirely fulfill the economic, social and cultural requirements for "the formation of a civic political culture." This is clear even without applying the more extreme theories that correlate economic and social development with democratic consolidation.[10]

The republican elites adopted a program of universal suffrage, anticlericalism and anti-British nationalism in defense of the colonial empire. Secularizing legislation was passed as early as 1910. It was accompanied by the emergence of a strong urban, anticlerical movement. These measures were modeled after those undertaken five years earlier by the Third French Republic, and they had a profound impact on the Catholic hierarchy. The extension of universal suffrage, however, was not decreed as promised, because of the dangerous monarchical revolts that broke out in Spain.[11]

The Democratic Party, successor to the Republican Party after the defection of key leaders in the wake of the revolution, inherited the electoral machine of the liberal monarchy and became the ruling party.

The political system became what Mattei Dogan (referring to Romania) has called a "mimic democracy."[12] The Portuguese system differs from Dogan's model in certain ways, however. First, the "political game" was not limited to the top of the social pyramid, as under the constitutional monarchy. Second, the landed gentry either lost access to the state or found new social and political mediators. Third, the state and the Church were not mutually supportive; this created a new political cleavage between the secular and religious arenas. Fourth, the state became more vulnerable to ideological pressure, and began to transcend its previous role as "traditional tax collector." Fifth, "semi-traditional" political clienteles changed. Finally, the urban world entered the political arena, thereby destabilizing it.

The establishment of a parliamentary regime with the approval of the 1911 Constitution was undertaken by a parliament dominated almost entirely by the Republican Party. According to the new constitution, the president was elected by parliament that he had no powers to dissolve. The republicans still did not implement universal suffrage, arguing that *caciquismo* in the countryside made such a policy impossible. Indeed, pressures for universal suffrage were very limited, if not entirely absent, at the Republican Constitutional Assembly of 1911. Pressure "from below" was also very weak, both because of the "absence" of the rural world from the political arena and the anti-participatory tendencies of the "active minorities" among the urban working classes.[13]

Curiously, it was the more conservative, dissident sectors of the Republican Party that occasionally debated the problem. Political participation was thus restricted to literate males. The electoral laws restricted proportional representation to Oporto and Lisbon, the electoral fiefdom of the Democratic Party. Majoritarian rule governed the rest of country (see table 1.1).

The republic put an end to the two-party system of the constitutional monarchy, replacing it with a dominant-party, multi-party system. The Republican Party had been the first quasi-mass party under the liberal regime. With the Revolution of 1910, dissident conservative members of the party created the Unionist and the Evolutionist parties. These, however, were never more than groups of notables.

TABLE 1.1
Ratio of Eligible to Actual Voters, 1911–1925

	Electorate	Voters	Percent
1911	846,801	250,000[a]	–
1913	397,038	150,000[b]	–
1915	471,560	282,387	59.9
1919	500,000	300,000	60.0
1921	550,000	350,000	63.6
1922	550,000	380,000	69.0
1925	574,260	407,960	71.0

[a] Only 26 electoral constituencies voted.
[b] Only 28 electoral constituencies voted.
SOURCE: F. F. Lopes, *Poder político e caciquismo na I* República* (Lisbon: Estampa, 1994).

The electoral hegemony of the Democratic Party was immediately established as it inherited the machinery of the Republican Party. It used the state to become "the main provider of patronage."[14] Limited suffrage enabled the Democratic Party to work out a compromise between its urban, petite-bourgeois electoral base and key provincial notables, who guaranteed its control of the system.

From the turn of century, the Democratic Party acquired a strong and stable electoral and political base (see table 1.2). It was the only truly national party. Radical petite-bourgeois and popular urban networks were central to its survival, both at the ballot box and in the streets, when it faced extra-parliamentary or presidential challenges. The party complemented the "legal" electoral system with violent attacks on monarchical, conservative republican and military opponents who operated in the electoral as well as the extra-parliamentary arena.

The political articulation between the urban and rural worlds was ensured through the "governmentalization" of local administration. The district governors sustained the clientelistic pacts that ensured the party's victory in rural areas. The Democratic Party thus acquired "a 'dual' structure and a 'dual' clientele with noncompetitive yet asymmetric ideological orientations."[15] Although this uneasy coalition between urban Jacobins and rural notables ensured the Democratic Party almost permanent electoral domination during the republican period, it was not "sufficient to ensure a genuine, permanent monopoly of political power... in the manner of dominant parties in semi-liberal politics."[16]

The Unionist and Evolutionist parties were both led by centrist or right-wing parliamentary factions that had left the Republican

TABLE 1.2
Distribution of Parties in Parliament, 1910-1917

	1911		1913		1915	
	Seats	%	Seats	%	Seats	%
Republican	229	97.9	–	–	–	–
Independent	3	1.3	12	7.7	13	8.0
Socialist	2	0.8	1	0.6	2	1.2
Democratic	–	–	82	52.6	106	65.0
Evolutionist	–	–	36	23.1	26	16.0
Unionist	–	–	25	16.0	15	9.2
Catholic	–	–	–	–	1	0.6
TOTAL	234	100.0	156	100.0	163	100.0

SOURCE: F. F. Lopes, *Poder político e Caciquismo na Iª República* (Lisbon: Estampa, 1994).

Party in 1912. As key "system" parties, they lobbied in favor of electoral constituency reform, and they advocated moderation in church-state relations. They also sought clienteles in the provinces, where they established local fiefdoms.

Left-wing opposition was insignificant: indeed, until the onset of World War I, the Democratic Party suffered no left-leaning splits. Furthermore, the two parliamentary seats in the hands of the Socialist Party were Democratic Party "gifts."[17] As far as the right was concerned, a semi-loyal conservative republican opposition operated until the establishment of the Sidónio Pais dictatorship in 1918. As all attempts to reform the political system and to unify conservative forces electorally failed during the 1920s, however, conservative elites came to believe that they would never achieve power, either electorally or constitutionally.

Endemic Cabinet Instability

Electoral stability and cabinet instability characterized the republican era. Between 1910 and 1926, 45 cabinets were formed. Of these, 17 were single-party cabinets, three were military, and 21 resulted from coalition governments.[18] The Democratic Party dominated cabinets between 1912 and 1917, but the conservative republican parties gained a foothold in some.

The first serious challenge to Democratic Party hegemony occurred in 1915 when the cabinet collapsed as a result of a military coup supported by the president and the conservative parties. In January 1915, under military pressure, the president nominated General Pimenta de Castro as prime minister. Pimenta de Castro headed a cabinet with a strong military component. Pressures to suspend parliament, to change the electoral law and to convene elections were strong. Only months later, however, an uprising was led by armed civilians backed by key military units, which reinstated the Democrats, caused 150 deaths, and left 300 wounded.

In June 1915, the Democratic Party won the elections again and began preparing for participation in World War I. From that time on, the party led successive coalition governments until Sidónio Pais's 1917 coup. The conservative republican parties supported these coalition governments, but whether conservatives, "neutrals" or a parliamentary Democratic majority led them, the coalition governments also proved unstable. Indeed, they experienced the greatest level of turnover and the lowest duration, lasting an average of 91 days compared with those of single-party governments, which lasted an average of 156 days.[19]

Although endemic throughout the Republican era, cabinet turnover peaked in the immediate postwar period. Postwar cabinet instability differed from prewar instability in two ways. First, economic policy issues, rather than issues of "political access," were the causes of instability, revealing the increasingly important role played by socio-economic cleavages and interest groups in political struggle. A study comparing cabinets and economic policy to see whether the former favored industry or agriculture, urban consumers or social pacts, shows that the attitude of economic interest groups was a key to the formation and fall of cabinets. The same study also highlights the role played by the "extra-parliamentary arena" in promoting cabinet instability.[20] Second, the postwar period was characterized by the increased fragmentation of the party system. Left-wing splits now afflicted the Democratic Party, and prewar Evolutionists and Unionists failed in their attempts to establish a conservative electoral machine.

Key Sociopolitical Cleavages

The first post-1910 cleavage was religious. Secularization had been a central republican propaganda theme, and during the first days of the Revolution, an anticlerical movement swept Lisbon. Convents were closed down and religious orders, such as the Jesuits, were expelled from the country. On 3 November, a divorce law was decreed; a month later, a law was passed that made marriage "exclusively civil." Strict limitations were imposed on non-Church religious ceremonies. All state religious rites in the courts the universities and the armed forces were abolished. By the beginning of 1911, approximately 150 priests were in prison, charged with various acts of disobedience.[21] When the Church hierarchy reacted to the new curbs, the government prohibited the reading of the pastoral letter: this led to the severance of Portuguese relations with the Vatican and of ties between bishops and the state.

The religious-secular cleavage became a focal point of Portuguese political life. It lasted until 1926, despite subsequent pacification measures. A new Catholic movement emerged from this conflict. It was authoritarian and closely linked to the hierarchy. The Catholic Center Party (CCP) naturally filled the "space" for a Christian-Democratic or "popular" party. Initially social-Catholic, the CCP became corporatist and authoritarian and supported the Pais dictatorship in 1917.

The second cleavage of this period was the republican-monarchical split, also known as the "regime question." It was expressed in the resistance to the republican regime of a small but relatively strong nucleus of monarchists, who were not connected with the liberal parties that had been dissolved in 1910.

In 1911 and 1912, two monarchist incursions, launched from Galicia, were led by a former officer of caesarist leanings, Paiva Couceiro, who had led the African occupation campaigns at the turn of the century. Paiva Couceiro was accompanied by a number of young men who later, on their return from exile in 1914, would create the *Integralismo Lusitano* (IL) movement. The Integralist movement was based on the Maurrasian ideology that had guided *Action Française*. It also influenced the CCP.

The third major cleavage of the 1910s was the urban-rural divide. It expressed a struggle for political access to the state and governmental decision-making, particularly after the war. It centered on a conflict between the rural, *latifundio*-based "traditional elite" and the leaders of industry. The inability of successive cabinets to deal with these divisions was central to the breakdown of the regime. This is why António de Oliveira Salazar later reshaped the political arena to protect the "traditional sector" and prolong its social and political power. Indeed, the *Estado Novo* (New State) used the political system, as well as state intervention and economic policy, to ensure the continued domination of the traditional sector.

Participation in World War I

The war had an immediate destabilizing impact on Portugal. The republicans had unanimously supported participation in the Great War, in the belief that it would guarantee the safety of the African colonies. But because Britain seemed prepared to "give" Germany some of those colonies, the Democratic Party concluded that neutrality was dangerous, and became the greatest champion of military participation on the European front. The Democrats believed, furthermore, that Portuguese participation in the peace negotiations would consolidate the country's international position.

In supporting participation, however, the Democratic Party also pursued its own internal political objectives. Ensuring the safety of the African colonies did not justify action on the European front, *per se*; Great Britain did not demand intervention on the basis of the Anglo-Portuguese Alliance: intervention in Africa alone, an option defended by conservative republicans, would have been sufficient. However, the Democratic Party sought to consolidate its control over the political system through nationalist and patriotic mobilization. It hoped to force the other parties to co-operate in a *union sacré* of sorts, to legitimate greater repressive control over political dissidents and to tone down political and social cleavages.[22]

The Democratic Party's expectations quickly collapsed. The issue of intervention divided the armed forces, leading to the emergence of a faction that favored intervention in Africa alone. Not trusting the army, the government set up a special intervention force, the Portuguese Expeditionary Corps, which was led by loyal republican military officers and manned by militia officers. In October 1914, however, a group of officers occupied a barracks and declared themselves against participation, foreshadowing the short-lived military government of 1915 and the coup led by Sidónio Pais in 1917.[23]

Despite the rebellion, the government was able to ensure participation in the war. In 1916 and 1917, approximately two-thirds of the army was dispatched abroad. Flanders received 55,000 Portuguese soldiers and the colonies 45,000. Of the former, 35,000 were either killed or wounded.[24]

The Democratic Party took it for granted that the rest of the republican parties would want to participate in its *union sacré*, but the Evolutionists, initially willing, soon abandoned the coalition. The Unionist Party on the other hand, was opposed to intervention in Europe from the start. Both parties feared the social and political effects of participation, which had already led to riots in Lisbon and raids on shops because of food shortages, and had brought more strikes led by revolutionary syndicalist unions opposed to the war. In response to these events, the government declared a state of siege in Lisbon on 12 July 1917, and harshly repressed a general strike in September of the same year, arresting revolutionary syndicalists *en masse*.[25]

An Authoritarian Interlude: the Pais Dictatorship (1917-1918)

Sidónio Pais put his military past at the service of his charismatic image, but his background was not really military; he was part of the conservative republican elite, a professor at the University of Coimbra and a Member of Parliament for the Unionist Party. He had held ministerial posts twice, and had been ambassador to Berlin in 1916 when Germany declared war on Portugal.

The 1917 coup was initially planned with the support of conservative republican notables from the Unionist Party, and it owed its success to the rapid erosion of support for the Democratic Party's war policy. Indeed, the military units that played a decisive role in the coup were preparing to leave for the front. An ambiguous coalition of groups adopted a position of "co-operative neutrality" *vis-à-vis* the coup. A delegation of unions visited Pais when he was directing military operations in the center of Lisbon, promising the future dictator their support in return for the release of political prisoners.

Not long after coming to power, Pais exiled a good part of the republican elite, broke with the 1911 Constitution and proceeded with the institutionalization of a plebiscitary, presidentialist dictatorship. Large crowds mobilized by the clergy proclaimed Pais the "savior of Portugal" during a triumphant tour of the provinces. Pais introduced universal male suffrage and became the self-elected president of the republic. He took control of the executive arm of the government, which the conservative republican parties had abandoned, and created a National Republican Party (NRP), the only republican party contesting the elections. Apart from the NRP, only the monarchists and the Catholics were represented in Parliament. The monarchists supported the regime and were reinstated in institutions such as the military; the Church supported Pais to the very end because he revoked the most radical anticlerical legislation and re-established relations with the Vatican.

The new political system constituted an experiment with corporatist representation. The bicameral system was maintained, but the new Senate included representatives of employers' associations, the trade unions, the industrial sectors and the professions. It was not long, however, before the Senate was sidelined; Pais sent both houses into recess and governed alone, increasingly confident of his charismatic leadership.

In the face of war provoked general shortages, Pais's political discourse was anti-plutocratic. It emphasized the struggle against party oligarchies and propounded a messianic nationalism. Pais brought the monarchists and the conservative republicans together; he also effectively attracted the support of a group of young army officers.

In late 1918, Pais was assassinated by a former rural trade unionist. The dictatorship did not survive the death of its leader and the outbreak of a monarchist revolt in the north heralded the end of the regime. A local military junta in Oporto proclaimed the return of the monarchy, and an insurrection erupted in Lisbon.

In response, the Republicans mobilized in the cities, and several military units declared themselves neutral, permitting the victory of the Democrats and a return to constitutional rule. The Democratic

Party promoted what was effectively its last popular mobilization in Lisbon against the monarchist revolt. Some military units handed out arms to party members, while others prepared to move north. By the end of January 1918, the provisional monarchical government in Oporto had been defeated. In Lisbon, rallies and demonstrations led to the dissolution of parliament and the pro-monarchist political police. The government took refuge in a barracks: a few days later, the Sidonistas resigned.

Thus, the collapse of Sidónio Pais's regime further disrupted an army divided and politicized by participation in the war. Many of the officers who had fought at the front had been unhappy with Sidónio's "war abandonment" strategy. They had also resented the monarchist officers who had joined the dictator. Military juntas were therefore set up in a number of cities after the assassination, emitting diverse political pronouncements, which forced the government's hand. Monarchical, Sidonist and republican "military barons" made their first and last appearance during this period of crisis. Finally, the re-emergence of the old "regime question" shattered the unity of conservative forces and almost threw the country into civil war.

This convulsive period was followed by several failed attempts to form a conservative party capable of opposing the Democratic Party in the elections. The Democrats won the elections of 1919, gaining 53 per cent of the seats in the House of Deputies and reinstated the Constitution of 1911.

The Crisis and Breakdown of the Republic

Participation in World War I did not seriously damage Portugal's productive or social structure, as had been the case in the countries of central Europe. Nor did it favor the emergence of groups able to form strong fascist movements. Portugal had suffered its war "humiliations" and the decimation of its frontline battalions midway through the Pais dictatorship, during which participation in the war had also ended. The republicans had managed to mobilize many veterans who felt betrayed by the monarchists and by the regiments that refused to leave for France. Nevertheless, this reaction did not lead to the emergence of a veterans' movement: either veterans were rapidly absorbed into rural society, or they opted for emigration. The *vitória mancata* was only moderately felt in Portugal, moreover, for the country had managed to safeguard its colonies and had no territorial claims in Europe.

In general, the prewar characteristics of the political system continued to prevail. Universal suffrage remained unimplemented and the formal political system was basically unchanged. Some changes did occur, however. The Pais dictatorship and the state of near civil war that followed its fall led to the first pact among political parties for a revision of the 1911 Constitution and for the stabilization of the political system. This pact led to a first, important change: in 1919 the Democrats granted the president powers to dissolve parliament after restricting the power of cabinets between dissolution and elections. This measure, however, established a direct channel for extra-parliamentary pressures over the presidency.

A second important change was the demise of the historic leaders of the pre-1917 period. Afonso Costa, the strongman of the Democratic Party, did not return from exile; António José de Almeida and Brito Camacho left the Evolutionist and Unionist parties.

A third change was an increasing fragmentation of the party system.[26] The Democratic Party suffered both left- and right-wing splits; small but highly ideological parties appeared in both the parliamentary (the CCP and the Democratic Left) and the extra-parliamentary arena (the Communist Party in 1921 and the Sidonists from 1919 on).

In 1919, the conservatives (including the Unionist, Evolutionist, and Centrist parties) united under the new Liberal Party banner. The Liberal Party became an embryonic electoral machine opposed to the dominant party. In 1921, for the first time in the electoral history of the republic, the Democratic Party was defeated and its monopoly on power jeopardized. The Liberal cabinets also fell, however, because of an insurrection led by the National Republican

Guard to dissolve the 1921 parliament. After 1921, conservative representation split again into several parties (*Governamentais, Nacionalistas,* and *Populares*) and authoritarian pressures increased.

Despite splits in the Democratic Party with the emergence of the *Reconstituintes* on the right in 1920, and the formation of the "democratic left" in 1925, the party maintained its dominant position. Nevertheless, its "asymmetrical," clientelistic machine caused it to suffer severe losses among urban voters. Manipulation and violence surrounding electoral activity increased dramatically. The lack of a well-defined party policy, resulting from two conflicting tendencies within the party structure, one moderate and another more left-wing, exacerbated divisions.

The Democratic Party survived the postwar economic and social crisis and the 1925 elections put it back in the seat of power. By this point, however, the main arena for political battle were already outside parliament. A new political actor emerged: a federation of employers' associations, the UIE, which supported a clearly antidemocratic platform, but which used elections and parliament to sell its ideas (see table 1.3).

In the extra-parliamentary sphere, the state, employers in urban industry and the trade and service sectors viewed 1919 to 1922 as the years of the "red threat". The "golden age" of the anarcho-syndicalist *Confederação Geral do Trabalho* (CGT—General Labour Confederation) was marked by a wave of strikes, which affected a range of sectors. As the union movement declined in strength, terrorism emerged. The conservative media demonized clandestine organizations, such as the Red Legion. The Democratic Party opened up the electoral machine, which allowed the Socialist Party to win eight parliamentary seats in 1919; however, all attempts to integrate the working class and the left failed.[27]

The employers' associations, affected by these almost exclusively urban movements, strengthened their federations and dramatically increased their intervention in political life. By the end of 1922, the "red threat" had been eliminated and labor confrontations were on the decrease. Studies linking the politicization of employers' associations and the authoritarian takeover of power prove that intra-

TABLE 1.3
Distribution of Parties in Parliament, 1919-1926

	1919-21		1921		1922-25		1925-26	
	Seats	%	Seats	%	Seats	%	Seats	%
Democratic	86	52.8	54	33,1	71	44.6	83	50.9
Evolutionist	38	23.3	–	–	–	–	–	–
Unionist	17	10.4	–	–	–	–	–	–
Independent	13	8.0	5	3.1	5	3.1	19	11.7
"Reconstituinte"	–	–	12	7.4	17	10.7	–	–
Socialist	8	4.9	–	–	–	–	2	1.2
Catholic	1	0.6	3	1.8	5	3.1	4	2.4
Liberal	–	–	79	48.5	33	20.8	–	–
Monarchist	–	–	4	2.5	13	8.2	7	4.3
"Dissidente"	–	–	3	1.8	–	–	–	–
Regionalist	–	–	2	1.2	2	1.3	–	–
"Popular"	–	–	1	0.6	–	–	–	–
"Governamentais"	–	–	–	–	13	8.2	–	–
Nacionalist	–	–	–	–	–	–	36	22.1
DemocraticLeft	–	–	–	–	–	–	6	3.7
UIE	–	–	–	–	–	–	6	3.7
TOTAL	163	100.0	163	100.0	159	100.0	163	100.0

SOURCES: A. H. Oliveira Marques, *A Iª República: as estruturas de base* (Lisbon: Iniciativas Editoriais, 1975); F. F: Lopes, *Poder político e Caciquismo na Iª República* (Lisbon: Estampa, 1994).

bourgeois economic conflict was more significant than bourgeois-worker conflict.[28]

Conservative republican parties and the groups of notables representing economic interests had become accustomed to using extra-parliamentary means to gain power. The radicalization of the small conservative republican parties was a key factor in the fall of the republic; it led them to appeal to the military when the Democratic Party won the elections of 1925.[29]

The most important factor unifying the new extreme right in the 1920s was the emergence of groups influenced by Italian fascism and the dictatorship of Primo de Rivera in Spain. A new generation of young Sorelian Integralists emerged, which postponed the republic-monarchy cleavage. Organizations such as the Nuno Álvares Crusade testify to this; it united Sidonistas, Catholics, Integralists, and fascists. The Integralists received significant support from members of the armed forces, who played an important antidemocratic role in some conspiratorial groups.

The Integralists themselves played a key role in conspiratorial and propaganda activities, unlike the CCP, which was linked to the Church hierarchy and was, therefore, more cautious. An important sector of the civilian radical right had lent support to the 1926 coup. Charismatic leaders emerged who joined the small and elitist extreme right-wing group supporting military intervention, and the formation of organized groups inside the armed forces. Francisco Cunha Leal, a leader of the Nationalist Party, is an example. Leal had advocated military intervention since 1923, negotiating a *post facto* political arrangement with military factions. Such groups were instrumental in giving the military a political program that transcended a mere call for "order in the streets and in the government."

Military intervention in republican politics predated the postwar period, as did persistent factionalism in the ranks of the military. The main difference between the prewar interventions and the 1926 coup lies in three factors: the proliferation of corporate tensions within the army, increasing tensions of the same kind within the government and the growing unity of the military when intervening in the political arena.[30]

Tracing the roots of the 1926 coup to previous conspiracies and to personalistic military players is an *evenementielle* trap. Indeed, as one US historian has said, Portugal had been living "in the kingdom of the *pronunciamento*" since 1918.[31] It is therefore important to find other explanations for the 1926 military coup.

The situation between December 1918 and February 1919 had been particularly devastating for the army, with military juntas emerging throughout the country and the renewed "regime question," particularly in the wake of the proclamation of the monarchy in Oporto. In addition to monarchist officers, the Sidonist regime had attracted an increasing number of young cadets and officers, all associated with the civilian radical right, which was involved in various conspiracies throughout the early 1920s. The Democratic Party was thus confronted with a new army after the war. This army had acquired a troop corps twice its 1911 size, with new, prestigious leaders who had returned from the battlefront. A new, militaristic ideology emerged.

The nearly 2,000 supposedly temporary militia officers were a key problem. Elsewhere in Europe, officer corps had been demobilized; however, in Portugal the government had incorporated militia officers into the regular ranks. In 1919, this "political" incorporation had increased the number of regular army officers to 4,500, while in 1915 they had numbered 2,600.[32] Whether this gesture was a response to the dangers of demobilization or an instrument of political patronage, it provoked tension between the army and the civilian government. This tension became particularly acute during a hyperinflationary period, when the purchasing power of a captain's salary in 1919, for example, had declined to 60 per cent of its 1914 value.

Its lack of trust in the army led the government to reinforce the staff and armament of the *Guarda Nacional Republicana* (GNR— National Republican Guard) between 1919 and 1921. The number of GNR officers increased from 5,000 in 1911 to 11,000 in 1922. The GNR "was strengthened as an urban defender of the state" against the working class and the army; it "became one more element of the bureaucracy associated with the Democrats' control of the government."[33] A second source of tension was thus created. The prime minister was later forced to weaken the GNR, not only to discourage insurrections, but also to calm the army.

On 18 April 1925, a group of military officers carried out the first open coup attempt in the name of the armed forces; however, resistance from some military units and the GNR led to the insurrection being aborted. A few months later, a military court sent those involved back to the barracks. Appeals for a military interregnum had reached a fever pitch.

The key difference between this coup and that of 1926 lies in the rise of an "anti-system coalition." The military coup that put an end to the parliamentary republic on 28 May 1926 was more than a praetorian intervention. An army that had been divided and politicized by participation in the war, and by conservative republican, social-Catholic and Integralist factions operating within it, overthrew republican liberalism. Fascist groups exerted a particularly important influence over young officers who had supported the dictatorship of Sidónio Pais.

The Rise of Fascism

The rise of fascism in postwar Portugal was characterized by the early adoption of the Italian model, and by fascism's feeble and fragmented party political expression.[34] Many of the groups that emerged, however, were not strictly fascist: in many cases, the concept of the radical right is more appropriate to characterize them. The composition of the Sidónio Pais Center Party in 1921 shows the rise of military participation in these groups: 19 of its 33 leaders were officers, mostly from the army. Many of the intellectuals involved, such as António Ferro, were active participants in the Portuguese futurist movement. Ferro later moderated his fascist ideas and served the Salazar regime as propaganda chief.

The first publications heralding "Portuguese fascism" emerged in 1923 when the first fascist party, *Nacionalismo Lusitano* (NL—Lusitanian Nationalism), was founded. NL was not just an ideological party: it was a militia movement. *Integralismo Lusitano* also developed fascist-type organizations. Rolão Preto, chief of the IL's "social" department, created a "syndicalist" party section and founded a newspaper called *Revolução* (1922-23). All attempts to establish fascist parties in Portugal were condemned to failure, however; these parties disappeared after the first serious military coup attempt against the liberal regime in April 1925.

Portuguese fascism was, nevertheless, ideologically and politically influenced by *Integralismo Lusitano*. Although the postwar crisis produced other movements that were not influenced by IL, the movement's ability to present a new reactionary ideological package was decisive. This package was, despite obvious foreign influences, legitimate in the Portuguese cultural context. IL's ideological vigor and its capacity to permeate the elites thus conditioned fascist development and penetration in Portugal. As a Portuguese sociologist has said, "[a]t a time when Italian fascist and Nazi models assumed 'world-historical' importance, those most predisposed to learn from and emulate them were all grounded in the teachings and intellectual style of the IL."[35] Indeed, almost all attempts to establish fascist parties—the last and most successful of which was National Syndicalism—were shaped by IL.

Integralism created durable foundations for a new reactionary nationalism in Portugal: it reinvented the "tradition" of an "organic" and corporatist society that was based on a vision of a medieval Portugal destroyed by "imported" nineteenth century liberalism. IL presented corporatism as the alternative to liberalism, acting as a launching pad for the restoration of the monarchy. Efforts to legitimate historically, and to develop the theoretical foundations of corporatism, however, were more than a reflection of Integralism's antiliberalism: this is apparent in the erudite studies published by its leaders.

IL constructed a coherent political and intellectual alternative. Its dogma was codified into a political program. A vision of a nation organized hierarchically according to tradition was held up in opposition to the notion of popular sovereignty. The idea of universal suffrage was replaced by a vision of the corporatist representation of the family, the city and town councils, and the professions. Parliament was rejected in favor of an advisory national assembly representing the nation's *forças vivas* (vital forces). In response to the liberal state's centralization, its destruction of local community life and uncontrolled urbanization, Integralism advocated an anti-cosmopolitan and ruralist decentralization that would allow an "eminently agricultural country to fulfill its historical mission." Corporatist representation became the antidote to a liberal economy and the "disastrous agitation of class struggle."[36]

Integralism was a typical reaction to modernization, hence its ability to infiltrate the areas most threatened by it, particularly after the destabilization of the fragile republican regime. IL was elitist, centered in a small university network and restructured provincial monarchical circles.

Although it suffered fascist-leaning changes in the postwar period, the ideology of the IL's founders remained traditionally antiliberal. Its "historical" nationalism was the expression of a rural reaction to industrialization. Socialism and communism were seen as variants of liberalism and democracy, undeserving of great attention. Masonry and anticlerical (or Jacobin) republicanism were its great enemies.

From the time it was founded, Integralism was embroiled in right-wing military conspiracies. In 1916, the pro-German IL took part in an antiwar uprising. Under Sidónio Pais, it forged closer ties with military academy cadets—the dictator's incipient praetorian guard. Young monarchical officers also supported Integralism, but it did not trust this group because they were prone to the "restorationist itch."

Sidónio's downfall and the return of the liberal regime, however, threw a good number of these officers into the orbit of the radical right. The monarchist revolt sounded the death knell for further restorationist revolts, and the Integralists began to back all right-wing military candidates campaigning for the overthrow of the republic. Integralists acted as "civilian links" in a number of coup attempts, such as that of 18 April 1925. Widespread civilian participation in the coup attempt permitted the consolidation of contacts with the more radical lieutenants, and with Manuel Gomes da Costa—the maverick general who led the 1926 uprising.

As he marched from Braga to Lisbon, Gomes da Costa negotiated his new powers with the conservative republicans, headed by Admiral Mendes Cabeçadas. There was barely any military resistance to the coup; civilian mobilization was similarly absent. The legacy of the liberal parliamentary republic, and the outcome of its legitimacy crisis led to the establishment of an unstable military dictatorship.

Although the Integralists played an important role in the first phase of this dictatorship, the new political situation divided them.

On the one hand, fascism was supported by a large part of the youth sector and by some military sympathizers. On the other, the hard-liners within Integralism's central junta remained faithful to the monarchy, and supported projects seeking to install a new and radically antiliberal corporatist order. This group viewed Salazar's subsequent rise to power and the hybrid political institutions he created with suspicion. A good part withdrew into various fascist-oriented organizations, later forming the core of *National Syndicalism* (1932); furthermore, many of those belonging to Integralism's so-called "second generation" supported Salazarism, including Marcello Caetano, Salazar's eventual successor in the late 1960s.

The Transition to Salazar's 'Estado Novo'

The most appropriate way to analyze the fall of the republican regime is to examine civil-military relations. Appeals to the military were a constant feature of postwar politics. By definition, the republican political system did not have a "loyal opposition." It was obvious to political actors that the possibility of achieving power through elections was virtually non-existent. The military coup of 1926 co-opted part of the liberal regime's political elite who, like many in the military, aimed for the establishment of a reformed constitutional order. The coup was also supported by what Juan Linz calls the "disloyal opposition," which aimed to remove the dominant party from power.[37]

The military dictatorship rapidly eliminated the republicans from the ranks of the regime, but it was unable to institutionalize itself. The small, pugnacious workers' movement, under anarcho-syndicalist hegemony, frightened the ruling classes who recalled the notorious failure of the republican regime to incorporate workers into the political system. The role of the Portuguese *bienio rosso* in the overthrow of liberalism should not be exaggerated, however. The old urban-rural and traditional-modern cleavages, typical of a "dual society" such as Portugal's, are more relevant than the divide between the bourgeoisie and the working class.

If the processes of the overthrow of democracy and the rise of fascism are indeed characterized by "the takeover of power by a well-organized disloyal opposition with a mass base in society, committed to the creation of a new political and social order, and unwilling to share its power with members of the political class of the past regime, except as minor partners in a transition phase," Portugal is notable for the absence of a fascist movement.[38] The crisis of Portuguese liberalism was a product of the complex relationship between fascism and the different political "families" that made up the conservative bloc during the first half of the twentieth century. Clearly, the rise of fascism in Europe was possible because of the emergence of coalitions of factions, parties, and voters previously represented by a variety of conservative parties. Yet this does not explain the distinct character of the two movements. As Martin Blinkhorn has stated, "[i]t cannot seriously be denied that as movements, parties and political ideologies, conservatism and fascism occupied very different positions within the early and mid-twentieth century European right, converging at some points and conflicting at others."[39]

It seems clear that the secondary role played by the fascists was particularly evident in countries such as those on the eastern and southern European periphery, with levels of economic development, social structures and political systems similar to Portugal's. The nature of the crisis of the Portuguese republic in the postwar period highlights the difficulties fascist movements faced in societies where the "massification of politics" was at only an incipient stage and where competitors had already occupied the available political space.[40]

The secularization cleavage was perhaps the most important one caused by the First Republic. The Portuguese case shows how, culturally speaking, the emergence of a "fascist intelligentsia" becomes very difficult when "the hostile response to modern society and the concomitant rejection of liberalism and democratization remain embedded in traditional religious forms, and reactionary or conservative politics is linked to the defense of the position of the

Church."[41] The Church and the CCP constituted a powerful obstacle to the "fascistization" of the university and intellectual elites, playing a key political role in the antidemocratic reaction.

Another enduring cleavage, the monarchy-republic cleavage or "regime question," also had an influence. "Restorationism" inhibited the development of fascism; it curbed fascist tendencies within the Integralist movement and Sidonism's attempts at populist mobilization. The "regime question" also highlighted the understanding between Integralists and social-Catholics, both groups defended authoritarian corporatism as an alternative to liberalism.

Following the mobilization of the urban working- and middle-classes—both increasingly distant from the Democratic Party—all traces of populist mobilization in the conservative countryside disappeared. The republic had not shaken the traditional structures of domination in the north where clientelistic pacts with local notables had been established. In the *latifundia*-dominated south, the rural unions had almost disappeared after brief periods of activity in 1910 and 1912. They were not part of the *bienio rosso* in the 1920s, and the social conflict that characterized the rise of rural fascism in Italy did not occur in Portugal. The nature of conservative political and social representation in the 1920s (mass parties had not yet emerged), and the existence of clientelistic relationships in the political system were decisive elements in the transition to authoritarianism.

As soon as the republican regime was overthrown, the military dictatorship found punitive solutions for some of the problems worrying the conservative bloc. The Democratic Party was ousted from power and its leaders exiled, the working class lost its right to strike and the unions were legally restricted. The republicans dominated revolutionary action against the dictatorship: the only exception being the failed general strike of 1934, the year Salazar established the corporatist system. The Catholic Church blessed the 1926 coup and, while suspicious of republican officers and civilians in the regime, immediately volunteered secular supporters for ministerial positions.

Salazarism was born out of a military dictatorship beset by a succession of conspiracies, palace coups and revolutionary attempts:

signs of the battle for leadership within the vast, pro-dictatorial conservative coalition. The consolidation of the authoritarian regime
met with difficulties because of the political diversity of the conservative bloc and its ability to penetrate the armed forces. Curiously,
it was under the military dictatorship that the fascists gained some
influence through the young officer class. They attempted to create
autonomous organizations and played a role in driving out republicans from the ranks of the military. This military-mediated, "limited
and self-devouring pluralism" was overcome only by Salazar.

The military regime has been characterized as a "dictatorship
without a dictator." It did not present an alternative to republican
liberalism; it arose from a tentative, military-brokered compromise
and experienced contradictory phases until the consolidation of
authoritarianism under Salazar. Between 1926 and 1930, it failed to
establish a firm hold on power. It was the target of several attempted *coups d'état* led by the pro-democracy opposition (the most serious on 7 February 1927), as well as by the far-right.[42] The conservative republicans, the Catholics and the far-right tried to convert
young officers, who were a parallel power in the barracks; their position was strengthened by the appointment of officers to local administrative posts.

At the governmental level, a more cohesive group of conservative
generals consolidated around General Oscar Carmona. In the wake
of a major financial crisis, Salazar was named finance minister, subsequently gaining ample powers over the other ministries.

The National Union (NU) was legally established in 1930 as an
"anti-party party" that aggregated the civilian forces supporting the
new regime.[43] In 1933, a new constitution declared Portugal to be a
"unitarian and corporatist republic," balancing liberal and corporatist
principles of representation. The former, however, were eliminated
through subsequent legislation, and the latter limited to the point of
insignificance.

The result was a dictatorship headed by a prime minister, and a
national assembly dominated by the UN through non-competitive
elections. To avoid any loss of power, even to a parliament domi-

nated by the government party, the executive was made almost completely autonomous. General Carmona was made president to guarantee military interests. Censorship eliminated any suggestion of political conflict, and censors devoted their attention to the opposition and, in particular, to the fascist minority led by Rolão Preto—a group that had initially challenged the new regime. The political police were reorganized and used with remarkable rationality.

All this was done "from above," and without fascistic demagoguery. It was a process that depended more on generals and colonels than on lieutenants, and more on the Ministry of the Interior than on "the mob." By 1934 liberalism had been eliminated, and the old republican institutions replaced.

The most rebellious of the fascist leaders were exiled; a majority, however, were appointed to minor positions, particularly after the ominous onset of the Spanish Civil War. The great republican figures were forgotten in exile after the brief optimism generated by the Spanish Popular Front. One by one, anarcho-syndicalist leaders went to prison or died in Spain, leaving the leadership of the clandestine opposition in the hands of the small and youthful Communist Party.[44]

The regime institutionalized by Salazar was admired by many on the fringes of the European radical-right, but above all by those of Maurrasian and traditional Catholic extraction, given its cultural origin. Its cultural identity was based on more than just an "order-promoting" program, but it did not have the "totalitarian," "pagan" elements of Nazi Germany or Fascist Italy. Salazarism was based on radical right-wing and antiliberal social-Catholicism.[45]

Salazar and the "Estado Novo"

The 1933 Constitution established the political institutions of the *Estado Novo*; it heralded an early compromise with the conservative republicans. Its liberal principles were weak, and its corporatist and authoritarian elements strong. Rights and liberties were formally maintained but were actually eliminated by government regulation.

De jure freedom of association existed, but parties were eliminated through regulation. Formally, the National Union never became a single party, although it functioned that way after 1934.

A "Constitutionalized Dictatorship"

As president of the National Union, António Salazar nominated the party's deputies to parliament. The constitution maintained the classic separation of powers, but the Chamber of Deputies had few powers, while the Corporatist Chamber had none. The government was thus freed of any domination by parliament.

Theoretically, the members of the Corporatist Chamber were designated by the corporations; however, in reality Salazar nominated most of them. The Constitution maintained the presidency of the republic, elected by direct suffrage, as well as the presidency of the Council of Ministers; Salazar was answerable only to the former. During the early years of Salazar's rule, the president posed the only constitutional challenge to his authority.[46] The president of the republic was always a general, given the legacy of the military dictatorship. This caused Salazar some problems after 1945. In short, to use a phrase of the time, the regime was a "constitutionalized dictatorship."

Together with the single party, the merely "advisory" Chamber of Deputies and Corporatist Chamber constituted the regime's "limited pluralism." The division between those favoring a restoration of the monarchy and the republicans, as well as that between Integralist and moderate corporatists, was reflected in both chambers. In the 1950s, moreover, different lobbies emerged to defend agricultural and industrial interests.

The *Estado Novo* inherited and strengthened the repressive apparatus of the military dictatorship. While censorship was established in 1926 and controlled by the propaganda services (as was the political police—the backbone of the system), the autonomy of the political police increased as a result of successive decrees until they were answerable only to Salazar. Apart from repressing the clandestine opposition, controlling access to public administration was of central importance. Mechanisms to control the judicial branch increased. Political crimes, for example, were placed under the jurisdiction of special military courts, and special judges were nominated. Furthermore, the political police were given ample powers to determine prison sentences.

In 1936, having completed the consolidation of the system, Salazar authorized the founding of a militia, the Portuguese Legion. He also set up youth and women's organizations dependent on the Ministry of Education. A fascist choreography emerged more clearly.

One important problem remained: relations with the military. This was the institution that Salazar feared most, yet the movement to co-opt and control the military elite was central to the consolidation of Salazarism.[47] The subordination of the military hierarchy to the regime was a fact by the eve of World War II, but the process was slow and fraught with tensions. Salazar's speech at an officers' rally in 1938 symbolically marked the victory of "a civilian police dictatorship" over the old military dictatorship of 1926.[48] This process of establishing control lasted from the time Salazar entered the War Ministry in mid-1936 to the reform of the armed forces in 1937, which General Carmona resisted. After taking charge of the War Ministry portfolio, Salazar could have the final—albeit tentative—word on all high-level promotions and transfers. Despite the "temporary" nature of his position, Salazar was Minister of War until the end of World War II; and it was in this post that he presented his reform bill for the armed forces in 1937.

This reform provoked the most important reduction in the armed forces since World War I. The officers' corps was reduced by 30 per cent. Already significantly affected by resignations and by the transfer to the reserves of those implicated in the dozens of attempted coups and revolutions, the number of officers reached "the lowest levels registered since 1905."[49]

Besides this control "from above," a number of legislative measures were passed that strengthened ideological and police control over the armed forces. These measures heralded the political hegemony of the undersecretary of state, Captain Santos Costa, whose power went unchallenged until the late 1950s.

Salazarism did not challenge the international order. Salazarist nationalism was based on a vision of the past and on Portugal's colonial patrimony. The Anglo-Portuguese alliance was never questioned, ensuring the British government's discreet support for the dictatorship. Geography, the evolution of the conflict and Salazar's commitment to maintaining Portugal's neutrality, as well as its old system of alliances, kept the country out of World War II.

As for the political system, little or nothing changed, despite the profound alteration of the international order after 1945. The only concession was the opening for the emergence of a legal opposition—a month at a time every four years—for which no constitutional reform was necessary. After 1958, when a "scare" was provoked by the presidential candidacy of a dissident general, Humberto Delgado, the president was indirectly and "organically" elected by the National Assembly and representatives of the municipal councils.

A Strong Dictator

Many studies of modern dictatorships ignore the figure of the leader. In the case of António Salazar, it would be a mistake to do so. Salazar had a worldview; he designed the whole institutional framework of the regime. Once he became the unchallenged leader, very little legislation—important or trivial—was passed without his approval.[50]

Salazar played no part in the 1926 *coup d'état*, nor was he listed as a candidate during the last years of the parliamentary regime. He was the son of a poor rural family from Vimieiro, a village in central Portugal. Salazar had a traditional Catholic upbringing and completed most of his intellectual and political education before World War I. He attended a seminary but abandoned the ecclesiastical path on the eve of the fall of the monarchy in order to study law at the University of Coimbra.

A reserved and brilliant student, he led the best-known Catholic student organization at Coimbra, the *Centro Académico de Democracia Cristã* (CADC—Christian Democracy Academic Center). His friendship with the future Cardinal Patriarch of Lisbon, Manuel Cerejeira, dates from this period. He pursued a university career as a professor of economic law, and his only political activity under the liberal republic took place within the strict limits of the social-Catholic movement. He was one of the leaders of the CCP, and was elected a deputy for them in the early 1920s.

Salazar's expertise in finance and his membership in the CCP made him a natural candidate for the post of Finance Minister immediately after the 1926 coup, and it was in that capacity that he joined the military dictatorship in 1928. His rise in the government was possible because of the ample powers he negotiated on arriving at the Finance Ministry.

The image Salazar cultivated was that of a reserved, puritanical and provincial dictator. It was an image that held sway until his death, and one that he never attempted to change. As a young Catholic militant he left Portugal only once, to take part in a Catholic congress in Belgium. After taking power, he made a single trip to Spain to meet with Franco. He ruled over a "colonial empire," but never visited a single colony during the 36 years of his rule. He never went to Brazil, Portugal's "sister country:" he flew only once, and did not like it.

Yet it would be a mistake to assume that his provincialism reflected a lack of political culture. Salazar was an "academic" dictator who closely followed international politics and the ideas of the times. He was ideologically and culturally traditional, antiliberal, and Catholic in a context of secularization and accelerated modernization. He was ultra-conservative, in the most literal sense of the term. He steadfastly defended his rejection of democracy, favoring an "organic" vision of society based on traditional, Catholic foundations. As the nation's leader, he was aware of the inevitability of modernization, but also acutely aware of the threat it represented.

The systematic, cartesian nature of his speeches provides a good indication of his political thought.[51] He always addressed the elite, never succumbing to populist mass appeals. He was a professor of finance, and had clear ideas about the management of a state's balance sheet. As a "strong" dictator, he rarely decentralized decisions, and he relied on a docile administration.

The National Union

The National Union was a variant of the political parties that Linz has called "unified parties." Giovanni Sartori considers such parties "single authoritarian parties," generally representing a "coalescence, from the top, of various elements to create a new political entity," obliging other forces either to integrate or to be excluded.[52] In some cases, such parties fulfilled a number of the functions of the single parties in totalitarian and fascist regimes. Their origins, ideology, organization and relationship with both state and society, however, were different. The determining factor is that these parties were created in an authoritarian situation, where political pluralism was already absent or severely handicapped.

The impetus for their formation came from the government, with decisive aid from the state apparatus. In general, their establishment entailed varying degrees of compromise on the part of other parties or pressure groups participating in the winning coalition.

In Portugal and Spain, parties of this type had precedents; they were modeled on those that had thrived under Sidónio Pais (the National Republican Party) and Primo de Rivera (the Patriotic Union).[53] Similar, and more or less successful projects had also been promoted in the 1930s by authoritarian regimes in Austria, Hungary (the National Union Party), Poland (the Camp of National Union) and Spain.[54]

Indeed, a single party similar to Portugal's was the one led by Franco. In 1937, Franco forced various previously independent parties, members of the coalition that ultimately won the Civil War, to unify under the banner of a single political party. He thus established an organization strictly controlled by him, but with distinct factions acknowledged by the party leadership.[55] The identity and

preponderance of intra-party groups were reflected in the ministerial elite.

Unlike Portugal's, however, Franco's single party was initially
closer to the Italian Fascist Party. In Portugal, the National Union
merged with the state apparatus and depended on it to the very end.
Its very existence was at times uncertain. This was, paradoxically,
most true during the "fascist era," when its survival seemed most
important.

Salazar created the National Union in 1930 when he was emerging as the dictatorship's main political leader. Its aims and membership criteria, however, were only vaguely stated. The government-
led NU welcomed all the dictatorship's sympathizers, whether
republican, monarchist or Catholic. For the first two years, the NU
was completely dependent on the Ministry of the Interior.[56] The district governors were influential in the establishment of local committees; the minister of the interior was initially responsible for
replacing local leaders, who normally depended on the district gov-
ernor.[57] Thus, the 1933 Constitution represented a formal commitment to liberal principles of representation, reflecting the political
weight of the conservative republican groups. The NU, on the other
hand, took on the political task of gaining the adherence and support of conservative republicans at the local level.

State dependency marked the life of the party. Contrary to what
one might expect, its lethargy was especially notorious in the 1930s.
Once its leaders had been appointed, its statutes established and its
National Assembly representatives chosen, the National Union practically disappeared. In 1938, the dictator himself recognized that the
NU's activity had "progressively diminished to near-vanishing
point."[58] It was only just before 1945, when opposition mounted and
disaster at the polls threatened, that the NU acquired visibility once
again.

The NU's internal structure was weak. It lacked the propaganda,
ideological, socio-professional and cultural departments of most
other authoritarian single parties. Salazar established state departments for propaganda, the Portuguese Youth, and the *Doppo Lavoro,*

but these were not linked to the party. Only occasionally did the state turn to the party network, and then only to carry out limited tasks.

The single party was not very important in the formation of Salazarism's political elite.[59] It did, however, strengthen Salazar's authority and limit the organization of blocs and pressure groups, as well as allow for a certain "technocratic" pluralism.

The first parliamentary elections in 1934 had clear legitimating aims. Elections were held regularly, but were not organized to achieve 99 per cent participation. Civil servants were mobilized and, despite the already restricted number of registered voters, electoral rolls were manipulated. The *Estado Novo* was never a "dual state;" Salazar governed over and through the administrative apparatus, relegating the truly "political" institutions to secondary positions. The National Union's key role was therefore to control central and local administration; to unify the diverse political factions that supported the regime and to supply the system with political officials—especially in the provinces.

The Corporatist Machine

The *Estado Novo* was essentially corporatist. Corporatism was written into the constitution and given a central role in determining institutional structures, ideology, relations with "organized interests" and the state's economic policy.[60]

Corporatism is not specific to fascism. Generally speaking, the term has covered a wide ideological spectrum within the authoritarian right since the beginning of the century. It is doubtful whether it can even be considered a characteristic of German Nazism.[61] It was, however, a key legitimating element for authoritarian regimes in Austria, Spain, Vichy France and Portugal.

Salazarism did not give the corporatist sector a monopoly on representation, despite pressures from the radical right to do so. Elections were held, but the Corporatist Chamber retained merely consultative status in a powerless National Assembly. The Portuguese corporatist edifice was never completed. Its influence on economic policy or its capacity to act as a buffer against social conflict, however, are worthy of detailed study. Although no "corporations" were created to represent the "organic elements of the nation" in the Corporatist Chamber, no intermediate organizations emerged either. The distance between the constituencies and members of the chamber was maintained. The procurators were chosen by the Corporatist Council, which consisted of Salazar and the ministers and secretaries of state of the sectors involved, such as the Ministry of Economy.

The lynchpin of the corporatist structure was the *Estatuto do Trabalho Nacional* (ETN—National Labor Statute) of 1933, along with the "industrial conditioning" law. Although tempered by the *Estado Novo's* strong Catholic leanings, the ETN owed a great deal to Italy's *Carta del Lavoro*. The statute, approved in September 1933, sought to establish a synthesis of the Italian model and the ideals of social-Catholicism. The founder of the Portuguese corporatist system, Pedro Teotónio Pereira, was a former Integralist who united young radical right-wingers as well as social-Catholic civil servants within his department (he was secretary of state for corporations).

Social engineering was undertaken only bureaucratically. The Rolão Preto fascists were explicitly excluded from the enterprise. Once the ETN was established and the appropriate control mechanisms created, the organization of labor was undertaken. The government gave the unions two months either to accept the new system or to disband. Substantially weakened after the 1926 coup, the unions accepted the new legislation, albeit by only a slight majority.[62] The most important unions were simply dissolved when they rejected the legislation. In January 1934 a strike took place to protest the so-called fascistization of the remaining unions; these were then re-created from the top down by officials from the corporatist apparatus.

The new unions were controlled by the National Institute of Labor and Welfare (INTP). Their governing statutes and prospective leaders were submitted to state approval. If they diverged from the ETN, they were summarily dissolved. Even members' dues came under official scrutiny. National representation was not permitted, so as to keep them weak and ineffectual.

The rural world was represented by the so-called *casas do povo* (community centers). The regime did not recognize social differences in a rural society overseen by "associate protectors," actually *latifundistas*. The old rural unions were simply abolished, particularly in the *latifundia*-dominated south. To ensure that the working classes were culturally provided for, the National Foundation for Joy at Work (FNAT) was created.[63]

The importance of the corporatist system becomes clearer when examining state economic intervention from 1930 onwards. The pre-corporatist institutions that could ensure smooth relations between the state and the emerging corporatist institutions, such as the organizations of economic co-ordination, were maintained. According to official rhetoric, they were to disappear gradually over time as the corporatist edifice neared completion. In practice, however, they became central features of the regime, gaining total control over the *grémios* (guilds) in the agricultural sector, the weaker industrial areas and the agro-food export sector. Wheat, flour milling, wine-making and related businesses: olive oil, wool and wool products, and canned products—including fish—depended heavily on the state for all decisions regarding production quotas, prices and salaries.[64]

The integration of the old employers' associations (*grémios*) into the new corporatist system was asymmetrical, especially when compared with labor. Decrees governing the *grémios* sought to reorganize employers and the liberal professions, but in a more moderate and prudent fashion. The employers' associations remained tentatively active. Although supposedly "transitional," some of them lasted as long as the regime itself. The *grémios* were led by the state in the name of "national economic interests." Economic intervention strategies, rather than corporatist coherence, determined their organization. Those in the more modern economic sectors enjoyed greater autonomy, but *grémios* in agriculture and associated trade sectors (wine, olive oil and cereals), as well as milling and agro-industry,

were rapidly forced to consolidate in the framework of the corporatist system.

Militia and Youth Organizations

Students of the *Estado Novo* have stressed the impact that the
electoral victory of the Spanish Popular Front and the outbreak of
the civil war had on Portugal. In response to the "red threat," the
regime developed a new political discourse and symbolism, and set
up two militia organizations. These steps have often been interpreted as the "fascistization" of the Salazar regime.

Until the Spanish Civil War, Salazar had refused either to create a
militia type organization or to permit the fascistization of the single
party. During the military dictatorship, a number of attempts to create such bodies had failed. In 1934, Salazar had crushed Preto's
National Syndicalism; in the same year, the first youth organization,
the School Action Vanguard (AEV—*Acção Escolar Vanguarda*), backed
by the philo-fascist propaganda chief, António Ferro, had been disbanded.[65] In 1936, however, the regime created a paramilitary youth
organization, the Portuguese Youth (MP—*Mocidade Portuguesa*), and
permitted the formation of a fascist-style militia group, the Portuguese Legion (LP—*Legião Portuguesa*).

The LP was founded in September 1936 in the wake of an anticommunist rally organized by the "national unions." It emerged from
the genuine "pressure" exerted by certain sectors that had recently
joined the regime. Salazar authorized its formation and decreed its
strict submission to the government. As was his custom, he moderated its declaration of principles and put the military in charge,
avoiding the selection of officers who had been prominent in the
radical right and National Syndicalism.[66]

Similar "pressures" led to the foundation of the MP. The Education Ministry had drawn up plans for various projects aiming to
unite different youth sectors in a paramilitary organization to
replace the moribund AEV. Between May and September 1936, in
response to the victory of the Popular Front in Spain, the MP indis-

criminately accepted new members, including young people who were not students in schools. Membership was voluntary, and the children of the "lower middle-class" business people, white-collar workers and laborers-could sign up. Thus, during its first months, the MP's social base "approximated that of the National Syndicalist Movement."[67]

The youth movement, however, was rapidly curtailed with the transfer of non-student volunteers to the Portuguese Legion. From then on, the MP accepted only school-going members. Participation became compulsory, and the MP became dependent on a strengthened Ministry of Education. In response to criticism from the Catholic hierarchy, the MP was rapidly "Christianized" and encouraged to interact with other, essentially Catholic, youth organizations.

Relations between the LP and the other regime institutions were not peaceful. This was particularly true with the National Union. Salazar separated the MP from the LP and rejected all proposals to place it under the control of the NU. Meanwhile, the single party, ever suspicious of militia organizations, continued to dominate local administration and to constitute the principal channel of communication between the state and society. Yet there was no formal link between the NU and the MP.

Certain differences between the LP and the MP are worthy of note. The MP was quickly depoliticized and Christianized, whereas the LP was vigorously politicized; its discourse, organizational structure and social composition were more typical of a fascist militia. Both groups were more modest in scale, and more dependent on the state apparatus, than their counterparts in other European authoritarian and fascist regimes. Their presence on the political scene, moreover, was only fleeting; and in choreographic terms (that is, in terms of rallies, parades and the like), they were never as fully developed. This holds true even when comparing Portugal with Vichy France, where the regime was ideologically and politically similar.

Salazar was pressured to maintain the LP after the Spanish Civil War. The LP claimed that "there is still much to do for our patriotic reinvigoration, and the Legion thus believes that its mission should not be terminated."[68] Salazar did not dissolve the LP, but it went into irreversible decline nevertheless.

State, Politics, and Society

In 1933 the regime created the National Propaganda Secretariat (SPN—*Secretariado de Propaganda Nacional*), headed by António Ferro. Ferro was a cosmopolitan journalist connected to futurist and modernist circles who had admired fascism since the 1920s.[69] He enjoyed the dictator's confidence. Salazar ordered him to create a propaganda machine that, in the end, greatly exceeded the needs of Salazar's image management. Although he had little to do with the leader's provincial integralism, or perhaps precisely because of this, Ferro provided the regime with a "cultural project" that skillfully combined elements of "modern" aestheticism with a "reinvention of tradition."

The SPN coordinated the regime's press, ran the censorship services and organized sporadic mass demonstrations, as well as leisure activities for the popular classes (in close association with the corporatist apparatus). It also organized numerous activities for the elites, and promoted cultural relations with foreign countries. The SPN skillfully recruited intellectuals and artists, thanks to Ferro's modernist links. Like other authoritarian regimes, Salazarism's cultural project sought the "systematic restoration of traditional values."[70]

The selective nature of censorship reflected the "organic" ideal of a conflict-free society. Because conflict had theoretically been abolished, nothing was published that might testify to its existence. The censors were ruthless when it came to compulsory "social peace." The regime did not ban or systematically dissolve opposition publications—they survived throughout the 1930s—but they reached only an isolated or reduced intellectual readership that was allowed to engage in debates about the social significance of art or the German-Soviet pact, as long as such debates stayed strictly inside Lisbon's cafes and well away from the working class. Salazar did not have to worry about his rural and provincial bastions because he trusted traditional structures, such as the Church, notables and the bureaucracy:

as he put it, "politically speaking, only what the public knows to exist, exists."[71]

The School System: "God, Fatherland, Family, and Work"

The *Estado Novo* was obsessive about education. This did not mean it wanted to modernize; modernization became an issue only in the 1950s when illiteracy debates abounded. In 1933, Salazar expressed the opinion that the constitution of elites is more important than teaching the people to read. At issue was the primarily ideological reorganization of what had been the pride of the liberal republican elites: the secular, state-run school—particularly the primary school. Instead of promoting the modernization of the school system, the *Estado Novo* controlled what it had inherited. Government spending on education remained stagnant from 1930 to 1960, while ideological control over teachers and students increased. The MP became an instrument for ideological training under the aegis of the Education Ministry; it trained youth in the high schools, to which—until the leap forward in the 1950s—only the urban middle class had access.

Salazarist ideology was based on the four-part doctrine of "God, Fatherland, Family, and Work." It shaped teachers' lives. Mandatory school textbooks were issued and special classroom decorations were created. The values of resignation and obedience, as well as the concepts of an "organic" conflict and a politics-free society, dominated primary school teaching. Christianization was another official obsession that affected everything from classroom decorations to school rituals.

From the 1930s on, the official version of Portuguese history was rigidly codified. History was revised and relative pluralism eliminated, pursuant to the slogan "Everything for the nation, nothing against it." As early as 1932, the Minister of Education drew up a new policy that greatly strengthened "the family as a social cell," "faith, as... an element of national unity and solidarity" and "authority" and "respect for the hierarchy" as "principles of the social life."[72]

State, Church, and Society

It is difficult to comprehend fully the political system and the ideological foundations of the *Estado Novo* without taking into account the determining influence of traditional Catholicism. The church affected all major texts and institutions, including the Constitution and the declaration of corporatist principles. Its influence explains the weakness of the National Union and the paramilitary organizations, as well as the nature of the regime's propaganda. "Clerico-fascism" definitions, also used to describe regimes such as those of Franco, Engelbert Dollfuss and even Vichy, attempt to account for this power. All these regimes received important support from the Catholic Church; they also followed republican secularization programs.

The Portuguese Catholic Church contributed to the Salazar regime's ideology. Not only did the regime use Catholic symbolism with the explicit approval of the Church hierarchy, but it also maintained an actual policy of "Christianizing" institutions and the school system. This close association between Church and state represented more than just a convergence of interests; it expressed a common ideological and political nucleus that was corporatist, antiliberal, and anticommunist.

Although the "Catholicization" of the *Estado Novo*'s institutions was a founding element of Salazarism, the Church feared the totalitarian bent of some state organizations after 1936, as well as an eventual "forced integration" of its youth organizations into official—albeit Catholicized—bodies. This fear turned out to be groundless.[73] The regime gave the Church control over the symbolic and ideological training of large sectors of society, particularly traditional rural society, and opened up social space for the Church's own organizations. The Catholic Scouts were not abolished, and they developed alongside the MP. Catholic Action organizations were linked to the corporatist system, but were allowed to maintain their autonomy. A significant Catholic private education sector emerged. The Church "defeated" conservative republican resistance and fascistizing tendencies with relative ease.

When the *Estado Novo* became institutionalized and the CCP was disbanded, Salazar gave the Church hierarchy the task of "re-Christianizing" the country after decades of republican and liberal secularization. The Catholic Center was restricted to the social arena and barred from the political arena. In 1940, the Concordat was issued, crowning close Church state ties and establishing the norms for *de facto* cooperation. The divorce law, the last piece of republican legislation to be abolished, was changed, prohibiting divorce in religious marriages. A subsequent constitutional revision made Catholicism "the religion of the Portuguese nation."[74] As Salazar himself stated, the *Estado Novo* gave the Church "the possibility to reconstruct... and recover... its leading position in the formation of the Portuguese soul." Pope Pious XII held Portugal up as a model: "the Lord has provided the Portuguese nation with an exemplary head of government."[75]

When the regime's ideological vitality began to fade after 1945, the Church gradually became an ideological haven, and the vitality of the Catholic organizations increased. In the early 1940s, Catholic Action organizations had almost 70,000 members, mostly in the youth organizations; by 1956, membership had reached 100,000.[76] Traditional Catholicism and the Church were, on the one hand, the dictatorship's most powerful weapons; on the other hand, they limited fascistization, becoming the driving force of the *Estado Novo*'s "limited pluralism."[77]

Salazarism, Fascism, and Authoritarianism

Many studies tend to emphasize the non-mobilizing nature of regimes such as the *Estado Novo*. If this is understood to be synonymous with the absence of extensive mobilization and totalitarian tendencies, the definition is correct. Even during the "fascist era," the *Estado Novo* was deeply conservative, and relied more on traditional institutions like the Church and the provincial elites than on mass organizations.

Salazar once said to Henry Massis that his aim was to "make Portugal live by habit."[78] This *maître-mot*, which so delighted his French supporter, perfectly sums up the traditionalism of the *Estado Novo*. It would be a mistake, however, to confuse Salazar's regime with a "pragmatic" dictatorship, particularly between 1933 and 1945. Salazarism officially instituted an "organic" vision of society and deployed all the ideological and social instruments of administrative, corporative, educational and propagandistic control, as well as the elite, the state and the Church, to make that vision a reality. On the other hand, it reinforced the presence of the state in the economy, limited the autonomy of the economic elites and disciplined them with an iron hand.

Culturally and ideologically, the dictatorships closest to Salazarism were those of Franco, Dollfuss and Vichy: Maurrasian and Catholic thinking dominated all of them. In comparing the agents of the transition to fascism, the fall of liberalism in Portugal and the military dictatorship that ensued can be seen as an integral part of the authoritarian cycle of the 1920s. This is especially true of the transitions brought about by military interventions supported by right-wing parties, such as in Hungary in 1919, and in Poland, Greece and Lithuania in 1926.

Nevertheless, of all the European dictatorships that emerged in the 1920s, Salazar's *Estado Novo* proved to be the most thoroughly institutionalized and the longest lasting. Had severe international constraints not hindered many of those dictatorships on Europe's southern and eastern periphery, they would probably have survived with features quite similar to Salazarism. Pilsudski's regime in Poland or Smetona's in Lithuania, Dolfuss's in Austria and Horthy's in Hungary encountered external, rather than internal, factors that froze the institutionalization of those regimes, leaving the process of "political engineering" unfinished.

All these dictatorships were established on the heels of traditional *coups d'etat*; they represented a compromise between civilian and military conservatives; they set up single-party or hegemonic party political systems; and the fascist parties were either minor partners in the coalitions that took power, or were entirely absent. The elites and political movements that inspired the dictatorships were influenced by fascism to a varying degree, but the principles, institutionalizing agents and types of dictatorships transcended fascism.[79] They were "the typical response to the pressures of mass politics and modernization in most of southern and south-eastern Europe during the interwar period."[80] They effectively became the dominant model for twentieth century right-wing dictatorships.

Resistance After 1945

In the period following World War II, the *Estado Novo* defined itself as an "organic democracy" and endeavored, without much difficulty, to conceal its resemblance to fascism. The paramilitary organizations, especially the *Mocidade Portuguesa*, became "former-student" or sporting associations. The SPN's name was changed to the National Information Secretariat (SNI—*Secretariado Nacional de Informação*) and its leadership replaced; it became more anodyne: a promoter of "tourism and information." The Portuguese Legion, downgraded after 1939 following Franco's victory, vanished from the streets and went into terminal decline. Institutional and decision-making changes were very limited. It was only after Marcello Caetano replaced Salazar in 1968 that a series of reforms took place and part of the political elite associated with the old dictator was removed.

Salazar's neutrality during World War II, his military concessions to Britain and the United States and the rapid onset of the Cold War ensured the survival of his regime in an unfavorable post-1945 international climate. Portugal joined the United Nations (after an initial veto from the Soviet Union) and NATO within the next ten years.[81] However, it was not easy for the regime to adapt to the new US-dominated international scene. The dictator had always feared and mistrusted the United States; this feeling was heightened as decolonization began and the UN's Afro-Asian bloc subjected Portugal's colonial policies to international condemnation. The Salazar regime survived by cultivating an external image of a benign and aging authoritarianism that stood as an "anticommunist bulwark of western civilization," and by efficiently controlling internal opposition.

After a period of internal turmoil in 1958, when the dissident general Humberto Delgado obtained significant results in the presidential "elections," members of the military establishment launched a coup attempt in 1961. Salazar neutralized the conspiracy and embarked "rapidly and forcefully" on the colonial war that eroded his regime and finally shattered it 13 years later.

The Economic and Social Changes of the 1960s

The colonial war occurred during a period of economic development when Salazar was, against his convictions, obliged to take liberalizing measures and open the country to foreign investment. Whilst, in common with much of southern Europe at this time, Portugal enjoyed substantial economic growth during the 1960s it nevertheless remained a relatively poor and backward country that was funding an expensive war.

Financing the war involved diverting substantial funds from two crucial areas during the 1960s: investment in the transport infrastructure in general, roads in particular; and education spending.[82] A relatively uncontroversial belief is that by the end of the 1960s, the colonies had come to represent an enormous burden on public finance, maintaining a huge debt in Lisbon at a time when, to cite a student of Portuguese colonialism, "Portugal no longer needed the colonies to pay its way."[83] Despite differences of opinion regarding the role the war played in Portugal's economic growth, the view that "the war was fought more to defend the regime than it was to save the economy," appears to be the most credible.[84]

The withdrawal of the Portuguese economy from Africa to Europe, which occurred precisely at the moment of the colonial wars, was an important factor. Portugal's export sector responded dynamically to the stimulus provided by EFTA, which absorbed an ever-increasing proportion of Portuguese produce—to the detriment of the colonies. "Inevitably, the changed economic realities of the 1960s and 1970s were progressively corroding the logic of imperial connections and of economic nationalism."[85] Portugal's economic growth during its first decade of EFTA membership reached six per cent, with foreign investment in Portugal also expanding. There was a significant growth in external trade—both in volume and direction—which was to have an extremely important political significance. During the 1960s, the importance of the colonies for Portuguese trade declined to be replaced by Europe, with both tourism and emigration having an important impact on economic growth.[86] During this decade the final destination for Portuguese emigrants moved from the American continent to Europe—France in particular—and expanded at an impressive rate.[87]

Marcelo Caetano inherited a very different country in the summer of 1968, one that was more European, at least in terms of economic exchange, leading him to sketch the outlines of a set of liberalizing policies. Caetano himself had been one of the dictatorship's few notables to propose, in 1962, the adoption of a prudent federalist solution for the colonial question; however, after obtaining power, he opted in both his political discourse and strategy promises to continue the war.

The war effort was redoubled, although now within the context of economic growth, and in 1970 Portugal spent a total of 45 per cent of its budget on defense and security. With a military force of 140,000 men, only Israel, and North and South Vietnam exceeded the proportion of the population under arms in Portugal.[88] Despite muted protests by the "Europeanists," who had precise data proving the very limited adverse effects that would be felt with the "loss of empire," the political authorities refused to prepare any initiatives for a peaceful resolution to the colonial problem.

One of the classic themes explored by studies of Iberian transitions to democracy in the 1970s has been the effect of the modernizing economic boom of the 1960s. Portugal underwent a qualitative modernizing leap at that time, albeit more modestly than Spain. According to one historian, Portugal "ceased to be dominated by the primary sector: the tertiary sector took over, marking the passage from a peasant to a post-industrial society."[89] Economic policy was marked by a gradual liberalization, accession to EFTA and increasing foreign investment in Portugal. Emigration to the more developed European countries from the rural interior increased. A new urban middle class emerged, with values that differed significantly from those of the regime. The "tourist boom" and emigrant remittances increased the pace of socio-economic change and development.

The 25 April 1974 military coup paved the way for the institutionalization of Portuguese democracy. Portugal's transition occurred at the height of the Cold War, at a time when there were few international pressures for democratization. The rupture provoked by the Portuguese military resulted in an accentuated crisis of the state, fuelled by the concurrence of democratization with the decolonization of the final European colonial empire.[90] The consolidation of Portuguese democracy was a complex process in which the prospect of membership of the European Union was to play an important role.

2 | Cultural Myths and Portuguese National Identity

Nuno G. Monteiro and António Costa Pinto

Most European states only fixed their frontiers and became autonomous political entities in the nineteenth or twentieth centuries, although the redefinition of pre-existing territorial frontiers has occurred throughout history. The 1990s can be seen as the continuation of a cycle of boundary redefinition, interrupted for almost half a century, with the international recognition of a significant number of new states following the collapse of the Eastern Bloc. The nineteenth century witnessed the unification of various territories under different political units; the twentieth century, on the other hand, has seen the logic of fragmentation prevail.

Britain, France and Spain are European states whose autonomous political existence was established long before the nineteenth century. Both before and after the French Revolution, significant tensions and conflicts emerged almost everywhere, including regions that had enjoyed political and institutional autonomy before their incorporation into larger state boundaries: these states subsequently preserved strong cultural and linguistic identities.

The above points are fundamental to understanding why, until recently, the theme of national identity has been virtually absent from Portuguese historiography.[1] The explanation for this is simple: Portugal is a political entity that has maintained stable frontiers since the thirteenth century. Its existence as an autonomous kingdom from the twelfth century on was interrupted only for little more

than half a century (1580-1640); moreover, Portugal has never confronted problems of linguistic diversity. All historians, and not just
those of a nationalist-corporatist bent, have generally taken the
nation's existence for granted.

Modern political nationalism, which first emerged during the
Liberal Revolution (1820-1834), never once questioned the existence of the nation and its unity; the central political question in
Portugal has always been the "decadence" of the nation. The image
of past grandeur associated with the middle-ages and the maritime
discoveries of the fifteenth and sixteenth centuries has permeated
erudite culture as well as national visionary currents of thought.
School socialization under the First Republic (1910-1926) and the
Estado Novo (New State, 1933-1974) reinforced these currents of
thought.

Portugal was also affected by the great intellectual and political
movements of the turn of the twentieth century: the vision of the
nation was redefined and consolidated during this period. Remote
historical periods and events, such as the middle-ages, were key in
creating that vision of the nation and of national identity given that
historians have invariably painted that period in heroic colors.
Throughout the nineteenth and twentieth centuries, the middle-
ages and the maritime discoveries were pet themes for Portuguese
writers and publicists.

The establishment of the kingdom in 1143 and the consolidation
of its frontiers in the thirteenth century have been portrayed by
nationalistic contemporary historians as epic events permitting the
early triumph of Christianity over the Moors in the western Iberian
Peninsula. A recent study of medieval Portugal has interpreted this
period in a new way. Because the author remains more preoccupied
with the question of the nation's origins, however, his interpretation
of events does not differ much from that of previous works. It is still
based on the idea that "the notion of national identity—that is, the
differentiation between the kingdom as a political unity defined by
monarchical power over a limited territory and its inhabitants—
seems clear from the first half of the thirteenth century on."[2]

The medieval period undoubtedly left unique marks on the modern monarchy. Unlike Portugal, seventeenth-century France has recently been described as a mosaic of imperfectly united particularities and languages;[3] Portugal's kingdom, by contrast, emerged not from the integration of territorial communities, but through conquest. Regional rights, provincial institutions, strong seigniorial powers or markedly divergent linguistic communities did not exist; Portugal had no *fueros* like those in Aragon until the period 1707-1716 and Navarre under the Spanish monarchy; nor did it have any parliaments or provincial rights, as existed under the French monarchy.

It is also important to emphasize that, from the middle of the eighteenth century on, Portugal had no ethno-cultural minorities. During the medieval period, Moorish and Jewish communities—the *mourarias* and the *judiarias*—had been very important. With forced conversion and the expulsion decree ordered in 1496 by King Manuel I, however, their legal recognition was terminated. For more than two centuries, the main offense against the faith persecuted by the Tribunal of the Holy Offices of the Inquisition in Portugal was "Judaism": the accusation directed at people suspected of practicing the Jewish religion. Converted Jews became known as New Christians, an infamous designation that their descendants inherited. During the rule of the Marquis of Pombal (1750-1777), however, the distinction between New and old Christians was finally formally abolished.[4]

The brief period of the Catholic peninsular monarchy (1580-1640) is a key point of reference in the contemporary vision of the nation. The medieval battle of Aljubarrota, waged when dynastic union was at risk, and the regaining of independence in 1640 are still celebrated today as fundamental moments in the affirmation of national identity against the eternal Spanish enemy. It was only in reaction to proposals for Iberian union during the second half of the nineteenth century, that the events of 1640 "became" a "national revolution," however.

This interpretation of events has been directly questioned by recent historical research. Actually the Restoration seems, funda-

mentally, to have been a reaction against attempts to impose institutional uniformity by the Count-Duke of Olivares: it was undertak-
en in the name of traditional institutions and not the nation; moreover, contemporary references to the nation, and to the feeling of
national belonging, competed with other equally important identities.[5] A combination of favorable circumstances in Europe (the
alliance with Britain and rivalries between the European powers),
along with the increase in income from Brazil, permitted the consolidation of the kingdom's autonomy.[6]

All that we have said to this point is not designed to underline
the precociousness of Portuguese national identity; rather, it seeks to
emphasize the absence of the competing historical legacies (regional identities or ethnic minorities in particular) and poorly defined
frontiers that cause difficulties in determining national identities in
the contemporary period. In our opinion, these factors lie at the
core of Portuguese national identity, and remain true to this day.
Nevertheless, some recent studies—those inspired by the "process"
theories in respect of the genesis of nations—have rejected the
"modernist" paradigms that hold to the idea that nations only
emerged during the modern era, and have sought to reaffirm the old
idea of there being a precocious national sentiment in Portugal,
whilst recognizing that the "dissemination of a national identity in
Portugal before the 1800s," particularly outside the elites, remains
"controversial." [7] Without seeking to deny the existence of "pre-
modern" aspects of national identity—in Portugal and elsewhere—
we believe that these aspects are not specific to Portugal in the same
way that the stability of its borders and the absence of strong competing historical legacies are.

The Rise of Nationalism: the Liberals

The nineteenth century began dramatically in Portugal with the
invasion by French troops in 1807 and the emergence of successive
nationalisms: anti-French nationalism emerged almost immediately.[8]
The period of the invasions was followed by a durable British mili-

tary presence, and anti-British nationalism decisively marked the genesis of the Liberal movement in 1820. Another key political question that dominated the first liberal triennium (1820-1823) was how to integrate Brazil by creating one nation on the basis of two kingdoms. The resolution of these difficulties favored Brazilian independence, which was finally proclaimed in 1822.[9] The first modern constitutional experiment was thus brought to a head.

It was also during this period that a discourse based on the themes of decadence and regeneration appeared that highlighted the grandiose period of the middle-ages, the discoveries and the decadence of the sixteenth century. According to this line of thinking, the continuous process of decline could be halted through the regenerative impulse of internal reforms that had become necessary after the definitive loss of economic control over Brazil.

The same images predominated after the 1832-34 civil war. Even the "ultra realist" discourse that reigned between 1828 and 1832 had a strong nationalist component.[10] Anti-British nationalism became a fundamental element of intra-liberal disputes: liberals were divided over Portugal's position in relation to Britain.[11]

Portugal participated in the intellectual and political movement to reformulate European nationalism at the end of the nineteenth century. As a Portuguese historian describes it, however, in the case of Portugal there were neither minorities nor citizens living in neighboring States on land that could be called national territory; but it was not just for this reason that the "national question" was not the sole point of reference to explain all problems between 1890 and 1930.[12]

The decisive role played by intellectuals in the search for the historical roots of Portuguese culture is a phenomenon that predates the nationalism of the end of the century. Decades earlier, key romantic and liberal writers—such as Almeida Garrett and Alexandre Herculano—had studied medieval history; they had done so in the name of a "patriotism" that "still maintained the classic sense of civic love of the common good, and not the sentimental adherence to a state."[13] This patriotism was in no way incompatible with Iberianism—the belief in a common political destiny for the diverse peoples of the Iberian Peninsula—a belief shared by various mid-century intellectuals. It was the advent of widespread Iberianist sentiment, combined with vague projects for the union of peninsular dynasties, that led to the 1868 commemoration of 1 December 1640—the date of the Restoration.[14] The timidity of the celebrations, however, contrasted sharply with those of later nationalist movements.

The "Generation of 1870" was also of key importance in the development of thought on the issue of national identity. A number of important writers radically criticized the realities of "triumphant" liberalism in Portugal. Their work was characterized by a keen national feeling. The "Generation of 1870" was very cosmopolitan compared with the exacerbated nationalism of the generations that followed—although some of its members later became key supporters of the more extreme form of nationalism.[15]

The Radicalization of Nationalist Thinking: the Republicans

The watershed signaling the decisive modification of Portuguese political culture occurred with the British Ultimatum of 1890.[16] Portugal had retained some African territories, but their political and symbolic importance increased when other European countries sought to gain a foothold in Africa during the 1880s. Britain directly opposed chimerical Portuguese projects to link Angola to Mozambique. The first large anti-British demonstration took place in 1890 to protest the Ultimatum. The Republicans capitalized on anti-British mobilization in 1890, and even organized a coup attempt in 1891. The uprising failed, but, from then on, political culture was marked by an imperialist nationalism.

Ten years earlier, the Republicans had taken advantage of nationalist sentiment when the tri-centenary of the death of Portugal's "national poet," Luís de Camões, was celebrated in 1880. At the beginning of that year, they proposed "three days of public holiday" to celebrate Camões's tri-centenary, to overcome the "crisis of spirits" and to promote a "national revival." They were proudly supported by their most influential positivist theorist, Teófilo Braga. The commemorative movement grew, transforming the 40,000-strong "civic" processions into protests against the liberal monarchy, and forming the basis for the republican movement.[17]

Republican indoctrination and propaganda were decisive for Portuguese nationalism at the end of the century. Braga's positivist republicanism provided the movement with a coherent doctrine, which had at its heart the "cultural construction of the nation."[18] The republican state was meant to represent collective beliefs on the grounds that it was "not ideas and interests" that united the Portuguese; rather, "the basis for all social agreement lies in affective impulses," and "the affective life, which is the basis for all national unity, needs to be disciplined by the most powerful sociability stimulus."[19]

In his 1884 book, *Centennials as an Affective Synthesis in Modern Societies*, Braga developed a theory of the production of symbols and national rituals. He affirmed that "centenaries of great men are festivals of national consecration. Each people chooses the genius that is the synthesis of the national character... Without knowledge of its history no people can fight for freedom."[20] In subsequent decades, when all contemporary Portuguese national symbols were produced, these ideas took root: they bolstered the 1910 republican triumph, and combined with contemporary political currents—including the corporatist conservatism that gained power after 1926. The cultural construction of the nation also accepted the declared objective of discovering the roots of a national identity within Portugal's historical legacy and its popular culture as the basis for the political order that they were seeking to create.[21]

Portugal confronted neither ethnic and linguistic minorities, nor unstable frontiers. Political instability arose in the urban centers and among a politicized minority. This point has recently been used to explain the liberal state's reduced investment in literacy programs.[22] Although some of the fundamental ingredients of contemporary nationalism were missing, the state was unable to integrate large masses of the rural population into the political system. The state had hardly any contact with this part of the population, and what contacts it had were channeled through *cacique*-based, "clientelist" networks.[23] The republican state project focused on overcoming multiple localisms and transforming the masses into citizens.[24] Although it did not succeed immediately, the integrating symbols and rituals of the nation triumphed in the long run.

The Republicans were the first political group successfully to mobilize the popular urban and middle classes that had, until then, been excluded from politics. They implemented their populist strategy in the name of a regenerating nationalism that would overcome both monarchical dependence on Britain and economic backwardness. Victorious in 1910, the republican elite prepared for Portugal's intervention in World War I bearing the profound effects of the British Ultimatum—as well as the fear that the Allies might use the African colonies as a bargaining chip with Germany.

Portugal's participation in World War I had disastrous political and social consequences. It cannot be dissociated from the nationalist aspiration to lessen dependence on Britain. Portugal hoped, at all costs, for a place at the victors' negotiating table. Recent research has shown, however, that Portuguese military intervention in Europe also sought to mobilize public opinion in favor of the new regime: thus, the "motherland in danger" was an appropriate slogan for the consolidation of the republic.[25]

Republican elites promoted a timid but radical "mass nationalization." They were always aware of the social and political stranglehold that the rural areas retained over Portuguese society. They created national symbols and undertook school socialization; they also sanctified the colonial empire—the key to Portuguese national identity. They inaugurated a national flag and anthem, created a new "civil liturgy" and declared bank holidays. Populist political mobilization and the "nationalization" of teaching accompanied the expansion of school education.[26] The anthem was anti-British, and was part of the propaganda against the British Ultimatum. The flag evoked "the two greatest moments in Portuguese history:" "the foundation of the nation and the maritime epoch." Both were regarded as "the national and colonial source of historic republicanism."[27] Initially targets of criticism, both the flag and the anthem were legitimated with participation in the war.[28]

In the postwar years, monuments to the dead and the great battles—as well as military intervention in politics—consolidated the break with the liberal, monarchist past. Neither challenges and monarchical revolts, nor the overthrow of the First Republic in 1926 eradicated the movement to link the "image of the republic with the image of the *patria*," as well as with the nation and the "sanctified" African colonies. The Republicans linked the national and the colonial questions: this modern nationalist linkage shaped Portuguese foreign policy until the transition to democracy in the 1970s.

The Rise of Authoritarian Nationalism: the New State

Authoritarian, traditionalist and corporatist nationalism emerged on the eve of World War I. The crisis provoked by Portugal's intervention in the war spread this vision in intellectual and military circles. Authoritarian nationalism differed from republicanism in its anti-cosmopolitan and socially reactionary outlook: it focused on a criticism of the liberal political system and the secularization undertaken during the Republic.

António de Oliveira Salazar's *Estado Novo*—Europe's most durable twentieth-century dictatorship—profoundly marked Portuguese politics.[29] Salazarism did not represent a clear break with modern Portuguese nationalism, however; the *Estado Novo* amply, coherently and totally defined a discourse on national tradition faithful to the positivist theoretical model—even whilst pursuing political objectives contrary to those of the republican movement that preceded it in power.[30]

Salazar tenaciously consolidated and "popularized" the idea of a "national regeneration."[31] This idea of "national regeneration" was based on the colonies, the empire, national independence and the discoveries that had made Portugal small in Europe, but large in global terms.[32] The reconciliation between traditional Catholicism and corporatism—a "national tradition" nearly destroyed by "imported" liberalism and secularization—also became important elements of this vision.[33] Catholicism was linked with the "nation's" formation: rituals and official discourse reinforced Portugal's medieval birth in the reconquest from the Moors. From the early 1930s on, furthermore, a process of "re-Christianization" was promoted. Corporatism aimed to "eliminate class conflict," it proposed a model of an "organic" Portugal based on medieval social organization. The *Estado Novo* thus hoped to create a society without conflict.

Under the *Estado Novo*, the movement to "reinvent the past" underwent a qualitative leap. School socialization, cultural propaganda and a policy of national monument restoration proceeded apace. Any memory of Moorish culture and cultural diversity (already weak in any case—even in the south) was silenced. The north was upheld as the "Christian cradle of nationhood," as was Guimarães—the capital of the medieval kingdom. The preservation of national monuments led to the reconstruction of "Christian re-conquest" symbols, with the restoration of castles and military fortresses. The "heroes" of the nation's founding or the maritime conquests were mythologized graphically, cinematographically and—literally—monumentally. The regime used all the propaganda of the "age of the masses" to sell this new vision of the nation.

The National Propaganda Secretariat (SPN—*Secretariado de Propaganda Nacional*) was founded in 1932 to promote an official political culture for the masses and the elites. The SPN restored or built most of the national monuments, and can also be credited with the introduction of popular "historical" cinema. The "reinvention" of Portuguese folklore also dates from this period.[34] Local dance and costumed music groups were selected by the state. Official competitions for "the most Portuguese village in Portugal," for example, aimed to "develop in the Portuguese the cult of tradition." These competitions expressed the *Estado Novo*'s traditionalist nationalism. The village was seen as a microcosm of a traditional conflict-free society, based on harmonious social relations between God-fearing individuals who were immune to urban vices.[35]

From the 1930s onwards, the official version of Portuguese history was rigidly imposed in the educational system. Although in some ways similar to the Republican nationalist vision, this version eliminated any existing pluralism. The slogan, "Everything for the nation, nothing against it," imposed a hegemonic cultural reality. Heroes were purged of all vices, and their perfection was gradually confirmed by "scientific research." The maritime discoveries were presented as an enterprise that had aimed exclusively to "spread the faith and the empire." The sins of positivism and of the discoveries as a "mercantile adventure" disappeared.[36]

In 1940, the *Estado Novo* organized the huge commemorative "Exhibition of the Portuguese World" to celebrate two national mythical dates: the founding of the nation in 1143, and the regaining of independence in 1640, following 60 years of Spanish occupation. The exhibition took place in Lisbon when the rest of Europe was at war, and marked the golden age of Salazarist nationalism. It sold the image of Portugal as an ancient nation with a glorious maritime past and an empire that extended from the north of Portugal to Timor.[37] The myth of empire was at the heart of the *Estado Novo*'s ideology; efforts to create a colonial mentality through the school system also peaked during this period.

As Salazar prepared to resist decolonization following the end of World War II, the word "colonial" was replaced with the description "multi-racial and multi-continental." The re-evaluation of theories on the unique nature of Portuguese colonialism dates from this period, officially, Portuguese colonialism was not racist. The search for colonial legitimacy occurred before the emergence of African resistance and developed in tandem with important economic and social changes in Portugal.

Up until the end of the 1950s, the structure of Portuguese society changed little. The economically active population and rates of urbanization remained almost static: in 1960, 43 per cent of the economically active population still worked in the primary sector, 22 per cent in the secondary sector, and 34 per cent in the tertiary sector.[38] Urbanization rates were low: only 23 per cent of the population lived in urban centers, with the remainder living in rural areas.[39]

Illiteracy rates were extremely high, and few children had access to what was, in any case, a very ideologically conditioned school system. Even fewer people had access to technical scientific training. In the rural areas, the Catholic Church was the most powerful socializing institution. The situation in the rural areas changed during the 1960s, however, with a wave of emigration, although the legacy of church domination lasted into the 1980s. During the 1960s, however, rural society fragmented further, shaken by modernization and rural-urban migration.

Also during the 1960s, Portugal underwent substantial economic and social change. A new wave of emigration occurred, this time heading for Europe. Economic growth was high and was accompanied by the progressive opening of the economy through membership of the European Free Trade Association (EFTA). With the expansion of the urban middle-class, a new public emerged that began to suspect the rationale for the endless colonial war.

European Portugal

The *Estado Novo* died in the wake of what was the last imperialist colonial war waged by a Western European nation. Portugal was diplomatically isolated during the 13 years of armed struggle against the African independence groups. The "imperial myth" gained strength during the 1960s, but its echo in Portuguese society was muted. Although decolonization was quick and dramatic for the thousands of Portuguese who had to abandon Africa, it did not lead to the rise of radical movements. With decolonization and the subsequent transition to democracy, furthermore, the central tenet of Portuguese nationalism came apart.[40]

After a precarious period in 1974 and 1975, the democratic parties joined together to unanimously support Portugal's European foreign policy—for economic and, more importantly political reasons. Integration with Europe was seen as a way to consolidate democracy and finally to take part in European democratic politics.[41] Despite the Communist Party's 1970s campaign—against membership of the European Economic Community (EEC)—opinion polls showed high levels of support for European integration.

Both the process of decolonization and the adoption of a pro-European political policy led to the production of a significant ideological output by some sections of the intellectual elite; although the often heralded "identity crisis" never appeared in any tangible form.[42] Following a period of recriminations criticizing the decolonization process—emanating mainly from conservative groups in the late-1970s, and which largely fell on deaf ears—smaller extreme right-wing parties sought to capitalize on the discontent felt within the small groups that had been most affected by Portugal's new found Europeanism: their target audience was those who had fled the colonies to settle in Portugal—the *retornados*.[43] The conversion of this conservative ideology into a discourse proclaiming the need to defend a "national identity" that was threatened by incorporation into the European Community also met with little popular success—even within the conservative milieu—as is evidenced by the fact that membership of the EEC was supported by the two main conservative Portuguese parties in the 1970s and the 1980s.

On the one hand, nationalist discourses, which were promoted by a conservatism that utilized—instrumentally—the country's exclusively Atlantic vocation, emerged during the 1970s as a reaction against the country's incorporation into Europe. On the other hand, the Communist Party promoted a more economistic defense of the "interests of the national productive forces" in the face of European capitalism; however, with the myth of the empire now ended, the democratic elites managed to consolidate the belief within public opinion that Europe was the only means through which Portugal could reconstruct any important relationships with the new Portuguese speaking African states—particularly since almost all economic links had disappeared and political relations had deteriorated following the granting of independence in 1975.

With the prospect of accession to the EC—and in the wake of it—new identity problems were to arise; the most important of which was the nature of Portugal's relationship with its neighbor, Spain. During—and particularly after—Portugal's attempts to negotiate accession separately, Spain regularly appeared in the public's mind as the powerful neighbor that had "invaded" Portugal's economy.[44] Having rapidly transformed itself into Portugal's major trading partner, Spain and the "Spanish menace" stood as a threat to the liberalization of the Portuguese market.

In 1978, three years after decolonization, almost 70 per cent of Portuguese believed that "Portugal had a duty to grant these countries their independence," although they also thought that "the rights of the Portuguese had to be protected." Only 2.2 per cent of those questioned were in favor of continuing the fight against the liberation movements;[45] nevertheless, even in 1978, a significant minority of 20 per cent thought that Portugal could not survive economically without the former colonies. The gradual diminution of this belief seems to be directly linked to the prospect of EC accession: "the accession process and membership itself, besides providing a substitute for the lost colonies, also represents an incentive for a change in the nature of the country's economic, social and cultural activities."[46]

The Portuguese case provides a good illustration of the thesis that regards the European Community as a reference for Europe's development, and acts as a "ready symbol" that the democratic elites could utilize in order to legitimate the new domestic order following the contested transition and the end of the colonial empire that had been so dear to the *Estado Novo*. On the other hand—and as it had in Spain—it led to the successful consolidation of a "democratic tradition" that was based on the "synchronization and homogenization of [national] cultures and institutions, with those of Europe" whose social and economic components had been changing since the 1960s.[47] This movement was consolidated during the 1980s by accelerated social change, economic growth and the influx of Community funds.

During the 1980s, Portugal underwent a second cycle of growth and social change. The movement of the population toward the coastal areas, as well as urbanization, increased again; although rates remained below the European average. More noteworthy, however, was the acute drop (to 12 per cent by 1992) in the number of workers actively engaged in the agricultural sector—a process that continued to break up traditional rural society in the northern and central areas of the country. Emigration was being replaced by a movement from the countryside to the cities. The growth of the middle-class and the tertiary sectors was also prominent during this period, and school attendance rates rose substantially. These factors delayed the development of any isolationist nationalism in Portugal.

EC membership has also changed domestic politics: the issue of regionalization is a good example. Before membership, a moderate but rapid project for the autonomy of Madeira and the Azores was written into the 1976 Constitution. On the mainland, debate on regionalization was sporadic, with the political parties wavering between centralism and moderate decentralization. With Portugal's entry into the European Community, however, pressures for regionalization have increased. Membership of the European Union (EU) has led to calls for the "regionalization" of what is, in reality, a small state with a centralist tradition, and which has experienced no historical or culturally legitimate decentralizing pressures.

Portugal's route to EU membership was promoted by the political elite with a great degree of political consensus, and without any attempt to measure public opinion through referenda. It was not until after accession had been secured that popular opinion began to exert pressure for more public participation in the reforms that were taking place within Europe. At the end of the twentieth-century, both opinion polls and the intelligentsia agreed on one point: the Portuguese were not experiencing a national identity crisis. National identity remained strong, and the expression of nationalist values and patriotism has not affected the majority's belief that EU membership has been a good thing.[48]

The Colonial Empire

3

Valentim Alexandre

The colonial question lies at the heart of modern Portugal's political life and of all fundamental national policy options. It has determined the fate of movements and regimes. Its weight is largely a product of the longevity of the Portuguese imperial tradition, initiated in the fifteenth century when the first trading posts and fortifications were established on the western coast of Africa. In the next century, the empire was based on Portugal's holdings in the Orient and India, and throughout the seventeenth and eighteenth centuries in Brazil. When the Brazilian portion collapsed in 1822 because of Brazil's secession, it was commonly held among Portugal's political elites that the country could not survive without an empire and would be absorbed by neighboring Spain if it did not possess one. In order to avoid this, it was thought necessary to create a "New Brazil" in Africa. The idea that the existence of the nation and its heritage would be guaranteed by the construction of a new colonial system left its mark on Portuguese nationalist thinking during the nineteenth and twentieth centuries.

It soon became apparent, however, that the task of creating a "New Brazil" would be more difficult than initially envisaged given Portugal's scarce resources and the African territories' paltry trade relations with Portugal. The African colonies were dedicated mainly to the slave trade supplying Cuba and Brazil.

The African colonial project was formulated during the third decade of the nineteenth century, but it became a reality only in the late 1880s, when the African empires of the other European powers came into being. Colonial frontiers were definitively established after the successive conflicts and negotiations of the decade following the 1885 Berlin Conference. The territory obtained by Portugal did not match the needs of a "New Brazil." It was a contiguous area stretching from coast to coast in Central Africa, including the area between Angola and Mozambique and a part of the Lower Congo.

Nevertheless, the empire embraced a vast area that far surpassed pre-existing occupied enclaves. It included Angola on the western coast, which occupied more than 1.2 million square kilometers, and Mozambique on the eastern coast that spread over 783,000 square kilometers. Additionally, there was Guinea, a small territory of approximately 36,000 square kilometers south of Senegal; the Cape Verde Islands, and São Tome and Príncipe in the Atlantic; and the minuscule remains of the Oriental empire, including Goa, Damão (Daman), and Diu on the Indian subcontinent; Macao, in southern China; and Timor in *Insulíndia*.

The "Pacification" of Africa

With the empire mapped out, it became necessary to transform formal sovereignty into effective dominion. This task was central to Portuguese colonial policy for more than three decades, from the middle of the 1890s onwards. The policy consisted of a series of "pacification" campaigns of varying scope undertaken in all three of the African colonies.

Military activity was not, in and of itself, a novelty. The overseas administration of Portugal's territories had been traditionally entrusted to the military. Its presence in Africa was marked by innumerable localized conflicts, as well as a few occupation campaigns of greater or lesser importance, such as the Congo campaign in the 1850s and the Zambezi campaigns initiated in 1869. Military occupation was thus a natural extension of previous policy. Operations now became more systematic, however. Military means were boosted by initial success, particularly the victory over the feared N'goni

Kingdom of Gaza in southern Mozambique in 1895. This culminated in the imprisonment of the N'goni ruler, who was subsequently paraded in the streets of Lisbon amid great patriotic fervor.

The leaders of the generation of 1895, António Enes, Mouzinho de Albuquerque, Paiva Couceiro, Aires de Ornelas, Freire de Andrade, Eduardo da Costa, Caldas Xavier, and other lesser personalities became national heroes. They left a strong imprint on colonial ideology in later years. These men justified the use of force to subdue "backward" or "inferior" races on the basis of Social Darwinism, popularized in Portugal in the 1880s. Da Costa, considered the leading ideologue of the group, put forward the most elaborate theory for the domination of the colonial territories. In his view, expeditious means had to be used to ensure occupation. The people who dared to resist had to be punished, and the subsequently pacified zones had to be placed under a regime of "mitigated despotism" that was characterized by the concentration of power in the colonial authorities; the absence of deliberative assemblies and the use of summary military trials as means of administration.[1]

Variations notwithstanding, this theory predominated in works on colonial matters at the time. The peaceful penetration of the colonial territories and harmonious civil administration was a vision espoused only by a very small minority. The traditional aims of Portuguese colonial policy—tax collection and labor recruitment—generated tensions that ultimately required the use of military force, such that the adoption of a peaceful path would not have been easy.

The process of occupation was characterized by a long series of localized conflicts punctuated by larger campaigns. The fragmentation of conflicts stemmed partly from the political pulverization of African societies, but also from the uneven pressure exerted by the Portuguese authorities and settlers. On rare occasions, conflicts would spread, affecting an entire ethnic group; a charismatic leader capable of uniting disparate populations sometimes provoked them. Such was the case of the revolt of the Ovimbundus on the Central Angolan Plateau in 1902 and the Bakongo revolt in north-eastern Angola from 1913 to 1915. Region-wide economic pressures also contributed to wider conflicts. The Ovimbundu revolt, for example, was also provoked by the fall in the price of rubber, a trading commodity for the region.[2] By contrast; the endemic state of war that affected Zambezi (the central zone of Mozamique) can be explained by the persistent action of traditional war chiefs.[3]

Some of the larger conflicts originated in decisions of the Lisbon government to rapidly occupy certain areas considered particularly sensitive for external security. The campaign against the Kingdom of Gaza in 1895 is a case in point. Its conquest was considered necessary for the domination of southern Mozambique in the face of Cecil Rhodes' expansionism. The majority of the small campaigns did not involve more than a few hundred men. In the Gaza conflict, more than 3,200 soldiers were deployed; approximately 2,700 of these were Europeans recently dispatched from Portugal. Mobilization continued over the following years as successive expeditions were launched, of which there were 12 between 1894 and 1901, raising the number of active soldiers in Mozambique to 7,000.[4]

The campaigns conducted both in Angola and Mozambique between 1914 and 1918 far-outstripped these numbers. Approximately 400 officers and 12,000 men were sent out to the Angolan territories; more than 19,000 were dispatched to the east coast. The mobilization of auxiliary African soldiers also increased; as did the recruitment of carriers used for military transport services.[5] This effort was also successful in Guinea, if on a smaller scale. By the end of the second decade of the 1900s, "pacification" had been achieved in the three African territories under Portuguese sovereignty.

The Empire under Pressure

Control over the empire as a whole was precarious, given that it was governed by a loosely structured and poorly organized military administration. As in the nineteenth century, the exploitation of the colonies after 1900 was ensured through the dominant trading circuits rather than by production itself (unless the limited, forced labor-based plantation sector is taken into account).

Once military occupation was established, the development and modernization of the colonies became the most urgent tasks of the 1920s, compelled mostly by external factors. The League of Nations defined the aims of colonization as the "civilization" of native peoples and the creation of wealth in overseas territories. Portugal consequently feared that poor performance in Africa would serve as an excuse for the League to partition Angola and Mozambique and eventually place them under the tutelage of more powerful countries. This fear led to the constitutional revision of 1920, giving the colonies greater economic and financial autonomy and permitting the nomination of high commissioners for Angola and Mozambique. The high commissioners were given vast legislative and executive powers and were charged with promoting the rapid development of their respective territories.

This policy was most fully implemented in Angola. After the transatlantic slave trade ended with the closure of the Brazilian and Cuban markets in 1851 and 1866 respectively, the Angolan economy turned to the export of products from the interior, such as coffee, wax and, from 1870 onwards, rubber. At the turn of the century, the plantation economy still consisted only of small areas of coffee and sugarcane cultivation. (The greater part of the latter replaced Brazil's production of *aguardente* destined for Angola's internal market.) Despite the abolition of slavery in 1869 and of servile labor in 1875, labor exploitation in this sector remained archaic and akin to slavery. Given the almost complete lack of roads and railways, the extremely onerous activity of the carriers took up much of the available manpower, with a detrimental effect on the development of agriculture.

This economic system went into crisis at the beginning of the 1890s, and was even more severely affected by the collapse of the Angolan rubber trade following the fall of international market prices in 1901 and 1913. Meanwhile, a prohibition on the manufacture of liquor damaged another important sector. These crises were only partially compensated for by the export of corn from the central plateau. Growing international pressure, moreover, made it increasingly risky to sustain forms of labor exploitation that resembled slavery.

It was against this background that General Norton de Matos, nominated high commissioner for Angola in 1921, appeared on the scene. The general had already governed the region once before, between 1912 and 1915. His plan was political: it aimed to reinforce Portuguese sovereignty over the territory. His efforts to replace the unstable and uneven military administration with a civilian one were undertaken in this spirit, aiming toward the organization of a "systematic, continuous, and constant administrative occupation" as did his policy of destroying the power of the "indigenous" chieftains.[6] The reinforcement of sovereignty entailed stricter control over the religious missions, particularly the foreign ones.[7] It also involved the encouragement of national "lay civilizing missions."[8] The maintenance of a Portuguese presence in Angola was, however, based on intensive colonization by families coming from Portugal, a process Matos sought to foster.[9]

None of these efforts would have been viable without the initially successful modernization of the Angolan economy. One aspect of modernization involved the elimination of all forms of forced labor, which Matos had already decreed during his first administration and which was subsequently reinforced by further legislation during his rule as high commissioner.[10] The process of modernization was also based on a massive program of infrastructure construction, financed mostly by loans contracted with foreign companies active in the colonies. In Angola, this role fell to Diamang (controlled by the Belgian Société Minière), which had controlled the diamond exploration concession in the territories since 1917.[11]

The Matos plan was aborted immediately, however, killed by a lack of financial resources, galloping inflation, and the territory's inability to keep up with the debt payment. The plan left few traces of its existence, apart from an increase in the number of settlers from 9,000 in 1900 to 44,000 in 1930 and a first, limited but nonetheless real, boost to the construction of communications networks. Politically attacked both inside and outside Angola, Matos was forced to retire in 1924. The modernizing path was short-lived. It could not overcome vested interests or the weakness of Portuguese capitalism, which could not sustain the voluntarism of the project.

In Mozambique, room to maneuver was more limited. High commissioner Manuel Brito Camacho, who was nominated in 1921, had even less impact. Approximately two-thirds of the territory under his aegis escaped the direct control of the Portuguese authorities. These areas had been administered since the end of the nineteenth century by two chartered foreign companies: the Niassa Company, operating in the north, between the Lurio and Rovuma rivers; and the Mozambique Company in the central region, between the Zambezi River and the twenty-second parallel. Both of these companies lived off tribute and the recruitment of labor for the Rand mines and the Sena Sugar Estate, which had established plantations in the region of the Lower Zambezi River. As a whole, the Mozambican economy maintained only tenuous relations with Portugal. It was strongly linked to South Africa by the trade passing through the port and railway of Lourenço Marques or Delagoa Bay, as well as by the emigration of laborers to the mining regions of the Transvaal.

This system did not function without tensions, as witnessed by a variety of factors: the massive periodic exodus of people fleeing forced recruitment; the protest of white settlers against emigration to the mines, which robbed them of labor; South African pressures to control the Lourenço Marques port and railway and even to annex the whole of southern Mozambique. In this context, Brito Camacho attempted to negotiate stable relations with South Africa. But he did not meet with success: in 1923, the South African government denounced the Convention of 1909 governing relations between the two regions. The question was left pending, but Cape Town did not abandon its expansionist aims.

By the mid-1920s, it was becoming obvious that the colonies were not fulfilling their promise. Even the relatively more profitable islands of São Tomé and Principe in the Gulf of Guinea, where a nucleus of planters had settled during the previous century, showed signs of decline. The production of cocoa had decreased from plant disease, soil erosion and falling prices. The bankruptcy of development plans, particularly those led by Norton de Matos, aggravated Portuguese anxiety over the colonial future.

The crisis revived the old specter of partition of the empire by the great powers. Apart from the South African threat to Mozambique (the most immediate and real one), it was feared that the colonial designs of Italy and Germany might lead to the re-division of the African continent, to the detriment of Portugal. A 1925 report by the American sociologist Edward Ross, accusing the Portuguese authorities of permitting labor practices akin to slavery in Angola and Mozambique, further darkened the horizon. In Lisbon, the report was regarded as yet another example of the international conspiracy to deprive Portugal of its overseas territories. Yet another threat, whether real or imaginary, the rumor of white separatism circulated in Lisbon on a number of occasions throughout 1924 and 1925.

All this was more than enough to reawaken the most radical forms of nationalist sentiment among the Portuguese elites. That led to the establishment of a "Movement for the Defense of the Colonies," which united personalities from a great variety of political backgrounds. The themes of the movement were those that had dominated colonial ideology from the last quarter of the nineteenth century onwards: the sacred nature of the empire, the "historical mission" of Portugal and national survival.

The colonial crisis and the nationalist upsurge it provoked were two of the decisive factors in the fall of the Portuguese First Republic with the military coup of 28 May 1926. The military dictatorship embodied the nationalist, centralizing reaction in the realm of colonial policy. The dictatorship promulgated a set of laws that aimed to make the colonial state machinery more consistent and efficient. The Organic Bases of the Colonial Administration (Decree Law 12.421 of 2 October 1926) limited the autonomy of the colonial governorships and reinforced the supervisory and fiscal powers of the central administration. The Organic Statute for the Portuguese Catholic

Missions in Africa and Timor (Decree 12.485 of 13 October 1926) gave overseas religious missions a free rein. As stated in the preamble, the aim was to combat the influence of foreign, particularly Protestant, missions, which were considered a threat to nationalization as well as being potentially subversive. The other aim of the legislation was to gain the institutional support of the Church for the exercise of an ideological control that the state had been unable to ensure.

The Political, Civil and Criminal Statute of the Natives of Angola and Mozambique (Decree 12.533 of 30 October 1926, later reformulated by Decree 16.473 of 6 February 1929) juridically distinguished between "civilized" and "native" peoples, a distinction that characterized modern Portuguese colonial practice. "Natives" were to be governed by traditional customs and usage under the tutelage of the state, rather than by the rule of law. Finally, the extensive and critically important Native Labor Code (Decree 16.199 of 6 December 1928) abolished the legal duty to work. This was an obligation that had been consecrated in the previous legislation; its suppression eliminated the legal basis for forced labor. It was a tactical retreat in the face of pressures from the League of Nations and the International Labor Organization. As such it was also heavily criticized by the more radical elements of the regime. Those criticisms, however, were unwarranted: all evidence indicates that compulsory practices were only very briefly affected by legal reforms.

The New State and the Imperial Mentality

The four laws of the military dictatorship laid the foundations for colonial policy in the following decades. It was only under the *Estado Novo,* however, that policy was systematized. The state apparatus was placed at the service of the construction of a colonial empire. The symbol of the transition to this new phase was the Colonial Act of 8 July 1930, which was promulgated by António Salazar as interim minister of the colonies and became part of the colonial constitutional order.

The aim of the Colonial Act was political: solemnly and constitutionally to reaffirm Portuguese sovereignty overseas. Its purpose was thereby to make the law permanent and irrevocable at a time of growing tensions with the League of Nations over the question of indigenous labor and the "internationalization" of the colonial territories. Hence the emphatic statement in the Act's second article: "It is part of the organic essence of the Portuguese nation that its historic function is to possess and colonize its overseas domains and to civilize the native populations contained therein." The issue of the defense of the empire, greatly popular among the Portuguese political elites, was thus taken up again.

The Colonial Act marked the beginning of a period in which the state actively pursued the creation of an imperial mentality among the Portuguese. It did this through an educational system that was at the service of the empire's cause, and through organized events that had an impact on public opinion: conferences of colonial governors; "Colonial Weeks," and various publications and exhibitions—all culminating in the visit of the President to the African colonies in 1938 and the Exhibition of the Portuguese World in 1940.

The Colonial Act, along with the Organic Charter of the Portuguese Colonial Empire and the Overseas Administrative Reform Act, also profoundly restructured the system of colonial power.[12] It centralized power, severely restricting the decision-making autonomy previously in the hands of the high commissioners (later replaced by governors) and concentrated a wide range of legislative and executive powers in the Ministry of the Colonies.

This new orientation was also reflected in the economic realm. The focus was on the "nationalization" of the exploitation of overseas territories. Strict controls over foreign investment and the prohibition or renovation of concessions to foreign companies were implemented, involving a delegation of sovereign powers (Colonial Act, articles 11, 12, and 13). It led to the progressive elimination of the concessions that occupied a great part of Mozambique. In this case, however, "nationalization" also entailed the establishment of complementary links between the various parts of the empire, through the so-called colonial pact regime. According to this system, the overseas possessions were to supply Portugal's industry with the raw materials it needed and to reserve overseas markets for Portuguese products.

This policy contained nothing new. The use of differential rights to protect Portuguese exports to the colonies was a tradition initiated almost a century earlier, and reinforced in 1892 with the establishment of a highly protectionist system, particularly for wine and textiles. The earlier regime was moderated somewhat in 1914, but the principle still applied at the beginning of the 1930s. The *Estado Novo* merely reaffirmed the system, fixing a 50 per cent minimum level of tariff protection and updating duties that had been devalued by inflation.[13]

The persistence with which the Salazar regime attempted to control imperial trade flows was new, however. Successive measures of economic intervention were tried. One was the establishment of exchange rate funds in Angola (1931) and Mozambique (1932), which gave the state control over the distribution of funds available for foreign payments. Another, the 1936 application of the principle of overseas "industrial conditioning," made governmental approval necessary for the establishment of industries otherwise restricted or even entirely barred. In 1937, the establishment of the so-called economic co-ordination mechanisms aimed to control exports of a variety of colonial products.[14]

The objectives of this policy were not very different from those pursued by other colonial nations after 1929. For Portugal, however, the results were very limited. Taking only the 1930s into account, trade between the colonies and Portugal never exceeded 15 per cent of the latter's foreign trade. The same was true for Portuguese exports to the colonies. In both instances, the figures were lower than those between 1890 and World War I.[15] It is important to note, however, the partial successes that were attained. The increase in textile exports to Angola and Mozambique was modest but real, as was the import of colonial products for consumption, including corn and sugar (the latter had exclusive rights to the market in Portugal, as prices were fixed above world prices from 1930 onwards).[16]

Perhaps the most important aspect of the imperial economy in the 1930s was the rapid growth of cotton cultivation in Angola and Mozambique.[17] Fostering the growth of this product had been a traditional aim of Portuguese colonial policy and had been unsuccessfully attempted on a number of occasions from the middle of the nineteenth century on. From the outset, the military dictatorship encouraged the cultivation of cotton, with the promulgation of a decree on 28 September 1926. This law followed the model already in use in the Belgian Congo. It provided for the division of the colonial territory into "zones of influence" under concessions that granted exclusive rights to buy cotton cultivated by the "natives." The real impetus for this policy, however, emerged only in 1932 after the fixing of minimum prices for cotton produced in the colonies for sale in Portugal.

Prices were fixed above international market levels.[18] In 1932, 2,378 tons of cotton was produced, rising to 7,048 tons by 1936.[19]

This system was based on the repression of African peasants, who were forced to cultivate a very low priced product grown to the detriment of subsistence crops or other more profitable products.[20] Forced cultivation was accompanied by more traditional forms of compulsory labor on the plantations or in the transport services, which were maintained despite their proscription by the Labor Code of 1928. It would be a mistake, however, to view Portuguese colonial society in the 1930s as a vast and uniform coercive labor camp. Depending on the economic situation, the pressure on labor varied from region to region (it declined overall in the 1930s, for example). That pressure also depended on levels of demand, and on the level of efficiency of the still weak Portuguese administration of that period. For this reason, many African societies retained a dynamic of their own, as well as a significant ability to adapt to external economic factors.

The Economic Takeoff

World War II lent renewed impetus to the policy of the 1930s, once initial difficulties caused by the closure of various markets and the scarcity of transport had been overcome. With the reorganization of international trade circuits, rising demand for the main colonial products increased the value of both Angola's and Mozambique's foreign trade. This reinvigorated domestic economic activity and increased pressure on the African peasantry through the forced cultivation of certain products or compulsory labor. At the same time, Portugal reinforced its control over imperial trade through specially established economic co-ordinating bodies. Control mechanisms already applied during the preceding decade were reactivated: protectionist duties, price tables for colonial goods (this time lower than international market prices), and fixed, compulsory quotas for the provision of the Portuguese market. Toward the end of the war, trade with the colonies accounted for approximately 20 per cent of Portugal's foreign trade, and Portugal was both Angola's and Mozambique's main trading partner.[21]

Overseas trade expansion lasted throughout the postwar period, benefiting from the high prices obtained for raw materials, and with the coffee boom in Angola. The intensity of relations between the colonies and Portugal peaked in this period, permitting the Portuguese state to achieve some of its traditional objectives. In the 1950s, for example, cotton textiles represented 90 per cent of the imports of Cape Verde, Guinea, São Tome and Príncipe, and Angola, and three-quarters of Mozambican imports. Wine production, which represented about 80 per cent of total exports, reached approximately 1,075,000 hectoliters per annum in the period between 1955 and 1959, in contrast with an average of 180,000 hectoliters between 1930 and 1934.

Apart from these products, the range of Portuguese goods exported to Africa increased to include beer, canned fish, chemical products, tires and machinery. On the other hand, a process of transferring industries to Angola and Mozambique was set in motion under the control of some of the most important Portuguese economic groups. From the mid-1940s on, these groups became interested in investing significantly, for the first time, in trade and finance as well as in productive activities. They invested in the plantation economy, taking advantage of the retreat of foreign capital in the wake of World War II.[22] The state's capacity to invest public monies overseas was also a novelty. Relatively high sums were set aside for infrastructure projects through the First Investment Plan of 1953-58.

In addition to these trends, emigration to Angola and Mozambique increased. Between 1947 and 1960, emigration represented half of all previous demographic flows from Portugal. Large settlements of European origin appeared for the first time in both colonies. In Angola, the number of white inhabitants increased from 44,000 in 1940 to 173,000 in 1960; in Mozambique, the numbers for the same dates rose from 27,500 to 97,000. The sudden attraction of the overseas colonies can be explained primarily by their economic development, but it was also a product of the efforts of the *Estado Novo* to spread the "mystique" of the empire from the 1930s on. That promotional effort rid colonial life of the stigma of exile and death that had traditionally characterized views of life in Africa. Apart from the obvious political importance of white colonization, the increase also contributed to the rapid growth of wine exports to Angola and Mozambique.

Until the end of the 1950s, the trading system between Portugal and the territories in Africa still followed the "colonial pact" model. The framework changed in the 1960s, however, with a new economic policy designed to create a single Portuguese market including Portugal and the overseas colonies, and to permit the free circulation of people, goods and capital. The policy was intended to support "national integration" consecrated with the constitutional revision of 1951. The evolution of the Portuguese economy, however, also rendered the previous model obsolete. The structure of industry was changing with the growth of the electrical, metallurgical, chemical and petroleum sectors. Textiles—which had up to then constituted the backbone of the "colonial pact" regime—lost their weight and influence, becoming less and less dependent on the overseas colonies either as markets or as sources of raw materials.

The creation of the "Portuguese Economic Space" also aimed to respond to the tensions provoked by European integration. By joining the European Free Trade Association (EFTA), and inaugurating a development policy that integrated all the empire's various territories, the Portuguese government hoped at least to gain time to negotiate a stronger position with the member states of the European Economic Community (EEC).

Within the framework of this new policy (although not necessarily because of it), the Angolan and Mozambican economies experienced relatively high growth rates. This was particularly true for Angola, which grew at an annual rate of 7 per cent between 1963 and 1973.[23] This allowed the colony greater access to the international economy under relatively favorable conditions. It also increased foreign capital investment between 1961 and 1965.

The colonial war that began in Angola in 1961, in Guinea in 1963 and in Mozambique in 1964 did not have the negative economic impact that might have been expected. Except for Guinea, the armed conflict affected only marginal areas and left productive activities in Angola and Mozambique intact. In fact, the conflict had an indirectly positive impact on the development of both colonies: not only did it lead to the elimination of the archaic forms of labor exploitation, but it also increased civil and military state investment.

Growth did not lead to national integration, however. On the contrary, the ties between Portugal and the colonies were weakened. Angolan imports from Portugal fell by more than 40 per cent of total imports during the first half of the 1960s, and again by 23 per cent in 1972 and 26 per cent in 1973. As for Mozambique, imports fell by more than 30 per cent by 1967 and again by 19 per cent in 1973. Portuguese exports overseas declined from 23.6 per cent of total exports in 1968 to 12.6 per cent in 1972.[24] These figures reflect Portugal's inability to absorb the increase in colonial production or to provide the colonies with the goods they needed.

The growth rate of the Portuguese economy accelerated, but its more modern and dynamic sectors (base metallurgy, chemicals, metal products, machinery and transport equipment) did not depend on the colonies.[25]

The Political Crisis

The economic centrifugal forces set in motion with international trade liberalization and the internationalization of the productive process forced the Portuguese empire to deal with an even greater political threat: the colonial crisis of legitimacy. It emerged in the wake of World War II, and it owed its origin to the reaffirmation of the principle of self-determination, the declining belief in the superiority of Western civilization and the discrediting of the tutelary role of European nations over races once considered inferior or backward.

The colonial powers' immediate reaction to this new context was to modernize the system. More shocking forms of exploitation, such as forced labor—widespread on the African continent during the war—were eliminated, and greater rights of political representation were conceded to local populations. Portugal was no exception: the first references in parliamentary debate to the need to adapt the juridical and institutional forms governing the empire to the new postwar situation date from 1944. In 1945, the colonial minister traveled overseas to eliminate the legislative and administrative practices most obviously based on racial discrimination, and to abolish forced labor.[26] Political concessions were minimal, however and did not transcend a slight softening of the highly centralized regime.

Such limited reform was manifestly insufficient to respond to the crisis, which shook the very foundations of the colonial system. This was demonstrated in 1947 with the struggle against Portuguese sovereignty over Goa, Damão, and Diu, three small territories on the Indian subcontinent that were claimed by the new state of India. This issue dragged on, as Lisbon consistently refused to allow a referendum to resolve the dispute.

Faced with these pressures, and predicting the deterioration of the situation in Africa, the Portuguese government decided to change the institutional and juridical foundations of the system rather than the system itself. In 1951, a constitutional revision altered the imperial vision that had predominated between the two world wars and that had been enshrined in the Colonial Act. It replaced that vision with the idea of assimilation, through which the colonies became "Overseas Provinces" and parts of a single nation.

In the same period, the regime adopted Lusotropicalism, a theory formulated by the Brazilian sociologist Gilberto Freyre, as the new official doctrine. This doctrine was based on the idea that the relations established between the Portuguese and the people of the tropical regions followed a particular model that emphasized understanding of, and adherence to, local values and which would give rise to a cultural and biological inter-penetration, permitting the creation of an integrated whole—a veritable "Lusotropical civilization."[27]

These new juridical and ideological bases barely affected the colonial political system, however. The Portuguese Organic Overseas Law, promulgated in 1953, only minimally altered overseas colonial administration. The Native Statute was maintained, countering the logic of assimilation. Although it was altered in 1954, the statute still deprived the overwhelming majority of the African population of access to Portuguese citizenship. The only exception to this rule was the "assimilated"—those who had adopted European values and lifestyles. But they were a minority that did not exceed 0.8 per cent of the population in 1961, when the statute was finally abolished.

That percentage also reflects the state's inability and, to some degree, lack of political will to create elites capable of mediating between the colonial power and African society. Portuguese colonial policy toward the traditional African authorities, from the occupation campaigns on, had always been to eliminate them rather than to take advantage of them as intermediaries. The creole groups that had traditionally played that mediating role up to the nineteenth century, moreover, had lost all their influence in the political system, a result both of the influx of Europeans and of the discriminatory practices of the Portuguese administration. Thus, a vacuum was gradually created between the state, which aimed to be omnipresent, and the African people.

This situation left little room for political maneuvering, particularly from the second half of the 1950s on, when African decolonization accelerated. Pressure on Portugal reached a critical point only after the Belgian Congo achieved independence in June 1960. This new state's geographical proximity to Angola and, more importantly, the shared ethnic identity of the people living in the border areas increased the likelihood that the conflict would spill over into Angolan territory. This is exactly what happened. At the beginning of 1961, a revolt erupted against forced cotton agriculture in the Cassang lowlands. It was fiercely repressed. An urban-based uprising broke out in Luanda in February, involving a frustrated attempt to liberate the regime's political prisoners. This event led to the indiscriminate persecution of the black population by the white militia. In March, the Congo insurrection infiltrated the north-eastern part of Angola, accompanied by a massacre of white settlers and mixed-blood, or "assimilated" people. This insurrection marked the beginning of the Colonial War.

The explosion of conflict in Angola profoundly shook the *Estado Novo*. For the first time in his 37-year rule, Salazar faced the threat of being removed from power: a military coup, which involved high-ranking officers—including the Ministers of Defense and of the Army—was attempted in April 1961.

The insurgency was defeated. African policy was subsequently redefined along three key lines: the rapid preparation of a military counter-offensive in the rebellious region of the Congo; the appeal to nationalist sentiment in Portugal; and the promulgation of a vast number of legislative measures. Among these were the abolition of the Native Statute and of forced cultivation and labor. Measures were taken to reinforce the colonial system so it could resist international pressures, and to rob the African movements of their social support.

Once again, however, alterations to the organization of colonial power were very limited. No new spaces were created for the population that had, up to then, been classified as "native." The native communities were regrouped under the *regedorias,* uniting "neighbors according to traditional law," directed by a *regedor.* chosen according to local custom.[28] The new legal formula merely reaffirmed existing practices; the *regedor* continued to depend on the Portuguese administrative authorities. On the other hand, the reforms aimed to integrate the white settlers—who had long railed against centralism—by establishing elections both for the local administrative bodies and for the legislative councils of each "Overseas Province."[29]

This strategy was initially successful and the political and military situation in Portugal was normalized. The mobilization of more military forces to Angola permitted the occupation of the rebel areas once again. Once the first great shock had been absorbed, however, guerrilla war began, spreading to the territory of Guinea in 1963 and to Mozambique in 1964.

The long colonial war took place against a complex background of greater conflicts experienced during the 1960s and 1970s. The emergence of African nationalism in the struggle against the imperial powers was, on a regional level, a battle between the "white bastion" of Africa and the countries of black supremacy. On a world scale, the African conflict was one of the most important of the Cold War. In this context, it was always possible for Portugal to garner military and diplomatic support to contain the guerrillas. Of all the Western nations, only the United States exerted real pressure on the Lisbon government to decolonize. But this pressure was short-lived; it was applied during the Kennedy administration and, above all, in 1961, the year the embargo on the sale of US military supplies to Portugal was decreed. From then on, pressure diminished, and the embargo was avoided on a number of occasions. The strategic importance of the Lajes base in the Azores (conceded to the United States for the first time in 1944 on a periodically renewable basis) prevented Washington from expressing its hostility toward Lisbon's African policy. Support from countries such as France and Germany, by contrast, was outright.

The majority of the African nationalist movements, on the other hand, sought support from the Communist bloc countries. Support and logistical bases allowed these movements to maintain a military presence in Angola, Mozambique and Guinea for many years. With the exception of Guinea, however, they did not significantly affect the economic activities, or even the daily routines, of the main population centers.

Only a fundamental shift in Portuguese policy could have brought the conflict to an end. However, the government of Marcello Caetano, who succeeded Salazar in 1968, made no change in policy. The "progressive autonomy" incorporated into the constitution in 1971 did nothing but transfer powers to the sovereign colonial institutions. The overwhelming majority of Africans were still excluded from the political arena and the right of suffrage. Instead of clearing a path toward a political solution for the colonial question, the constitutional reform of 1971 signaled the regime's inability to find one.

Meanwhile, the progressive disintegration of the bloc sustaining the regime was aggravated as a result of the economic development process itself. Economic interests with more links to the European market than to the "Portuguese Economic Space" emerged. Prolonged war cracked the edifice of the institutions that had been the great pillars of the system: the Church and the armed forces. This process finally culminated in the military coup of 25 April 1974, which was accompanied by a popular uprising and a subsequent process of rapid decolonization.

Conclusions

Foreign observers usually see the Portuguese colonial empire, dependent on a poor country that missed the Industrial Revolution of the nineteenth century, as an abnormal case; one that escaped what appears to have been the normal course of history. Two temptations emerge from this view. The first, which re-emerges periodically, is to see modern Portuguese colonialism as a simple conduit for the aims of the great powers, or a merely formal political sovereignty exercised in the name of outside interests. Portugal's semi-peripheral status makes this theory particularly attractive; however, nothing in the above account confirms it. The presence of foreign capital was always tolerated as a necessary evil, rather than actively promoted. Lisbon's colonial policy, moreover, was always defined in strictly national terms, often to the detriment of the economic development of the overseas territories.

The second temptation is to consider the Portuguese empire as an anachronism, a survivor of the slave-trading era, its existence secured by inertia. Again, analysis discredits this preconceived notion. As noted, the Portuguese empire was constituted during the "scramble for Africa," and it subsequently followed a similar path to that of the other European colonial systems in Africa: the consolidation of frontiers; military and administrative occupation; economic exploitation. The "archaic" forms of labor exploitation found in the Portuguese colonies—forced labor and cultivation—were also found in many French or Belgian territories in Africa, and were therefore not exclusive to backward Portuguese capitalism. From an economic point of view, the difference between the Portuguese empire and the others is one of degree rather than of substance.

Another less obvious difference is perhaps more important. It stems from the particular weight the colonial question held in Portuguese politics. For historical reasons, the imperial project was connected with the image of the nation itself, the "sacred heritage" of the "Golden Age of Discovery" and the country's own independence in relation to Spanish power on the Iberian Peninsula.

This view led to the "deification" of the empire, a process that reached its culmination in the last quarter of the nineteenth century, casting a long shadow over the period to follow. It robbed anticolonial currents of any political space. These never acquired more than a tiny following in Portugal except during the final years of the *Estado Novo*. Whereas nationalism in other colonial countries was divided into pro- and anti-overseas expansionist currents, Portuguese nationalism was, with rare exceptions, imperialist.

Hence the voluntarist nature of Portuguese colonial policy: it sought to mold the social forces and economic interests involved in the colonial process in the name of national goals that were considered transcendent. This voluntarism peaked during the *Estado Novo* and lay at the root of the creation of an "imperial mystique" in the 1930s and the tenacious defense of the colonial system in its final years, against the general trends of the times.

4 | Between Africa and Europe: Portuguese Foreign Policy, 1890-2000

Nuno Severiano Teixeira

Portugal is both a European and an Atlantic country. As a small, semi-peripheral power with only one land border, it has always experienced an unstable geopolitical balance, caught between the devil of continental pressure and—literally—the deep blue sea. Geopolitical conditions, as well as the constant search for balance, have informed the strategic options and the historical characteristics of Portuguese foreign policy.

It would not be true to say that Portugal's foreign policy and diplomacy changed substantially at the end of the nineteenth century and during the twentieth century. Portuguese foreign policy principles were always marked by the constant search for a peninsular equilibrium and a concomitant balance between Europe and the Atlantic; in other words, between the weight given to relations with Spain, on the one hand, and extra-peninsular alliances and strategic options, a preferential alliance with the maritime powers—and a special emphasis on the colonial project, on the other. It was only with the advent of decolonization and the emergence of the "European option" that this historical framework changed.

From the diplomatic point of view, Portugal was still at the mercy of the power games and projects of the great powers. The country's diplomats sought to maintain a balance between Portugal's multiple dependencies and to adapt to new, evolving, international circumstances with short-term policies subject to rapid alterations.

The Constitutional Monarchy

Throughout the first half of the nineteenth century and up to the 1870s, Portuguese foreign policy was unequivocally and forcibly dominated by the alliance with Britain. Initially, the primacy of this alliance was ensured in a direct and violent way by a political-military tutelage imposed after the French invasions and the economic hegemony ensured through the Anglo-Portuguese Treaty of 1810. Subsequently, it was imposed in a less direct, albeit equally effective, fashion through the Quadruple Alliance, and through the integration of the peripheral and dependent Portuguese economy into the British economic system. Nevertheless, British hegemony over Portugal was sometimes visible during the first half of the century, notably during the emergence of liberalism in 1834, the September 1836 revolution and the Patuleia Civil War, which culminated in the Gramido Convention of 1847.

It was only with the unification of Germany, in 1871, and the resulting emergence of a new power in the international arena that an important alteration took place in the balance of power that had been in place since the Congress of Vienna in 1815. Although still dominant, Britain was no longer alone in the international sphere. Portuguese foreign policy thus had an alternative. At the very least, mitigating the overwhelming hegemony of the alliance with Britain became a possibility. Portuguese diplomats attempted to make use of the German alternative when the first colonial conflicts with Britain emerged in the 1880s. The British Ultimatum of 1890 was a direct result of Portugal's attempt to decrease its external dependence. The ultimatum was a highly symbolic moment in Portuguese history, in both foreign and domestic political terms. It signaled the end of the monarchy.

International public law governing colonial issues was, until the Berlin Conference of 1885, based on a Portuguese juridical principle: the principle of historically established rights. Indeed, it was according to this principle that the first colonial disputes between Portugal and Britain had been settled through international arbitration. The Guinean Bolama Bay question had been settled by President Grant of the United States in 1870, and the dispute over Lourenço Marques Bay in Mozambique had been mediated by President MacMahon of France in 1875.

Still, as interest among the European powers for the colonial territories increased—leading to the "scramble for Africa"—the rising tension not only threatened the colonial territories Portugal claimed on the basis of historical rights, but also challenged the very juridical principle of historical rights in the international arena. The Berlin Conference of 1885 had a dual impact on Portuguese foreign policy. First, the partition of Africa forced Portugal to limit its sphere of influence on the African continent through the signing of two conventions in 1886: the Franco-Portuguese and the Luso-German—both limiting treaties. Second, Portugal was forced to occupy the territories it claimed by historical right through the international consecration of the new principle of effective occupation.[1]

Faced with Britain's explicit refusal to support Portugal's project, either politically or diplomatically, at the Berlin Conference, and confronted with the emergence of Bismarck's Germany as an extra-European power, Portuguese foreign policymakers could not resist a rapprochement with Germany. They sought from Berlin the support on colonial matters that was not forthcoming from London. For Portugal, it was not a question of altering its policy of foreign alliances; instead, Portugal sought a diplomatic alternative and greater room to maneuver in relation to Britain's oppressive hegemony.

It was in this context that Portugal developed its "Meridianal African Portuguese" project, famous from its cartographic embodiment in the "Pink Map." It was a project that linked Angola and Mozambique horizontally through the interior of the African continent. The Pink Map opposed British imperial projects aiming to vertically link Cape Town with Cairo.

The combination of the rapprochement with Germany and the colonial dispute with Britain lay at the heart of the diplomatic conflict between Portugal and Britain that culminated in the British ultimatum on 11 January 1890. London demanded the immediate withdrawal of Portuguese troops from the disputed area under threat of a break in diplomatic relations.

Faced with the ultimatum, and strategically weaker than its opponent, Portugal gave in to the demand. Its initial diplomatic strategy was a vain attempt to mitigate the effects of defeat by appealing for international arbitration, as provided for by the 12th article of the final act of the Berlin Treaty. Britain, however, did not accept the solution, nor did Germany accept a mediating role. Portugal then had no choice but to agree to direct negotiations with Britain. After eighteen months of discussions, and the collapse of a first treaty on 20 August 1890, Portugal and Britain signed a second treaty in June 1891 that put an end to the conflict, and drew what became the political map of Portuguese Africa until the era of decolonization began in 1975.

The treaty imposed onerous conditions. Despite a parliamentary debate on revising the country's policy of alliance—on possibly seeking German support for colonial matters—and on establishing an Iberian Union, the crisis of the ultimatum did not lead to radical changes: the alliance with Britain went unchallenged as the lynchpin of Portuguese foreign policy. Another consequence of the ultimatum was more important: Portuguese nationalism became colonial. With nationalist sentiment affronted by the treaty, and with part of the African territories amputated, the ensuing imperial project, and Portugal's "African vocation," shaped collective political myths for a century after the ultimatum.[2] From then on, Portuguese foreign policy developed on two parallel, but clearly interdependent fronts: the European, centered on the alliance with Britain; and the colonial, centered on the African empire.

During monarchical rule, Portugal's diplomacy was notable for a number of European state visits by King Carlos, and by visits to Portugal by King Alfonso XIII of Spain, Britain's King Edward VII, Germany's Kaiser Wilhelm II and President Emile-François Loubet of France.

Portuguese historians have passionately debated the meaning of these state visits, as well as King Carlos's foreign policy. The monarchists have assessed the latter positively, even suggesting that Portuguese diplomacy had a formative impact on the establishment of the *Entente Cordiale* and the *Triple Entente*. The republicans, on the other hand, have minimized the political value of these diplomatic trips as mere tourist or technical visits. If it is unreasonable to attribute great weight to Portuguese diplomacy in the international political arena, however, it is equally exaggerated to rob the latter of any diplomatic or political meaning. The aim of these initiatives was to ensure the inclusion of Portugal in international politics and to influence the foreign policies of the great powers, whose interests and objectives affected Portuguese interests and aims in two regions: the colonies and Europe.

Following the British ultimatum, the alliance with the United Kingdom went through a particularly critical period that culminated in the Anglo-German agreement to partition the Portuguese colonies in 1898. The Boer War and other international events radically altered the situation, however, favoring an Anglo-Portuguese rapprochement. The secret declaration of 1899—inappropriately named the Treaty of Windsor—marked the renovation and reinforcement of the alliance with Britain. The British fleet's visit to Lisbon in 1900 was the first public indication of that rapprochement; its consummation was the visit of the newly crowned King Edward VII in 1903. The arbitration treaty of 1904—the Second Treaty of Windsor—finally consecrated this shift. Relations with Spain were also normalized in the aftermath of the polemic over the Iberian Union and the difficult period of Iberianism.

With its relations with Britain and Spain thus improved, Portugal regained its traditional geopolitical equilibrium. After the critical period of the last decade of the nineteenth century, the first years of the twentieth were particularly favorable for Portuguese foreign policy.

In Europe, Portuguese interests conflicted with those of the Great Powers in the western Mediterranean and, more importantly, in the Atlantic. The Morocco question polarized opinion. The Portuguese position was not a matter of indifference to the Great Powers, as evidenced by the visits of Kaiser Wilhelm and President Loubet to Lis-

bon precisely on the eve of the Algeciras Conference of 1905.
France sought support, and Germany neutrality. The Portuguese
position, as expressed in the instructions to the delegates from the
Ministry of Foreign Affairs, was quite clear: the delegates were to
vote with Britain without arousing German hostility. The results
were highly beneficial for Portuguese diplomacy: having supported
the position of France and Britain, Portugal reaffirmed its international status in relation to the *Entente Cordiale*. On a regional level,
Portugal stood by the powers with a particularly keen interest in
Morocco—namely, France and Spain.

The Atlantic and the archipelagos of Madeira and the Azores
were also fundamental to foreign policy.[3] Portugal's Atlantic territories were strategic points because they permitted the establishment
of a privileged logistical position, with control over maritime routes
as well as the installation of submarine cables. These territories had
been historically important for Britain, and they became critical for
Germany when the latter began to dispute the former's naval hegemony.

It was in this context that Britain demanded preferential access to
the islands after the secret declaration of 1899; Britain wanted formal guarantees that these territories would not be handed over to a
third power. After King Edward's visit in 1903, the Treaty of Windsor of 1904 and, above all, the Moroccan crisis of 1906, the British
government redoubled its efforts to obtain such guarantees. Later
that control would permit the establishment of military installations,
including naval and airforce bases, in the Azores archipelago during
the two world wars and the Cold War. The bases were later handed
over to the United States with the establishment of a tripartite agreement between Portugal, Britain and the US in 1917.

Although this favorable progress was made in Europe, Portuguese
interests and strategic objectives came into conflict with those of the
Great Powers in the colonies, putting Portugal's colonial project and
its colonial foreign policy at risk. International stability depended in
great part on Anglo-German rivalry to ensure the European balance
of power, Britain was often forced to negotiate with Germany on

colonial matters. In particular, the Portuguese colonies became pieces of the negotiating currency.

International historians have long debated the role of the colonial question in Anglo-German relations. Were the colonies a strategic objective in and of themselves, or merely a tactical means to ensure appeasement and a bilateral rapprochement? Whatever the aim, for Portugal the result was one and the same: a threat to its African empire. The threat reared its head twice: in 1898, during the monarchy; and in 1912-13, during republican rule. On both occasions the cause was an Anglo-German agreement to partition the Portuguese colonies.

The 1898 partition agreement must be seen in light of two distinct factors. The first was the international repercussion of the colonial situation during the second half of the 1890s—especially the imperial projects of Britain and Germany. The second was the difficult financial situation of the Portuguese state, which worsened progressively with the declaration of bankruptcy in 1892.

To resolve its public finance problems, Portugal proposed that Britain grant a loan, to be guaranteed by Portugal's colonial customs revenues. When Germany got wind of the proposal, it declared its interest in the operation to the British government. The situation was favorable for an Anglo-German rapprochement. The loan issue became the pretext for the opening of bilateral negotiations between the two countries, culminating in an agreement that not only ensured that Portuguese colonial customs revenues would guarantee the loan, but which also provided for the immediate sharing of customs revenues between Britain and Germany. Foreseeing the possibility of debt default on the part of Portugal, moreover, the agreement provided for shared German and British "zones of influence" in the colonies themselves.

Two conditions had to be met for the agreement to work. First, Portugal had to fail to service the debt and, second, both powers needed the political will to cooperate. Neither condition was met: Portuguese diplomats in London learned of the supposedly secret agreement, and Lisbon reacted by canceling the loan. On the other hand, although Germany wanted to see the agreement succeed, the same was not true for Britain. The latter was troubled by the obvious contradiction between the Anglo-German agreement and the obligations imposed by the Anglo-Portuguese alliance. A more ambiguous solution was desirable for Britain; it wanted an agreement that would neutralize Germany without alienating Portugal.[4]

The unfolding of the Anglo-Boer conflict and the evolution of the international situation favored Portugal.[5] Britain urgently required use of the port at Lourenço Marques, and the railway line situated in Portuguese Mozambican territory. It called for the diplomatic support of Lisbon, and for the use of its colonial resources. Informed of the Anglo-German agreement, Portuguese diplomats took advantage of London's request to make a masterly move: they offered support, but on the condition that the British reaffirm the Anglo-Portuguese treaties of 1642 and 1661. Hence the secret declaration of 1899 and the Treaty of Windsor of 1904; hence, too, the period of cordial relations during the final years of King Carlos's reign.

The alliance with Britain was, however, the cause of new problems for Portugal's foreign policy during the last years of the monarchy—this time in Europe and on the Iberian Peninsula. Since Alfonso XIII's accession to the Spanish throne in 1902, Portugal's neighboring power had abandoned its traditional isolationism and had initiated a diplomatic rapprochement with the *Entente Cordiale*—and with Britain in particular. After Algeciras, Britain needed Spanish naval cooperation to ensure its position in the western Mediterranean. This reinforced a diplomatic rapprochement at Cartagena in 1907.

Cartagena became a specter for Portugal. Spain's extra-peninsular system of alliances, its relations with Portugal's old ally and the re-emergence of the "traditional threat" upset Portugal's fragile geopolitical balance and increased its vulnerability. Not only did it reduce Portugal's importance in the peninsula—devaluing its political importance compared with Spain—but more fundamentally, it weakened the value of the alliance with Britain as a guarantee of national sovereignty. Had Britain not already negotiated with Germany over the colonies? What was to stop it from doing the same with Spain?

These were the fundamental questions that confronted Portuguese foreign policy toward the end of the constitutional monarchy. The similarity of the political regimes and the family connection between King Carlos and Edward VII mitigated the impact of the Cartagena meeting. The regicide of 1908 drastically altered the situation, however. Republican Portugal adopted the same foreign policy principles of the monarchical regime; it confronted the same difficulties and challenges, but now without the advantage of similar regimes and connected royal dynasties.

The Democratic Republic

During the period of anti-monarchical propaganda, the Republican Party had no defined foreign policy. Its ideas were vague and diffuse, based on Iberianism—a legacy of traditional Republican ideology that combined republicanism, municipalism and federalism. At the same time, they were also based on an exacerbated nationalism, which, because of the British Ultimatum, was Anglophobic and strongly linked with the colonial project.

Only with its gradual rise to power, and its concomitant shift from a tradition of oppositionist political culture to political realism, did the Republican Party abandon its Iberianist ideology and Anglophobia. Indeed, even during the last days of the monarchy, Republican diplomatic policy was still based on traditional precepts. Nevertheless the first official Republican ambassadorial missions to France and Britain—visits that aimed to prepare the international community for the formal recognition of the future republic—transmitted an already realistic and moderate message that was conveyed within the historical framework of Portuguese foreign relations. In the name of the future regime, the Republican Party re-affirmed its commitment to previous international political and economic agreements—including the alliance with Britain and strict neutrality *vis-à-vis* Spanish domestic politics and the Iberian question.

While French foreign policy was conditioned by the *Entente Cordiale*, London's position was of critical importance. The Republican "embassy" in London achieved its first diplomatic victory for the future republic: republican leaders gained assurances—albeit unofficial—that the regime question in Portugal would be treated as an internal affair. The British Foreign Office also implicitly assured the Republicans that the Anglo-Portuguese alliance was not between royal dynasties, but between peoples. Britain's non-intervention and the survival of the Anglo-Portuguese alliance thus seemed secure. The path towards the international recognition of the future Portuguese republic promised to be smooth. Nothing, however, could have been further from the truth.

The international situation was not at all favorable to the establishment of a republic—a republic that, moreover, seemed to be assuming an increasingly radical and Jacobin face. Europe at that time was dominated by monarchies, and the only two republican regimes in existence could neither promise significant international support nor provide alternatives for Portuguese foreign policy. Switzerland was a small power with little weight in the international arena, and France was diplomatically linked with Britain through the *Entente Cordiale*.

Although Britain stuck to its promise not to intervene in Portugal's internal affairs, when the monarchy was toppled on 5 October 1910 the new republic was received internationally with a coolness that quickly descended to hostility. Gaining official recognition was a difficult and complex process involving three distinct phases that dragged on for 10 months, and which had a serious impact on Portugal's domestic and international situation.

The first wave of official recognition occurred almost immediately, led by the South American republics—with Brazil and Argentina at the forefront. The second wave, between June and August 1911, was led by the United States and France. The delay in extending recognition was different in each case; the United States successively postponed it, breaking with the Monroe Doctrine that traditionally advocated the automatic recognition of *de facto* regimes.

Washington sought assurances as to the constitutional legality of the regime, so as to maintain a certain leeway when confronted with the recognition of the various Latin American dictatorships. France, on the other hand, was guided by the British attitude. Being linked to Britain by the *Entente Cordiale*, its recognition was conditioned by all the political-constitutional guarantees the British government demanded of the republican regime.

The final wave of recognition was initiated by the British monarchy, followed by the other great European monarchies. London made recognition of the republic conditional on a series of demands—the fulfillment of which successively delayed the process. First, it demanded that elections be held and that the normal functioning of the Constituent Assembly be ensured. Once the Assembly had been elected, it demanded that the head of state be elected. Once the president had been elected and was exercising his powers, Britain delayed recognition yet again. The cause of this delay was not the juridical-constitutional nature of the republic, but the dispute between the Portuguese Republic and the Anglican Church in Portugal over the Law of Separation of Church and State. The problem was finally resolved only on 11 September 1911, when Britain and the remaining European monarchies finally extended their formal recognition.

Official recognition was undoubtedly an important step, but it did not by any means imply international acceptance of the regime. The establishment of the republic did not alter the orientation of Portuguese foreign policy or the strategic options of the state, which remained centered on the alliance with Britain and the African colonial project. The other threats and challenges persisted as well.

Despite its international isolation, the republic was still a part of the dynamics of international politics in both Europe and Africa. Portuguese interests still intersected with those of the European powers in the Mediterranean and the Atlantic.[6] British interest in the Azores continued, regardless of the change of regime. Although a British Admiralty report of 1912 questioned the strategic value of Portugal on the Iberian Peninsula, interest in the Atlantic islands was maintained, and London renewed its request for guarantees of exclusive access to the islands whenever a new Portuguese foreign minister took office.

Portugal was a presence in the Mediterranean: it adhered to the Franco-German agreement of 1911 that put an end to the Agadir crisis. Portugal adopted an attitude of support for the *Entente Cordiale* powers, so it could not openly confront Spain—which had not resolved its differences with France. The difficult relations between the two peninsular states forced Portugal to engage in what turned out to be a successful diplomatic exercise involving a postponement of adherence to the 1911 agreement until the Franco-Spanish agreement of May 1912.

Despite the success of Portuguese diplomacy in this process, the rapprochement between Spain and the other powers of the *Entente Cordiale* raised the specter of Cartagena once again, and gave renewed importance to the geopolitical balance between Spanish continental pressure and the compensatory weight of the alliance with Britain.

The pro-annexation lobby in Spain was powerful and—although the idea did not reflect the position of Spanish foreign policy—Alfonso himself did not entirely reject it. Portugal's political instability facilitated the possibility. In this context, was the alliance with Britain an adequate diplomatic and military instrument to guarantee Portuguese security? This was a very delicate question: the British Foreign Office preferred not to intervene directly in the peninsular issue, favoring a bilateral understanding between the two protagonists. In the periods of more acute animosity, nevertheless, it was unable to abstain.

While London did not go so far as to accept Spanish military intervention and annexation of Portugal, it did demonstrate a special degree of tolerance toward Spain during the monarchical incursions. On two occasions (in 1911 and 1912), pro-monarchy troops marched into Portuguese territory with the knowledge and assent of the Spanish authorities, proclaiming their intention of restoring the monarchy. These incursions were military fiascos;

nevertheless, they aggravated the specter of the "Spanish threat."[7] Portugal persistently tried to gain formal guarantees regarding the alliance from the British Foreign Office throughout 1912 and 1913, but never received more than a verbal guarantee because of the colonial question.

In a repetition of the events of 1898, a second Anglo-German agreement to partition the Portuguese colonies was signed in 1912-13. This agreement arose from the prevailing tension in the international arena, with the arms race and the increasing Anglo-German rivalry before World War I; it also stemmed from Portugal's own continuing post-revolutionary international isolation and domestic political instability.

In the wake of the total failure of the Haldane mission to Germany in 1912, the only way to maintain the dialogue between Britain and Germany was through the colonies. Compensating Germany overseas was the only means available to Britain for maintaining the fragile equilibrium of European forces and to avoid conflict. The domestic and external vulnerably of the Portuguese republic also favored an Anglo-German rapprochement. Therefore, in 1912, the two powers renewed the terms of the 1898 agreement. The partition of zones of influence was re-negotiated and, more importantly, the basis for legitimately intervening in Portugal's overseas territories was broadened. Like the first agreement, however, the second failed under autonomous but simultaneous pressure from Portugal and France. The outbreak of World War I finally rendered it obsolete; yet one thing about it was certain—this instrument for international stabilization, which the British did not hesitate to adopt when it appeared to serve its interests and aims, constituted a real and concrete threat to Portugal's imperial project.

At the beginning of World War I, Portugal faced a threat from Spain in Europe and from Germany in its colonies. Its vulnerability resulted from British intransigence over Spain and the peninsular question, and Germany's persistence with regard to the colonial question. These two factors were at the heart of Portugal's decision to enter the war.

Portuguese historians have usually explained the nation's participation in World War I on the basis of two distinct theories. One is
the colonial thesis that argues Portugal entered the war to save the
colonies.[8] There is no doubt about this explanation: the Portuguese
colonies were the object of economic and strategic interest on the
part of the Great Powers; more importantly, they had already been
twice used as "currency" in the negotiations between European
powers. During the war, interest in the Portuguese colonies
increased. Germany attacked them militarily, and incited the population to rise up against Portuguese rule. Britain used them strategically as supply bases for wartime operations. Above all, there was no
guarantee that Britain would not place the Portuguese colonies on
the negotiating table should that become necessary to resolve the
conflict advantageously. The threat was real, as was the risk to Portuguese sovereignty over its colonies.

For Portugal, the colonial question was both a weighty consideration and a mobilizing factor: indeed, it was the one issue that produced consensus in Portuguese society. However, the colonial issue
is not sufficient—in and of itself—to explain the decision to enter
the war: it cannot account for Portugal's active belligerence and military intervention in the European theater. Sovereignty and imperial integrity could have been assured by an undeclared neutrality and
by a concentration of war efforts in the African theater.

The second explanatory theory is the peninsular European thesis.
It argues that Portugal entered the war to ensure a place for itself in
Europe and to ward off the "Spanish threat."[9] There is no doubt about
this motivation either: the country's international situation had been
difficult before the war, and did not change during the conflict. The
"Spanish threat" was a *de facto* threat, all the more so when Britain
warned Portugal that the alliance merely guaranteed the security of
the colonies and Portugal's maritime coast, but not its land frontier.
Faced with Spain's neutrality, Portuguese belligerence on the side of
the Allies—under the umbrella of the British alliance—constituted a
double guarantee: first, it ensured a strong alliance with Britain by
weakening the Anglo-Spanish link; second, it increased Portugal's

international status, affirmed its preponderance in the peninsular context, and thereby did ward off the "Spanish threat."

This second thesis doubtless explains Portugal's belligerence, but it too fails to provide a reason for military intervention in the European theater. To explain Portugal's entry into the European war, it is therefore necessary to take up a third explanation: the republican regime's lack of political consolidation and national legitimacy.[10] Given the social cleavages and political instability of the new nation, only an external threat and military intervention in the central theater of war alongside the Great Powers could enable the regime to promote national unity and build support. Thus it simultaneously achieved both its foreign objectives and the consolidation and democratic legitimacy of the republic. Portugal entered the war on 9 March 1916.

Voluntary intervention was undoubtedly the safest way for Portugal to achieve all its objectives—safeguarding the colonies, warding off Spain, and consolidating the republic—yet it was also the most difficult way, because it meant meeting more stringent conditions, and it demanded greater means. That very voluntarism betrayed Portugal's realistic evaluation of the strategic situation. Not only did it fail to achieve the consensus and national unity the regime hoped for, but it actually aggravated internal cleavages, fostering a political movement that aimed to shift war policy. That movement led Sidónio Pais to power in December 1917. Furthermore, voluntarism wrongly assessed the correlation between aims and means; in other words, the objectives were too ambitious compared with the economic, financial, military and even political means available.

The results were plain at the Treaty of Versailles in 1919. Portugal paraded alongside the victors under the Arc de Triomphe, but the Peace Conference left it far from attaining its war objectives.[11] The colonial question was not resolved: Portugal's sovereignty over its colonial territories had depended almost directly on its intervention in the war; but even the restitution of Kionga—the small territory on Africa's east coast that the Germans had occupied since the end of the nineteenth century—was not part of the war compensations. It merely represented the restoration of the international legal order.

The aims of peace were different from the aims of war. They were related to the imperious need to reconstruct the country's economy. Portuguese foreign policy therefore concentrated on achieving financial objectives; namely, war debt forgiveness and the right to reparations and indemnities from Germany. Portugal's place in the "concert of nations" and the resolution of the peninsular question were still on the agenda.

If the economic and financial objectives were achieved, the same cannot be said for Portugal's international position, which was now shaped by participation in the reorganization of the international system and in the League of Nations. This is where Portuguese foreign policy suffered its greatest defeat: not only was Portugal's application for membership to the Executive Committee of the League of Nations not even considered but, more importantly, Spain managed—despite its neutrality—to gain the position Portugal's belligerence had failed to achieve.

In any case, during the final phase of the democratic republic, the League of Nations became a reference point for Portuguese foreign policy. Apart from bilateral relations based on the geopolitical balance of the Lisbon-London-Madrid triangle, a new institutional arena for multilateral relations had opened up that gave Portugal's foreign policymakers a wider margin for diplomatic maneuvering and for diversifying the republic's foreign relations with Brazil, Belgium and South Africa.

The colonial project was still Portugal's key strategic concern—albeit in different international circumstances. In accordance with the dictates of the League of Nations and the British Foreign Office, Portugal adopted a new colonial political-administrative regime that was institutionalized through the establishment of high commissioners, and which granted the colonies greater autonomy. The republic's treatment of colonial issues on an international level had two further characteristics. First, Portugal's presence was ensured in the Permanent Commission of Mandates of the League of Nations. Second, an active and versatile diplomacy was undertaken—sometimes in London and sometimes in Brussels—in defense of Portuguese colonial interests in Mozambique and Macao, where the issue of sovereignty was raised in 1921.

The military dictatorship that overthrew the democratic republic on 28 May 1926 did not alter Portugal's foreign policy. Overwhelmed by financial crisis and domestic political conflicts, the dictatorship retained republican foreign policy. The colonial project and the alliance with Britain were dominant; the diversification of foreign relations—as well as multilateral initiatives in the "international assembly in Geneva"—were maintained. The Financial Commission of the Council of the League of Nations was even involved in a foreign debt issue in 1927-28. It was only with the rise of the *Estado Novo* in the 1930s that Portuguese foreign policy underwent a significant shift.

The *Estado Novo*

When Antonio Salazar rose to power in 1932, his views on international politics were not yet known. In 1933, the year his regime was institutionalized, he gave an interview expressing his views on foreign policy matters. He protested openly and critically against the "international parliamentarism" of the League of Nations and declared his loyalty to the alliance with Britain.

This seemed to herald a return to the traditional precepts of Portugal's foreign policy: indeed, Salazar's initial assessment of the country's international situation confirmed that tendency. First, he condemned "assemblyism" in Geneva, which he considered to be the center of continental politics. He countered it by affirming Portugal's Atlantic vocation, and distancing the country from continental issues. Secondly, he reaffirmed the alliance with Britain. Thirdly, he emphasized the reinforcement of Iberian friendship. Finally, he intransigently defended the integrity of the colonies.

By 1935, the political objectives and the diplomatic principles that would govern Portugal's foreign policy during both the Spanish

Civil War and World War II wars had been defined. Such was the importance of these two events that Salazar personally conducted foreign policy from 1936 to 1947, directing the Foreign Affairs Ministry while acting as president of the Council of Ministers.

Indeed, the deliberate distancing of European affairs, also, and the affirmation of Atlantic Portugal and the African colonial project, constituted Salazar's strategic options. Furthermore, the traditional balance based on the diplomatic triangle between Lisbon, London and Madrid was revived—it became the central focus of Salazar's foreign policy throughout the 1930s and 1940s.[12]

Between 1931 and 1939, Portuguese foreign policy was completely dominated by the "Spanish question." Salazar had a very particular understanding of the "peninsular friendship:" not only was it a desirable principle, it was an important way to achieve a geopolitical balance—albeit strongly conditioned by the political nature of the regimes in question. The size of the Iberian Peninsula, its division between two states and the varying nature of the political regimes in each country all represented a menace to Portugal—especially to the survival of Salazar's regime. Indeed, between 1931 and 1936, Salazar saw the Spanish Republic as a dual threat: in addition to the permanent Iberian threat, there was the danger of revolution. The specter of left-wing victory in Madrid loomed large in Lisbon: the triumph of the Popular Front in February 1936 heightened Salazar's fears of the incompatibility of two opposing regimes cohabiting peninsular space.[13]

Given these concerns, Portugal's foreign policy during the Spanish Civil War aimed to reconcile two imperatives: it continued to reaffirm the alliance with Britain—an instrument Salazar knew to be essential for safeguarding the African colonial project in a European context already dominated by the expansionism of nascent totalitarian regimes—and it also worked discreetly but generously to support the Spanish nationalists. This support was considered indispensable to ensure the installation of a regime in Madrid that would not threaten the survival of the *Estado Novo*.

Despite the divergences and reservations that affected Salazar's negotiations with London, he always respected the alliance with Britain and coordinated his policies with the British Foreign Office. Salazar participated in the London Commission for Non-Intervention in the Spanish Civil War; he agreed to the demand that Portugal's borders be monitored: he did not even officially recognize the Burgos regime until Britain had done so.

On the other hand, he did not spare any effort in aiding Franco's nationalist troops unofficially. He gave them logistical and financial support, and granted them safe passage into Portuguese territory where they could find material support and mobilize volunteers.

The duplicity of Portugal's foreign policy succeeded throughout almost the entire Civil War. It was only with the Munich crisis of 1938 that the conciliation of official and informal Portuguese policy was challenged.

With the end of the Civil War, Franco's victory created the conditions for the establishment of "peninsular friendship" along the lines Salazar had espoused, initiating a period of good relations and political solidarity between the two authoritarian regimes. This solidarity found diplomatic expression in the signing of the Luso-Spanish Treaty of Friendship and Non-Aggression—the Peninsular, or Iberian, Pact—in March 1939.[14] This pact, together with the alliance with Britain, constituted the basic diplomatic instruments that governed Portuguese foreign policy during World War II.

On 1 September 1939, immediately after the invasion of Poland and before Britain had declared war on Germany, Salazar hastened to declare Portugal's neutrality. He was undoubtedly moved to do so by the memory of the detrimental, ambiguous and undeclared neutrality of the First Republic during World War I; moreover, Salazar wanted to distance Franco's Spain from the Axis powers and to ensure its neutrality. The move also took account of the low degree of efficiency and readiness of Portugal's armed forces.

Between 1939 and 1942, Salazar's worries centered on Spain's possible entry into the war on the Axis side, which could have dragged Portugal into the conflict on the side of the Allies. The maintenance of neutrality and the concomitant establishment of conditions favorable for Spain's neutrality were therefore the key objectives of Portugal's foreign policy—a policy that was buttressed by the alliance with Britain and the Iberian Pact.

Respecting the alliance with Britain—and following the British example—Portuguese diplomacy insistently pressured Franco to comply with the policy of non-belligerence and to fulfill the conditions of the Iberian Pact, especially the Additional Protocol of 1940. Between 1940 and 1942, Portugal's neutrality effectively favored Spanish non-belligerence.

The success of Portugal's foreign policy is undoubtedly attributable to Lisbon's political will and its diplomatic action. Things could have turned out differently, however, had it not been for a series of events that favored such a policy. In the first place, the Great Powers took an interest in the strategic neutrality of the Iberian Peninsula. Second, Nazi Germany shifted its military objectives, which, from 1940 on, focused on the Soviet Union rather than on the British Isles and the Mediterranean. Third, the internal situation in Spain itself—the state of penury inherited from the Civil War that was aggravated by the economic blockade imposed by the Allies—destroyed the strategic reserves indispensable for conducting a war.

In the autumn of 1942, the strategic situation in the Iberian Peninsula changed significantly. With the Allied victory in North Africa and the opening of the fronts in Sicily and Normandy, the Iberian theater became peripheral. From 1943 on, Spain abandoned its non-belligerent status, and the Iberian Peninsula as a whole became neutral. With peninsular neutrality ensured, Portugal was in a position to diversify its foreign policy objectives, and it now turned to the defense of its economic interests and, above all, the integrity of the colonies. The controversy over Macao and the maintenance of sovereignty over Timor, which had been successively invaded by the Dutch, the Australians and the Japanese, became a key concern.

In this context, Atlantic foreign policy and relations with the Allied powers were reinforced. Portugal, Britain and the United

States initiated tripartite negotiations for the concession of bases in the Azores archipelago. The talks culminated in the establishment of British and North American military bases on the islands in 1943 and 1944. As part of the same policy, Portugal ceased to sell wolfram to the Axis powers.

Although it maintained a formal position of neutrality, Portugal's foreign policy went through a period of "cooperative neutrality" or—as the British would have it—"continental neutrality."[15] Portuguese historians have extensively discussed neutrality and Salazar's World War II foreign policy. The traditional thesis explains Portuguese neutrality on the basis of the "statesman" theory: neutrality was successful because of Salazar's political acumen. More recent hypotheses differ, however: they tend to "relativize" the importance of the "statesman" and to give weight to objective factors, such as the situation in Franco's Spain and, above all, the strategic evolution of the war. The strategic neutrality of the Iberian Peninsula—a geographic extension of neutrality on the western Mediterranean coast with Vichy France—served not only Portuguese foreign policy interests but also those of Britain, and even of Germany.[16]

With the end of the war, Portugal, as a neutral country, was peripheral to the diplomatic efforts to restore peace and reorganize the new international diplomatic system. Although the authoritarian regime survived the wave of postwar democratizations, the nation experienced a period of international marginalization and it lacked a defined foreign policy between 1945 and 1949.

The first sign of marginalization dates from April 1945, when Portugal was not invited to participate in the San Francisco conference for the foundation of a new international organization. Portugal was not a founding member of the United Nations, and the Soviet Union vetoed its first application for membership in 1946; it finally achieved membership in 1955.

The lack of a well-defined foreign policy reflected an inability to adapt to a new world order. Salazar appeared neither to understand nor to accept the profound transformation that had occurred in the international sphere with the end of World War II: the bipolar division of power between the West and the Soviet bloc, the emergence of the two superpowers, the demise of Britain and the concomitant rise of the United States as the great maritime power. The shift was confirmed by the emergence of the North Atlantic Treaty Organization (NATO) in 1949.

Salazar also did not seem to accept the importance of the United Nations as the new world organization, or the demise of the Europe of old and of the European powers as protagonists in the world arena. The reconstruction of Europe was no longer possible on a national basis; it would have to be undertaken within a framework of international cooperation. Finally, Salazar did not comprehend that the two new superpowers were both anti-colonial (albeit for different reasons). Indeed, the right to self-determination was a dominant principle of the United Nations and, given the cooperation of many colonial peoples with the Allied war effort, decolonization was now an irreversible process.

The first moments of hesitation in the face of the new postwar reality occurred in June 1947 over the Marshall Plan. Salazar's limited understanding of the international situation and traditional mistrust of the Americans led him to reject their offer of aid, thereby distancing Portugal from the so-called first exercise of the Marshall Plan in 1947-48. With the onset of the Cold War and the decline of Portugal's financial and exchange rate balance, the nation changed its stance and eventually applied for participation in the second phase of the Marshall Plan in 1948-49.[17]

The Cold War clearly defined the new Soviet threat, the new Atlantic security framework and, consequently, US protagonism. The first sign of Portuguese acceptance of this new strategic order was the bilateral military cooperation agreement between Portugal and the United States in February 1948. Unlike that of 1943, this new agreement institutionalized the permanent nature of the North American air base on the Azores archipelago.

Salazar's hesitation regarding the Marshall Plan and concession in the Lajes Agreement reveal two contradictory orientations in Portugal's foreign policy: one, a distancing from the process of European integration; and the other participation in the Atlantic security system. These, together with the intransigent defense of the colonial territories, were the strategic concerns of Portugal's foreign policy virtually until 1974.

In June 1948, faced with the Soviet threat and the need to define a new Atlantic security framework, the United States, Canada and the European countries that had signed the Treaty of Brussels initiated negotiations with a view to creating a North Atlantic security system—the future Atlantic alliance. In December of that year, contacts were established with Lisbon to explore the possibility of Portugal's participation in the project. A complex diplomatic process eventually culminated in the signing of the North Atlantic Treaty in April 1949.

Portugal's accession to NATO immediately raised three fundamental questions.[18] First, why had Portugal been invited to join? It had an authoritarian regime, it had remained neutral during the war, it did not yet belong to the United Nations and it had been peripheral to the reorganization of the international system in the postwar period. Second, as far as Portugal was concerned, the question was why it had accepted the invitation. To do so meant a radical shift in foreign policy—the abandonment of a neutrality that had been constructed with such difficulty during the war and had been the crowning glory of the regime's propaganda. Given that drastic change, the third question was, naturally, how Portugal's membership in NATO would affect the country's future foreign policy.

The answer to the first question was simple: it was related to geostrategic issues. The regime's political authoritarianism and its international situation were of less concern than the strategic importance of Portugal's territory in the new Cold War context. The Azores were particularly significant in this situation. An Atlantic security system based on two pillars—one European and the other North American—made the Azores bases a fundamental link for the articulation of the system and for the so called rapid reinforcement of Europe. The strategic value of the Azores and the Lajes Agreement were thus confirmed and reinforced within a multilateral framework.

The answer to the second question was more complex. It derived from Portugal's reduced margin for political maneuvering, and from the need to establish an alternative foreign policy in the context of the Cold War. When Portugal was formally invited to sign the NATO treaty, Salazar—mistrusting the United States—looked on the proposal with suspicion. Deploying his usual negotiating tactics, he voiced some diplomatic reservations as a way to gain some negotiating power and more decision-making time. He made two formal observations on the formulation of the treaty: concerning its references to democracy and to the United Nations. He also expressed three reservations of substance. He argued that the 20-year period during which the treaty would be in force seemed too long; that the Spanish question— that is, the affirmation of the strategic unity of the Iberian Peninsula and the importance of Spain in the defense of the West—required the joint integration of Portugal and Spain in the alliance; and finally, that the geographical zone covered by the treaty did not include the Portuguese colonies. Salazar attempted to include the colonies as a means of guaranteeing the security and sovereignty of Portugal over its colonial territories through the 5th article of the treaty.

All Portugal's claims were rejected because none of them really affected the Great Powers. From then on, two contrary pressures were exerted on the Lisbon government. Invoking the Iberian Pact, Spain applied pressure on Portugal not to join NATO or, rather, to create the conditions for Spain itself to join. At the same time, the United States and Britain insisted on Portugal's adherence to the NATO treaty through diplomatic pressure exerted personally by the British prime minister and the US secretary of state.

Despite Salazar's reservations and the divisions within the executive branch of the government, Portugal's alternatives were minimal. In a bipolar world, Portugal's refusal to participate could have created fissures in the Western bloc that would favor the Soviet Union. The responsibility was too great and, in the final analysis, Salazar did not want to shoulder it: necessity triumphed over conviction and on 4 April 1949, Portugal became a founding member of NATO.

What were the consequences of Portugal's entry into NATO? Despite Salazar's suspicions and reservations—one of the ironies of history—joining the alliance constituted a victory for the country's foreign policy. The regime could return to the traditional guidelines of Portuguese diplomacy: the Atlantic vocation and a preferential alliance with a maritime power. The novelty lay in the new choice of ally—the United States. In the Iberian context, the Western powers' refusal to accept Spain favored Portugal's position. Portugal's inclusion and Spain's exclusion reinforced Lisbon's status on the peninsula and turned Portugal into a privileged interlocutor.

Portugal's entry into NATO in 1949 thus initiated one of the most favorable periods in the foreign policy of the *Estado Novo*. It ended only when Portugal joined the United Nations. It was admitted in December 1955, together with a number of other countries—Spain among them. From then on, the international position of the Iberian countries underwent a reversal. Spain's entry into the UN put an end to the international isolation of the Franco regime: it also signaled the end of tolerance toward the *Estado Novo*, and the beginning of international opposition to the regime's colonial policy.[19]

Portugal's entry into the UN led to immediate confrontation with the anti-colonialist spirit of the Afro-Asian and Non-Aligned Movement that then dominated the General Assembly. Indeed, the colonial question became a dominant preoccupation in Portuguese foreign policy between 1956 and 1961. During this period, Portugal sought external support for the country's overseas policy; one initiative was a series of state visits begun in 1957 with President Juscelino Kubitchek of Brazil, in an attempt to create a Luso-Brazilian community. Subsequent invitations were accepted by the president of Pakistan, Britain's Queen Elizabeth II, President Sukarno of Indonesia and Emperor Haile Selassie of Ethiopia. In 1960, the initiative was repeated with visits by the presidents of Peru, Nepal and Thailand, culminating in those of the Secretary General of the United Nations, Dag Hammarskjold and, most significantly, of President Eisenhower.

Despite these attempts, the international attitude toward Portugal's colonial policy degenerated, and Portugal faced a military and diplomatic battle; first with India, then later with the African liberation movements. The new state of India had already presented a diplomatic memorandum to Lisbon in 1950 that formally claimed Indian sovereignty over the territories of Goa, Damão and Diu, and proposed negotiations to terminate Portuguese domination.

Salazar directly confronted the problem of decolonization for the first time. He had great difficulty accepting the principle of a peoples' right to govern themselves. For that very reason, he could not accept its political consequences: self-determination and independence. Now, moreover, he was confronted with a real problem, and not just a theoretical principle. If he accepted Indian sovereignty over Goa, Damão and Diu, with what legitimacy could he then defend Portuguese sovereignty over its other overseas territories?

Salazar therefore defended the integrity of the colonies with intransigence. His policy attempted to deprive the Indian Union of all political and diplomatic alternatives. It was based on the assumption that the explicitly pacifist position of Indian leader, Jawaharlal Nehru, would prevent him from resorting to military alternatives. If Nehru did militarize the conflict, Salazar believed that Portugal could count on the support of its closest allies. The calculation was doubly wrong: in December 1961 India invaded the three Portuguese territories, and not even the old ally, Britain, or the former colony, Brazil, supported Portugal. Franco's Spain had already established diplomatic relations with Nehru's India in 1956, a first sign of a break in the peninsular friendship. Not one of Portugal's NATO partners supported it: the international community generally looked on the events with indifference, and the UN General Assembly did so with some enjoyment.

Between 1961 and 1974, the international isolation of the *Estado Novo,* and international hostility towards it increased. With the loss of the territories in India, the problem now centered on Africa. In 1961, the war in Angola began, and it was not long before Portugal became embroiled in decolonization conflicts in three different theaters: Angola, Guinea and Mozambique.

In April 1961, a group of military officers led by General Botelho Moniz, attempted a coup against the Salazar regime with the knowledge and assent of the US government. Their aim was to alter policy toward the colonies, to abandon the military path and to seek a political solution to the conflict.

Later that year, the Kennedy administration tried to promote an agreement between Lisbon and Washington, with a view to negotiating a solution to the Portuguese colonial question.[20] The US proposal suggested a third path between Salazar's integrationism and the UN's Afro-Asian movements demand for the complete independence of Portugal's colonies. Salazar rejected the proposed self-determination formula, thereby rendering agreement impossible.

Between the failed coup and the attempt to come to an agreement, the US administration was able to elaborate a list of countries with which Portugal had the best relations, and which were therefore in a position to apply pressure on Lisbon to shift its position. These included Britain, Spain, Brazil and the Vatican. All attempts by these countries were in vain, however: Portugal resisted every one. As it had in the Indian question, Britain distanced itself from Portugal over African decolonization. Under pressure from the Brazilian administration of Jânio Quadros, Spain distanced itself from Portugal on a number of occasions. Even the Vatican abstained from supporting Portugal: Pope Paul VI received the liberation movements of the Portuguese colonies at the beginning of the 1970s, despite making his own visit to Fátima in 1967. Portugal's policy of "proudly standing alone" peaked.

Salazar regarded Africa as a natural extension of Europe. The colonies were seen as an inseparable part of the old continent and, both economically and strategically, as part of the defense of the Western bloc. Salazar had made this argument in vain when Portugal joined the North Atlantic Alliance.

Given the primacy of Atlantic policy, and the wholehearted defense of colonial integrity, Europe had a merely secondary place in

Portugal's foreign policy during this period. Salazar was always manifestly skeptical of—and frequently hostile towards—the process of
European integration. Portugal's traditional distance from continental issues was compounded by its deep suspicion of processes such as
integration, supra-nationality and involvement that might threaten
the survival of the authoritarian regime. Thus, when Portugal participated in European affairs, it did so less from adherence to the
political ideal of constructing Europe, and more for pragmatic reasons. Despite the weight of the United States in the Atlantic framework since Portugal's entry into NATO, Portugal's European foreign
policy continued to follow closely the positions of its old ally,
Britain.

With the second Marshall Plan, Portugal had participated in
European economic cooperation through its membership in institutions such as the European Economic Cooperation Council
(EECC). In 1957, Britain distanced itself from the negotiations that
would lead to the Treaty of Rome, and initiated talks for the creation
of the European Free Trade Association (EFTA), of which Portugal
became a founding member. Experience of Europe through EFTA
led to the emergence of a pro-European current among the country's economic elites and characterized its foreign policy. In 1961,
when Britain changed its mind and decided to request admission to
the Treaty of Rome, Portugal also asked that negotiations with the
European Economic Community (EEC) be initiated with a view to
the establishment of an association agreement; this was formalized in
May 1962.

De Gaulle's veto on Britain's accession necessarily slowed down
negotiations with the other EFTA countries—Portugal among
them. It was only in 1969, after the Hague Summit and the end of
de Gaulle's rule, that Portugal asked the European Community to re-
open negotiations. Begun again in May 1970, negotiations lasted for
almost two years. In March 1972, after Britain had already gained
accession, the trade agreement between Portugal and the EEC was
finally signed;[21] however, the shift towards the "European option"
had to wait for the transition to democracy.

The Transition to Democracy
and the Democratic Regime

With the end of the authoritarian regime and the transition to democracy—initiated on 25 April 1974—Portugal's foreign policy underwent a profound redefinition in accordance with the program of the Armed Forces Movement (MFA—*Movimento das Forças Armadas*). The MFA's program was basically represented by the formula, "Democratization, Decolonization, Development." Although the MFA program declared and guaranteed the fulfillment of all of Portugal's international commitments, it became apparent that the two simple principles—democratization and decolonization— implied a reinterpretation of these commitments and a profound change in the external orientation of the Portuguese state.

Negotiations on decolonization began in 1974: indeed, decolonization constituted the first great foreign policy challenge for the new regime.[22] Various ideological perspectives on the issue were debated. A first tendency, based on General Spínola's book, *Portugal and the Future*, continued to insist on a federal option. A second one, inspired by Melo Antunes—leader of the moderate left-wing elements of the MFA—sought to create an axis of non-aligned Third World neutrality. Finally, Prime Minister Vasco Gonçalves supported a pro-Soviet tendency.

From a political perspective, these ideological nuances can be divided into two basic positions: the first argued that self-determination did not mean automatic independence, and it strongly defended Portuguese sovereignty over the territories until a referendum could determine their destiny. The second position was based on a direct link between self-determination and independence, and argued for the immediate transfer of powers to the liberation movements as legitimate representatives of the colonial people.

The second position won the battle in a complex process that had an important impact on domestic politics. While the cease-fire was being implemented on the ground, the Portuguese Foreign Office initiated the first round of diplomatic negotiations. In August 1974 Guinea-Bissau, which had already unilaterally declared its independence in 1973, became the first country to receive international recognition from its former colonial power. Between that date and January 1975, the same process of power transfer took place in all of the former Portuguese colonies.

While the process of decolonization unfolded, Portugal also established diplomatic relations with the Soviet Union, the eastern European countries and the Third World. Albania and China presented greater difficulties, and relations were established only in 1979.[23]

Decolonization, the widening of diplomatic horizons and the end of international isolation, however, were not sufficient to define the new foreign policy guidelines of Portugal's democracy. On the contrary, a silent battle over the objectives and strategic options of the country's foreign policy underlay the noisy struggles of the internal democratization process. Between April 1974 and January 1986, Portugal's foreign policy oscillated between two fundamental orientations that also characterized two distinct phases: the transition to democracy—which corresponded to the pre-constitutional period—dominated by the revolutionary process; and the consolidation of democracy—corresponding to the constitutional period—marked by the institutionalization and stabilization of the democratic regime.

The pre-constitutional period was characterized by a battle over the strategic options the country should adopt, by the exercise of parallel diplomacies, and by a concomitant lack of foreign policy definition. Despite the struggles, hesitations and lack of clarity under the provisional governments—especially those dominated by the military—Portugal's foreign policy at this time was largely pro-Third World, favoring privileged relations with the new countries that had recently emerged from Portuguese decolonization. This was a replay of Portugal's "African vocation" that had been so dear to Salazar, only now it had a socialist bent.

The constitutional period was characterized by the clarification of foreign policy, and by the unequivocal and rigorous definition of the country's international position. Portugal fully assumed its role as a Western country—simultaneously European and Atlantic. The Atlantic dimension implied the continuation of the historical aspects of Portugal's foreign policy and played an important role both at the level of foreign policy orientation and at the level of internal political stabilization. On the bilateral level, Portugal's Atlanticism was embodied in the strengthening of diplomatic relations with the United States and the renewal of the Lajes Agreement in 1979 and 1983. With these agreements, Portugal extended the use of the Azores bases to the United States until 1991. In return, it was promised economic and military aid on a multilateral level. The Atlantic policy was expressed in the redefinition and renewal of Portuguese military commitments to NATO, which the African war effort had forced the country to abandon in the 1960s. The new commitments led to the organization in the army of the Independent Mixed Brigade (*Brigada Mista Independente*), which was later converted into the Air-Transported Brigade (*Brigada Aero-Transportada*) that replaced and reactivated the old Independent Army division whilst essentially maintaining its old objectives in NATO's missions in the southern flank of the Alliance. As for the navy and the air force, patrol missions were reinforced in the framework of NATO's IBERLAND and CINCIBERLAND, which a Portuguese officer was permitted to command.[24]

The "European option", however, was the great novelty in foreign policy after 25 April, as well as the greatest challenge for democratic Portugal.[25] After conquering anti-European resistance, the authoritarian African option and the Third World temptation of the revolutionary period, Portugal clearly adopted the "European option" from 1976 onwards. Now, however, it adhered to the political project; transcending the merely economic focus that had characterized the association agreements of 1972.

Portugal's rapprochement with the process of European integration began in 1976 with the country's entry into the European Council and the signing of the Additional Protocols to the 1972 agreement, which constituted a first step toward accession. Following a cycle of negotiations in various European capitals between September 1976 and February 1977, the first constitutional government formally requested accession to the European Community in March 1977. The formal request for accession signaled the abandonment of hesitations concerning a Portuguese formula for integration (pre-accession status or "privileged association"). It also signaled the firm establishment of the "European option." It was a strategic option that decisively marked the future of the country.

Two objectives lay behind this strategic option. First, entry into the European Community ensured the process of democratic consolidation. Second, it enabled modernization and economic development. The request for accession was followed by a long and complex process of negotiations that lasted for almost a decade. The process culminated in June 1985 when Portugal signed the Treaty of Accession to the EEC. On 1 January 1986, Portugal became a full member of the European Community and signed the Single European Act.[26]

The development of relations and ties of friendship and cooperation with other Portuguese-speaking countries was a continuing preoccupation for Portugal from 1976 until the end of the 1980s. Both the government and the president spared no diplomatic efforts to improve relations with the African Lusophone Countries (PALOP—*Países Africanos de Língua Oficial Portuguesa*). The truth, however, is that Portugal's strategic option was shifting from Africa to Europe.

Without altering the nature of its international insertion, Portugal has nevertheless altered its strategic priorities. Traditionally, Portugal developed Atlanticist and colonial priorities, and sought continental compensations when the weight of the maritime vector became excessive. Now the reverse is true: the priority is Europe and the European Union, and, to obtain greater influence, Portugal has sought to rediscover and strengthen its Atlanticist position and its relations with its former colonies.

The European Union, NATO, its relations with its former colonies through the multilateral Community of Portuguese Speaking Countries (CPLP—*Comunidade de Países de Língua Portuguesa*) and the participation of Portugal's armed forces in UN peace-keeping missions now constitute the fundamental direction and strategic priorities of Portugal's foreign policy and its international position.

Continuity and Change

What has remained the same and what has changed in respect of the continuities and ruptures in Portuguese foreign policy before and after democracy?

The continuities that exist are concerned with structural and geopolitical elements, and are found primarily in those areas of strategic interest that Portugal has maintained: the Atlantic, Europe and post-colonial relations.

There have been at least four changes: Firstly, the antinomian logic has changed from the Atlantic to Europe. As far as Portuguese foreign policy is concerned, to be Atlanticist has greater value within Europe, just as to be European has great value in the Atlantic— particularly in the South Atlantic where Portugal is developing its post-colonial relationships.

Secondly (as we have seen), in the Europe-Atlantic binomial the geopolitical element has been retained—although the strategic priorities have been inverted. Traditionally, Portugal developed Atlanticist and colonial priorities, and sought continental compensations when the weight of the maritime vector became excessive. Now the reverse is true: the priority is Europe and the European Union, and to obtain greater influence Portugal has sought to rediscover and strengthen its Atlanticist position and its relations with its former colonies.

Thirdly, the democratization of Portugal and Spain has brought the two Iberian states closer in terms of their international positions. Between 1974 and 1975 Portugal decolonized: in 1979 Spain moved closer to EFTA, and in 1982 it joined NATO. In 1986, both Portugal and Spain joined the European Community. In 1990, both countries joined the WEU (Western European Union). In 1997, Spain

entered NATO's military structure. This signifies that not only did
Portugal's geo-economic machinery become more continental with
its entry into the European Community, but also that the diplomatic strategies of both Spain and Portugal became ever closer—to the
extent that they now coincide. Put another way, nowadays Portugal
and Spain both share—for the first time ever—the same extra-
peninsular alliances: the European Union, NATO and the WEU.

Finally, as a result of the increased interdependence of international relations and the increased importance of multilateral diplomatic organizations, bilateral Portuguese diplomacy has progressively diminished in favor of multilateralism, which has resulted in Portugal's presence in strategically important multilateral organizations—such as the European Union in Europe, NATO in the
Atlantic, and the CPLP in post-colonial relations.

5 | The Portuguese Economy in the Twentieth Century: Growth and Structural Change

Pedro Lains

Introduction

Throughout the twentieth century, the poor economies of the European periphery entered the club of countries in which there was a convergence of per capita income levels. For the first time since industrialization began, there were substantial reductions in the gaps between average incomes in Europe. However, this convergence occurred with different degrees of intensity across time and space. In fact, during the inter-war period, convergence was relatively slow and confined to countries that were less affected by World War I. After World War II, economic growth gained momentum, and the rate of convergence was considerably faster—not only in places such as Portugal and Spain, but also in Greece, Yugoslavia and other central European countries. After the first 1973 oil shock, the European economy entered a period of slower growth, and the rate at which the less developed economies converged was substantially reduced.[1]

The evidence shows that there is no clear relationship between convergence patterns and phases of international economic integration. In fact, some of the southern countries—such as Portugal—expanded at higher rates than the average of the more industrialized northern countries during the inter-war years, which was a period of high trade barriers and autarky. This fact has not received enough attention in the literature on European economic growth, and Portugal's experience is most relevant in order to understand how growth was achieved under tariffs and other forms of protection. During the "golden age" of European growth—from 1950 to 1973—convergence in the south was quite considerable and was clearly associated with increasing international economic, financial and institutional integration. During this period, the southern economies expanded very rapidly—particularly in the industrial and services sectors—and quickly caught up with the average productivity levels of Western Europe. However, the institutional and political integration of the European economies, particularly within the European Union, increased after 1973, although the convergence of per capita income levels did not follow suit.

In order to explain economic growth within Europe we need to take into account national developments, and in particular the conditions of the domestic economies. By doing so, we may conclude that convergence in Europe was at least facilitated by the fact that the poor southern economies had high growth potential that accrued from the fact that productivity gains from shifting resources from agriculture to industry were still quite large. The same happened with the industrial sector, as there were large potential gains from shifting resources from traditional and labor-intensive sectors to modern and capital-intensive ones. Thus, structural change was a major source of convergence during the European "golden age" and, after 1973, the scope for structural change was substantially reduced. More importantly, as we shall see, the opening up of the poor southern economies implied further specialization towards the sectors where these economies had comparative advantages in the European markets. In the case of Portugal, the increase in specialization level led to the growth of sectors with lower labor productivity, which contributed to reducing the growth of the country's average productivity, and to its lower convergence rates. The understanding of the decline in the rate of convergence in Europe after 1973 is a major theme in European economic history, and the study of Portugal provides some useful insights.

Traditional explanations of growth and slowdown in the Portuguese economy have put more emphasis on economic policy options that would have shifted in important ways. To start with, the financial indiscipline that characterized the Republican period (1910-26) would have been responsible for alleged economic stagnation. The emergence of the *Estado Novo* in 1933, although it enhanced monetary and financial stability, did not lead to higher levels of economic growth because of agrarian and industrial policy options that, according to some authors, would have shifted domestic resources towards the "wrong" sectors. Following the same line of reasoning, growth resumed after World War II because, unlike during the previous period, the dictatorship imposed a "strategy aimed at economic growth and structural change."[2]

The higher growth of the post-World War II period is also traditionally attributed to the fact that Portugal engaged in the emerging international institutional framework that both regulated and fostered the resurgence of the international economy, and that it was a founding member of EFTA.[3] However, some authors argue that the economy did not expand as much as it could have done, because opening-up policies were not backed by a more interventionist stance by the government, which kept the budget balanced for most of the years prior to the end of the dictatorship in 1974.[4] The slowing down of economic growth that followed is attributed to the revolution in 1974 and the nationalization spree in 1975. The privatization of major financial and industrial firms from 1982 onwards, and Portugal's accession to the European Union in 1986, would have set the economy in a good direction once more. In more recent times, the emphasis has been placed on the lack of institutional reforms that would promote higher levels of education, a more efficient judicial system and more flexible labor markets, among other things.[5] The relation between changes in economic and other policies, and changes in trends in economic growth and convergence is, however, weaker than is often claimed.[6]

The prevalence of internal factors in shaping the pattern of growth of the Portuguese economy has been scrutinized. Lopes recognizes that both internal and external factors were relevant for "the acceleration of economic development, macroeconomic stability and increasing openness of the economy [during 1950-73]," but he stresses that "it was above all because of foreign stimuli that the Portuguese economy expanded as it did and became more open to foreign relations." The same author holds that the economic growth slowdown after 1973 was also mainly a consequence of "external factors."[7]

This chapter analyses the causes of changes in rates of growth and convergence during the twentieth century. Convergence is defined as the rate at which Portugal's level of per capita income increases in relation to an average of nine more developed Western European countries. Following the analyses of convergence trends, we examine the major structural transformations of the economy in terms of growth of output and labor productivity in agriculture, industry and services. Rapid economic growth trends were reversed after 1973, and in order to understand why that happened, we analyze structural changes in Portugal's industrial sector.

The remaining parts of the chapter are organized as follows: the next section sets down the main periods of growth and convergence of the Portuguese economy in a comparative framework. This is followed by an analysis of economic growth within a growth accounting framework and an exploration of the effects of structural change on economic growth. The final section presents the main conclusions.

The Portuguese Economy in the European Mirror

The evolution of the Portuguese economy during the twentieth century has some common points with the evolution of the European economy, as the country's economic performance was—to a great extent—related to what happened across the border. Nevertheless, economic growth trends and fluctuations in Portugal and the rest of Europe also show many important differences, which were the outcome of changes in Portugal's growth potential related to

TABLE 5.1
Growth of Real Income per Capita in Portugal and Europe, 1910-90
(% peak-to-peak annual growth rates)

Portugal		Average 9	
1910-34	1.57	1913-29	1.35
1934-47	1.15	1929-39	1.28
1947-73	5.03	1939-73	2.67
1973-90	2.32	1973-90	2.05
1910-90	*2.77*	*1913-90*	*2.08*

Notes: 'Average 9' is based on an unweighted average index for the following European countries: UK, France, Belgium, the Netherlands, Germany (West Germany to 1991), Italy, Denmark, Norway and Sweden.
SOURCE: Lains, "Catching-up."

FIGURE 5.1
Growth of Income per Capita: Portugal and Average 9, 1910-98
(1990 dollars; semi-logaritmic scale)

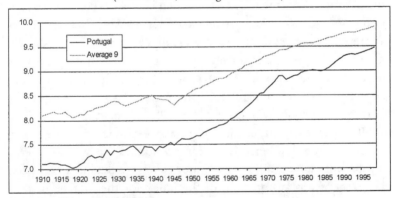

SOURCES and NOTES: See Table 5.1

changes in the structure of the economy. Figure 5.1 depicts an index for the growth of Portugal's real per capita income and another for the growth of an unweighted average per capita income for nine European economies.[8] Table 5.1 shows annual growth rate trends between peak years of the two series.[9]

According to this data, both the Portuguese and the European economies were in a depressive cycle during World War I, with per capita income reaching a trough at the end of the war. From then on, both indices increased, with the European index peaking in 1929, and Portugal's in 1934 (although there was a blip in the series in 1927). The Portuguese economy managed to expand during this period; notwithstanding the negative consequences for the balance of payments accruing from the fall of remittances from emigrants to Brazil and the fall in colonial re-export revenues.[10] A period of stagnation followed that lasted until the end of World War II. The fact that the Portuguese economy performed better during the 1920s and early 1930s than it did during the decade after 1934 should be taken into account when evaluating the stabilization programs that followed the advent of Salazar and the *Estado Novo*. In fact, stagnation in Portugal's income series lasted throughout the 1930s, precisely when the new regime achieved its first phase of consolidation. Growth resumed shortly after, and another peak in the per capita income series was reached in 1947.[11] Portuguese economic growth was comparatively high during World War II, whereas the European economy—as represented by our average index for nine countries—was negatively affected by the war, hitting a trough in 1945. However, recovery started earlier in Europe, with economic growth resuming immediately after 1945. In contrast, the Portuguese economy remained virtually stagnant from 1947 to 1950. From then on, economic growth expanded consistently in the nine more developed European economies—as well as in Portugal—until a new and coincident peak was reached in 1973. After 1973, there was an inflexion of the index for the average of nine European countries, rather than a period of slowdown until 1986, followed by rapid growth until 1998, which was also the case in Portugal.

Table 5.2 shows growth rates according to Maddison's phases of twentieth century economic development.[12] We may observe that Portuguese per capita income increased at a faster rate than the index for the average of Europe in every phase except the periods 1929-38 and 1973-86. The table also shows growth rates for Spain and Greece. Within this group of countries, Portugal had a better performance during the inter-war period. The fact that Spain was

TABLE 5.2
Growth of Real Income per Capita in the European Periphery, 1913-98
(Maddison's phases of development; % annual growth rates between 3-year averages)

	Portugal	Spain	Greece	Ireland	Average 9
1913-29	1.35	1.65	2.45	0.33	1.39
1929-38	1.28	-3.53	1.50	0.87	1.16
1938-50	1.56	1.48	-2.72	0.94	1.00
1950-73	5.47	5.63	5.99	2.98	3.55
1973-86	1.52	1.31	1.75	2.47	2.01
1986-98	3.45	2.65	1.39	5.42	1.88
1913-98	2.79	2.20	2.29	2.19	2.06

NOTES AND SOURCES: see Table 5.1

ravaged by a civil war (1936-39), and that Greece was directly affected by World War II and the subsequent civil war is crucial for explaining their poor performance. After World War II, growth rates in these three countries were fairly similar, with Greece expanding at a slightly faster rate. After 1973, the Portuguese economy fared better. Finally, Table 5.2 shows data for Ireland, which depicts a different pattern of growth throughout the twentieth century.

Table 5.3 reports income convergence rates for the same growth periods.[13] As we can see, Portugal's rate of convergence during the period 1950-73 was quite exceptional. In fact, on average, Portugal got closer to the median level of per capita income of the nine European countries here considered, by 1.85 per cent annually. During the period 1913-50 the Portuguese economy also converged, albeit at the very low rate of 0.19 per cent per annum. It should be noted that Portugal was the only country in the table that converged. Between 1973 and 1986, Portugal and the other two southern countries in Table 5.3 diverged from the more developed European countries. However, after 1986, Portugal converged at a considerable rate again. The Portuguese rate of convergence during 1950-73 was inferior to that of Spain and Greece, whilst convergence in the period 1986-98 was higher. Ireland was again an exceptional case.[14] Yet, Por-

TABLE 5.3

**Convergence of Real Incomes per Capita in the European Periphery,
1913-98**

(Maddison's phases of development; % annual growth rates between 3-year averages)

	Portugal	Spain	Greece	Ireland
1913-29	-0.04	0.26	1.04	-1.04
1929-38	0.12	-4.64	0.33	-0.29
1938-50	0.55	0.47	-3.69	-0.06
1950-73	1.85	2.01	2.36	-0.55
1973-86	-0.49	-0.69	-0.26	0.45
1986-98	1.54	0.76	-0.48	3.48
1913-98	0.72	0.14	0.23	0.13

NOTES: convergence defined according to: $\phi = [(y_i/y^9)_{(t+1)} / (y_i/y^9)_{(t)}][1/(t+1-t)]$
where y_i is income per capita for the 4 countries in the table and y^9 is the average for 9 core
countries as defined in Table 1.
SOURCE: Lains, "Catching-up."

tugal's level of per capita income, relative to the European average
attained in 1974, was only achieved again in 1990.

Following the period of higher growth and convergence (1950-
73), Portugal's per capita income growth entered a new period of
slower growth, which has lasted to the present. However, after 1973,
the growth rate trend of the Portuguese economy was higher than
the growth trend prior to 1950. Portugal fits what Crafts and Mills
(1996) have termed the "reverse Janossy hypothesis." In other words,
despite the slowdown in Portuguese economic growth, the rate at
which the economy expanded after 1973 was higher than the rate of
economic growth before the 1950-73 period. Such a result implies
that during the period of high growth there was a "greater accumulation of technological capability," as well as infrastructures and economic institutions, which helped the increase in the Portuguese
economy's growth trend.[15] In the appropriate comparative framework, the slowdown of the Portuguese economy after 1973 appears
less spectacular, and is at least partially explained.

Economic Growth and Structural Change

Any explanation of economic growth implies the choice of a set of relevant explanatory variables that can be quantified, and a model that posits the relations between those variables and economic growth. The use of a properly defined quantitative model allows a clear definition of the possible direct causes of growth, which can then be analyzed more closely and put in a historical context. This is the best procedure for analyzing the effect of economic policies, for example. If we conclude that the growth of capital investment was crucial for the growth of the economy, then we can analyze what policies led to the growth of investment and assess their role in the process. One such model is provided by neo-classical growth theory, which attributes the sources of output growth to the accumulation of human and physical capital and to exogenous technological change. Sources of growth are measured through a production function with constant elasticity, which implies that the effect of each factor input on total output is constant along the production function. By taking technological change as exogenous and not explained by the growth process itself, and by taking constant elasticity of substitution, we are simplifying the real world. Yet, the fact is that such growth accounting models provide a fairly good explanation as to how the industrialized western European countries caught up with the higher average productivity level of the US during the twentieth century. The model shows that most European economies converged because they had higher growth rates of *both* capital stock and total factor productivity than the US during the years 1950-73.[16] That was also the case for Spain between 1965 and 1990.[17]

Table 5.4 sets down the evidence on the growth of factor inputs for Portugal. The data shows that both human and physical capital expanded more rapidly after 1947. In the case of human capital, which is measured as the average years of schooling for the active population, it increased by 2.08 per cent per annum during the 1910-34 period; 1.14 per cent during 1934-47; 2.47 per cent during 1947-73 and 4.83 per cent during 1973-90. Such behavior in the human capital index

TABLE 5.4
Growth of Factors and GDP, 1910-90
(% peak-to-peak annual growth rates)

	Labor	Human capital	Capital	GDP
1910-34	1.00	2.08	1.25	2.17
1934-47	1.31	1.14	3.89	2.09
1947-73	0.70	2.47	7.73	5.17
1973-90	0.05	4.83	5.21	3.92

NOTES: 'Labour' is total employment. 'Human capital' is the average years of schooling of active population; 'Capital' is the stock of capital based on the growth of gross domestic capital formation (residential capital excluded).
SOURCE: Lains, "Catching-up."

is not surprising if we take the efforts made in the educational sector during the second half of the century into account. This was true during the *Estado Novo* period, and even more so after 1974, as is shown by the fact that the secondary enrolment ratio increased from less than 10 per cent before World War II to 18 per cent—on average—from 1947 to 1973, and 62 per cent from 1973 to 1990. Similarly, the primary enrolment ratio tripled to full enrolment at the end of the century.[18] Although the levels of Portuguese education remained low by Western European standards, the fact was that they increased at relatively high rates throughout the century, and that that had positive effects in the conditions for economic growth. The rate of growth of physical capital also increased significantly throughout the century: in fact, it doubled twice between 1910 and 1973, from 1.25 per cent per year, between 1910 and 1934, to 3.89 per cent, between 1934 and 1947, and 7.73 per cent, from 1947 to 1973. After 1973, the rate of growth of capital stock declined but still remained higher than before World War II. Thus, the share of investment in Portugal's GDP expanded rapidly from less than 8 per cent before World War II to 21 per cent between 1947 and 1973, and 30 per cent from 1973 to 1990. Portuguese domestic savings and capital imports led to levels of investment typical of middle income countries, worldwide.[19] The observed trends in the growth of human and physical capital were a major characteristic of twentieth century Portugal, and their impact on the growth of the economy needs to be properly assessed. The growth accounting framework is crucial for this.[20]

Table 5.5 shows growth accounts for twentieth century Portugal. In that table, we use an average production function that relates the growth of factors of production, namely, labor, human and physical capital, as well as the growth of the productivity of the same factors, to the growth of total output.[21] The first striking conclusion we may draw from the table is that total factor productivity growth did not have a paramount role in accounting for Portuguese economic growth during the century. The highest contribution to the growth of factor productivity was in the 1910-34 period, whereas between 1934 and 1947 it was slightly negative. The comparatively small contribution of productivity growth in Portugal in the period to 1973 contrasts with what happened in the rest of Western Europe. Portuguese economic growth was more dependent on capital deepening. That happened particularly in the period from 1934-47, but also in the periods 1947-73 and 1973-90, when capital growth accounted for 49.9 and 44.3 per cent, respectively, of domestic output growth.[22] The contribution of human capital growth was relatively small in the years to 1973, increasing to 41 per cent during the last period in the table. The contribution of total factor productivity declined after 1973. This is in accordance with what happened elsewhere in Europe.[23]

Portugal's growth accounting shows that the country's experience was more akin to that of most of the Asian "tigers," in the second postwar period, where the growth of human and physical capital made a greater contribution to total output growth than the growth of productivity. In the case of Portugal, the growth of the labor force was not as important as it was in the Asian countries because of lower demographic expansion and higher levels of emigration.[24] This form of "extensive growth" was also common in some eastern European countries (e.g. Czechoslovakia and East Germany), and was in opposition to the "'intensive growth' model which was predominant in Western Europe during the postwar period."[25] After 1973, the contribution of capital growth to total output growth declined only slightly, and the decline in the rate of growth

TABLE 5.5
**Growth Accounting for Portugal: Sources of Growth
and Output Growth, 1910–90**
(% annual growth rates between 3-year averages)

	Annual growth rates					As percent of output growth			
	Labor	Human capital	Capital	TFP	Output	Labor	Human capital	Capital	TFP
1910-34	0.33	0.70	0.42	0.72	2.17	15.4	32.1	19.2	33.3
1934-47	0.44	0.38	1.30	-0.02	2.09	20.8	18.2	62.0	-0.10
1947-73	0.23	0.82	2.58	1.53	5.17	4.5	15.9	49.9	29.7
1973-90	0.02	1.61	1.74	0.56	3.93	0.5	41.0	44.3	14.2

NOTES: Sources of growth are based on factor growth rates from Table 4 weighted by factor shares of 1/3, according to Nehru and Dhareshwar (1994). See Lains, "Catching-up."
SOURCES: see Table 5.4

of total output can mainly be attributed to the decline in the contribution of total factor productivity growth. This implies that we need to explain the fall in total factor productivity growth in order to understand the reduction of Portugal's overall economic growth after 1973. In other words, the main reasons for the decline in the rate of growth of the Portuguese economy after 1973 cannot be satisfactorily explained by what happened in education or in investment behavior: the two factors that most contributed to high growth rates in the periods before that year.

Our findings can be confirmed by other studies on Portuguese economic growth. Afonso (1999) provides an alternative growth accounting model where output growth is a function of investment per worker, imports of machinery per worker, and exports per worker. The author also adds, as an exogenous variable, average total factor productivity growth of the Europe Union (12 members), in order to capture the convergence effect.[26] According to this author, in the 1960-73 period, the growth of the Portuguese economy was led by the growth in capital stock and total factor productivity. The contribution of these two factors of growth amounted to 93.4 per cent of output growth. Afonso further concludes that the growth of total factor productivity was mainly due to growth in labor "efficiency," which was positively affected by the four exogenous variables in his model. On the other hand, the contribution of the growth of capital "efficiency" is negligible. For the 1974-85 period, the author finds a reduction in the explanatory power of capital deepening and labor productivity growth, and a negative contribution of capital productivity. For the period after 1986, capital and total factor productivity are again the two main sources of growth, although at a lower rate of total output growth.[27] Afonso's findings on the declining contribution of factor productivity growth after 1973 are in accordance with those based on the growth account exercise presented in Table 5.5.

Levine and Renelt propose another model to estimate elasticity in income growth with respect to a series of exogenous variables—including initial income levels—for a sample of 103 countries in the 1960-85 period. The variables used by these authors are, for each country, the initial income level relative to the leader, investment shares, primary and secondary enrolment ratios, the weight of the government sector in GDP and the growth of population.[28] Their model predicts the growth of European economies from 1923 to 1938 and from 1950 to 1973 relatively well, but it underestimates growth for 1973-89. The major difference between the periods before and after 1973 is the higher negative effect of initial per capita income levels, which have decreasing importance over the periods as the average income of the sample of European countries approximated the US level. Secondly, the government expenditure share also had a higher negative effect.[29] The Levine-Renelt model can be used to determine to what extent Portugal's growth performance mirrored a world "norm." We can conclude that the model is a relatively good predictor of Portugal's per capita income growth from 1910 to 1934 and 1947 to1973; although in the second period it slightly underestimates the actual growth rate. However, the model does not account for the slowing of Portugal's economic growth during the interwar and post-1973 periods. The reason for the best performance predicted by the model is that Portugal's investment and school enrolment ratios remained relatively high after 1973.[30] Thus, the observed reduction in Portugal's income growth after 1973 cannot be attributed to the performance of the investment ratio, or to the investment in human capital as measured by the school enrolment ratios.

The models we have just mentioned do not take into account the role of foreign trade. Yet, despite the generally held assumption that foreign trade is a major factor for growth in small open economies, export growth did not have a paramount role in Portugal's economic growth during the twentieth century.[31] The openness of the Portuguese economy throughout the second half of the twentieth century occurred in two phases. The first phase followed membership of EFTA, and the ratio of foreign trade to GDP increased from about 17 per cent to 30 per cent (1960 to 1973). In the next period, up until 1986, the ratio remained constant. The second phase (1986-1994) followed Portugal's entry into the EEC when the ratio increased from 30 per cent to nearly 55 per cent.[32] In 1994, Portugal was ranked as the fourth most open economy in the European Union.[33] The fact that the increase in foreign trade was more rapid in the 1986-94 period—which had slower growth than during the period 1950-73—is indicative of the small explanatory effect of trade in Portuguese growth. In fact, according to Mendes, the effect of European integration on Portugal's economic growth was relatively small. He estimates that participation in EFTA and the 1972 trade agreement with EEC explains between 2.0 and 2.5 per cent of Portugal's per capita income growth during the 1960s and 1970s, while gains from joining the European Union accounted for 10.1 per cent between 1986 and 1992.[33]

Both the growth accounting framework and Afonso's and Levine and Renelt's models point to the conclusion that trends in investment ratios in respect to both physical and human capital explain the increase in growth rates after World War II, but they fail to explain the slowdown after 1973. In fact, there were significant investments in human and physical capital in Portugal between 1950 and 1973; investments that either increased during the following period, or only marginally declined. Yet after 1973 there was a sharp decline in the overall growth rate of the Portuguese economy.

After 1973, there was a decline in the rates of growth of output from agriculture, industry and services, as is demonstrated in Table

5.6. As the labor force in the agricultural sector continued to decline, labor productivity in the sector increased from 3.5 per cent per annum from 1950 to 1973, to 4 per cent per annum from 1973 to 1990. In the industrial sector there was a sharp decline in labor productivity growth, from 5.8 per cent (1950-73) to 0.7 per cent (1973-90), whilst in the services sector the decline was also very significant, from 4.4 per cent (1950-73) to −0.1 per cent (1973-90).[35]

Yet the single most important factor in the slowdown of Portuguese economic growth after 1973 was the decline in the rate of growth of total factor productivity. The performance of factor productivity in both the industrial and the service sectors was the main cause of the fall in the growth of total factor productivity, as productivity growth in the agricultural sector increased slightly after 1973.[36] Taking into account the behavior of total factor productivity in the three sectors of the economy, we may conclude that the decline in the Portuguese economy's growth rate after 1973 was due to the decline in the performance of the industrial and the services sector.[37]

In order to explain the fall in industrial factor productivity growth, we need to take into account the major distinctive features of growth in the periods before and after 1973.[38] The high levels of industrial growth during the period 1960-73 were due to the expansion of external demand caused by European growth and Portugal's participation in EFTA, as well as by the overall favorable performance of the economy and, in particular, of domestic demand. According to Lopes, the growth of industrial sector output in the period to 1973 was enhanced by growth inducing government policies, including: protection from foreign competition that was granted to some branches of industry; fiscal incentives; public investment in social overhead capital and in key capital intensive industrial sectors; as well as wage and price controls and low interest rates.[39] EFTA membership meant Portugal had to open up to external competition; however, the Portuguese government managed to negotiate gradual and selected reductions in tariffs and other forms of domestic protection, while Portuguese industrial exports took advantage of the opening up of foreign markets.[40]

TABLE 5.6
Sectoral Output and Productivity Growth, 1950–90
(annual growth rates between 3-years averages; per cent)

	1950-73	1973-90	1950-90
AGRICULTURE			
Output	1.3	1.2	1.3
Employment	-2.2	-2.8	-2.4
Productivity	3.5	4.0	3.7
INDUSTRY			
Output	7.6	2.5	5.4
Employment	1.8	1.8	1.8
Productivity	5.8	0.7	3.6
SERVICES			
Output	6.0	3.7	5.0
Employment	1.6	3.8	2.5
Productivity	4.4	-0.1	2.5
TOTAL GDP			
Output	5.7	2.9	4.5
Employment	0.2	1.7	0.8
Productivity	5.5	1.2	3.7

SOURCE: Lains, *Os progressos*, chapter 6.

After 1973, there was a shift in the industrial sector towards an increase in the output of some more labor-intensive sectors. In fact, the contribution of the foodstuffs and textiles sectors in the industrial sector increased between the periods 1950-73 and 1973-80, and even more to the period 1980-90. The contribution of more capital-intensive sectors to total output growth declined. Foodstuffs and textiles accounted for half of total industrial growth between 1973 and 1980, and over two-thirds between 1980 and 1990. The more capital-intensive sectors accounted for 42 per cent of industrial growth between 1973 and 1980, and 30.7 per cent from 1980 to 1990. It is worth noting that the performance of total factor productivity in the industrial sector was more favorable in the 1973-80 period than it was from 1980 to 1990.[41] This indicates that the growth of the foodstuffs and textile sectors had a negative impact on industrial productivity growth compared to the impact of the more capital-intensive sectors.[42]

According to Peres Lopes, Portugal's industrial labor productivity in relation to the United Kingdom's was comparatively higher in the "traditional" sectors, namely: textiles, clothing, leather and footwear, wood products, paper and electrical appliances.[43] This explains why the opening up of the Portuguese economy led to the increase in the weight of the lower labor and capital productivity industrial sectors and, consequently, to the reduction of overall industrial output growth.

To fully understand the causes of the fall in factor productivity growth in the industrial sector after 1973, we have to explain what caused the observed shifts in the output structure. One of the main reasons for the shift was the increasing openness of the industrial sector to foreign trade. According to Barbosa *et al.*, the structure of Portugal's industrial sector in 1993 was in tune with the structure of revealed comparative advantages. Yet, according to the same authors, labor productivity in the industrial sectors with better export performance and higher output growth rates, was below the average for the sector.[44] The fact that the Portuguese industrial sector adapted to the changes in the structure of demand imposed by increasing integration with the European Union economy, led to an increase in the weight of industrial sectors with higher levels of comparative advantage. However, that was achieved with lower levels of labor and capital productivity. This structural transformation led to a reduction in the average productivity level of the Portuguese industrial sector.

Conclusions

Over the past decades, economic historians have shown that there is a wide diversity of economic growth experiences across frontiers. Different experiences stem from the fact that the conditions for economic growth can be very different from country to country. Such a conclusion has a corollary that has not been sufficiently exploited in long-term economic growth studies, which is that conditions for economic growth also vary substantially across time. The Portuguese experience of growth during the twentieth century is a good example of this.

Many authors have recognized that the *external* conditions for Portuguese economic growth changed throughout the century. Those changes are associated with transformations in the international and, in particular, in the European economy, which can be described as Maddison's phases of development. Less attention has been paid to the fact that *domestic* conditions for the growth of the Portuguese economy have also changed substantially. Although the consequences of changes in industrial, monetary and fiscal policies—as well as overall political conditions—have largely been accounted for, less attention has been paid to changes in the structure of the economy and the consequences that those changes may have had in the potential for growth of the economy.

The Portuguese economy went through an intensive process of structural transformation during the period to 1973. While in 1950 Portugal was largely an agrarian economy, with about 50 per cent of the population employed in the agricultural sector, by 1973 the growth of the industrial and the services sectors had substantially transformed the economy. The sheer shift of labor from agriculture to the other sectors of the economy was a source of growth, as the labor productivity in agriculture was about half that of industry and services. The potential gains in term of growth accruing from shifts of resources to industry observed in 1950 were thus much reduced after two decades of intense industrialization and the growth of the service sector.

This chapter has put together evidence showing that high levels of investment in human and physical capital were the main instruments for rapid economic growth up to 1973. The fact that Europe was expanding rapidly was also of considerable help. After 1973, however, the overall conditions for growth were less favorable, as most of the gains from structural change had already been reaped. The fact that the European economy slowed down imposed further restrictions on rapid growth. More importantly, the Portuguese economy opened up to the external world more rapidly during the last decades of the century, for which accession to the EEC in 1986 was, of course, of paramount importance. The increasing degree of openness implied that the economy had to evolve according to its pattern of comparative advantages, which led to an overall reduction in the growth of factor productivity, income per capita, and convergence to the levels of the more developed European economies. Not enough time has yet passed to enable us to conclude whether the short-term losses from specialization along the structure of comparative advantage will be offset by long-term gains of a more open and more competitive economy. After two decades of intensive growth between 1950 and 1973, the Portuguese economy was substantially altered and, despite the fact that the potential effect of structural change on economic growth had died out, the fact was that the various forms of capital and capacities acquired in the period of rapid growth pushed the economy into a stage of growth at rates higher than those observed before 1950. Hopefully, the process of adaptation to the structure of the European economy that Portugal is presently undergoing will set the economy on a renewed higher pace of growth.

6 | Portuguese Emigration After World War II

Maria Ioannis B. Baganha

The northern Portuguese landscape is dotted with old houses that are architecturally exotic, with plenty of small, picturesque towers and innumerable decorative elements. One also finds new houses, architecturally reminiscent of northern European cottages, with black roofs and large windows. Then there are expensive suburban houses, which their owners have covered with colorful tiles. A significant number of these are currently being built or enlarged.

These are the houses of former or present-day emigrants. The older ones are known as Brazilian houses and the more recent as French. Seemingly out of context, they dot the traditional landscape and constitute the most obvious material evidence that emigration has been a constant feature of modern Portuguese life.

Although Portuguese migrated to the United States, Venezuela, Germany and Luxembourg (to name just a few of the countries where sizeable Portuguese immigrant communities have settled historically), the labeling of these houses is rooted in the country's migratory experience. Up to the 1950s, Brazil received more than 80 per cent of Portuguese migratory flows, and France approximately half from that period on.

The objective of this chapter is to present a general overview of the Portuguese migratory experience from World War II to the 1980s. It is, however, important to emphasize that Portuguese migration has been a significant historical process for centuries, one that has changed not only the country's landscape but also its way of life and its people's mentality.

The analysis presented here is based on the assumption that Portuguese emigration is essentially an international labor flow, which has changed according to the demand for labor in the international market of the macro-geographical system to which the country belongs. Its evolution has depended not only on the potential migrants' assessment of available rewards for labor abroad, but also on the political sanctioning of the recipient nations and the strength of the migrant network active at both ends of the trajectory.

Migration Policies: The Legal Framework

The Marshall Plan gave Western Europe the means with which to launch its postwar economic recovery.[1] Southern Europe and other peripheral regions covered the initial labor shortages resulting from war casualties, and later substituted native labor in the so-called dirty and low-paid jobs. Thus, between 1958 and 1973, the six countries of the European Economic Community issued eight million work permits to facilitate a mass transfer of labor from the peripheral south to the industrialized north of Europe.

It was only from the 1960s that Portugal began to participate substantially in this intra-European transfer of labor. This can be shown with an analysis of foreign arrivals in France between 1950 and 1974. France was a major destination for migration in this period, and the preferred destination for Portuguese emigrants. Between 1950 and 1959, Italians represented more than half of the total foreign inflow. In 1960, Spaniards equaled the number of Italians entering France, with each of these nationalities contributing 30,000 migrants to a total of 72,600 arrivals. The Spaniards replaced the Italians as France's main suppliers of foreign labor from 1961 to 1965, and were in turn replaced by the Portuguese from 1966 to 1972. From 1962 on, Portugal's share grew constantly, peaking in 1970 and 1971. In an overall total of 255,000 arrivals in 1970 and 218,000 in

1971, the Portuguese contribution represented 53 per cent (136,000) and 51 per cent (111,000 migrants) respectively.[2]

The Portuguese did not simply replace the Italians and the Spaniards numerically: they also took up jobs left vacant by them in public works, construction, and the domestic and personal service sectors, as well as in agriculture.[3] An analysis of the structure of the active native and foreign labor force in France also suggests that the labor market was segmented, with certain jobs specifically taken up by foreign laborers in the public works and construction sectors.[4]

The oil crisis of 1973-74 and the restrictive immigration policies of receiving countries halted the influx of foreigners. Up to then, however, the major European recipient countries had "open door" immigration policies. The same cannot be said of Portuguese migratory policy. Indeed, until 1974, individual freedom to emigrate was subordinated to the economic and imperial aims of the state. According to Article 31 of the 1933 Constitution: "The state has the right and the obligation to co-ordinate and regulate the economic and social life of the Nation with the objective of populating the national territories, protecting emigrants, and disciplining emigration." The *Estado Novo* tried to attain three key goals with this policy: to meet the country's own labor needs, to satisfy its interests in Africa and to benefit from emigrant remittances with a supervised export of labor.

In order to ensure the attainment of these goals, the *Estado Novo* enacted several policy measures concerning emigration. Thus, in 1944, the issuing of ordinary passports to any industrial worker or rural labor was interdicted; in 1947, after a temporary total ban on emigration, a special government agency—simultaneously dependent on the Foreign and the Interior ministries— was created to regulate and supervise emigration. The *Junta da Emigração* (Emigration Committee) aimed to implement a quota system that defined the maximum number of departures by region and occupation, after taking into account regional labor needs and the structure of the active population.

According to the same logic, several bilateral treaties were signed in the 1960s with the Netherlands, France and the Federal Republic of Germany. These treaties, which explicitly aimed to maximize economic returns from emigration to these countries, were accompanied by an order to the emigration services to allow a maximum of 30,000 legal departures a year, and by a total ban on the legal departure of those engaged in specific occupations.[5] The combined effect of these policies was to ensure a migratory flow that the state considered beneficial to both the country's labor supply and its economic development.

The rationale behind this last set of government policies has to be linked to the new economic model of development endorsed by the *Estado Novo* during the 1960s. In fact, while the previous model of economic development favored the labor-intensive traditional industries in northern Portugal and rural development, the new model favored the creation of a leading modern industrial sector in the metropolitan area of Lisbon. It was thought that this new industrial sector, in conjunction with emigration, would absorb the rural surplus. It was also thought that this industrial sector, along with the banking and insurance sectors that are also centered mainly in the Lisbon area, would absorb the majority of skilled or highly skilled workers and professionals. In fact, neither of these groups was particularly inclined toward emigration.

On the eve of the 1974 Revolution, the state was ready to promulgate an unprecedented liberal law, justified on the grounds that emigration was highly beneficial for Portugal because it promoted gains in productivity and the rationalization of production methods. The law concluded with the following statement: "Emigration, which acts as a positive factor in modernization and the rationalization of labor, contributed greatly to the progress and development of the country."[6] Individual freedom to emigrate and return were finally written into the 1976 Constitution. By that time, however, most European countries had shifted to a "closed-door" policy.

The Evolution of Migration Flows

Between 1950 and 1988, the Portuguese Emigration Bureau, the *Secretaria de Estado de Emigração*, registered 1,375,000 legal departures.[7] Of these, five countries absorbed 82 per cent (see Table 6.1). This official picture should be compared with French and German sources, which state that 1,259,000 Portuguese migrants entered these two countries during this period.[8] Even revising Portuguese emigration figures taking into account only these two destinations, emigration between 1950 and 1988 totaled at least 2,152,000. This means that during this period, at least 36 per cent of Portuguese migrants left the country illegally.[9]

No systematic study has ever been made of clandestine migrants. The study of illegal Portuguese migration in other historical periods, as well as available information on illegal departures to Europe after World War II, however, indicates that clandestine flows differ significantly from legal ones. Illegal Portuguese migrants tend to be isolated and unskilled males in their prime: this increases the likelihood that legal flows do not accurately reflect actual migratory flows between 1950 and 1988.[10]

One corrective for the discrepancies in the official figures is to examine the relative attraction of the principal recipient countries.

TABLE 6.1
Principal Destinations of Portuguese Legal Emigration, 1950–1988
(thousands)

	Legal Departures	Percentage
France	347	25.0
Brazil	321	23.0
United States	193	14.0
Germany	135	10.0
Canada	138	10.0
Other	241	18.0
Total	1 375	100.0

SOURCE: SECP, *Boletim anual* (1980-81, 1988).

TABLE 6.2
Principal Destinations of Portuguese Emigration, 1950-1988
(thousands)

	Legal and illegal Departures	%
France	1 024	48.0
Brazil	321	15.0
United States	193	9.0
Germany	235	11.0
Canada	138	6.0
Other	241	11.0
Total	2 152	100.0

SOURCES: see Table 6.6

According to French and German records, we can correct the distribution in Table 6.2. Table 6.1 (Legal Departures) shows that the two preferred European destinations (France and Germany) attracted 35 per cent of the total between 1950 and 1988, and that the three overseas destinations (Brazil, Canada and the United States) attracted 47 per cent. Table 6.2 (Legal and Illegal Departures), by contrast, indicates that the two key European destinations accounted for 59 per cent of the total, and the three overseas destinations for just 30 per cent, in the same period.

We can also correct the annual totals by destination (see Table 6.6), which helps to obtain a better sense of the evolution of the "true" Portuguese migratory flow. The first remarkable change, indicated in Table 6.6, is the intensity of growth of the total migratory flow. The annual average number of departures jumped from 33,000 between 1955 and 1959 to 55,000 between 1960 and 1964, 110,000 between 1965 and 1969, and 134,000 between 1970 and 1974. The average declined drastically to 37,000 in the period 1975-79, the same level of average annual departures attained in the initial period (1950-54). Numbers decreased even further to 17,000 average departures between 1980 and 1988. This intense and sustained growth in the 1960s and early 1970s can be attributed to the Portuguese migratory flow to Europe, particularly to France, which absorbed 60 per cent of the total flow in this period.[11]

FIGURE 6.1
Portuguese Emigration by Destination
(thousands)

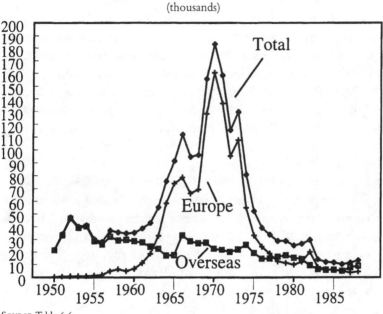

The data from Table 6.6 can be visually summarized in Figure
6.1. Both Table 6.6 and Figure 6.1 show that Portuguese emigration
grew constantly and substantially from 1950—when departures
numbered 22,000—to 1970—when departures numbered 183,000.
It declined from 1971 to 1988, as departures dropped from 158,000
to 13,000. The peak years of Portuguese emigration after World War
II occurred between 1965 and 1974, when the annual average number of departures reached 122,000.

It can also be inferred that three major changes in preferred
destinations took place between 1950 and 1979. In the first decade
(1950-59), the overseas flow was clearly dominant. Indeed, of the
350,000 departures, 327,000 (93 per cent) went overseas. A single
country, Brazil, absorbed 68 per cent of the global total of departures.
In the following decade (1960-69), the overseas flow lost its relevance. Europe attracted 68 per cent of the total number of depar-

tures, with France absorbing 59 per cent of the global total. This shift occurred in 1962-63. In 1962, total departures numbered 43,000, of which 24,000 went overseas (57 per cent) and 19,000 went to Europe (43 per cent). In 1963, the total number of departures numbered 55,000, of which 22,000 (41 per cent) went overseas and 33,000 (59 per cent) to Europe. Europe clearly dominated between 1963 and 1977, but from then on, overseas destinations became dominant again. The European share fell from 56 per cent in 1977 to 43 per cent in 1978 and 39 per cent in 1979. In the last period, 1980-88, overseas destinations accounted for 51 per cent of all departures.

The change in the relative weight of migratory flows overseas is not the only noticeable shift. Although they tended to decrease in absolute terms, overseas flows did not register any dramatic fluctuation before 1979. They did, however, register a major change in the absolute and relative weight of the receiving countries. In the early 1960s, the contraction of the flow to Brazil was quite dramatic: the average annual number of departures to that country fell from 12,000 to 3,000 between 1960 to 1964 and 1965 to 1969. The United States and Canada took Brazil's place during this period: the annual number of departures to the United States rose from 3,000 in the period 1960 to 1964 to 10,000 between 1965 and 1969, and to Canada the total rose from 4,000 to 6,000.

It is thought that lack of information on illegal migrants creates a bias in the relative weight of each sex, in the distribution by age group and in the distribution by marital status. Origin and distribution by economic activity are meant to be the characteristics least affected, if not in absolute then, at least in relative terms. This analysis will therefore focus on the more reliable factors. Table 6.3 shows the distribution of Portuguese emigration by region of origin.

Because the contributions of the islands and the mainland are quite different in terms of their respective shares in total flows, their direction and the characteristics of their migrants, they will be treated separately. Between 1950 and 1988, the islands' migratory flow accounted for 21 per cent of the total, and was overwhelmingly directed overseas. The Azorean flow went to the United States and grew markedly during the 1960s and 1970s, particularly after the United States passed the 1965 amendments favoring family reunification in the concession of US immigrant visas, and revised the national origin quota system that had been in place since 1968. These measures increased the share of southern European migration and the Portuguese quota of entry with it.[12] Madeira's flow contracted markedly after the 1950s, when Brazil ceased to be a major destination, and has remained at a relatively low level since.

TABLE 6.3
Percentage of Portuguese Emigration by District, 1950-1988

	1950-59	*1960-69*	*1970-79*	*1950-79*	*1980-88*
Aveiro	10.74	6.62	7.32	7.84	10.93
Beja	0.18	1.08	2.04	1.13	0.45
Braga	6.04	9.31	6.24	7.63	4.01
Bragança	6.32	3.78	1.81	3.85	1.06
Castelo Branco	1.43	5.17	1.94	3.33	1.15
Coimbra	4.80	2.84	3.78	3.59	3.65
Évora	0.10	0.38	0.73	0.41	0.24
Faro	2.25	3.69	2.45	2.98	1.28
Guarda	6.76	5.80	2.29	5.04	2.22
Leiria	3.98	7.66	6.88	6.53	4.95
Lisbon	2.17	8.10	12.14	7.78	18.91
Portalegre	0.15	0.37	0.31	0.30	0.20
Porto	10.47	8.55	7.73	8.79	7.76
Santarém	1.94	3.79	3.42	3.23	3.50
Setúbal	0.32	1.75	3.08	1.77	5.19
Viana do Castelo	4.64	5.63	2.97	4.63	3.52
Vila Real	5.54	3.88	3.98	4.32	4.21
Viseu	10.59	4.73	5.39	6.37	3.26
Total mainland	*78.41*	*83.12*	*74.51*	*79.51*	*76.50*
Azores	6.14	11.17	19.30	12.23	21.21
Madeira	13.75	5.63	6.17	7.80	2.29
Unknown	1.70	0.08	0.01	0.46	0.00
Total	**100.00**	**100.00**	**100.00**	**100.00**	**100.00**
Total number of emigrants	**342 928**	**646 962**	**392 5171**	**382 407**	**89 562**

SOURCE: SECP, *Boletim anual* (1980-81, 1988).

The flow from the mainland in the period 1950-88 represented 79 per cent of the global flow. It was essentially directed toward Europe, particularly to France and Germany. It is possible to conclude from Table 6.3 that three regions of the mainland—the Lisbon interior, the Alentejo, and the Algarve—were poor sources of emigration. Together these three regions supplied only a total of 111,000 migrants between 1950 and 1988. This figure is lower than the total of any of the other five regions considered individually. The heaviest suppliers of the period were the coastal regions—always contributing more than half the total migrants. The northern coast alone provided 305,000 migrants (26 per cent of the total mainland flow).

An analysis by periods shows that the most remarkable change is in the numbers leaving from the Lisbon coastal region. During the 1950s, this region had only 8,500 emigrants. The number rose to 64,000 and 60,000 during the 1960s and 1970s, respectively, when France and Germany became the preferred countries of destination. The Lisbon coastal region became the country's main migratory area between 1980 and 1988, representing 24 per cent (22,000 migrants) of total mainland legal flows.

This change seems to be connected to a major difference between the composition of migration flows overseas and to Europe. When directed overseas, migration was essentially from rural areas, both on the mainland and on the islands. When directed to Europe, it was increasingly linked to the most urban and industrial areas. Current trends show an even clearer intensification of this pattern, as documented by the growth of the Lisbon coastal region.

Key Migrant Characteristics

An analysis of the economic characteristics of the legal migrants will help complement the characterization so far. Table 6.4, which summarizes legal migrant characteristics between 1955 and 1988, indicates that of the economically active migrants who left the country legally, 26 per cent between 1955 and 1959, 38 per cent in the 1960s, and 50 per cent in the 1970s were engaged in the sec-

TABLE 6.4
Characteristics of Legal Migrants, 1955–1988

	1955-59		1960-69		1970-79		1980-88	
	No.	%	No.	%	No.	%	No.	%
GENDER								
Male	96 357	60.35	378 080	58.44	210 347	58.79	50 253	56.11
Female	63 300	39.65	268 882	41.56	147 455	41.21	39 309	43.89
AGE								
<15	37 376	23.41	171 434	26.50	99 757	27.88	21 695	24.22
15–64	120 104	75.23	468 994	72.49	254 163	71.03	66 165	73.88
>65	2 177	1.36	6 534	1.01	3 882	1.08	1 702	1.90
MARITAL STATUS								
Single	93 066	58.29	307 161	47.48	166 593	46.56	39 545	44.15
Married	63 608	39.84	329 594	50.94	185 894	51.95	47 789	53.36
Other	2 983	1.87	10 207	1.58	5 315	1.49	2 228	2.49
ECONOMIC SECTOR[a]								
Primary	43 634	56.43	140 730	50.05	54 175	32.39	6 157	16.86
Secondary	20 245	26.18	105 908	37.67	84 101	50.29	23 421	64.15
Tertiary	13 448	17.39	34 539	12.28	28 969	17.32	6 932	18.99
TOTAL ACTIVE	77 327	100.00	281 177	100.00	167 245	100.00	36 510	100.00
INACTIVE	52 425	40.40	240 399	46.09	163 155	49.38	53 052	59.23
TOTAL	129 752		521 576		330 400		89 562	
TOTAL	159 657	100.00	646 962	100.00	357 802	100.00	89 562	100.00

SOURCE: SECP, *Boletim anual* (1980–81,1988).

[a] Emigrants aged 10 or over

ondary economic sector. Equally relevant is the increase in the annual number of departures from this sector, which rose from 5,000 between 1955 and 1959 to 10,600 between 1960 and 1969, clearly pointing to the greater attraction that European labor markets exerted over the urban and industrial sectors.

As noted earlier, inferences from the legal registers on sex-, age- and marital-status are risky. Nevertheless, Table 6.4 permits two conclusions. First, the flow overseas that was dominant in the 1950s was more male-dominated, and tended less towards family reunification than the European flow. Second, the European flow experienced a first wave in the 1960s, a flow dominated by isolated departure of single or married males in their prime, followed by a second wave in the 1970s, consisting largely of family reunification flows, as suggested by the growing share of children under 15 years of age and the number of married female migrants.

French sources confirm this change in composition. Between 1960 and 1971, workers represented 68 per cent of the Portuguese arrivals to that country. From 1972 to 1979, on the other hand, they represented only 37 per cent, and from 1980 to 1988 just 36 per cent.[13] Both Portuguese and receiving country data also indicate that after 1970, a growing number of Portuguese immigrants either decided—or were forced—to return to Portugal.

Return Migration

The myth of the return is deeply embedded in Portuguese emigrant culture. It plays a role in the decision to leave, and it is an important reason why, before World War II, men migrated while women stayed, even though many men never returned.[14] Portuguese emigration to Europe in the 1960s initially fits this traditional pattern. After a decade, however, family reunification became a new trait of Portuguese emigration because of the proximity of the host societies, new means of transportation and labor opportunities for women in the receiving areas.[15] Yet even then, the desire to return was not abandoned.

The number of returnees, their socio-demographic characteristics, their social reintegration and its economic impact are perhaps the most researched topics in recent migration studies.[16] From these studies, it is possible to make several observations. After 10-14 years of working permanently abroad, the objectives that led a significant number of men to leave Portugal, and later to call their families to join them, apparently were attained. Various factors, moreover, seem to indicate the culmination of a cycle of family migratory projects. For example, the number of annual returnees grew from 7,000 during the 1960s, to 13,000 during the 1970s, and 52,000 during the 1980s.[17] Among the returnees, 25 per cent in 1970 and 32 per cent in 1980-81 were between the ages of 1 and 19, while 86 per cent of returnees were already married when they first emigrated.

Predictably, returnees were mostly male (71 per cent of the total). This was because migratory flows were male-dominated until the 1970s, and because, for a significant number of migrants, family reunification and second-generation educational prospects in host societies made staying there appear more favorable than returning.[18] Most returnees were originally connected to agriculture in Portugal, and 90 per cent returned—even if not to agriculture—to their communities of birth. More than half were over 45 years old, and one-third were older than 56. Of those who went to France, 56 per cent worked in construction and public works.

Returnees followed a dominant economic trajectory. Before emigration, 45 per cent worked in agriculture and 18 per cent in construction. As emigrants, 37 per cent worked in construction and 32 per cent in manufacturing.[19] On returning, 38 per cent worked in agriculture, 18 per cent in construction, and 17 per cent in small trades or catering. It is important to note that only 59 per cent of returnees opted for an active life, and that the majority of those working in agriculture or small businesses were self-employed.

For the majority of these returning migrants, emigration was a success story.[20] A house, major appliances, a car, a small trade or restaurant, the opportunity for wives to stop working, the return to the region of departure, and a varying, but frequently reasonable, level of savings all guaranteed upward mobility.

As far as the Portuguese economy is concerned, however, returnee contributions are debatable. The overwhelming majority of returnees were either illiterate (12 per cent), had no formal schooling (24 per cent) or had attended only primary school (56 per cent). New skills acquired have not been easily transferable; nor are former emigrants interested in taking up the same jobs they had abroad. They have used their savings primarily for consumption rather than productive investment. It is undeniable, however, that they have made a major contribution to regional development and that with more adequate policies, their contribution could increase.

We have described the main features of Portuguese emigration and return migration. In the last part of this section, we will try to assess its impact on the Portuguese economy and demography.

In demographic terms, the impact of emigration between 1960 and 1979—the heaviest period—represented 47-55 per cent of the country's natural population growth. Annual migration rates during that period varied from 5.3-6.1 migrants per thousand inhabitants, while the annual average number of departures was 82,419. In the same period, returns are estimated to have been between 30,000 and 37,000: Portugal's natural annual population growth was 95,693. Thus, net migration can be estimated at between 45,400 and 52,400. Based on the 1970 census (total population 8.569 million), the annual migration rate between 1960 and 1979 must have oscillated between 5.3 and 6.1 migrants per thousand.[21]

TABLE 6.5
Demographic Evolution, 1951-1981
(thousands)

	Natural growth	Effective growth	Net migration
1951-60	1 090.8	410.0	– 680.8
1961-70	1 720.6	– 282.6	– 1 355.2
1971-81	838.7	1 284.1	445.4

Source: 1981 Census; SECP, *Boletim anual* (1980, 1981).

For inter census periods the numbers were as shown in table 6.5. It is important to note that these figures do not account for total impact, because migration caused a significant part of the country's demographic potential to go unfulfilled.

In economic terms, between 1973 and 1979, emigrant remittances represented 8.22 per cent of gross domestic product; between 1980 and 1989, this figure rose to 10 per cent. As a percentage of the GDP, remittances varied between 5.6 in 1975 and 12.1 in 1979, according to the National Statistic Institute. Considering the relative weight of remittances in relation to the country's exports, the figures are even more impressive. Remittances increased from 13 per cent of the country's exports in the 1950s to 25 per cent in the 1960s and 56 per cent in the 1970s.

These crude indicators illustrate the impact of Portuguese emigration on the country's economy and demography, but they do not tell if that impact was beneficial. The latest econometric simulations to measure the trade-off between emigration and remittances suggest that "past emigration had positive welfare effects, which means that the positive effects of remittances dominate the negative welfare effects of depopulation. However, the annual growth of domestic production has been slowed down by about half a percentage point."[22]

Changes in the 1970s

With or without state permission, by the mid-1960s and early-1970s, Portuguese were leaving the country in increasing numbers. Sociologists and historians working during those years have stressed the duality of Portuguese society, and the imbalances of the country's economic structure as being the main factors driving a growing number of migrants out of the country.[23] Economists prefer to emphasize pull factors, and they name the wage differential between Portugal and the receiving countries as the main factor driving Portuguese emigration.[24] According to one recent study, changes in the productive structure in the 1960s created high natural rates of both unemployment and chronic underemployment in the agricultural and family craft sectors, thereby giving a growing number of Portuguese men in their prime strong reasons to migrate to improve their lives.[25]

The push-pull factors analyzed in these works were obviously important, but for the most part, they ignore the condition that if international labor flows are indeed demand-oriented, the response of each individual does not depend on the evolution of the labor market in the host country alone. Indeed, the evolution of migration after 1974 clearly reflects the impact of other factors, namely, the political sanctions of the recipient nations and the strength of migrant networks active at both ends of the trajectory. Without taking these factors into consideration, how can the extremely low migratory flows of the period be explained?

Economic recession in most of the Organization for Economic Cooperation and Development (OECD) countries after the mid-1970s, and conditions in Portugal in the aftermath of the 1974 Revolution, was aggravated by the forced return of 400,000 Portuguese from the former African colonies, along with 100,000 troops. Emigration was abruptly halted by the receiving societies in the early 1970s, which aggravated the economic situation. All these factors, plus the legal prohibition on dismissing employees, led the private sector to avoid new permanent labor contracts. This change, in turn, brought about major changes in the national labor market.[26]

Unemployment jumped from 86,000 in 1974 to 222,000 in 1975, and continued to grow. In 1980 the number of unemployed was 340,000, and by 1983 the figure had reached 446,000 thousand, or 6.5 per cent of the active population. Furthermore, as economists José Barosa and Pedro Pereira note: "[measured] unemployment does not tell the whole story, as a survey of the Ministry of Labor found 95,000 workers in 1983 to be wageless."[27] As they also point out, the labor market began to show signs of recovery in 1979, after new legislation in October 1977 gave the private sector flexibility to hire workers over a fixed period. Unemployment finally decreased, dropping to 8.5 per cent in 1985, to 7 per cent in 1987, and to 5.7 per cent in 1988. Even today, an increasing number of new jobs are still based on short-term contracts.

As noted earlier, Portuguese migratory flows to Europe peaked in 1970 and tended to decrease thereafter, but it was only after the 1973-74 oil crisis that large and sudden reductions were observed. The decrease in migrant workers was even greater, at least until 1986. For France, the data indicates that workers dominated the migratory flow to that country until 1971. Between 1972 and 1977, their relative share fell but remained significant. From 1978 to 1985, the flow was overwhelmingly composed of family members. For 1987 to 1989, the last three years for which information is available, workers were dominant, although less than before: they represented 74 per cent of the 17,000 immigrants arriving in France.

Deteriorating economic conditions and mass return migration from the former colonies undoubtedly increased migratory pressure in this period; however, annual average departures fell from 122,000 per annum between 1968 and 1975 to 22,000 per annum between 1976 and 1988. Economic factors alone cannot explain the contraction in flows in the latter period. Restrictive migratory policies in the traditional recipient countries, and the lack of sizeable migratory networks functioning in other destinations, left potential migrants temporarily without alternatives.

Portuguese scholars wrote the obituary for Portuguese emigration to Europe in 1985 at an international meeting entitled "Portugal and Europe: The End of a Migratory Cycle."[28] It was too soon, however. Indeed, Portuguese emigration to Europe is once again a significant phenomenon. In fact, a new European migratory cycle, this time mainly directed to Switzerland, took off during the 1980s. Between 1986 and 1993 alone more than 117,000 Portuguese permanent immigrants entered that country.[29] It should come as no surprise if in the years to come we see the Portuguese landscape enriched with a new set of houses, perhaps labeled Swiss houses. When they appear, they will once again provide evidence of Portugal's most constant modern historical phenomenon: emigration.

TABLE 6.6
Portuguese Emigration by Destination, 1950-1988

	Brazil	USA	Canada	Total overseas	France	Germany	Other Europe	Total Europe	Total	%
1950	14 143	938	–	21 491	319	1	81	401	21 892	1.83
1951	28 104	676	–	33 341	418	2	254	674	34 015	1.98
1952	41 518	582	–	46 544	650	4	209	863	47 407	1.82
1953	32 159	1 455	–	39 026	690	–	246	936	39 962	2.34
1954	29 943	1 918	–	40 234	747	4	205	956	41 190	2.32
1955	18 486	1 328	–	28 690	1 336	–	121	1 457	30 147	4.83
1956	16 814	1 503	1 612	26 072	1 851	6	167	2 024	28 096	7.20
1957	19 931	1 628	4 158	32 150	4 640	5	99	4 744	36 894	12.86
1958	19 829	1 596	1 619	29 207	6 264	2	127	6 393	35 600	17.96
1959	16 400	4 569	3 961	29 780	4 838	6	130	4 974	34 754	14.31
1960	12 451	5 679	4 895	28 513	6 434	54	158	6 646	35 159	18.90
1961	16 073	3 370	2 635	27 499	10 492	277	304	11 073	38 572	28.71
1962	13 555	2 425	2 739	24 376	16 798	1 393	435	18 626	43 002	43.31
1963	11 281	2 922	3 424	22 420	29 843	2 118	837	32 798	55 218	59.40
1964	4 929	1 601	4 770	17 232	51 668	4 771	1 905	58 344	75 576	77.20
1965	3 051	1 852	5 197	17 557	60 267	12 197	1 467	73 931	91 488	80.81
1966	2 607	13 357	6 795	33 266	63 611	11 250	3 868	78 729	111 995	70.30
1967	3 271	11 516	6 615	28 584	59 597	4 070	2 461	66 128	94 712	69.82
1968	3 512	10 841	6 833	27 014	58 741	8 435	2 037	69 213	96 227	71.93
1969	2 537	13 111	6 502	27 383	110 614	15 406	2 269	128 289	155 672	82.41
1970	1 669	9 726	6 529	22 659	135 667	22 915	1 964	160 546	183 205	87.63
1971	1 200	8 839	6 983	21 962	110 820	24 273	1 418	136 511	158 473	86.14

1972	1 158	7 574	6 845	20 122	68 692	24 946	1 785	95 423	115 545	82.59
1973	890	8 160	7 403	22 091	63 942	38 444	5 255	107 641	129 732	82.97
1974	729	9 540	11 650	25 822	37 727	13 352	3 958	55 037	80 859	68.07
1975	1 553	8 975	5 857	19 304	23 436	8 177	1 569	33 182	52 486	63.22
1976	837	7 499	3 585	14 762	17 919	5 913	598	24 430	39 192	62.33
1977	557	6 748	2 280	14 826	13 265	4 835	750	18 850	33 676	55.97
1978	323	8 171	1 871	16 307	7 406	4 509	636	12 551	28 858	43.49
1979	215	8 181	2 805	17 532	5 987	4 400	807	11 194	28 726	38.97
1980	230	4 999	2 334	15 281	5 200	4 000	692	9 892	25 173	39.30
1981	228	4 295	2 196	14 498	8 600	3 100	409	12 109	26 607	45.51
1982	187	1 889	1 484	9 420	17 900	1 900	285	20 085	29 505	68.07
1983	197	2 437	823	6 242	6 300	1 500	166	7 966	14 208	56.07
1984	121	2 651	764	5 747	4 600	1 400	116	6 116	11 863	51.56
1985	136	2 783	791	5 842	4 000	1 600	109	5 709	11 551	49.42
1986	91	2 704	983	5 024	1 800	3 100	280	5 180	10 204	50.76
1987	28	2 643	3 398	7 757	400	3 100	158	3 658	11 415	32.05
1988	21	2 112	5 646	8 934	600	3 600	198	4 398	13 332	32.99

NOTE: The special legalization from 1963 to 1968 was deducted.
SOURCES: France: 1950–79, "Statistiques de l'immigration"; 1988, ONI, in Antunes, "A emigração portuguesa desde 1950: Dados e comentários," *Caderno GIS*, 7 (Lisbon, GIS, 1973), 14; Stahl et al., *Perspectivas da emigração portuguesa*, 61. Germany: "Statistiches Bundesamt" 7-B, 182, in Stahl et al., 63. All other countries: SECP, *Boletim anual* (1980–81, 1988); *Système d'observation permenent des migrations* (Paris: OECD, 1980, 1986, 1988, 1990).

7 | Social Change in Portugal: 1960-2000

António Barreto

Portuguese society has undergone dramatic and rapid change in the last four decades.[1] It is one of the mysteries of nationality and cultural identity, however, that, despite rifts and profound change, citizens still feel they belong to the same country as they ever did. As we shall see, some essential traits of the Portugal of 1960 have disappeared: from structural aspects of population and society to traditional characteristics of their behavior and mentality. First, though, we must look at some historical events of that period to put some of these changes into context.[2]

A Historical Background

The period between the late 1950s and early 1960s was decisive in Portuguese history. In 1959, Portugal was one of the founders of EFTA (European Free Trade Association); the response by a group of countries to the creation of the European Economic Community.[3] This was to have important repercussions in the immediate future. It would not only lessen the relative isolation of Salazar's authoritarian regime in terms of international relations, but, principally, it initiated a process of opening the economy up to the outside world, particularly to other European countries.[4] In just a few years, external investment in Portugal grew as never before. Foreign assembly and manufacturing plants were set up to export to developed economies.

Trade exchanges with European countries—mainly of industrial products—were moderately liberalized.[5] During some years, industrial production grew by more than 20 per cent. For the first time, there appeared to be an industrial alternative to agricultural employment, offering Portuguese workers new working environments, higher wages and employment for most of the year.[6] Between 1960 and 1973, the national per capita income grew by more than 6.5 per cent on average each year, and at times by more than 10 per cent.[7] This period saw the greatest economic growth in the country's history.

Emigrants leaving Portugal had traditionally tended to gravitate towards Brazil, other Latin American countries, the USA, Canada, South Africa and the Portuguese colonies in Africa (mainly Angola and Mozambique). In the early 1960s, they began to move to European destinations, especially France. The total number of emigrants leaving Portugal each year climbed to previously unknown heights. From the mid-1960s, the annual net migration canceled out the natural population increase, which meant, in absolute terms, that the population decreased.

This migratory flow coincided with the beginning of mass tourism in Portugal. Tourists, mostly of European origin (Britain, Germany, Spain, etc.), headed towards the Algarve in the south of the country. In just a few years, the annual number of tourists visiting Portugal reached several million. Tourism was important not just for the balance of payments, but also for the development of several activities (hotels, business, construction, real estate, etc.) in coastal regions where the country's industrial boom—at that time only really in evidence around the metropolitan areas—was not yet offering alternatives to agriculture.

Politically, 1961 was crucial in Portugal's recent history. In the first three months, independence movements started an armed struggle in Angola. The Portuguese government sent in the armed forces. Thus began the colonial war, which later spread to Guinea and Mozambique.[8] The war was to last almost 13 years. It consumed close to 50 per cent of public spending, and involved, on average, approximately 200,000 armed forces personnel at any one time.[9]

Also, in December 1961, after several years of diplomatic wrangling and border incidents, the armed forces of the Indian Union invaded Portuguese possessions in India (the enclaves of Goa, Damão and Diu). It constituted the first colonial loss for Portugal in the twentieth century and the beginning of the end of the empire.[10] For more than ten years, the colonial war would play a pivotal role in national life. It conditioned all political life, took up a considerable part of budget resources and strengthened the severity of a dictatorship based on one party; the use of political police, censorship of the press and state recognized trade unions. After Marcelo Caetano succeeded Salazar as prime minister, the colonial war continued to determine politics, acting as a barrier against pressures for political liberalization coming from both society and even from within the government.[11]

The end of the colonial war came with the military coup of 1974. The revolution lasted from 1974 until 1976, radically altered political life and had enormous social, cultural and economic repercussions.[12] Rapid decolonization caused around 650,000 European settlers to return from Africa, mainly from Angola and Mozambique.[13] Thus Portugal's colonial age ended. Overseas links were cut—perhaps irrevocably.[14] Economic links with the newly independent African states were drastically reduced.[15] Prospects of emigration from Portugal to Africa—a constant in the recent history of the country—disappeared. The Portuguese state was now limited to its European territory.

An immediate consequence of the revolution was the nationalization of vast sectors of the economy, spelling destruction for most private company groups. A large part of the country's farmland was also subject to nationalization and occupation in a complex, collectivist process of "agrarian reform."[16] For a period of one or two years, an inversion of political and social powers took place. Workers, political groups, trade unions and revolutionary soldiers exercised authority legally or by their own initiative. Leftists and members of the revolutionary military dominated successive governments. However, after a political process that was rapid and peaceful (as the revolution was)—based on elections, the approval of a constitution and the restoration of constitutional administrative and legal authority—a democratic and parliamentary regime was founded. This gradual "normalization" meant that legal guarantees to fundamental rights were returned, including rights of ownership. All those who had been exiled for various reasons returned to Portugal, and economic life reverted to free market conditions.

Almost immediately after the political revolution, Portugal put forward its candidature to the European Economic Community (today the European Union, EU). It was first accepted in 1977 and full membership came into effect in 1986. Then began the "second European push" of the economy and Portuguese society, following the first—that of EFTA and the emigration of the 1960s. This new stimulus, however, was more radical and today the EU accounts for three-quarters of the Portuguese balance of trade. Portuguese companies are very closely linked to multinational and European companies. Economic protectionism has practically disappeared and Portugal is now one of the most open economies in Europe, as measured by the proportion of its external trade relative to its national product. Moreover, at the beginning of the twenty-first century, Portugal was among the countries that adopted the Euro as the single currency.[17]

It was during this second phase—from 1976 until the end of the century—that, for the first time in Portugal's history, a political system was founded and consolidated that was based on fundamental civic and parliamentary rights, including universal suffrage and freedom of political activity.[18] It was in this period that the independence of the judiciary was guaranteed and that most of the media became entirely independent of the state and free of any political censorship. Perhaps for the first time in two centuries, a kind of "constitutional consensus" is evident: most voters and most elected members of parliament agree with the general idea of the constitution.[19] Contrary to what went on during most of the nineteenth and twentieth centuries, the nature of the regime is not in question, and its democratic foundations are accepted by almost the entire electorate. There is no "religious question," as distinct from other periods in the last two centuries. For the first time in many decades there are neither political exiles nor prisoners of conscience, nor is there the concept of "political crime." These things may not seem much, but in the modern history of Portugal they are novelties.

Social Change

With these events forming the historical and political backdrop, we shall now look at the main trends of social change that have taken place during the past 40 years. In 1950, Portugal had the youngest population in Europe. Today, though not the oldest, it is one of the populations that is aging fastest. Since the late 1990s, the proportion of the elderly (i.e. those over the age of 65) in the total population became higher than that of children under 15.[20] Life expectancy has increased considerably, rising from 60 and 66 years (men and women, respectively) in 1960 to 73 and 79 in 2001. Largely responsible for the aging of the population is the fall in the birth rate; it has become one of the lowest in Europe (11 per thousand currently), having been the highest in the 1960s (24 per thousand). The same has happened with the fecundity index (currently 1.4 per woman of child-bearing age; it was 3.4 in 1960). General mortality (6.6 per thousand) remains relatively stable, but infant mortality has been drastically cut: from more than 80 per thousand in 1960, to less than seven per thousand today.

Family size has reduced considerably, and now hovers at around 2.8 people per household. As a cause and effect of this, the nature of the family has also changed. Essentially, the strictly nuclear family of one or two generations, in which the father and the mother work, is now predominant. There are fewer and fewer families where more than two generations live together under the same roof. Also reduced in number are the family households that comprise more than five or six people. Growing in number are common-law marriages, single parent families and households consisting of just one person. The number of divorces has increased (currently one divorce in every four marriages) as has the number of second marriages.[21] The number of children born outside marriage is growing significantly: one in four births belong to this group.[22]

Traditionally, the country had a high rate of emigration, but now the flow has reversed and it has become a net recipient of migrants. This is perhaps one of the most dramatic changes occurring in Portugal in the last few decades.[23]

Between 1960 and 1973, more than 1.5 million Portuguese left the country to work abroad. Breaking with a centuries old tradition, these emigrants abandoned Brazil and other Latin American countries as their favored destination, preferring instead Europe—specifically France, closely followed by Germany, Belgium, Luxembourg and Switzerland (and later, the UK, the Netherlands and Spain). The urge to migrate was so great that the number of "illegal" emigrants began overtaking that of legal emigrants.[24] In the first half of the 1970s, emigration slowed down, partly due to the international economic and social climate (recession and the oil crisis). Decolonization prompted the return of several thousand people who had previously been resident in the colonies (for many it was their first time in Portugal, since they had been born in the colonies and had never even visited the mother country). Their social and economic integration was rapid, and without any problems worthy of note. Emigrants continued to leave Portugal, but in greatly reduced numbers.[25]

Then, within a short time, a complete inversion of population movement took place. Effectively, during the 1980s, a flow of immigrants originating in Brazil and the old colonies was gradually consolidating. A growing number of Europeans were also choosing Portugal for their home or as a base for work (those connected with foreign business and new investments, farmers, retired people, etc.). By the mid-1990s, the (legal) resident foreign population was close to 2 per cent of the total population. Some emigrants continued to leave Portugal, but on average there were no more than 10,000 permanent emigrants and 15,000 temporary emigrants per year. Gradually, starting in the years 1995-97, the migration balance became positive: that is, the number of immigrants overtook that of emigrants.[26] Since then, a new wave of immigration has sprung up, and with surprising speed: workers are arriving from eastern and central Europe—specifically Ukrainians, Russians, Romanians, former Yugoslavians and Moldavians. Less than 10 years later, the resident foreign population has reached 4 per cent of the total resident population.

Although Portugal was already a fairly homogeneous country in terms of currency, language, the law and the armed forces, and although administrative power had long since been enforced over the whole territory, a large part of the country did live to a different rhythm than that of the capital and the other main urban areas.[27] Several factors contributed to national integration, including the mobilization of conscripts to the colonial wars, the expansion and broadening of television coverage, the expansion of health services and social security and the establishment of school, postal and bank networks that would eventually cover the country. The most important factor in the homogenization of the country, however, was certainly the expansion of the economically active population, especially with the inclusion of women. Women can now be found in all jobs and professions, and at schools and universities.[28] There has been a profound change in the presence of women in society and in the public arena.[29] At the start of the 1970s, women represented around 20 per cent of the economically active population; three or four decades later, this has risen to practically 50 per cent. In many sectors, such as public administration and public services (especially in health and education), women are in the majority. The university student population consists of more women than men (around 56 per cent) and, every year, it is women who receive most of the university diplomas (65 per cent). This change, linked to the cultural evolution of the last few decades, has been responsible for an important alteration in the distribution of the power of the sexes: a patriarchal and masculine society has given way to one with a more visible balance between the sexes.[30]

The young have also benefited from further inclusion in society. With the development of a "youth culture" and of "youth" as an age group and social category, a new, active generation group of voters, consumers and producers has been born. The evolution of the economy and the education sector helped the younger generation delay their entry into professional life by some years, which in turn helped to increase the size and number of colleges of further and higher education. They are virtually excused from military service, freeing them from that bond to the state. With the right to vote at 18 (since 1976), they are subject to special attention from the political parties and the authorities. The youth branches of the political parties try to attract them to take part in political campaigns and they are targeted by advertising and business. Making an indelible mark on the towns and cities, the "young" have their own meeting places, leisure spaces and cultural venues, and animate the nightlife of bars and clubs.

The process of creating a tertiary economy was rapid, with a drastic reduction of the primary sector and the stagnation of the numbers of industrial workers. The primary sector, still the largest sector during the 1960s, became the smallest (accounting for less than 8 per cent of the total workforce in 2000). Contrary to the situation in other Western European countries, industry has never been the most important employer of the working population in Portugal. It was the tertiary sector that passed directly from last to first place in hiring manpower. Public administration grew strikingly: the 196,000 or so employees of the local and central administrations in 1968 increased to 516,000 in 1983 and to more than 716,000 in 2001. The number of employees in the education and health sectors also increased significantly. There has been a visible expansion of business, restaurant and hotel activity, of the bank system and of telecommunications services. Along with "tertiarization," "coastalization" and urbanization have also intensified. Population movement within the country has continued, concentrating populations along the coast and in the urban centers, especially in the two large metropolitan areas of Lisbon and Oporto, but also around some foci of urban growth which have resisted the pull of the two largest cities: Braga, Aveiro, Coimbra, Viseu, Évora and Faro.

The employment rates among the three sectors have, of course, changed significantly according to the evolution of the sectors themselves. According to the census, the population employed in the primary sector fell from 43.6 per cent (in 1960) to 6.9 per cent (in 1991) and currently to 7 per cent. The number employed in the secondary sector rose in the same period, from 28.9 per cent to 37.9 per cent, and stands today at between 34 and 36 per cent. The number employed in the tertiary sector jumped from 27.5 to 51.3 per cent and might be 55 per cent in 2002. As we have seen above, the secondary sector has never been the main employer of the active Portuguese population, which makes Portugal a unique case in European terms.[31]

Today, women make up the majority of the active population in the primary and tertiary sectors, though they are still in a minority in the secondary. Overall, women comprise half of the active employed population. Although we do not have a consistent series from the 1960s until 1974, existing estimates show that it was in this period that women were definitively included in the active population. In 1960, women represented between 20 and 25 per cent of the total. Industrialization and "tertiarization" are partially behind their integration, but, more significantly, emigration and the colonial wars forced women into the workplace.

During the last 25 years, the active population has increased by around one million people (maybe as many as 1.2 million). Today it totals around five million, which is equivalent to more or less half of the resident population. The increases were mainly in the tertiary sector (781,000 more women and 397,000 men), followed by the secondary (304,000 more men and 150,000 women). Meanwhile, the primary sector has lost at least 650,000 workers—if, as well as all the farmers and laborers, we count their families and the supporting rural society, over 1,630,000 have left agriculture since 1968.[32]

The social and professional composition of the working population has also changed. The proportion of employers more than doubled (from 2.6 to 5.8 per cent) whereas that of self-employed/independent workers (from 16 to 19 per cent) and of employees (from 65 to 70 per cent) increased less drastically. More important were the changes within the active female population. The proportion of female employers (in each category of the active population including both sexes) rose from 10 to 26 per cent; that of the female self-employed from 22 to 46 per cent; and that of female employees from 35 to 45 per cent. On the other hand, in the case of household workers (domestic staff), there was a considerable fall from 80 per cent to 58 per cent.

Unemployment, usually correlated with economic cycles, reflects sometimes more deeply rooted structures and trends. It is worth emphasizing that, during the last 25 years, overall unemployment has never exceeded 10 per cent of the active population (in contrast to what happened in most of the European Union). There is a tendency for the rate of female unemployment to be consistently higher than that of male unemployment (normally 15 to 20 per cent higher). In periods of economic crisis and greater unemployment, the difference can be 50 per cent more women unemployed. Also, the rates of unemployment tend to hit the following categories harder: young workers in industry and transport; women employed in domestic service; workers on short-term contracts; and workers who possess no qualifications or have only a basic level of education.[33]

As for employment contracts, the majority of employees have a permanent contract or a contract with no time limit. Only around 12 to 20 per cent of the total workforce work under short-term contracts; however, this situation fluctuates considerably according to the state of the economy.[34] There is a trend, despite some fluctuation, towards more negotiated regulation of working conditions, affecting a growing number of workers. In the last two decades, there has been a noticeable trend towards a decrease in work conflicts, as measured by the number of strikes, number of workers involved and number of days of strike action.

As far as it concerns the comparison between Portugal and the other European Union countries, the evidence shows that, in respect of demographic, health and educational indicators, Portugal's social structures are approaching European standards.

Rates of male and female activity, overall and per age group, are similar to European averages. The same is true for the rates of employment. The annual rate of variation in employment reveals some interesting facts, however: between 1960 and 1990, they were lower than the EU average, and at times the lowest of all. One should remember that those years encompassed the greatest migratory flow from Portugal to Europe. From 1987 until the late 1990s, Portugal's annual rates of variation in employment were higher than the European average in most years. In this respect, Portugal ranks alongside Spain, the Netherlands, Ireland and Luxembourg.

The structure of employment by sector of activity, shows a marked difference between Portugal and the majority of European countries. Portugal has the second highest rate of agricultural employment (13.7 per cent of total employment) after Greece (17.7 per cent). The European average is 4.6 per cent, and in almost all countries it is below 6 per cent. The rate of employment in industry (36 per cent) is the highest of all (the European average is 29.5 per cent), whereas other countries employ between 20 and 30 per cent. The rate of employment in the service sector (50.2 per cent) is the lowest in the EU (average 65.7 per cent). Also, the rates of female employment in agriculture and industry are the highest in the European Union.

Portugal was among the four countries with the lowest rates of unemployment in the 1980s and 1990s (the others were Austria, the Netherlands and Luxembourg)—the EU average in the 1990s was almost always above 10 per cent, a figure never seen in Portugal or these other three countries. On the other hand, however, regarding age, duration of unemployment, activity sector and profession, Portuguese unemployment seems not to have any specific patterns.

Wages remain far lower than in the richest countries, and below the European average—even lower than in Spain and Greece. Portuguese figures in 1998 (using Purchasing Power Parity), stood at 63 per cent of the European average, 71 per cent of that in Spain, 91 per

cent of that in Greece and 57 per cent of that in France. This situation, however, is already considerably better than in 1980. At that
time, Portuguese wages were 45 per cent of the European average,
67 per cent of that of Greece and 41 per cent of that of France.

Similarly, Portuguese average hourly rates of pay for the manual
worker in industry can be one-half or one-third of other countries,
even including Spain and Greece. It is likely that the differences in
earnings between countries are more pronounced in the less-quali-
fied occupations. An indicator frequently used (average disposable
monthly earnings of a couple comprised of two manual workers, in
manufacturing, with two salaries, without children) reveals a huge
gap between Portugal and other countries: earnings are 48 per cent
of those in Greece, 40 per cent of those in Spain and 34 per cent of
those in France.[35]

The generalization of the system of social protection began even
before the 1974 political revolution. For example, the number of
pensioners rose from 56,000 in 1960 to 2.5 million in 2000.
Whether or not they have contributed during their working life, all
citizens have the right to an old age retirement pension, as well as to
invalidity benefits or widowed person's pensions. In the late 1960s
and early 1970s the governments of Marcelo Caetano took initiatives
towards increasing the number of contributors to, and beneficiaries
of, the system. It was at that time that many rural elderly and domestic workers were first included as beneficiaries. After that, almost all
governments in the new democratic regime, because of their principles or because of electoral concerns, aimed to increase the number
of people included, as well as creating new mechanisms of support
targeting some special segments of the population (the disabled,
women, children, unemployed, retired, large families, etc.). In the
mid 1990s, the "minimum income guarantee" was created, including
around 145,000 families and a total of close to 430,000 people.[36]

As has happened in other countries, Portugal is now suffering
from financial problems associated with the mechanisms of public
social security. For several years now, the accelerated growth of the
system, together with the rapid aging of the population, have made

it necessary for the state to make up the system's deficit each year.[37] Currently, the number of active employees (contributors) per pensioner is 1.7, the lowest in the European Union.

Illiteracy has finally almost disappeared from Portuguese society and there is a guarantee of universal education, but the average level of education attained remains relatively low in comparison with other European countries. Illiteracy survives only among the elderly. From levels of 40 per cent in 1960, illiteracy fell to around 8 per cent currently.[38] The school system expanded hugely, for the first time in history reaching the whole territory and the whole population. Compulsory education (consisting of nine years) has been effective since the 1980s. Despite high rates of repetition, failure and early leaving, almost all children up to the age of 15 go through the school system. In 1960, the number of students attending the final term of further education was slightly over 8,000; it is currently around 380,000. The expansion of the system of higher education has been similarly remarkable, especially given its small size at the start: between 1960 and 2000, the student population attending higher education rose from 26,000 to more than 400,000.

It is worth noting, however, that because of birth rate decline, the numbers attending basic and further education, after a significant growth in the 1970s and 1980s, have begun to decrease in a marked way: in the first cycle of basic school (the equivalent of junior school) by one-half; in the second cycle (equivalent to the first years of secondary school), they are 60 per cent of what they were in 1985; and in the third cycle (equivalent to the last years of secondary school), 80 per cent of what they were in 1992.[39] In further education, at first a huge increase was seen—from 8,000 in 1960 to more than 475,000 in the 1990s—but it has been in decline since 1997.

The public health system also became universal. After a slow evolution, already visible during the 1960s, the health system underwent a rapid expansion, covering all the territory, and is apparently within the reach of the whole population, regardless of region or locality, profession or social condition.[40] In the late 1970s, when the National Health Service was created, around two-thirds of the population were already covered by some or other system of sickness support. The reduction in infant mortality and death from contagious disease (including tuberculosis), as well as the increase in life expectancy, attest to the positive effects of the expansion of public health services. One indicator adequately reflects this evolution: medical attendance at births, for example, rose from 15 per cent of all births in 1960 to 99.9 per cent in 2001.

The expansion of the welfare system has been continuous and rapid since the end of the 1960s, accelerated by the effects of the revolution and of democracy. There are, however, problems and imbalances that accompany this swift "universalization." Social security payments are relatively low: around 200 euros per month for the old age pension and around 150 euros for the widowed person's pension. Furthermore, as already mentioned above, the combined effect of the aging population and the reduced number of contributors per pensioner, difficulties in financing the system are likely in the short or medium term.

In spite of notable progress in the health sector, there are many cases of delay and inefficiency—a constant object of political debate and media attention. The waiting lists for surgery or consultants' appointments, acknowledged by the public authorities themselves, represent many months or years of waiting for patients. These failings cannot be blamed on a lack of equipment, hospitals or staff. The number of doctors per citizen, for example, is today higher in Portugal than in several European countries.

Similarly in education, despite the formidable expansion of the system, the truth is that rates of early leaving and repetition are very high (implying a high waste of resources) and the efficiency of the school system is frequently questioned. In the case of higher education, for example, the public system was so incapable of responding to student demand that, in just 15 years, more than a dozen private universities and tens of private higher education colleges were created.[41]

The inefficiency of the welfare state, measured as much by the low pensions paid to the beneficiaries of state aid, as by the dysfunctional systems of health and education, is certainly not only due to a lack of organization and experience, but also to a real lack of resources.[42] This may seem paradoxical, since public expenditure, under the so-called "state social function" heading, today reaches levels equal to or higher than those in developed European countries. On health and education, the Portuguese state spends a greater proportion of the national product than several of its EU partners.[43] In absolute terms, however, the lack of resources is real.[44]

In any case, the past four decades represent a period of progressive and almost constant increase in collective and individual well-being. Today's situation must be compared to the situation of real backwardness in which the country found itself in 1960. In an initial phase, up to the mid 1980s, emphasis was put on the installation of the basic infrastructures: in the 1960s, electricity, water, sewers, etc. reached less than one-half of all households, while today practically all benefit. According to the official census, mains water was available to just 28 per cent of inhabitants; it is now available to 87 per cent. Nineteen per cent of inhabitants had a shower or bath; today 82 per cent have. Forty-two per cent had a domestic toilet, and now 89 per cent. Only 41 per cent of Portuguese had mains electricity in 1960; today the percentage is 98 per cent. Only 38 per cent benefited from mains sewerage and today 91 per cent do so. Then, between the 1980s and the late 1990s, was the time to acquire personal and domestic consumer goods. Telephone, television, white goods, cars, photographic and music equipment, computers and mobile telephones became commonplace in the majority of family households, some (television and telephone) being present in almost 100 per cent. As for cars, 60 per cent of households own one. Home ownership has reached levels that are rare in Europe (more that 65 per cent of households are homeowners).[45]

Thus, a society of mass consumption has been born and the middle-class has expanded. At the same time, social inequalities have increased.[46] All the social groups have experienced an indisputable rise in their earnings, but the gap between the highest and lowest earners has widened. It is possible that rapid modernization has played a part in this, but institutional, political and cultural factors may have had as much influence in the distribution of wealth. After all, greater or lesser inequality does not essentially, or simply, depend on the level of affluence of a given society.[47]

Apart from the years 1975, 1984 and 1993, the Portuguese experienced a consistent increase in the national product and income per inhabitant. Using current prices, national income increased per capita around four-and-one-half times from 1960 to 1999. Earnings from work increased at almost the same rate. The rates of annual variation of the national product and national product per capita fluctuated, showing a strong performance from 1962 to 1972. There was also a period of solid growth, although not as strong as before, from 1986 to 1992.

The rates of annual variation of earnings from work per capita confirm this evolution: the most consistent growth was that of the period 1961 to 1974, with values higher than those of the growth of the product. There were eight years in which its evolution was negative: 1976 to 1979, 1983 to 1985 and 1994. Since 1974, there have been few years in which growth of per capita earnings from work was greater than that of the national product: 1974, 1981, 1982, 1989, 1991, 1992 and 1993.[48]

The percentage of wages and salaries comprising disposable income (in other words, the share of work in the national income) also fluctuated, not only according to the economy, but also determined by the political situation. The values from the late 1990s, at around 46 per cent, are very similar to those of the early 1960s (47 per cent). From 1960 to 1974 there was a gradual climb, with a sharp acceleration in 1974 when it reached 60.1 per cent. This drastic mutation in the distribution of income was an immediate consequence of the political and social revolution. In 1975, the workers' share of the national income reached its maximum—62.3 per cent— and then decreased consistently until 1987. From then on, that share recovered slowly, but never attained the levels of 1974-75.

The evolution of the national minimum wage for industry and services, created in 1974, is interesting. At current prices, it went from being 3,300 escudos to around 60,000 in 1999; but at constant prices, the national minimum wage for industry and services is slightly lower today than it was in the 1970s. It grew gradually until 1980, fell drastically until 1984 (a fall of more than 25 per cent) and then began climbing again—very slowly—until the end of the 1980s.

The evolution of household incomes from 1981 to 1995 shows, at constant prices, a consistent climb, proportional to the national product. However, observation of its distribution among the socioeconomic categories reveals some important differences. Despite real growth in all groups, some of them enjoyed far slower growth in their income than others. In 1995, the families of agricultural producers and workers earned far less than the national average. Families of factory operators, who in 1981 found themselves above the national average, are now slightly below it. Also, relative to the national average, office workers have found their situation worsening (125 per cent of the national average against 130 per cent previously), as have the liberal professions (208 per cent of the national average against 242 per cent previously). Those seeing a real and relative improvement were the technical and scientific experts, managers and non-agricultural entrepreneurs.

As for the origins of household incomes, it should be emphasized that the proportion of households relying on income from employed work has declined slightly. The same happened to those dependent on self-employment, income from property and emigrants' remittances. On the other hand, the percentage of households relying on social security and insurance has risen.

The evolution of average monthly *income* per sector of activity reveals that, between the four main sectors of activity, only "banking and insurance" grew distinctly above the national average. The gap between that and other sectors continues to increase. Below the national average are sectors like "agriculture and fisheries," "manufacturing" and "commerce." Of these, *income* from agricultural employment is decreasing in relative terms, whereas income from manufacturing is stabilizing, and from commerce is improving slightly.

If we turn now to levels of qualification in relation to income, we can see that top and medium level managers saw their monthly earnings increase in absolute and relative terms, and that non-qualified professionals saw the least improvement. Once again, it was in banking, insurance and commerce that earnings climbed higher at all levels of qualification, and in agriculture and industry that they grew the least.

Average monthly earnings for women, by sector of activity and level of qualification, saw absolute increases at constant prices. In terms of national averages and men's earnings, they have improved slightly in the last decade.[49] Average monthly earnings for women (in all sectors of activity and at all levels of qualification) were, in 1986, 80 per cent of the national average (men and women together); 79 per cent in 1991; and 82 per cent in 1996.

Comparisons with the other 14 countries of the EU allow for some interesting observations. In the final years of the 1990s, the national product per inhabitant in Portugal was still only three-quarters (75.3 per cent) of the European average.[50] however, in the 1960s it was less than one-half (45.2 per cent). In 1960, and largely until the 1980s, in respect of national product per inhabitant, Portugal took last place. Currently lying next to last, it overtook Greece during the second half of the 1980s.[51] Portugal is gradually closing the gap between itself and Europe, an objective proclaimed by almost all political parties: in 40 years, solely from the perspective of national product per inhabitant, around 30 percentage points have been recovered. The Portuguese GNP starting point was 55 per cent of the European average.

During this 40-year period, Portugal registered the second highest rate of growth of GNP per inhabitant (after Ireland) among the 15 EU countries. If we only consider the first three decades (1960 to 1990), then Portugal occupies first place. In the 1990s, there were only two years in which Portuguese growth was lower than any of the other European countries: in 1993 and 1994.[52]

In 1960, in terms of private consumption per inhabitant (using PPP), Portugal was in last place (46.3 per cent of the average of the countries of the present EU), followed by Greece (57.3 per cent) and Spain (63.4 per cent). Its evolution, until 1999, is parallel to that of the national product, taking Portugal to 74.4 per cent of the EU.

However, Portugal maintains its last place, since in Greece private consumption represents 77.5 per cent of that of the Union, and in Spain 79.2 per cent.

Socio-economic changes were accompanied by transformations in all other areas: politics, law, culture, etc. The legal formalization of social relationships increased due to the integration of most people into the active population, and the consolidation of a modern market economy. The democratic regime and schooling have helped citizens to be aware of their rights and to find legal means of defending and guaranteeing them. Thus, there has been an enormous growth in litigation between 1960 and 2000, and especially between 1975 and 2000. The number of legal proceedings initiated annually has almost tripled. The number of judicial magistrates and public ministry magistrates per inhabitant has increased by a factor of almost 4.5, and there has been an eight-fold increase in the number of lawyers. The number of legal proceedings initiated and completed annually per magistrate approximately halved (1,000 to 500), but the number of proceedings pending per magistrate remain at similar levels.

The new configuration of citizenship, resulting from the founding of the democratic state, ensured public liberties, the affirmation of individual rights and their respective guarantees, and the establishment of political rights. Possibilities have opened up for political, social and civic participation. For the first time in history, all Portuguese men and women—civilian or military, educated or illiterate, professional or unemployed—can elect the head of state, members of parliament, local leaders and local council assemblies.

With new liberties and a greater openness to the outside world, Portuguese society became more permissive and secular. The Church, the armed forces and the large state bodies have far less influence in today's society; or rather their influence is now shared and discussed, and occasionally contested. Also the Church itself has changed.[53]

Portuguese society has seen a process of cultural, ethnic and religious diversification, accompanied by the establishment of political pluralism. For the first time in several centuries the Catholic Church co-exists with other churches, other forms of worship and other religions. The Islamic, Hindu and animistic religions have thousands of followers, and their forms of worship are free and public. Other forms of Christian worship (including what are commonly known as "sects," originating in the United States and Latin America) have, in two decades, secured success, attracting tens of thousands of faithful, acquiring buildings for worship and holding their meetings in public places. In the streets, even in agricultural areas and small villages, can be heard a great variety of languages (Latin languages, Creole, African, Slavic etc.), a real novelty in the recent history of the country. This environment of linguistic and religious pluralism—largely a result of decolonization and immigration—accompanied the opening up of politics and the diversification of political parties that began in the mid 1970s. At the same time, in this era of globalization, the influence of foreign cultures is daily asserted through television, cinema, music, the press, the Internet, overseas travel or by the presence of foreign tourists in Portugal. Gone are the days of a closed, homogeneous society of controlled information, traditional culture and single ethnicity.

The new democratic climate, established after what was an agitated revolutionary period during 1974 and 1975, caused social and functional relations in all kinds of organizations and institutions to change. Willingly or by force, the whole of society adapted to democratic principles, rules and decision methods. Habits of participation and consultation were created. Many public institutions, such as schools, universities, hospitals and others, adopted systems designed to promote participation and consultation from citizens and service-users. Gradually, negotiated contractual social relations were developed. Indisputable principles of state authority and of constitutional powers declined to the point of affecting democratic authority itself. The reverence and subservience that, by atavism or fear, were so evident in Portugal for most of the twentieth century, slowly gave way to a society, not necessarily of equal opportunities, but of equal conditions. In the early 1970s, mainly after the establishment of democracy, institutions and mechanisms concerned with the defense of rights and representation visibly grew in number: trade unionism, consumer defense, defense of specific interests, etc.[54] After a period of great social and political conflict (during the years of the revolution and those which immediately followed), social agreement and collective negotiation predominated. Strikes and other labor conflicts have become rare, a phenomenon not unconnected with the decline in union recruitment. Today, the main labor conflicts are currently ongoing in the public sector, or what is left of it (e.g. transport). An indicator of this atmosphere of agreement must be the relatively peaceful climate in which the reprivatization of companies and the public sector was carried out. In 1975, an enormous number of companies, making up the most important part of the country's economy, had been nationalised.[55] However, from the end of the 1980s a huge program of reprivatization, and the opening up to private capital of previously state-owned sectors began, which was carried out by the governments of two different parties. Despite intense disagreements, the process did not cause political conflicts or any social rupture.[56]

The expectations of the legislators and the authorities in terms of an increase of civic and political participation do not seem to have been fulfilled, however. It is very difficult to engage parents in the running of primary and secondary schools. Companies and other interest groups do not show much interest in being associated with the universities. The participation of town councils and private associations in the "consultative" and "general" councils of various public institutions (such as large hospitals, for example) is practically non-existent, despite the fact that the law allows it. The links of "service users" and consumers with the public services are—when they exist at all—rare and fragile. Electoral abstention is a good indicator of the general climate of participation. Portugal registered extremely high rates of electoral participation in the 1970s and 1980s. Since then, abstention has grown significantly: in fact, of all the member countries of the European Union, it was in Portugal that it grew the fastest.[57]

With the foundation of the democratic state, there were pressures from the whole of society to democratize all community/collective activities, not just political life. With relative speed, the old ways of paternalism, bureaucratic despotism, secrecy in public administration, social segregation and favoritism have all declined. Everyone became acquainted with their rights, and equality before the law was guaranteed. Comparing the situation today with the situation 40 years ago, it is easy to conclude that political, civic and social participation has increased considerably, thanks mainly to the establishment of democracy. If one looks at a more recent period, the last 10 or 20 years, the conclusions will be different. In fact, a very marked decline in civic and social participation can be detected, not only at the level of trade unions and professional associations, but also at the level of local and district clubs and associations, including cultural and sports associations and friendly societies. The new mass culture, the growth of suburban areas, the separation of work from the home, the expansion of television and other factors, has largely destroyed a previous network of associations. In other words, comparing the situation now with the situation 40 years ago, two apparently contradictory processes can be seen. Firstly, in sectors related to political life, the defense of professional and economic interests, trade unionism and employers' associations, there has been an increase in participation and respective institutions and associations. Secondly, there has been a visible decline in social and cultural voluntary activity, based in local communities.

Some forms of civic and social participation are equally in recession, trade unionism being the most evident. We now know that the level of union membership is far lower than it was in the late 1970s. The ability of the unions to mobilize and recruit continues to decrease. Among other phenomena at the root of this trend, it must be noted that the privatization of state owned companies has been a significant factor in demobilizing the unions, since the most energetic union activity, including strikes, has been seen in the public sector. Apart from this, the very considerable influx of foreign immigrants has caused—as in many other countries—a relative decline in trade unionism. Employment in the "black market" and short-term contracts has had the same influence.

Other forms of civic, social and even religious participation—as much at a national level as at a local level—have undergone a different evolution. There are areas in which the progress in participation and the resultant will to intervene, attempt to influence and defend interests are noticeable: namely some forms of volunteering; international, ecological and environmental aid; cultural expression; consumer defense, etc.[58] But many old associations have come to an end. In old towns and neighborhoods, most of the associations have closed their doors and it is difficult for the remaining few to find support or even members. The new "mass culture" has cooled the associative spirit in many people.

From the mid-twentieth century until the end of the 1960s, Portugal was in many respects different from most Western European countries. It had the oldest and most durable overseas colonial empire, the only one in existence at that time, and the longest running modern dictatorship. Portugal was also the country with the highest rates of illiteracy and infant mortality. The Portuguese population was the youngest in Europe, with the highest birth rate and the lowest life expectancy at birth. Portugal had the lowest number of doctors and nurses per inhabitant; it had the lowest wage per inhabitant; the lowest productivity per worker; the highest agricultural population; and the lowest rate of industrialization. It had the lowest number of pupils in primary education and students in higher education, and the lowest number of people included in social security systems. There was one more characteristic to add to all these: in the mid-1970s, Portugal was the country that experienced—as it was seen by its protagonists and consecrated in the constitution—the last "socialist revolution" in Europe, a revolution that was rapidly defeated, ending up simply as a democratic revolution.

It is possible that some development indicators still put Portugal in the last place in a European rank. But most social indicators show that Portugal is today much closer to the European average than in the past. Portuguese society has seen a process of change of extraordinary speed, marked by political events of primary importance, like the breakaway of the colonies and the foundation of a democratic regime. Apart from other factors which will have been responsible for this process of change, the opening up to the exterior (due to a free trade policy, emigration, tourism and entry into the EU) is at the source of the most important transformations, including the economic growth of the 1960s.

The speed of change, together with the peripheral position of Portugal and the general paucity of resources, are among the primary causes of the imbalances created in the meantime. At the end of 40 years of accelerated evolution, and the constant closing in on European levels of development, the country finds itself at the beginning of the twenty-first century in the grip of a constantly low level of productivity and suffering from lack of capital and a shortage of public financial resources. However, the expectations and aspirations of the Portuguese today are those of any citizens of any of the most developed and richest European countries. The gap between the aspirations and the possibility of fulfilling them is certainly a common trait in all societies. In Portugal, however, it is more pronounced than in any other Western European country.

For the first time in its recent history, Portugal's economic, social and political life is strongly linked to that of Western Europe, with which it shares institutional and development patterns. Portugal has ceased to be different from the rest of Europe. This change occurred in a short time: Portuguese society revealed that it was far more flexible than might have been expected after many decades of authoritarian paternalism; however, imbalances and insufficiencies are still very much in evidence: in terms of productivity, the efficiency of the systems for social protection and in respect of the social and human capital available. In any case, the country's opening up to the outside world seems to have been the greatest stimulus for social change.

8 | Elections, Parties and Policy-Making Institutions in Democratic Portugal

Pedro C. Magalhães

From democratic transition in the 1970s to the mid-1980s, Portugal functioned under a proportional electoral system, exhibited a multiparty system with a sizeable Communist Party and was characterized by endemic cabinet instability. However, since 1987 all of this has changed. Some aspects of this change have been described as, "by far the most dramatic shift" experienced by any new southern European democracy.[1] It consisted in an abrupt "majoritarian turn," through which the number of relevant political parties was drastically reduced, cabinet stability substantially increased and policy-making power increasingly concentrated in the executive. More importantly, this transformation from "consensualism" to "majoritarianism" cannot be attributed to any fundamental change in institutional framework of politics such as the one that, for example, gave birth to the French Fifth Republic. Instead, and in spite of important constitutional amendments in the 1980s regarding the military reserve powers and the economic legacies inherited from the Portuguese transition and revolution, the institutions regulating elections and legislative-executive relations have remained mostly intact.

This chapter describes some of the basic features of this "majoritarian turn" in Portuguese politics, particularly at the level of the party system and legislative/executive relations. It also dwells upon some of its potential causes. The dramatic party system change that has taken place in Portugal (regardless of electoral system stability) was made possible both by the organizational weakness of political parties in Portugal and by their lack of roots in society. This created the conditions that made easy electoral realignment possible, allowing the progressive concentration of votes and parliamentary seats in the largest parties and fostering their alternation in power. However, in spite of their stability, political institutions were not irrelevant in the country's majoritarian turn. On the one hand, it is arguable that although the mechanical effects of the electoral system have remained constant, the psychological effects of electoral rules—both for the presidency and the legislature—have been delayed and prolonged in time, increasingly fostering strategic voting in the dominant political forces in each ideological bloc. On the other hand, policy-making rules in Portugal—which had been designed in order to foster greater governability in the face of what was predictably going to be a fragmented party system—ended up contributing to an exponential concentration of power in the executive as soon as disciplined single-party majority government emerged.

The Electoral System

The electoral system that has prevailed in Portugal to this day was designed for the purpose of electing a constituent assembly in 1975, in the first fully democratic elections following the 1974 military coup that put an end to authoritarian rule. Unfortunately, very little research has yet been conducted on the specific political and institutional bargaining process that led to the adoption of the election rules that have prevailed more or less intact. The first electoral law was drafted by a committee appointed by the provisional government in May 1974, and the avowed rationale behind the adoption of a proportional representation formula was to allow "the constituent assembly to be the image of the electorate, reflecting as much as possible its currents of opinion and significant political trends."[2] However, a closer look at the system's other relevant institutional features suggests that the motivations and goals behind the institutional design of the electoral system may have been somewhat more complex, and its legacies enduring.

To some extent, the option for a proportional representation formula seems to have resulted from the unanimous rejection of the past among the new democratic political actors.[3] That past had been the use of a plurality electoral formula, combined with a rigid list system which, together with electoral fraud and political repression, contributed to preserve single-party rule for more than four decades. Moreover, and perhaps more importantly, the decision to adopt proportional representation (PR) took place following a democratic transition through rupture, where all political actors connected to the previous authoritarian regime were delegitimized and simply vanished from the political arena. In this context, the new political parties—created either shortly before or immediately after the April 1974 coup—had little notion about their future electoral support. Under this particular context, the option for proportional representation predictably emerged as a way for parties to hedge their bets against an uncertain future.[4] Finally, electoral districts were designed to match a previously existing administrative division of the country into provinces (*distritos*), and the number of deputies elected has been kept roughly proportional to the population eligible to vote in each district.[5] The use of these more or less "objective" and stable criteria has prevented the kind of gerrymandering problems that have been frequent in countries such as the United States, Australia, France, Japan or Spain.[6]

However, the goal of turning the constituent assembly into an "image of the electorate" seems to have been complemented (and, to a certain extent, mitigated) by other aspects of the electoral rules. First, among the formulas that could have conceivably been selected, the d'Hondt system, which is known to produce a greater bias in favor of larger parties than any other PR formula, was chosen in an apparent effort to prevent the kind of excessive party system fragmentation and instability that had characterized the First Republic during the early part of the twentieth century.[7] Second, the general proportional rule of allocation of deputies to each electoral district according to population size led to important variations in district magnitude; from the extremely large ones of Lisbon and Oporto (48 and 38 deputies, respectively, from a total of 230 in the 2002 elections), to the extremely small ones of Beja, Évora and Portalegre in the Alentejo region in the south of the country (three deputies each). Since levels of disproportionality in the conversion of votes into seats vary according to district size, the fact that about half of those districts elect only five deputies or less has contributed to reduce the overall proportionality of the system. In fact, the combination between the reduction of the size of parliament from 250 to 230 deputies in 1989, and demographic changes in the south has increasingly put the very notion of proportionality under stress as it applies to the smallest districts.[8] Finally, the electoral system also seems to have been designed taking into consideration the weakness of the recently founded Portuguese political parties, which lacked any significant local roots and national organization. Thus, in order to strengthen party leaderships and preserve them from external or internal competition, parties were given a monopoly over the presentation of candidates for the constituent assembly and a strictly rigid list system was adopted.[9]

The combination of these institutional rules has produced two main observable consequences. First, although the Portuguese electoral system can be clearly placed in the "proportional" side of the distribution among existing democratic regimes, the effective threshold of representation it imposes, and the levels of disproportionality it engenders, have presented important barriers to the representation of smaller parties. From 1975 to 2002, the average effective threshold of representation in Portugal has been 6.5 per cent, above those legally imposed in countries such as Germany or New Zealand (post-1996), and also above the effective thresholds found in many other PR systems, including Austria, Belgium, Finland, Sweden, Norway, Luxembourg, Israel, the Netherlands, and, for that matter, most of the new eastern European democracies.[10] On the other hand, the average electoral disproportionality in Portuguese elections from 1975 to 2002, as measured by the Gallagher index, has been 4.6

per cent.[11] Among western European countries with PR systems, only Iceland, Norway, Greece and Spain have exhibited higher average levels of disproportionality.[12]

The second main consequence of Portuguese election rules has been felt in the patterns of candidate selection and the overall level of internal democratization within political parties. As predicted by most of the comparative literature (and, in all likelihood, by the framers of the Portuguese electoral law themselves), the adoption of the closed list system has contributed to increase the control of party leaderships over individual candidates.[13] Although there is some variation between the major Portuguese parties in this respect, there is no single case in which rank and file members play any institutionalized role in legislative recruitment, which has typically remained a centralized process in which national party organs have complete control over list composition or, at least, the power to make final decisions.[14] As a result, the occurrence of "parachuting" in national leaders as candidates into districts with which they have no visible political ties is relatively frequent, and party discipline remains very strong.[15]

By the end of the 1980s, a consensus around the need to reform this electoral system began to emerge. The closed list system in particular has been blamed for providing little incentive towards the establishment of strong representation and accountability links between the individual deputies and their constituents, and is seen as being responsible for neutralizing the role of the former in parliament. Proposals have ranged from splitting up the largest electoral districts—potentially allowing voters a better awareness of list compositions—to the adoption of a mixed-member proportional system, where single-member districts could be combined with low levels of disproportionality in the conversion of votes into seats. However, such proposals have repeatedly failed to muster the required qualified majority support in parliament. The reasons for this can probably be reduced to four main factors: partisan fears about the unintended consequences of electoral reform for the allocation of seats; the constant overloading of the electoral reform agenda with many other unrelated issues; the potential disturbances in the organization of parties at the local level that a redrafting of districts might cause; and—perhaps more importantly—the lack of incentives for party leaderships to abandon a closed list system that, after all, still brings them obvious advantages.[16]

Parties and Elections

Considering this lack of fundamental change in the electoral rules since the 1970s, one of the most striking aspects about the evolution of electoral preferences and behavior in Portugal is the dramatic party system change that took place in the 1980s, from a multiparty polarized system towards a two-party system. Figure 8.1 reveals the basic indicators of the magnitude of such change.

As we can see, changes in the effective threshold of representation imposed by the Portuguese electoral system have been very small since 1975. Its slight reduction after 1976 is related to the elimination of several single-member districts in the autonomous regions of Madeira and Azores, while the increase after 1987 is mainly related to the reduction in the number of deputies from 250 to 230. However, these minor changes have co-existed with important fluctuations in disproportionality levels and, most notably, with a strong reduction of party system fragmentation since 1987. In fact, the drop in the effective number of parties is even more relevant than that suggested by the figure, since the low levels of party system fragmentation in 1979 and 1980 were caused by the formation of pre-electoral coalitions, an explanation that does not apply to the post-1985 period. Furthermore, while disproportionality levels dropped again in 1995, the fundamental trend towards fewer significant parties in comparison with the 1970s and early 1980s persisted, revealing Portugal to be a singular case among consolidated democracies.[17]

This change has occurred simultaneously with high levels of electoral volatility. As Gunther and Montero note for the 1945-2000 period, two Portuguese elections (1987 and 1985) rank among the ten most volatile European elections between these years. Further-

FIGURE 8.1

Operational Properties of the Electoral System and Party System Fragmentation, 1975–2002

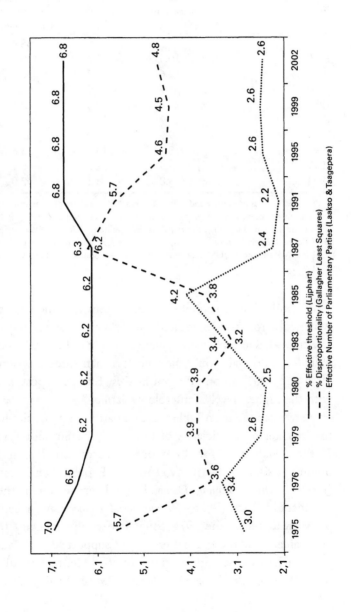

TABLE 8.1
Total and Interbloc Volatility in Portuguese Elections

Election	Total volatility	Interbloc volatility	Interbloc volatility as percentage of total volatility
1975-76	11.3	6.6	58.4
1976-79	10.5	3.2	30.5
1979-80	4.6	1.7	36.9
1980-83	11.2	7.7	68.7
1983-85	22.5	0.5	2.2
1985-87	23.2	15.4	66.4
1987-91	9.5	1.2	12.6
1991-95	18.2	13.8	75.8
1995-99	3.9	2.2	56.1
1999-2002	8.8	8.1	92.0

SOURCE: 1975-99, R. Gunther and J. R. Montero, "The anchors of partisanship: a comparative analysis of voting behavior in four southern European democracies," in P. N. Diamandouros and R. Gunther (eds.), *Parties, politics and democracy in the new Southern Europe* (Baltimore: Johns Hopkins University Press, 2001). Data for 2002 are my own calculations. PS, PCP, BE, MRPP and POUS were treated as left-wing parties, and PSD, CDS-PP PPM as right-wing.

more, "interbloc" volatility—i.e. the extent to which electors have switched across parties located on different sides of the left-right cleavage—has also been comparatively high: if the 2002 election was included, Portugal would have no less than three elections (1987, 1995 and 2002) among the ten in West European post war history with the highest level of interbloc volatility.[18]

As we can see from Table 8.2, two parties in particular have been the long-term beneficiaries of this trend: the Socialist Party (PS— *Partido Socialista*), a social-democratic party founded in 1973 by political exiles in Germany; and the Popular Democratic Party (PPD—*Partido Popular Democrático*)—later renamed the Social Democratic Party (PSD—*Partido Social Democrata*)—a center-right party created after the 1974 coup. Two complementary trends are detectable. First: the gradual erosion of support for the smaller parties, such as the Social Democratic Center/Popular Party (CDS/PP—*Centro Democrático Social/ Partido Popular*) on the right,

TABLE 8.2

Distribution of Seats and Votes in Legislative Elections

(percentage of the vote between parenthesis; spoiled and blank votes excluded)

	PS/ FRS	PPD/ PSD	CDS/ CDS-PP	PCP/ APU/ CDU	PRD	BE	Others
1975	46.4	32.4	6.4	12.0	—	—	2.8
	(40.7)	(28.4)	(8.2)	(13.4)			(9.3)
1976	40.7	27.8	16.0	15.2	—	—	0.3
	(36.6)	(25.6)	(16.8)	(15.1)			(5.9)
1979	29.6	51.2		18.8	—	—	0.4
	(28.1)	(46.5)		(19.3)			(6.1)
1980	29.6	53.6		16.4	—	—	0.4
	(28.4)	(48.7)		(17.1)			(5.8)
1983	40.4	30.0	12.0	17.6	—	—	0.0
	(36.9)	(28.0)	(12.9)	(18.6)			(3.6)
1985	22.8	35.2	8.8	15.2	18.0	—	0.0
	(21.3)	(30.6)	(10.2)	(15.9)	(18.4)		(3.6)
1987	24.0	59.2	1.6	12.4	2.8		0.0
	(22.7)	(51.3)	(4.5)	(12.4)	(5.0)		(4.1)
1991	31.3	58.7	2.2	7.4	—	—	0.4
	(29.7)	(51.6)	(4.5)	(9.0)			(5.2)
1995	48.7	38.3	6.5	6.5	—	—	0.0
	(44.6)	(34.8)	(9.3)	(8.7)			(2.6)
1999	50.0	35.2	6.5	7.4	—	0.9	0.0
	(45.0)	(33.0)	(8.5)	(9.2)		(2.5)	(1.8)
2002	41.8	45.7	6.1	5.2	—	1.3	0.0
	(38.6)	(41.0)	(8.9)	(7.1)		(2.9)	(1.5)

and the Portuguese Communist Party (PCP—*Partido Comunista Português*) on the left. This trend is particularly visible since the early 1980s for the CDS (following two coalition cabinets with the PSD that rendered the party undistinguishable from its larger partner), and since the late 1980s for the PCP (following internal strife in the aftermath of the fall of the Berlin Wall). The second trend is, obviously, the increasing concentration of votes in both the PS and the PSD. In 1975, the two parties combined obtained about 78 per cent of seats and 69 per cent of votes. By 2002, those percentages had risen to about 87 and 80 respectively.

The most recent historical cause of party system change in Portugal was the creation of the Democratic Renewal Party (PRD—*Partido Renovador Democrático*) in the early 1980s. The PRD was mainly a creature of President Ramalho Eanes, conceived in order to dispute the center-left vote with the PS and, more crucially, to provide Eanes with the means to remain a protagonist in Portuguese politics following his second (and final) term as President. As it happened, the entrance of the PRD onto the political scene in 1985 caused an electoral earthquake, through which the party obtained 18 per cent of the valid vote and almost displaced the PS as the major party of the left. The 1985 elections were just the first step in the transformation of the party system. Two years later, following a period of extensive acrimony and mutual obstructionism in relations between the PSD minority cabinet and the opposition, the PRD supported a motion of censure and thus effectively overthrew the PSD government. However, it did so during a period in which the PSD was popular with an electorate that yearned for governmental stability after thirteen years during which there were no less than ten different cabinets. As a result, the PRD was severely punished in the 1987 elections, while the PSD was richly rewarded. While the latter won Portugal's first ever single-party majority in 1987, the former's support—which had been obtained mostly at the expense of the PS and the PCP—shifted massively to PSD and, to a lesser extent, back to the PS.[19]

However, if the 1985 and 1987 elections are crucial for an understanding of the actual mechanics of party system change in Portugal, they still tell us little about the deeper underlying factors that made such change possible. Those factors seem to be both institutional and socio-political in nature. First, the increasing concentration of votes in the two largest parties may have been fostered by the Portuguese semi-presidential regime, which is based on a majoritarian electoral system. This created "a tendency for the party system to split into two blocs, each behind one of the candidates. Therefore, successive presidential elections have encouraged parties to converge within their own bloc, underlining a greater bipolarity in the system."[20] Besides, although the basic features of the electoral system have remain unaltered, it is likely that, particularly in the smaller constituencies where disproportionality is higher, the system has produced increasingly stronger psychological effects in the direction of strategic voting.[21]

Second, the realignment of the Portuguese electorate in the direction of the two largest parties in the mid-1980s (and the high levels of electoral volatility behind it) has been made possible by the weakness of the parties' organizational grounding in society, and the increasing shallowness of social-structural vote anchoring. Portuguese parties lack both substantial mass-membership bases and strong organizational apparatuses, a consequence of the fact that, in the historically recent democratic transition, what were (in most cases) newly created parties were immediately called to assume functions in both parliament and government. In this context, they preferred to focus on building social support from *within* the state apparatus, rather than through the extra-parliamentary institutionalization of true mass-based parties.[22]

Moreover, although Portugal continues to display important socio-economic cleavages (expressed in levels of economic inequality that rank among the highest in Western Europe, for example), social-structural variables have never been strong predictors of partisanship.[23] This weak grounding of electoral support in social cleavages is arguably a legacy of the revolutionary period, which has been reinforced by later socio-economic changes. In the early 1970s, the highly left-skewed political environment, and the complete delegitimization of the right, prevented parties from establishing clear links with their "natural" social constituencies in that crucial formative period.[24] Moreover, the legacy of a "revolutionary" constitutional text and of military intervention in politics systematically forced all parties to the right of the Communists to form alliances around most fundamental institutional and policy issues throughout the 1970s and 1980s, obfuscating their ideological distinctions and further uncoupling them from social bases with potentially conflicting interests. The only partial exception to this pattern was, predictably, the vote for the Communist Party, whose social bases had been constituted primarily by the urban proletariat in the Lisbon region and rural wage laborers in the south.[25] However, even that peculiarity has been slowly fading as levels of economic development and standards of living have risen dramatically, and the employment structure has been transformed since the mid-1980s, further diminishing the already low impact of social cleavages in political behavior, allowing electoral volatility and facilitating electoral realignment.[26]

Political Institutions and Policy-Making

How has party system change played out in the ability of executives and the parties that support them to convert their preferences into policy? In fact, Portuguese democratic political institutions have always favored some amount of autonomy of the executive *vis-à-vis* parliament. For example, although—as in any parliamentary system—the Portuguese cabinet is responsible before the legislature, cabinet formation and survival does not require explicit and continuous endorsement by a parliamentary majority. On the one hand, there is no need for a formal investiture that would require the support of an absolute majority in parliament for a new cabinet to take office. Instead, all that is necessary is for the new cabinet *not* to have its program rejected by an absolute majority. On the other hand, unseating a cabinet requires either support for a motion of censure by an absolute majority in parliament or, conversely, the lack of plurality support for a motion of confidence presented by the government itself.[27] Furthermore, and with very few exceptions, passing bills requires only a simple majority—rather than an absolute majority—on the floor, and the executive additionally enjoys what can only be described as extremely vast decree powers in comparison with most Western democracies.[28] This Portuguese brand of "rationalized parliamentarism" was designed precisely to compensate for what was expected to be a fragmented and highly polarized party system with unlikely absolute majorities, thus fostering governability and allowing the formation and survival of single-party PS and PSD minority cabinets during the 1970s and early 1980s.

TABLE 8.3
Portuguese Cabinets since 1976

Prime Minister	Partisan composition	Size of partisan support (% of MP's)	Duration	Reason for termination
Soares I (1976-77)	PS	40.7	17 months	Rejected motion of confidence
Soares II (1978)	PS; CDS	56.7	6 months	Dismissal by President
Nobre da Costa (1978)	Nonpartisan	—	1 month	Rejection of government program
Mota Pinto (1978-79)	Nonpartisan	—	7 months	Resignation of Prime Minister
Pintasilgo (1979)	Nonpartisan	—	5 months	Elections
Sá Carneiro (1980)	PSD; CDS; PPM	51.2	11 months	Elections following death of Prime Minister
Balsemão I (1981)	PSD; CDS; PPM	53.6	8 months	Resignation of Prime Minister
Balsemão II (1981-82)	PSD; CDS; PPM	53.6	20 months	Resignation of Prime Minister and elections
Soares III (1983-85)	PS; PSD	70.4	2 years	Resignation of Prime Minister
Cavaco Silva I (1985-87)	PSD	35.2	18 months	Approval of motion of censure
Cavaco Silva II (1987-91)	PSD	59.2	4 years	Elections
Cavaco Silva III (1991-95)	PSD	58.7	4 years	Elections
Guterres I (1995-99)	PS	48.7	4 years	Elections
Guterres II (1999-2001)	PS	50.0	2 years	Resignation of Prime Minister
Barroso (2002-)	PSD; CDS	51.8	—	—

SOURCES: L. S. Matos (1992), "O sistema político português e a Comunidade Europeia," *Análise Social*, 27 and M. C. Lobo, "The role of political parties in Portuguese democratic consolidation," *Party Politics*, 7 (2001)

However, by the late 1980s, these and other institutional rules have interacted with party system change in order to dramatically reinforce the concentration of power in the executive. The first manifestation of that phenomenon was a shift from endemic cabinet instability to stable single-party government.[29] The trend is clearly visible in Table 8.3, which lists all Portuguese cabinets since the 1976 elections, including their duration, partisan composition and parliamentary support. Starting in 1987, and lasting throughout the 1990s, all Portuguese cabinets were supported by a single political party and stayed in power throughout the duration of the legislature. The exception concerns the more recent 1999-2001 Socialist cabinet, led by António Guterres, and its succession by a PSD-CDS coalition. However, since Guterres' fall was a result of his own resignation following negative results in local elections (rather than as a result of any concrete threat of parliamentary defeat), it is not clear that the basic balance of power between executive and legislature has experienced any major change from this point of view.

Single-party government—and particularly majority government—has been associated with a transformation of legislative-executive relations that caused "majoritarian criteria... [to have] replaced consensual ones in deciding on the distribution of rights and responsibilities."[30] This is a result of the fact that legislative policy-making institutions in Portugal place few obstacles in the path of a cabinet supported by a cohesive majority. Although the rules determining the plenary agenda do not favor the parties supporting the executive *per se*—unlike in countries such as Ireland, Greece, France and the United Kingdom—they also fail to give minorities agenda-setting powers in cases of majority governments, since majority rule ultimately prevails in the body in charge of setting that agenda, the *Conferência de Líderes* (Leader's Conference). Furthermore, the articulation between the use of available urgency and/or priority procedures for a government's legislative initiatives, the executive's monopoly over the presentation of bills that increase expenditure or taxation, and the availability (and abundant use) of decree powers, have reinforced the government's dominance over the entire legislative process.[31]

Although the Portuguese parliament has a specialized committee system with important formal legislative powers, and proportionally allocated chairs—a pattern that sets it apart from the extreme majoritarian institutions and practices found in typical Westminster-style democracies[32]—it is doubtful that this has made any significant difference to policy outcomes, particularly during periods of majority government. The strong party discipline that has prevailed—stimulated, as we have seen, by the closed list PR system, has rendered legislative behavior in committees highly partisan and totally compliant to the overall correlation of forces in parliament,[33] turning them into little more than "miniature parliaments" with reduced autonomous impact on the extent to which parliament as a whole is actually able to influence policy.[34] Finally, this concentration of power in the executive has been compounded by the concentration of power at the *head* of the executive. There has been a visible increase in the organizational and budgetary resources placed in the hands of the prime minister, accompanied by the conversion of the presidency of the Council of Ministers into an increasingly institutionalized agency within the executive.[35]

One way in which this "majoritarian turn" in Portugal could conceivably be mitigated would have been through the role of the popularly elected President of the Republic. Although the head of state, the president holds no executive powers in Portugal's semi-presidential system. While the president can still dissolve parliament, dismiss the executive, and veto bills passed by parliament and governmental decrees, for example, presidential powers have been increasingly constrained, not only by means of constitutional amendments, but, more crucially, by changes in the political environment. First, presidential legislative veto powers do not make a direct difference to the extent to which an executive supported by a parliamentary majority is able to convert its preferences into policy. On the one hand, an absolute majority in parliament can override the presidential veto—in which case the president is constitutionally forced to promulgate the previously vetoed bill in its entirety; on the other hand, although the president's veto over government decrees is final

TABLE 8.4
Presidents and Cabinets, 1981-2002

Periods	President of the Republic	Parties that had supported winning presidential candidate	Ruling parties
January 1981 – June 1983	Ramalho Eanes – 1st term (military)	PS, PSD, CDS	PSD/CDS/PPM majority coalition
June 1983– November 1985	Ramalho Eanes – 2nd term (military)	PS, PCP	PS/PSD majority coalition
November 1985– January 1986	Ramalho Eanes – 2nd term (military)	PS, PCP	PSD minority
January 1986– August 1987	Mário Soares – 1st term (Socialist)	PS, PCP, PRD	PSD minority
August 1987– January 1991	Mário Soares – 1st term (Socialist)	PS, PCP, PRD	PSD majority
January 1991– October 1995	Mário Soares – 2nd term (Socialist)	PS, PSD	PSD majority
October 1995– January 1996	Mário Soares – 2nd term (Socialist)	PS, PSD	PS minority
January 1996– January 2001	Jorge Sampaio – 1st term (Socialist)	PS, PCP	PS minority
January 2001– March 2002	Jorge Sampaio 2nd term (Socialist)	PS, PCP	PS minority
March 2002 –	Jorge Sampaio – 2nd term (Socialist)	PS	PSD/CDS majority coalition

and cannot be overridden, a cabinet supported by a cohesive majority can simply reintroduce the previously vetoed decrees as bills in parliament, and have them relatively easily approved. In fact, the only type of legislation in which a president facing an absolute majority is a veto-player, is that which regulates elections and referenda, national defense, state, of emergency and the Constitutional Court, in which a presidential veto can only be overridden by a two-thirds majority. In all remaining issues, the president cannot be counted as an effective veto player.[36]

Thus, what is left is the case in which the president faces a cabinet supported by a parliamentary minority. However, as we can see in Table 8.4, this has only occurred in two periods since the 1980s, and the longer of them (1995-2002) was one in which the cabinet and the president belonged to the same party—the PS. The only period of "cohabitation" between a president affiliated to one party and a minority government of another party took place during the 16 months from January 1986 to August 1987.

The remaining presidential powers have been subjected to institutional and, more importantly, political constraints since the 1980s. In 1982, the first revision of Portugal's democratic constitution limited the president's cabinet dismissal powers, converting the cabinet's direct "political responsibility" before the president to a mere "institutional responsibility" of somewhat undefined contours.[37] It is true that the power to dissolve parliament remained discretionary, and that the new constitutional provision that the president can only dismiss the cabinet "in order to assure the regular functioning of democratic institutions" may be subject to various interpretations, allowing the president substantial leeway. In other words, the fact that the successive holders of this office have interpreted these powers in rather restrictive terms seems to have much less to do with any fundamental change in institutional rules than with new shared social expectations about what the role of the president should be: facilitators rather than impediments to governability and institutional stability, and mere impartial arbiters in relation to everyday politics.[38]

This does not mean that, in practice, the Portuguese semi-presidential regime has swung more or less permanently to the "parliamentary" side of the presidential-parliamentary continuum along which Duverger and others assumed semi-presidential regimes could be positioned.[39] In fact, unlike the situation in France, there has been no clear and predictable alternation between "presidential" and "parliamentary" phases in Portugal—at least since the 1980s. Instead, even in periods where cohesive parliamentary majorities have supported cabinets, Portuguese presidents have retained means of intervention in everyday politics that render the regime "not quite parliamentary." On the one hand, legislative vetoes and referrals of legislation to the Constitutional Court, although of uncertain effectiveness in terms of actually preventing majorities from passing their preferred policies, can and have been used as weapons in "wars of attrition" against parliamentary majorities: they are aimed at swaying public opinion against the cabinet. On the other hand, presidents can resort to their privileged media access in order to voice discontent with the government (as well as those of unions, the military, the judges and other interest groups).[40]

It is unclear, however, whether such political and institutional resources are likely to make a systematic difference in the way policy is made in Portugal. The use of such weapons on the part of presidents seems to be constrained by the potential electoral punishment to which they themselves can be subjected by endangering either stability or governability: and although "lame duck" presidents need not feel such constraints—as was demonstrated by Mário Soares during his second term, *vis-à-vis* the majority PSD cabinet of 1991-95—what has, until now, been a relatively peaceful cohabitation between Jorge Sampaio and the center-right PSD-CDS/PP cabinet seems to suggest that even the combination of ideological divergence and electoral unaccountability are not sufficient conditions to foster "presidential interventionism."

Consequences and Uncertainties

There are very few doubts that the "majoritarian turn" we have described above has produced a series of welcome developments in Portuguese politics and society. Party system fragmentation and rampant cabinet instability throughout the 1970s and early 1980s were associated with failures in economic performance, short-term political manipulation of the economic cycles and difficulties in both passing and implementing badly need economic and social reforms. This has been replaced by government stability and a pattern of alternation between the two main centrist parties, whose record during the late 1980s and 1990s has been one of steady and often rapid convergence with Europe, both in terms of economic development and social welfare expenses.[41] Furthermore, polarization and acrimony in government-opposition relations have been sharply reduced in comparison to the early years of democracy, while electoral choices seem to have moved in the direction of a model in which the electorate is more clearly able—and willing—to hold leaders and governments accountable for past performance.[42] All this has occurred simultaneously with a rise in public support for democracy as a regime from the 1980s, reaching levels comparable to those found in most European democracies.[43]

However, at the same time Portugal has begun to display some of the symptoms that are typically associated with majoritarian democracies, such as increased levels of electoral abstention.[44] From the 1970s to the 1990s, average abstention rates have risen from 13 to 25 per cent, the highest rate of increase of all OECD countries, and already above the average of those countries without compulsory voting.[45] Moreover, while public support for democracy as a regime has indeed increased, and there are little signs of an incomplete allegiance to basic democratic values and freedoms, political discontent—as measured by indicators such as "satisfaction with democracy"—is clearly on the increase.[46] Levels of confidence in political institutions are not only low, but they are also strongly dependent upon perceptions of economic performance, suggesting that a more detached and cynical view of political officeholders is replacing previous attachments and loyalties.[47] To some extent, these developments are common to many other contemporary Western democracies.[48] Nevertheless, the speed and intensity with which they have manifested themselves in Portugal since the 1980s has given rise to increased concerns among observers and politicians about the quality of Portuguese democracy, leading to continuous calls for institu-

tional reform. It is likely that the fact that such reforms have systematically failed to materialize—such as in the case of the electoral
system—has contributed to increase rather than mitigate some of
those symptoms.

Nevertheless, it may also be the case that the Portuguese political
system is again "reforming itself," regardless of any institutional tin-
kering. The 2002 elections illustrate some aspects of this potential
development. Although they were among the most competitive
elections ever—with the PSD and PS separated by less than 4 per
cent of the vote—some of the smaller parties displayed a surprising
resistance to the pressures for strategic voting this time. In fact, the
inability of the PSD to obtain an absolute majority, and the CDS-
PP's electoral resilience, were the main causes behind the formation
of a center-right coalition government, breaking with the 17-year
old single-party "tradition." It is true that the orthodox Communist
PCP remains outside the realm of possibilities for future pre- or
post-electoral coalitions with the PS; however, the sharp decline of
the Communists (which is creating internal pressures for a change in
the party's political strategy and discourse), the slow rise of the new
left-libertarian Left Bloc (BE—*Bloco de Esquerda*), and a PS leadership that is apparently more willing than ever to build bridges with
parties to its left, are creating incentives and opening opportunities
for power-sharing arrangements on the left of the political spectrum.
If that was to happen, a new "turn" in Portuguese politics might take
place: a return to power-sharing practices without necessarily endangering governmental stability, and a revival of ideological competition between blocs of parties without necessarily resulting in the
excessive party system polarization and political acrimony of the
1970s and early 1980s.

9 | Legitimizing the EU? Elections to the European Parliament in Portugal, 1987-1999

Marina Costa Lobo

There is a paradox regarding the Portuguese relationship with the European Union(EU).[1] On the one hand, diffuse attitudes towards it are overwhelmingly positive. According to *Eurobarometer* data, since 1986 more than half of the population considers the EU to be "a good thing," and an above-EU average majority agrees that Portugal has benefited from membership. On the other hand, electoral participation in elections to the European Parliament is below the European average, which itself has been declining. The views of Portuguese citizens towards the EU have been the focus of relatively recent studies,[2] while very few studies have sought to analyze the elections to the European Parliament in Portugal.[3] In this chapter we propose to analyze the latter as evidence of the relationship with the EU.

Having experienced four elections over 12 years—elections that have been held under both center-left, PS (*Partido Socialista*—Socialist Party), and center-right, PSD (*Partido Social Democrata*—Social Democratic Party), and single-party governments—there is sufficient data to undertake a longitudinal analysis of European Parliament elections in Portugal.[4] Also, Portugal has been included in the "European Election Studies" project that analyses behavior in the European Parliament elections since 1989.[5] These post-election studies are very useful to understand certain aspects of the way in which European Parliament elections work, and will be used selectively throughout this chapter.

The objectives are to try to ascertain the degree to which each of these elections have functioned less as second order elections, seen solely in the perspective of national politics, and more as elections of a *sui generis* political system to the institution that behaves as a co-partner in legislative decisions in the EU. To this end, we will analyze the context of the various European Parliament elections held in Portugal in order to understand what has been at stake. Then, the various characteristics that are assigned to second order elections will be tested in order to understand whether elections can be considered consistently second-order elections, or whether there is any visible trend that enables us to discern the nascent traits of a European political system.

Between 1987 and 1999, the EU experienced profound transformations. From the mid-1980s onwards, successive treaty revisions have deepened integration between member-states. This has involved a supra-nationalization of policy-making in key areas such as agriculture, transport, training, common market regulations and monetary and fiscal issues, to mention some of the most important. Europeanization of policy-making has gone hand-in-hand with changes in the balance of power among supranational institutions, to the benefit of the European Parliament.[6] In effect, ever since the first direct election of the European Parliament in 1979, it has sought to increase its powers. The Single European Act saw the establishment of the cooperation procedure ensuring that the Parliament had to be heard on all initiatives presented by the Commission to the Council; the Maastricht Treaty introduced the co-decision procedure, which made the Parliament a partner of the Council of Ministers; and the Treaty of Amsterdam has widened the ambit of co-decision, as well as given the Parliament more leverage within this legislative procedure. Some have thus argued that, since Maastricht, the Council and the Parliament are best understood as two legislative chambers sharing unequal power.[7]

First, however, it is necessary to understand what exactly is meant by the term "second-order" election, as well as the electoral system within which these elections took place. European elections have been characterized as "second order national elections" where there is "less at stake as compared to first-order national elections."[8] These elections are predominantly about the political situation of the first-order arena at the moment when it is being held, even if nominally second-order elections are about something quite different (European representation, local affairs, etc.). As a result, Reif and Schmitt consider that turnout will be lower in second-order elections; that incumbent national parties will do worse; and that larger parties will also do worse and smaller parties better. A corollary of the latter is that since smaller parties tend to belong to the extremes of the party system, these will have greater representation in the European Parliament. All premises follow from the secondary nature of these elections, which makes voters less inclined to assume the costs of going to the voting booth, induces them to use these elections to send a warning message to the incumbent government in order for it to try to improve performance in preparation of the following legislative elections, and also allows electors to "vote with their hearts," rather than tactically for the larger party within their own bloc, as may occur in legislative elections. According to Marsh and Franklin, until 1994 the European record is that, indeed, on average turnout is lower, government parties do lose votes and the party system does become more fragmented. However, apart from the case of turnout, the differences are not large, and in every case—including turnout—the standard deviation approaches or exceeds the mean: indicating that there is a great deal of variance unexplained.[9] In this paper, we will analyze these three indicators of "second-order elections" and see their evolution in the Portuguese context in turn.

To some extent, the way in which the nature of second-order elections actually plays out depends, in large part, on the electoral system employed. Since 1994, Portugal has used the d'Hondt system of proportional representation to elect 25 members to the European Parliament.[10] However, unlike in the legislative elections, in European Parliament elections the whole country is a single constituency.[11] For the first time, Portuguese citizens living elsewhere in the EU, or EU citizens with Portuguese residency, were allowed to cast their vote for one of the lists presented in Portugal at the 1994 election.[12] Despite this possibility, relatively few Portuguese citizens living elsewhere in the EU actually voted on that day; a tendency that was maintained in 1999. Parties have to present closed lists with 15 candidates, and between 3 and 8 replacement candidates (art. 7).[13] Electoral systems across the EU have varied: in 1999, various systems of proportional representation were used in all member-states.[14]

In the Portuguese case, what are the consequences of this election system on proportionality *vis-a-vis* the legislative elections' 22 electoral circles? According to Blais and Massicote, a single electoral district is most conducive to accurate representation, thus increasing proportionality.[15] The single constituency lowers the organizational costs associated with running an election with multiple electoral circles, a factor that may also benefit the smaller parties. Finally, since executive power is not at stake, the benefits of being an incumbent will be less important in contesting an election, thereby favoring smaller parties. Thus, in the Portuguese case we would expect this difference in district magnitude to improve the smaller parties' chances of success in European Parliament elections. Yet it is worth bearing in mind that differences in the number of deputies to be elected (25 in European Parliament elections as opposed to 230 in national parliamentary elections) makes the number of votes required to elect a deputy much greater in the European than in the national parliamentary elections.

The paper will proceed tas follows: firstly, the degree of polarization between the main parties on EU issues, the election campaign and the election results will be analyzed. The underlying objective is to understand, from a longitudinal perspective, whether these elections have become more European. Then, the main characteristics that second-order elections are supposed to have, will be analyzed in turn, once again to detect whether there is any trend either increasing the degree to which these elections can be considered second-order or not. In this way, we will consider turnout, the degree to which the European Parliament elections are seen as an occasion to punish incumbent parties and the performance of smaller parties in these elections.

The Making of a Cleavage:
Ideological Positioning vis-à-vis the EU

In Portugal until 1985, the process of European integration was used as an "alternative model" by the pro-pluralism parties, to the "left-wing revolutionary" model that was mainly presented by the PCP (*Partido Comunista Português*—Portuguese Communist Party);[16] indeed, a study on party positions in the pre-accession period shows that in Portugal, the PS, the PSD and the conservative CDS (*Centro Democrático Social*—Social Democratic Center) made European integration a fundamental part of their program.[17] The PCP, on the contrary, was opposed to European Community membership for economic, political and foreign policy reasons.[18] According to this party, membership of the European Community would be disastrous for small- and medium-sized Portuguese firms, and would lead to higher unemployment. Moreover, it would contribute to the reversal of some important revolutionary achievements, namely the process of nationalization and the collectivization of agriculture. Furthermore, they argued that membership would diminish national sovereignty and turn Portugal into an instrument of "imperialist" neo-colonial policies.[19]

By 1987 there was a split on the left; separating the Communists from the relatively Euro-enthusiastic group that included the PS, PSD and CDS. The CDS and the PS also emphasized their membership of the largest and most emblematic parliamentary groups in the European Parliament—the European People's Party and the European Socialists, respectively—and denounced the presumably ideologically inconsistent affiliations that the PSD and the PRD (*Partido Renovador Democrático*—Democratic Renewal Party) had negotiated.[20]

Still, despite this important cleavage on the left, the 1987 European Parliament election campaign was completely subsumed in the legislative one. Not only were the elections simultaneous, but the national election was, arguably, the most important legislative election since democratization. The PSD was poised to obtain an absolute majority, and on the left there was much anxiety concerning whether the PRD would retain the representation it achieved in 1985.[21] When on the eve of the election the weekly newspaper, *Expresso*, questioned the main party leaders on what would be a good result, only Adriano Moreira—leader of the CDS—mentioned his party's objectives for the European elections: all other leaders referred only to the legislative election results.[22]

The 1989 election saw continued support for European integration by the three pro-European parties (the CDS, the PSD and the PS), with only minor differences between them. The main change occurred on the left, with the relative convergence of the PCP towards the position of the other parties. The previous year, the PCP had begun to acknowledge some of the inherent benefits of Portuguese accession to the EU, even though it continued to criticize the way in which the governing parties (PS and PSD) approached the process of integration.[23] In a document prepared for the upcoming party congress, the authors argued that the European elections would have internal political consequences and, therefore, the PCP should contest these elections to its maximum ability. This important redirection of Communist policy should not be overemphasized: they ceased to be anti-EU since it became evident that Portugal would not withdraw from it; nevertheless, they continued to be highly critical of the EU and its policies.

The Communists' U-turn has to be understood in the context of attitudes towards the EU at this time. In 1989, as well as during the previous European election, attitudes towards the EU were extremely positive in Portugal.[24] As has been shown elsewhere, Portuguese attitudes towards Europe during the mid-1980s were more positive than they ever had been in countries that had been members since the 1970s (e.g. Denmark and the UK).[25] This elite and mass consensus contributed to a lukewarm campaign, and pundits agreed that European themes were not really discussed: instead, it became a test of the government's declining popularity[26] and of the firmness of the PSD electorate to discover whether it was solidly behind the government and the party, or whether other parties would benefit from a transfer of votes. All parties—the Socialists in particular—attempted to "nationalize" the elections: transforming them into a referendum on the performance of the government.

The 1994 European elections were held in a very different public opinion context. While attitudes towards Europe remained largely positive, they had, nevertheless, reached their lowest level since accession.[27] These were, of course, the first post-Maastricht Treaty elections, which arguably introduced a European cleavage in several hitherto "national" party systems.[28] It has been seen above that, in Portugal, a European cleavage existed previously; one that split the PCP from the remaining parties. However, Maastricht did have a significant impact on the Portuguese party system: this was so not only due to divergences regarding the treaty itself, but particularly concerning the government's economic policies during the early-1990s in order to fulfil the so-called Maastricht Criteria,[29] which consisted of stringent financial objectives that the government had to comply with in order to qualify for European Monetary Union.

Thus in the early 1990s, the newly renamed CDS-PP (*CDS-Partido Popular*—CDS/Popular Party), under the new leadership of Manuel Monteiro, refashioned itself as a Euro-skeptic party. This strategy had seemed to be the only alternative for the party if it was to avoid disappearing during the PSD's second absolute majority government (1991-95). This programmatic change had consequences at the national level, and also for the European Parliament elections. In 1992, the CDS-PP left the EPP (European People's Party) parliamentary group, and joined EDA (European Democratic Alliance), which included the French Gaullists and the Irish *Fianna Fail*.[30] In the following European elections, the CDS effectively reversed its pro-European stance: emphasizing inter-governmentalism, and promoting policies that upheld national governments' decision-making powers (such as reducing decisions by majority rule).[31]

On the left, the Communists were also extremely critical of the Maastricht Treaty. Firstly, due to the fact that it endowed the EU with a juridical nature, thus opening the way to federalism and to the diminution of national sovereignty. Secondly, the PCP rejected the goal of European monetary union, since it would only serve international capital. Thirdly, the party objected to the European military bloc that was provided for under the terms of the Maastricht Treaty. Finally, they criticized the double democratic deficit, i.e. the lack of power of both the national parliaments and of the European Parliament in community affairs.[32] The Socialists were rather more cautious in their approach. Given their governmental and European vocation, they defended the main principles of the Maastricht Treaty.[33] The main issue for this party was the way in which the objective of monetary union was being pursued by the government, namely the excessive attention given to financial issues to the detriment of social convergence concerns. In effect, the Socialists used this campaign as a test to what might be achieved in the 1995 legislative elections: the whole party united in its efforts behind the campaign, with Guterres, the party's leader, being present in all party rallies, and concentrated on the failures of the government's European policy. Among the larger parties then, the issue was hardly the performance of the MEPs, but a dress rehearsal for the 1995 legislative elections.

In the 1999 European elections, the PSD was, for the first time, not the incumbent party. This time there were few dividing issues between the two main parties. Thus, the European elections effectively became an opinion poll for the forthcoming legislative elections, which most Portuguese would decline to take part in. A survey in early June attributed 57 per cent of voting intentions to the Socialists in a legislative election, and also showed that the change in PSD leadership, with Durão Barroso as new leader, had not increased the PSD's popularity.[34] With this type of result, the real issue was whether the PS would, in fact, obtain an absolute majority in the European elections or not. It is important to note that the 1999 European elections were held shortly after Portugal had become one of the founding members of EMU(European Monetary Union): an event that was considered a success both by the PS and the PSD. Moreover, the election occurred in a positive economic context, at a time when—once again—Portuguese attitudes towards the EU were climbing back up to levels approaching those of the 1980s.[35] In the meantime, the PCP and the CDS-PP maintained their critical stance with respect to the EU.

Thus it can be seen that a European cleavage has existed since democratization; one that has split the Communists from the rest of the parties with parliamentary representation. After the Maastricht Treaty, the CDS-PP became a Euro-skeptic party, and strongly politicized the issue of European integration. Yet, the two main parties have been committed Europeanists. Given that together the PS and PSD have polled over 72 per cent of the vote since entry into the European Community, it is obvious that the European cleavage is not very salient in Portugal.

Regular non-Events?
Interest in European Election Campaigns

The fact that the two main parties, which between them obtain two-thirds of the vote, chose not to politicize a pro- or anti-integration cleavage, may have influenced the lack of interest that resulted in high abstention rates in Portuguese elections to the European Parliament. Using data compiled in *European Election Studies* of 1989, 1994 and 1999, Table 9.1 shows interest in the election campaign and the exposure that respondents' say they had to the European election campaign during the weeks preceding each election. Between 1989 and 1999, the interest in the campaign is virtually identical—and low. On average, 30 per cent of respondents declared that they had been "somewhat" or "very interested" in the campaign. One decade of changes to the European Parliament's powers, together with an increase in awareness of EU issues (due both to the length of membership and deepening integration) have *not* led to any increased interest in European election campaigns. It is a pity that 1994 was excluded since, as we have seen above, this

Table 9.1
Interest in European Election Campaign and Media Exposure to it
(%)

	1989	1994	1999
somewhat or very interested in election campaign	29.6	na	31.0
not very or not at all interested in election campaign	64.6	na	69.0
Did you...			
...Watch a program about the election on television (1994 includes radio)?	55.3	72.9	90.4
...Read a newspaper report about the election?	15.1	20.2	53.2
...Talk to friends or family about the election?	26.0	16.4	70.2
...Attend a public meeting or rally about the election?	3.5	na	2.6
...Look into a website concerned with the election?	na	na	0.6

Source: European Election Study 1989, EB1994 and European Election Study 1999.

was the election in which the differences between parties were greatest.

What appears to have risen considerably during these 10 years is the degree to which the Portuguese are exposed to media content on European elections. The greatest rise is in the percentage of those who admit they have discussed European elections with friends or family (Table 9.1); additionally, exposure to newspaper reports and television programs on European parliamentary elections has also increased substantially. Finally, it is necessary to give a general overview of the party developments that have occurred by presenting the results of the four European elections.

Results of Elections to the European Parliament

In 1987, the election to the European Parliament was held simultaneously with a general election. As a consequence, parties assumed that electors would vote similarly in both ballots; following the pattern in local elections, where, despite the existence of three ballots, voters almost always cast their vote for the same party.[36] The extent to which electors split their vote was unexpected; indeed, the PSD's absolute majority in the general election

TABLE 9.2
European Parliament Election Results, 1987-99

Year	CDU	PS	PRD	PSD	CDS
1987					
%	**11.50**	**22.48**	**4.44**	**37.45**	**15.40**
Votes	648, 700	1, 267, 672	250, 158	2, 111, 828	868, 718
Mandates	3	6	1	10	4
1989					
%	**14.40**	**28.54**	—	**32.75**	**14.16**
Votes	597, 759	1, 184, 380		1, 358, 958	587, 497
Mandates	4	8		9	3
1994					
%	**11.19**	**34.87**	—	**34.39**	**12.45**
Votes	340, 725	1, 061, 560		1, 046, 918	379, 044
Mandates	3	10		9	3
1999					
%	**10.32**	**43.07**	—	**31.11**	**8.16**
Votes	357, 671	1, 493, 146		1, 078, 528	283, 067
Mandates	2	12		9	2

SOURCE: *Comissão Nacional de Eleições* (http://www.cne.pt/).

was not reproduced in the European election (Table 9.2), in which it obtained almost 700,000 fewer votes, 37.45 per cent of the vote, and ten MEPs. The PS's electorate remained largely faithful over the two ballots. The PRD confirmed its ephemeral nature, obtaining 4.44 per cent of the vote and electing one MEP. The CDS performed very well in the European election, where it received 622,000 more votes than it did in the general election: obtaining 15.4 per cent of the vote and four seats. While the CDS's tactic of fighting for the so-called "strategic vote" did not work for the legislative elections, it did have a substantial impact in the European ballot, with the PSD failing to replicate the general election result at that level. The Communists, who had lost votes in the general election, experienced a further decline in their vote in the European election: obtaining 11.5 per cent and three mandates.

The greatest novelty of the 1989 European election was the largely unforeseen high rate of abstention. All parties registered an absolute decrease in the number of voters (Table 9.2 and Table 9.3);

however, the biggest loser of the election was the government party
(the PSD), which saw its share of the vote decline to 32 per cent;
resulting in the loss of one MEP. All other parties increased their
percentage share of the votes; with the greatest increase accruing to
the PCP, which managing to elect an additional MEP (Maria Santos). Despite losing an MEP, Lucas Pires, who led the CDS candidate list ran a successful campaign that saw his party's share of the
vote reach 14 per cent, even though this led to the loss of one MEP.
Finally, the PS, which had agreed a pre-election coalition with the
PRD, slightly increased its share of the vote, thus narrowing the difference between itself and the PSD, and elected an additional MEP.
The abstention rate could be interpreted as a partial warning to the
government; although it did not signal any wholehearted disap-
proval of it to the extent that it would have consequences in national politics. In an effort to improve the government's image, the
prime minister, Cavaco Silva, undertook—shortly after these elections—the most far-reaching government reshuffle since taking
office.

In 1994—at a time when opinion polls were predicting that the
PSD would obtain around 30 per cent of the vote—the actual results
were received with relief by that party and with some apprehension
by the PS (Table 9.2). In this election, official abstention was the
largest winner, reaching 64.5 per cent—the highest in the EU. Once
again, all parties lost a substantial number of votes in absolute terms
(Table 9.2). The Socialists won by a very narrow margin with 34.8
per cent of votes cast, while the PSD managed to obtain 34.4 per
cent. These results were better than the previous European election
results for *both* parties, implying a redirection of the vote towards the
larger parties to the detriment of the smaller ones. The smaller parties saw their percentage of the vote decrease slightly from the previous European election, with the CDS-PP receiving 12.5 per cent,
and the CDU 11.2 per cent of the vote. In mandate terms, the PSD
managed to maintain its nine MEPs, the PS elected a further two—
raising its total to ten—while the CDS-PP retained its three deputies
in Strasbourg, and the PCP lost one.

The actual results were very positive for the Socialists in 1999, both in absolute and in percentage terms, but did not result in the absolute majority they had hoped for and expected given the pre-election opinion poll results. The PS increased its share of the vote to 43 per cent from 34.8 per cent, and elected 12 of Portugal's 25 European deputies. Despite its decreased share of the vote—which dropped from 34.6 to 31 per cent—the PSD held onto the nine MEPs it had elected in 1994. At the EU level, the trend was the opposite: the 1999 elections resulted in the European Socialists becoming the second largest party in the European Parliament after the Conservative EPP. Following successive fusions, in 1999 the EPP won the greatest percentage of votes (37.72 per cent).[37] Both the smaller parties, unable to resist the strong tendency for bipolarization in these successive elections, lost votes in absolute and in percentage terms, and each lost one MEP. As for abstention rates, the record level experienced in 1994 was not exceeded in 1999; in fact, there was a slight decrease, from 64.3 per cent to 59.6 per cent. This is, nonetheless, hardly a heartening result given that, notwithstanding the updating of the electoral register, close to 60 per cent of those registered to vote abstained.

Following this contextualization of the European election campaigns from 1987 to 1999, three themes stand out that require further examination. The first is an analysis of the breakdown in participation during that period (which has been extremely large). The second is the degree to which these elections have, in fact, resulted in the fragmentation, or bipolarization, of the electorate. The third is the extent to which the government party has been punished.

Turnout in Elections to the European Parliament

As has been widely documented, the systematic reinforcement of the European Parliament's power has been accompanied by a *decrease* in rate of participation in European elections; indeed, perhaps the most notable characteristic of European elections is their low turnout. As we shall see, Portugal is no exception. In this section, we present EU-wide data on abstention rates; then the individual-level influences on turnout will be analyzed in Portugal during the period 1989-99, partially following van der Eijk and Franklin's turnout model.[38]

Undoubtedly, one of the most important factors concerning the level of turnout in European elections is their timing relative to legislative elections: "turnout should be lower when national elections were recent, at the start of the electoral cycle, changing to a comparatively high level of turnout when national elections were imminent."[39]

It is necessary to discuss the issue of data reliability on participation rates in Portugal. Due to the lack of constant updating mechanisms, it has been estimated that the Portuguese electoral register was grossly inflated between 1987 and 1998.[40] Deceased voters were not deleted from the register, and neither were changes of addressnotified, resulting in the multiple registration of individual voters. This contributed to widening the gap between official levels of abstention (as measured by the electoral register), and real levels of abstention (as measured by the numbers of citizens over 18 years of age living in Portugal), with the former being greater than the latter. This situation has apparently been largely dealt with and, since 1999, it has become possible once more to accept official participation levels as real participation.[41] A recent study of the nature of Portuguese abstention shows that it has increased in all elections, and that its rate of growth in the legislative elections has been considerable.[42] Thus, the European Parliament elections are not an exception to this recent Portuguese trend (Table 9.3). Even despite this national trend, lack of turnout in European elections does stand out when compared to other elections in Portugal,[43] as well as when compared to European elections in other EU member-states (Table 9.3).[44]

The exception to this was the first election, which took place on the same day in 1987 as the national general elections. If we discount this election due to its artificial coincidence, turnout was significantly lower in the three subsequent elections than in the preceding legislative elections—which have themselves suffered from declining

TABLE 9.3
Participation in European Parliament Elections in EU Member States

Country	1989	1994	1999	Change 1989-99
United Kingdom	36.92	36.49	24.02	-34.9
Denmark	46.15	52.92	50.46	9.3
Netherlands	47.53	35.69	29.95	-37.0
France	48.79	52.71	46.76	-4.2
Portugal	**49.70**	**35.67**	**40.03**	**-19.5**
Spain	54.72	59.14	64.38	17.7
Germany	62.30	60.02	45.19	-27.5
Ireland	68.28	43.98	50.70	-25.7
Greece*	79.97	71.24	70.27	-12.1
Italy	81.60	74.77	69.76	-14.5
Luxembourg*	87.60	88.54	86.63	-1.1
Belgium*	90.73	90.56	90.96	0.3
Sweden	-	41.62	38.84	-6.7
Finland	-	57.59	30.00	-47.9
Austria	-	67.73	49.40	-27.1
EU12/15	56.17	56.66	49.62	-12.4

*Countries where voting is mandatory in European Parliament elections.
SOURCE: Delwit 2000.

participation rates. As a trend, Portuguese participation rates are well below the EU average, which was 56, 57 and 50 per cent in 1989, 1994 and 1999 respectively (Table 9.3).[45] In fact, Portuguese turnout in 1994 was the lowest in the entire EU, its lowest ever participation in a European election: the 1999 turnout showed a slight increase, reaching 40 per cent.

Can abstention in European elections be explained by the same factors that traditionally explain abstention in first-order elections? In order to answer this question we have used the three post-election studies fielded after 1989, 1994 and 1999. Given the data differences in these surveys, different statistical tools were used.[46] Logistic regressions were performed on the 1989 and the 1994 data, broadly following Marsh and Franklin's model, although disaggregating the variables employed. Firstly, the model includes variables that are

TABLE 9.4
**Measuring the Individual Level Effects on Turnout
at European Parliamentary Elections**

INDEPENDENT VARIABLES	DEPENDENT VARIABLES 1989(Voted: 0 Did not vote: 1)	DEPENDENT VARIABLES 1994(Voted: 0 Did not vote: 1)
Block 1:		
Age (nr. Exact age)	-0.12[2]	-0.026[3]
	(5, 270)	(29, 456)
Education (nr. Years in Education)	n.s.	n.s.
Income (- - to ++)	n.s.	n.s.
Subjective Social Class (wkg class to upper class)	n.s.	n.s.
Church Attendance (never to several times a week)	n.s.	n.s.
Nagelkerke R^2	**0.024**	**0.093**
Valid N	(595)	(782)
Block 2:		
Political Interest	-0.794[3]	-0.514[3]
	(19, 541)	(20, 093)
Strength of party attachment	-0.770[3]	-0.629[2]
1- sympathiser, 3- very close	(21, 699)	(7, 119)
Nagelkerke R^2	**0.199**	**0.183**
Valid N	(546)	(573)
Block 3:		
Habitual Voting	-2.502[3]	- 1.788[3]
	(58, 157)	(35, 673)
Nagelkerke R^2	**0.380**	**0.261**
Valid N	(437)	(564)
Block 4:		
Membership a good thing 1- bad thing, 3- good thing	n.s.	n.s.
Membership benefits P 1= benefit, 2 = not benefit	n.s.	n.s.
Satisfaction with Dem in EU 1- not satisfied, 4- very satisfied	n.s.	n.s.
Nagelkerke R^2	**0.347**	**0.287**
Valid N	(304)	(518)

n.s. = not significant
[1] $p < 0.1$
[2] $p < 0.05$
[3] $p < 0.01$

known to be important for turnout in national elections—namely demographic and socio-economic background factors. The second block of variables includes motivational and attitudinal variables that are not specifically related to turnout in national elections, but which are related to the individual's interest in politics. The third block is voting in the previous election. The fourth block of variables includes orientations, attitudes and evaluations pertaining to European integration.[47] We present the data for each individual independent variable, allowing us to assess which of these are the most important, both generally and within each block, and also to understand which variables have become more important over time.

Given the limited sample for the 1999 data, a different statistical tool was used: an independent-samples *t-test*. This test compares the mean score on some continuous variable for two different groups of subjects. Unlike the logistic regression, which gives an indication of which independent variables explain a greater percentage of variance in the dependent variable, this test only tells you if there is a statistically significant difference for the two groups (in our case, "voters" and "non-voters").

Table 9.4 shows that, in both 1989 and 1994, the same determinants are useful in explaining voter turnout—even though the importance of the variables have been somewhat altered. Among the socio-economic variables, only age explains turnout. As has been documented elsewhere,[48] younger people are less inclined to vote in general elections: an attitude that is maintained in European elections. In 1989, however, variables that reveal the respondent's involvement with politics (namely political interest and party attachment) are more important in explaining behavior than age. In particular, whether or not the respondent voted in the previous legislative election (coded as "Habitual voting") explains a full 18 per cent of the turnout variance. What can be seen from the values for 1994 is that the importance of age has increased relative to the "political variables," and the overall level of variance explained is slightly lower. This may signal the growing structural nature of turnout, rather than being a result of more conjunctural political variables. In both cases, attitudes towards membership are not relevant in either year as an explanation for turnout in European elections; confirming Marsh and Franklin's 1996 findings. The analysis of the 1999 survey goes some way to further confirm these findings. Although it is not possible to say what variables are more important, it is clear that the same variables vary significantly with the "turnout" dependent variable, namely: age, interest in politics and party attachment. As in 1989 and 1994, there is no significant relationship between attitudes towards the EU and participation in elections to the European Parliament.

A Different Party System?

Having seen the way in which Portuguese elections to the European Parliament confirm the second-order election hypothesis with respect to participation rates; to what extent do Portuguese electors also conform to the other two hypotheses: namely punishing the incumbent and benefiting smaller parties? Before we turn to the evidence on Portugal, it is worth noting what the conclusions regarding these effects on a Europe-wide scale are.

The authors of the 1996 study found it useful to differentiate between large and incumbent parties, and small moderate and extremist parties. Whilst there is evidence that larger parties are negatively affected by elections to the European Parliament, government parties are not.[49] The corollary of this is that smaller parties do rather well in these elections. However, whether it is small radical parties that benefit most depends to a large extent on the timing of the election. When elections to the European Parliament are held soon after national general elections there is less incentive to express a protest vote, and so it is moderate small parties, rather than the radicals, that obtain most votes. Thus, the time difference between national and European elections seems to be a determining factor in European election results. Larger parties are particularly hurt when the most recent national elections are held up to two-and-one-half years prior to the European election. Converse-

TABLE 9.5
**Party Share of the Vote in National
and European Parliamentary Elections** (%)

	1987 (Euro)	1987 (Nat)	1989 (Euro)	1991 (Nat)	1994 (Euro)	1995 (Nat)	1999 (Euro)	1999 (Nat)
Larger Parties and Incumbents:								
PSD	**37.45**[*]	**50.22**[*]	**32.75**[*]	**50.60**[*]	**34.39**[*]	34.12	**31.11**	32.32
PS	**22.48**	22.24	**28.54**[1]	29.13	**34.87**	43.76[*]	**43.07**[*]	44.06[*]
Total Large Parties	**64.37**	72.46	**61.29**	79.73	**69.26**	77.88	**74.18**	76.38
Smaller parties:								
CDS-PP	**15.40**	4.44	**14.16**	4.43	**12.45**	9.05	**8.16**	8.34
PCP-PEV	**11.50**	12.14	**14.40**	8.80	**11.19**	8.57	**10.32**	8.99
PRD	**4.44**	4.91	–	–				
PSN				1.68				
BE								2.44
Total Small Parties[2]	**26.90**	21.49	**28.56**	14.91	**23.64**	17.62	**18.48**	19.77

[1] In 1987 the PS presented a joint list to the European Parliament election with the PRD
[2] This refers to small parties that have representation in Parliament
[*] Incumbent party
SOURCE: Comissão Nacional de Eleições (http://www.cne.pt/).

ly, when the interval between a European election and the previous national one becomes larger, the differential advantage of small over large parties diminishes.[50]

With respect to the punishment of incumbents, it seems that there are differences between PS and PSD governments. For the elections of 1987, 1989 and 1994, the PSD government lost a greater percentage of votes than any other party. Between 1987 and 1995, the PSD managed to obtain 50 per cent of the votes in national general elections. During the same period, its best electoral score in European elections was 37.45 per cent (in the simultaneous election of 1987 (Table 9.5)). Interestingly, the PS, having been the incumbent government since 1995, was not similarly punished in 1999. Due to the very large abstention levels, it is also interesting to note the differences in absolute levels of voting for the incumbent parties. Even taking into account absolute changes in vote levels, the trend is similar. Between 1989 and 1994 the PSD lost the greatest proportion of votes in absolute terms. In 1999, even though all parties lost votes—including the incumbent PS—the PSD was once again the greatest proportionate loser in absolute terms. Thus, insofar as incumbency is concerned, 1999 clearly stands out from the other elections in that no incumbent punishment is evident.

Confirming the "second-order" election hypotheses, in three out of the four European elections the smaller parties have, in percentage terms, fared better than in national general elections (Table 5). The greatest difference occurred in 1994; in the European elections the two smaller parties combined obtained 23.64 per cent of the vote, whilst in the 1991 national general election they polled a combined share of 14.91 per cent—an increase of 36.9 per cent. However, 1999 stands out, since the share of smaller parties increased only marginally vis-a-vis the 1995 general election. The CDS-PP was responsible for most of the difference between election results at the European and national level. In the 1987 and the 1991 elections, the PSD absorbed much of the CDS electorate, with this latter party seeing its share of the vote decrease to 4.4 per cent. In the elections to the European Parliament, however, the CDS's electorate remained largely faithful.

Thus, in 1987, 1989 and 1994, there is evidence that both the "punishment of incumbent" and the "benefits to smaller parties" occurred in Portugal; however, 1999 stands out in that neither of these phenomena appears to have ocurred. There are two types of explanation for this phenomenon, and they are not necessarily mutually exclusive. One is the long-term decline of small parties that has occurred at the legislative and structural level—also having an impact at the European Parliamentary election level. Another is the timing of the election. We shall consider both of these in turn.

At the national legislative level, smaller parties have systematically lost their percentage share of the vote during the 1990s: this can be explained by the emergence of a majoritarian trend in the Portuguese party system at the national legislative level.[51] Indeed, since 1987, the vote has tended to concentrate in the PS and the PSD,

Table 9.6
Number of Effective Parliamentary Parties in National and European Parliamentary Elections in Portugal and the EU, 1976-1999 [1]

Election Date	1987	1989	1991	1994	1995	1999
Euro elections:						
EU	5.3	5.0		4.6		4.2
Portugal	3.3	3.4		3.1		2.7
National elections:						
Portugal	2.4		2.2		2.6	2.6

[1] The effective number of parliamentary parties is derived from the following formula:
$$N = 1/\Sigma \ s_i^2$$
In which si is the proportion of Assembly seats won by the 'ith' party. This formula was developed by M. Laakso and R. Taagepera, "Effective number of parties: a measure with application to West Europe," *Comparative Political Studies*, 12 (1) (1979), 3-27.
Source: Lobo (2000), and own calculations based on data in G. Grunberg, P. Perrineau and C. Ysmal, (2000).

with the smaller parties—the CDS-PP and the CDU (a coalition of the Communists with the small Green Party)—having increasing difficulties combating their long-term decline. The appearance of the extreme- left-wing *Bloco de Esquerda*—a coalition of existing extreme- left-wing parties—has added some electoral success to small parties since 1999; however, at least at the national legislative level, this has not been sufficient to reverse the trend of the low number of effective parliamentary parties in Portugal since 1987 (Table 9.6).[52] This national trend has been mirrored at the European Parliamentary election level: between 1987 and 1999 the smaller parties have lost 31 per cent of their share of the vote. The CDS-PP is responsible for the largest proportion of this decline; in 1987, led by a popular candidate, Lucas Pires, the party obtained 15.4 per cent of the vote (the second best result in that party's electoral history after the 1976 legislative election result, when it obtained 16.6 per cent (Table 9.5)). With 8.16 per cent in 1999, it fared worse than it had in the previous national legislative election, where it had obtained 9.05 per cent. The Communist vote has not swung as much, however. With the exception of 1989, when the party achieved 14.4 per cent of the vote, its score has hovered around the

11 per cent mark (Table 9.5). Looking at Table 9.6, the decline in the number of effective parliamentary parties (NEPP), measured for the elections to the European Parliament in Portugal demonstrates this. Whilst the NEPP was 3.3 in 1987, in 1999 it was 2.7—approaching the value for the legislative elections.

Beyond the long-term evolution of individual parties, the decline in small party voting that took place in 1994, and especially in 1999, can be explained by the difference in the timing of those elections *vis-a-vis* the national general elections; indeed, these two elections were held once the national legislative elections were in sight, and could thus be used as markers for the following election. According to Oppenhuis *et al.*, this favors small extremist parties, but not small moderate parties.[53] It is too early to say whether the poor results for smaller parties and good performance by the incumbent party in 1999 was, in fact, a function of the timing of the election, or whether it is a reflection of the general decline in the electoral appeal of smaller parties that has been occurring at the national level, or whether it is a combination of both. If the 2004 elections—which will be held in mid-cycle and should thus favor a strong showing by small parties—reproduces the 1999 results, it will contribute to consolidate the characterization of the Portuguese party system as a majoritarian one.

Conclusions

This chapter has sought to analyze the electoral context of elections to the European Parliament, as well as the electoral behavior of the Portuguese in these elections. To do so, we first contextualized the elections to the European Parliament in order to understand the extent to which it can be considered that successive campaigns have had a larger European content. Both the 1994 and the 1999 elections can be considered more European for two reasons. Firstly, European themes achieved more prominence in debates than had been the case during the previous elections, in part due to conjunctural reasons. Secondly, European themes were given greater visibility because in these two elections there were already a substantial number of MEPs who were running for re-election and, thus, it was possible to compare performances within the European Parliament—a possibility that had been very limited in the previous elections. The survey data presented on the awareness of the election campaign attests to this.

Next, we analyzed whether or not the Portuguese elections to the European Parliament can be considered to be second-order elections. With regard to participation levels, the "real," as opposed to the "official," level of abstention was presented. The analysis of individual-level factors to explain low participation levels shows that the most important factors in explaining this phenomenon coincide with the explanatory factors at the legislative level. Thus it is youth, lack of political interest and low party attachment that foster abstention. Conversely, voting in the previous election, strong party attachment, high political interest and age foster participation. Voters do not seem to attribute separate legitimacy to European elections: they are seen through the lens of national institutions. After all, it is national parties that compete for the European vote, and the impact of the EU is overwhelmingly mediated through governmental actions.[55] As such, it is natural that the same factors affecting participation in national legislative elections should also be present at the European Parliament election level. The conclusions may be that EU democratic legitimacy feeds on the legitimacy of national institutions, such as parties.

Concerning the punishment of incumbents and the weight of smaller parties, there is a different party system at the European Parliamentary level. Until 1994, in contrast to what occurs at the national legislative level, there had been no absolute majorities at elections to the European Parliament, and the smaller CDS and CDU have managed to obtain relatively high scores. Nevertheless, 1999 proved to be a different election: in it, not only was the incumbent unpunished, but the smaller parties lost both votes and mandates.

Has the steady decline that these parties have experienced at the legislative level finally caught up with them at the European level?

Or can all the differences seen in 1999 be attributed to the timing of the election, held three months before the national legislative election? It will only be possible to answer some of these questions more fully after the next elections.

At the outset of the chapter, we set out to find evidence of the growing "European" nature of elections to the European Parliament. Our findings confirm, very firmly, that these elections may be considered as being second-order: i.e. they are really not about what they are nominally supposed to be about. As they presently stand, elections to the European Parliament do not serve to legitimize the EU in Portugal: in fact, they even seem to damage national parties' and institutions' credibility. Each election has been transformed into a show of non-compliance by voters who prefer to go away for the (normally long) weekend.

10 | Contemporary Portuguese Literature

João Camilo dos Santos

Whenever evaluating literary works, one needs to bear in mind aesthetic criteria on the one hand, and ethical criteria on the other. Aesthetic criteria oblige us to invoke notions like that of literary genre, style, technique or linguistic competence. The ethical criteria force us to situate the work as a "discourse" in its historical context, obliging us to invoke notions like that of "ideology," "society" or the "class struggle," for example. In both cases (whether aesthetic or ethical values) the quality of the experience to be identified, analyzed and interpreted is a fundamental element in the evaluation of the importance of literary works.

Literary works are never purely aesthetic objects; they are also always, inevitably, a "speech" and an "act" where the problematic relationship of the individual with language and with him/herself, with others, and with history (and consequently with values, with "truth," with the law) takes shape.

In the case of Portugal, given the continuity that exists between the two time-periods, it seems difficult to understand the literature of the twentieth century without bearing in mind the literature of the second half of the nineteenth century. Portugal's most important nineteenth-century authors and works marked out the mythical heritage, the world vision and the language of their successors. Therefore, they are undoubtedly still worthy of our attention and demand closer and more informed readings, and more complex ways of understanding.

Modernity in Portuguese literature seems to begin in the most obvious way with Almeida Garrett (1799-1854) and his *Viagens na Minha Terra* (1846), reaching its height with the publication of the works of Fernando Pessoa (1888-1935) and Mário de Sá-Carneiro (1890-1915). In between there were notable steps backwards. However, progress in literature is an arguable notion, as the survival and eternal modernity of authors like Camões, or the consistent appeal of forms like Galaico-Portuguese lyric poetry prove, among other reasons.

When we consider things from an "end of the twentieth century" perspective, however, everything that came after Pessoa and Sá-Carneiro may be considered as an intensification and development of the aesthetic and literary, linguistic, ethical and social "questions" already formulated in and by the works of the two geniuses of modernism. Pessoa and Sá-Carneiro mark a limit, show a rupture and announce another future already. Portuguese literature since Pessoa and Sá-Carneiro, although we understand it in some ways and knew that it came to bear upon our existence, is also, in part, still our modernity or "post-modernity," and it still remains to be better understood.

The Influence of Liberalism

The prose fiction of Almeida Garrett, Alexandre Herculano (1810-1877), Júlio Dinis (1838-1871), Camilo Castelo Branco (1825-1890) and Eça de Queirós (1845-1900) seems to have begun the process that brought us to the end of the twentieth century and the beginning of the twenty-first. The philosophical and political concerns of Antero de Quental (1824-1891), and the poetry of Cesário Verde (1855-1886), however, fit coherently within the world vision created (or staged) by the aforementioned writers, completing it, enriching it, clarifying it and being clarified by it in turn. The works of these novelists and poets seem to have created and imposed, in a solid and unmistakable way, the modernity that had already been glimpsed and initiated by Garrett. To these names we should add that of the poet António Nobre (1867–1900), who wrote the collection *Só* (1892).

The nineteenth century in Portugal was marked by the Liberal Revolution of 1820 and by both its immediate and long-term consequences. The democratization of political, economic and social life gathered impetus—despite opposition—paving the way for new forms of competition and social mobility. Works of fiction and poetry from this period evoke and recount the nature of social and economic conflicts or power struggles that developed within this context, offering at least a partial view of the causes of these struggles, rather than simply describing them. Love relationships between men and women, in which marriage played a dominant but not exclusive role, are difficult to distinguish from struggles for social success. The search for social status is one of the forms taken by the battle for identity, for the conquest of one's own place in society, one that can serve as a refuge from the difficulties and uncertainties of existence. Thus, the optimism of some, contrasted with the frustration and despair of others. Nothing, however, happened calmly.

In *Viagens na Minha Terra*, Almeida Garrett "invented" a new narrative form that imitated the unpretentious spontaneity of everyday speech,[1] as well as having practically invented the interior monologue in modern Portuguese literature.[2] He also gave us the first romantic hero: a man confused by his emotions, but well aware of his confusion and of the "impossibility of defining things." Human contradiction, the insufficiency of language and the human mind-set and vision of the world—none of these escaped Garrett's sharp eye. Nor did he miss the inability of literature and the novel to render faithfully the inexhaustible complexity of reality.

Garrett's poetry speaks of love with a simplicity that seems almost excessive today. But *Viagens na Minha Terra* is unapologetically fictional and quite conscious of its "literary" discourse.[3] The modernity of the older Garrett is also apparent in the courage and clarity with which he criticizes the destruction wreaked by liberal ideology, by the "Regime of Matter"—proof that disenchantment with the Liberal Revolution affected the more enlightened classes relatively quickly. In Garrett, political clarity becomes entangled with linguistic, aesthetic and literary lucidity. In *Viagens*, the story of Carlos—who ends up a rich baron—is one that denounces the irresolvable and tragic conflict between romantic fulfillment through love, and material fulfillment through success. Lesser-known, and even unfinished, prose works attest to Garrett's tendency towards the experimental and innovative. He sometimes wrote with an "indecision" similar to that acknowledged over half a century later by Mário de Sá-Carneiro in his *Céu em Fogo* (1915).

Herculano's most obvious contribution towards the creation of modern prose fiction in Portugal can probably be found in the solid construction of the plots of his novels. In them the action gives us the impression of progressing austerely from chapter to chapter without straying from a previously drawn up plan. In spite of the weighty, didactic style of most of his works (which also show what a great historian Herculano was), his intelligent reflections on narrative—like those we find in *O Pároco de Aldéia* (1851)—the sense that he was describing problems that considered the relationship between the individual and the institutional on one hand, and history on the other, and his capacity for psychological analysis, all go to show that Herculano was another contributor towards the birth of the modern Portuguese novel. Although he looked to the past to provide lessons and models for the present, he also skillfully presented conflicts—such as struggles for power, frustrations born out of the relationship between the individual and society and dominant values—in works such as *O Bobo* (1843), *Eurico o Presbítero* (1844) and *O Monge de Cister* (1848). As liberal as Garrett, the austere Herculano seems to have traced the same path of disillusionment. Liberalism did not solve the social question or the question of self-fulfillment.

The work of Júlio Dinis seems to represent the mentality of the liberal period that was still hopeful, if not as euphoric as it once had been. In novels like *Uma Família Inglesa* (1868) and *A Morgadinha dos Canaviais* (1868), for example, he describes love marriages that span the social classes: virtue, on one hand, and education and culture on the other, allowed characters from humble backgrounds to improve their station, impose respect and finally "deserve" happiness. Although he expressed—with an apparent naïve optimism—hope in the liberal vision of social betterment, he belied the claim of those who accused him of writing sentimental, romantic novels, and denounced the political and social vices of the liberal political system: uncovering the lack of scruples, the cynicism, corruption and opportunism in the struggle for power. The scenes of violence that disturb the calm universe of his novels prove that Dinis, while believing in liberalism, was not blind to what went on around him. On the other hand, his novels show a surprising and wonderful talent for psychological analysis, and an eye for the description of landscapes, interiors, action scenes, domestic environments and romantic intrigues. By moving the setting from the city to the countryside in *A Morgadinha dos Canaviais,* for example, he expresses nostalgia for the "natural" life that becomes an obsession in the works of his contemporaries, Camilo Castelo Branco, Eça de Queirós and Cesário Verde.

Although conscious of the limitations and vices of liberalism, Dinis believed that the new political climate allowed individuals to pursue fulfillment and more readily to find happiness. Camilo Castelo Branco had a less optimistic vision of the age in which he lived. Conflicts are more acute in his novels. His characters, blinded by passion, forget their long-term interests and appear committed more to anarchic and irrational self-destruction than to eventually becoming part of a promised new order. Love relationships and marriage (inseparable from social relationships, struggles for social prestige and the ambiguous notion of honor) do not lead to peace and happiness as they do in Dinis's novels, but act as the catalyst for crime, disaster and tragedy. In Castelo Branco's view, liberalism does not offer the conditions that can justify the optimism that dominates Dinis's work. His novels consistently show that the new potential for individual fulfillment does not eliminate class conflict but is instead conditioned by the old notions of nobility and superiority. The question of individual identity was still, therefore, a burning issue, for it seemed impossible for individuals to overcome the contradictions of fate and raise themselves above the chaos unleashed by passion. Finding peace in an existence dominated by the permanent interference of the social "order" on individual destiny was an arduous task. The old Portugal and the new were locked in a tragic battle. Characters from this period seem to be marked as much by the passions of the past that they were trying to overcome as by ambitions for the future opening up ahead of them. Plentiful amounts of blood were shed. If Júlio Dinis's particular brand of romanticism was, in the main, idyllic—reconciling itself with domestic life and already showing modern characteristics in its relative sobriety of sentiments—Camilo's was brutal, excessive, so extreme that it seemed to want to ignore the limits of the human and never ceased to accuse the different forms of social conditioning. The former was civilized, the latter a savage. Júlio Dinis' protagonists belong to a bourgeoisie with moderate customs and passions. Camilo's characters, even when they belong to the bourgeoisie, show glimpses of primitive forces that explode after attempts to contain them. Furthermore, just as Camões's *Os Lusíadas* carries within it criticism of the discovery epic, Camilo's *Amor de Perdição* presents a *crime passionel* that is also a critique of passion itself and a reflection upon the kind of love that makes the need for tragedy real. So what did love actually mean to Camilo? What conclusion can we draw when we realize that the hero, Simão, is presented as a hotheaded youth (the victim of his temperament and, perhaps, of his ambiguous relationships with his mother, father and brother) rather than the model of a responsible romantic hero?

The world of Eça de Queirós lies closer, in general terms, to that of Júlio Dinis than that of Camilo Castelo Branco (*O Crime do Padre Amaro*, written in 1876, but revised considerably in 1880, is the most Camilo-like of Eça's novels). Eça tends to highlight the demystification of social conflicts. They do not disappear from his plots altogether; but they no longer give rise to great public tragedies or crimes. Instead, parody and irony dominate, and the romantic disappointments of Eça's characters do not lead to revolt. In this way, and particularly with *Os Maias* (1888), Eça can be considered more modern than the Flaubert of *Madame Bovary*. From the other side of the Atlantic, Machado de Assis also showed himself to be more lucid, profound and amusing than the French author with his obsessive concern with stylistic perfection.

The dilettantism that dominates Eça de Queirós' characters expresses an ironic vision of reality. When overbearing ambitions and grandiose projects fail; when ingenuousness, the intent to save the world and the need to resolve the problems of existence by extraordinary means fall flat, Eça's characters resign themselves to the modesty of their fate. If there is an element of intimate tragedy, it is repressed. Absolute happiness and fulfillment do not exist—the ideal is unattainable—but Eça's characters find their consolation in sumptuous meals, accompanied by the finest wines and nights on the town, along with amorous adventures. Therefore it is not surprising that there are hardly ever any "normal" relationships between men and women in Eça's novels. With the exception of Jacinto in *A Cidade e as Serras* (1900), his main characters are often idealistic, occasionally cynical, bohemians who never get married, nor even entertain the idea of marriage (only politicians and the bourgeoisie get married). Eça's heroes are allergic to the idea of marriage and would rather have affairs with other peoples' wives (the wives of the politicians and the bourgeoisie, Spanish girls, singers and dancers). Male friendship, on one hand, and the attraction of adulterous love, on the other, are characteristics of Eça's novels too evident to pass unnoticed. In 1856, Eça was present at the ceremony of the opening of the Suez Canal. Might he have met Ibsen there, and talked to him about love, marriage, the relationships between men and women and many other topics? If he did, the two authors would certainly have had plenty of impressions to exchange.

Eça died in Paris in 1900, but a large proportion of his work was published posthumously. The author of *A Capital* (1925), *A Relíquia* (1887) and *A Ilustre Casa de Ramires* (1900), left indelible marks on the literature and mind-set of the Portuguese, whatever the claims of his detractors. Until 1915, the year the first issue of the journal *Orpheu* came out, all the important literary developments that took place in Portugal were mere reworkings of Eça and the legacy of the nineteenth century, representing a pause before the momentous arrival of Portuguese modernism. The fact that Eça, Garrett, Herculano, Júlio Dinis and Camilo can be read one hundred years later, and their works still reveal dimensions that seem not to have been understood or explored, providing us with original experiences and new pleasures, is due to what? To the existence of new analytical perspectives that allow us to see in their works aspects of reality that had not been noticed before, to understand things hitherto misunderstood? To the fact that the twentieth century lived through the mental constructions and the myths elaborated by the nineteenth century, digesting them, developing them and commenting on them, in an obsessive cannibalistic impulse? For these reasons certainly: and others.

The Poets' Perspective on Liberalism

Antero de Quental had a huge influence on Eça de Queirós and other members of the generation of 1870 (which nonetheless did not stop Eça, who was always as lucid and disenchanted as he was cheerful, referring with subtle irony and admiration to the utopian, serious and tragic idealism of the author of *Odes Modernas*). But the constant and tortured ambition to rationalize and theorize, which allowed him to be—at least in part—the ideological mentor of his generation, hampered him from becoming a great modern poet. The only Portuguese poet of the nineteenth century whose talent matches that of the above-mentioned novelists is Cesário Verde. His poetic vision of Portuguese reality completes the portrait painted by the novels of Eça. Although firmly rooted in the nineteenth century, the works of Cesário, a poet whose loyalties are torn between city and countryside, constitute the first bricks in the edifice of modern poetry. The conflict between romanticism and realism emerges in Cesário's work, not as a theory, nor as a lesson to be learned, but rather as the thrilling experience of the Self. This Self, while feeling the temptation of abandonment to the "absurd desire to suffer," imposes up on itself a rigid discipline based on the objectivity of "realism." Verde's poetry repeatedly mentions the struggle between *desire* (the urge to abandon oneself to feeling, to plumb the depths of inexplicable and intimate pain, to enjoy the "sickness" of existence) and *need* (to survive in a liberal society of commerce, capitalism and production). For having had the courage to consider poetic realities and ways of speaking that at the time were passed over as prosaic, only after his death was Verde read and recognized. With his rhyming quatrains and sonnets he created poetry of new rhythms: agile, nervous, thorough, austere. The "desire to suffer," which is emphasized by Verde's anti-sentimentalist realism, coexists with a descriptive talent that reminds some readers of the paintings of Eduard Munch, or the somber atmosphere of German expressionism. Verde also seems to express the sense of civic duty later emphasized by the neo-realists, and reveals the existential pessimism arising from the obligation to be productive. His melancholy is repressed in the name of the "virile" obligation to maintain full control over a reality dominated by economic laws. Verde knew that reality from his experience of working with his father, who was a trader and fruit exporter.

The works of António Nobre and Camilo Pessanha, along with Cesário Verde, can also be considered precursors of the Portuguese modernist movement of 1915. They show characteristics of decadentism and symbolism. But Nobre's most important contributions to modern poetry are his colloquial style, the simplicity with which he expresses common feelings, the ingenuousness and subtle irony of his "poetic" voice, an obsession with and nostalgia for ancient lost purity. Like the realist novelists and Verde, he used his descriptive skills to create tableaux of provincial life in the north of Portugal. Although he used traditional meters and not free verse, Nobre, like Verde, changed the "tone" of literary language, and paved the way for modernity in Portuguese poetry. When he was a student exiled in Paris (as Mário de Sá-Carneiro was to be years later), Nobre cultivated a mythical nostalgia for Portugal and for certain traditional values threatened by social change. His nostalgia is a form of conservatism—the lament of a class that has lost its privileges in the changes wrought by the Liberal Revolution. But readers today might interpret that nostalgia as a reaction to the emergence of a liberal social order that threatened traditional human values, as well as the ingenuous and "pure" happiness of childhood. Similarly, heightened competitiveness threatened the peace of the individual. For that reason, rural settings and ways of thinking gradually became utopian symbols of a former, relatively peaceful existence. As was the case with Mário de Sá-Carneiro's work, the poetry of Nobre and Verde reveals the suffering resulting from the conflict between the need to be an exemplary, productive and socially integrated individual, and the desire to create an alternative existence based on an acute sensibility and spiritual values.

The Years of the Republic

Long foretold by the conflict and disturbances that followed the Liberal Revolution of 1820, the Portuguese Republic was finally proclaimed in 1910. The beginning of the twentieth century, while not entirely lacking in literary achievements, was clouded by idealistic nationalist ambitions and misunderstandings. The historical novel was revived or sustained, and currents that are now considered old-fashioned and conservative emerged: neo-Garretism, *Lusitanismo* and *Integralismo*. Other currents of nationalist thought, such as the *Renascença Portuguesa* and *saudosismo*, developed an "emphasis that is markedly more rationalist, agnostic, progressive and, at times, linked with a more down-to-earth and realistic sense of things."[4] Teixeira de Pascoaes, a poet with philosophical pretensions, was the leading light of *saudosismo*. He gathered together the founders of the journal *Águia* (1910-1932) and brought together a group of intellectuals from Oporto, the *Renascença Portuguesa*—members of which were to become renowned figures: the historian Jaime Cortesão; the philosopher Leonardo Coimbra; the poet Afonso Duarte; and the essayist António Sérgio. Mário de Sá-Carneiro and Fernando Pessoa were also briefly seduced by *saudosismo*.

The journal *Seara Nova* was launched in 1921 as the voice of the republican ideology of progress. Members of the Lisbon National

Library group were associated with the periodical: Jaime Cortesão; the writers Raul Brandão and Manuel Teixeira Gomes; the novelist Aquilino Ribeiro; and the thinkers and essayists António Sérgio and Raul Proença.

Manuel Teixeira Gomes followed a diplomatic career (he was the Portuguese Republic's first ambassador to London) and became president of the Republic from 1923 to 1925; however, disenchanted with both political life and his country, he went into voluntary exile. He wrote prose works of "Hellenic" elegance and sensuousness imbued with romanticism, paganism and a desire for social justice. Teixeira Gomes was one of the most lucid, independent and progressive figures of his time. *Inventário de Junho* (1899), *Gente Singular* (1909), *Novelas Eróticas* (1935) and *Maria Adelaide* (1938) count among his most representative works.

The best prose of Aquilino Ribeiro follows on from the colloquial language and apparently relaxed style of Camilo Castelo Branco. In his fascination with crude and primitive customs and characters, Aquilino anticipated Miguel Torga and some of the social preoccupations of neo-realism. Brutal in their passions, succumbing to primitive instincts and capable of the best and the worst of acts, the characters in Aquilino's *Terras do Demo* (1919) and *Malhadinhas* (1922) show readers how he imagines a "return to one's roots" and his understanding of the "national soul"—neither of which had anything to do with the ideals held up by the conservative nationalists.

As well as his plays: *O Doido e a Morte* (1923); *O Gebo e a Sombra* (1923); and *O Avejão* (1929), Raul Brandão wrote obsessive narrative works that are hard to categorize. Among them we have to mention the extraordinary "prose poems:"[5] *A Farsa* (1903); *Os Pobres* (1906); *Húmus* (1917); and *O Pobre de Pedir* (1931). Critics have identified the key aspects of this writer's work: a sensitiveness to, and a preoccupation with the fate of the poor and humble; a heightened sense of guilt (similar to that found in Tolstoy and Dostoyevsky); traces of *fin de siècle* decadence; and an acute awareness of the ridiculous and pathetic. The contradictions within the human being tormented him: traits such as hypocrisy, problems like the fate of women crushed by marriage and the wretched situation of individuals in bourgeois capitalist society. The pessimism in Brandão's work presents a tragic vision of reality that reminds the reader of the works of Cesário Verde and António Nobre, but contrasts strongly with the ironic vision of human failure and the death of ambition offered by Eça de Queirós. In fact, the work of Raul Brandão reveals a sensitivity that is closer to Antero de Quental.

The poet Florbela Espanca stands out during this period for the intensity of her erotic lyricism: love poetry written from the woman's point of view. Apart from Cesário Verde and António Nobre, however, it is the work of another important precursor of modernism—Camilo Pessanha—that deserves closer attention. Pessanha lived in Macao for many years, and was the author of *Clepsidra* (1922). He was influenced by the French poet Paul Verlaine, and is generally considered to be the most important Portuguese symbolist. His poems express an existential pessimism born of frustration. Just as would appear to have been the case with Luis de Camões and Bernardim Ribeiro, his frustration is rooted in the mutability of life: the human being has no sense of permanence, and is constantly traveling; the voyage—a metaphor for existence—is arduous. The images Pessanha used, which he claimed passed before his eyes but could not be pinned down, transmit the impossibility of capturing a sense of "the real," or of discovering within it any comfortable or stable coherence. The difficulty, or impossibility, of knowing and of loving are further causes of dissatisfaction and metaphysical disquiet. Hence the poet's desire to die: death would be an end to the torments provoked by the endless mutability of reality and feelings on one hand, and by the inability of the individual to attain the "absolute" to which the thirst for love and knowledge is directed on the other hand.

Camilo Pessanha was not a poet lacking in willpower, however. The frustration, disenchantment and pessimism in his poems are reactions to experiences, and it seems as though the individual spirit struggled against those experiences before considering himself defeated. Thus human limits and destiny are questioned. Pessanha's poetry escapes banality and insignificance due to the rigor of his structures and the music of his verse. What would otherwise be a conventional style and theme is made different by the skill with which he gave allegorical and symbolic value to common situations, to episodes that signified the self's relationship with others and with the real. The juxtaposition of the apparent (the vague, indefinite, the virtual) and that which *was* and no longer *is*, inspired in Pessanha some of his best poems. The modernity of his poetry stems largely from his questioning of the world order, and opposing to it an uneasy individual incapable of entering into a stable, peaceful and satisfying relationship with himself and the world around him.

Twentieth-Century Literary Movements: Modernism, *Presença* and Neo-Realism

Three important literary movements emerged in twentieth century Portugal: modernism in 1915, which developed around the founding and launch of the journal *Orpheu*; the *Presença* movement, based around a journal of the same name published between 1927 and 1940; and neo-realism, which took off in the 1930s.

Fernando Pessoa and Mário de Sá-Carneiro were the greatest exponents of Portuguese modernism. The writer and painter Almada-Negreiros, and Santa Rita Pintor were also important members of the movement. The fact that Fernando Pessoa had received a British education in South Africa, that Mário de Sá-Carneiro had lived in Paris from 1913 to 1915 (when he committed suicide), and that Almada and Santa Rita had also spent time in Paris and been in contact with the most advanced artistic currents of the period, may explain why Portuguese modernism represented such a decisive break with tradition. Although the modernists were influenced by futurism, the evolution of modernism in Portuguese literature was unique and original.

Along with the two issues of *Orpheu* published in 1915, other short-lived journals published between 1915 and 1935 were also mouthpieces for new ideas and means of expression. These included *Eh real!*, *Centauro*, *Exílio*, *Ícaro*, *Portugal Futurista*, *Contemporânea*, *Athena*, *Revista Portuguesa*, and *Sudoeste*.

Portuguese modernism irreverently attacked the dominant values of the petty bourgeoisie of the liberal period. It should therefore be understood as the first serious attempt to revolutionize not only literature and language, but also actual ways of life and ways of thinking. Because it had the courage to distance itself from the dominant ideologies and the values of social prestige, and because it attacked the various social manifestations of "stupidity," it shocked the public and provoked a scandal.

The poetry and fiction of Sá-Carneiro includes *A Confissão de Lúcio* (1914), *Céu em Fogo* (1915) and *Poesias* (published posthumously in 1946). His works express a profound dissatisfaction with bourgeois life and the inability of the individual to adapt to the vulgarity of a daily life without horizons. Aspiring to unrealistic and intangible goals excites the imagination and the senses, but frustration of that ambition is inevitable and forces the individual to live through the senselessness of an empty and mediocre daily life. Although attracted by extreme and utopian forms of individual fulfillment, Sá-Carneiro knew how to confer mystery and dignity upon the pleasures of simple daily life and its more banal moments (time spent in a café, for example). Simplicity and daily pleasures were not, however, sufficient to cure Sá-Carneiro of the nostalgia for extraordinary ideals or to satisfy his anxieties. Having discovered his vocation for fulfillment, and aware of the desire that projected him into a sensuous paradise, the poet chose to commit suicide rather than have to conform to the banal existence that bourgeois society offered him. Sá-Carneiro shows the reader that the modern city affords the most intense pleasures, but falls short when it comes to honoring its promises. This is partly what happened in *A Cidade e as Serras,* by Eça de Queirós. The hero of the novel, Jacinto, ends up choosing the Portuguese "mountains"— which he yearns for with melancholy—over Paris, "the city of progress". It is in the countryside that he finally achieves happiness.

The theme of social climbing and decline also clearly marks the work of Sá-Carneiro. It reveals the exacerbated and hysterical experience of deception that was already present in the work of Camilo Pessanha, Cesário Verde and António Nobre. Above all, the poetry and suicide of Sá-Carneiro reveal an overweening pride. Instead of giving in to useless and despicable romantic laments, the author of *A Confissão de Lúcio* (1914) adopts provocative attitudes and the ironic self-destruction of his own image and idealized objects is expressed with a sarcastic masochism. Sá-Carneiro appropriated his own death, as it were, disdainfully and proudly rebelling against the insignificance of human destiny.

Identity crisis and the fragmentation of the self also characterize the work of Sá-Carneiro's friend Fernando Pessoa. Pessoa and his heteronyms also felt that reality was unsatisfactory. Like the characters created by Eça de Queirós, Pessoa knew that romantic revolt and the sentimental portrayal of tragedy made no sense because they had no real purpose. This is why Pessoa's poetry and prose consist of a series of questions about, and approaches to the lack of reality in reality—the absence of meaning in the world and in life. Pessoa and his heteronyms—Alberto Caeiro, Álvaro de Campos, Ricardo Reis, and Bernardo Soares, to cite only the most important—cultivate a negative vision of existence *ad nauseam*; they question language and common-sense values in a schizophrenic manner. For them, the imperfection and the absurdity of existence are beyond repair and deserve nothing less than scornful laughter. This is deception with no hope of contradiction.

The masks of the heteronyms represent attempts to describe reality from a variety of perspectives and in a range of styles. The masks are pure fiction, but they are also the only reality we are allowed to glimpse. It is as though Pessoa, unable to believe in one vision of reality that necessarily excluded others by its very nature, wanted to leave us with multiple variations on the theme of the relationship (imaginary, yet real) between man, existence and the world. Pessoa forces us to understand that the meaning of the world lies within us. Although abandoning himself to language, literature and life, he is still aware that everything is a game, a form of fiction. On the other hand, death inevitably transforms that game and all human activity into useless and futile passion.

If the relationship we establish with reality is arbitrary (it might be different from what it actually is; but this would not matter), and if that relationship is difficult to define—despite linguistic pretensions to truth (everything is highly questionable)—how can a lucid spirit allow the reader to see that his suffering is serious and his life tragic, even when he wears literary masks? Pessoa's lucidity denies him a rhetorical expression of tragedy; it is only through irony that the latter is revealed. In some ways, he seems to deny the ironic-tragic vision of life. Despite the impossibility of achieving truth and the absolute, despite the unhappy awareness that existence is gratuitous fiction, both Pessoa and Sá-Carneiro leave us with images of Lisbon and our daily lives that reconcile us to our fate. It is in the works of these authors, but particularly Cesário Verde, Pessoa and Eça, that the city of Lisbon—its neighborhoods, its streets, its colors, its skies, the geometry of its houses and their views over the Tagus—acquires its mythical status. Such are the contradictory consolations of literature.

Like Sá-Carneiro, Pessoa was unheroically proud and rebellious in the face of the imperfection of the world, a fictitious world that Alberto Caeiro, in contrast, saw as being only "an example of reality." Pessoa's work is far removed from the nineteenth century novel; the language that he uses to describe the individual's inability to adapt to reality emerges in the form of a radical protest. It is no longer a study of the order imposed by social mechanisms. No longer is one social class guilty and another innocent (as neo-realism will have it, following on from the tradition of nineteenth-century realism and naturalism). There are no longer even guilty or innocent individuals, but we all become simultaneously guilty and innocent. The same fate—the same limitations—explains our woes and conflicts, just as they explain our hopes and joys. The tragic element in this vision of reality (more philosophical than historical), the helpless inability of the individual to adapt to the world, is understandably diluted by an irony that reveals a minimal instinct for self-conservation.

The struggle, the complaint and the reflection found in Camões's poetry reveal a Self that either accuses itself or holds others—the gods, destiny, the ruling order (the "disorder of the world")—responsible for its own suffering. By finding someone or something to blame for his misfortunes, Camões could hope (hopelessly) for a change of fate. But the conflict between the individual and the world, the existential malaise that neither in Camões nor the nineteenth century novel are incompatible with hope, emerge in Pessoa as irresolvable—and they are accepted with scorn and a bitterness always charged with irony. Pessoa already knew that one could expect nothing from the gods, from others, from history, from language or even from poetry.

The modernist movement of 1915 was prolonged with the posthumous publication of Pessoa's works. They brought to an end a process that was initiated with the romantic perplexities of Almeida Garrett and that culminated with the modern theme of disappointment. For Pessoa more than for Sá-Carneiro, nothing was "worthwhile," except perhaps telling the story of our disillusionment, to mark out the path of hope and deception, making it very clear that we had, at last, unmasked the fiction that had lulled us into the belief that it was reality. We could not be fooled, we would never be fooled again; fate did not even exist, only nothingness and chaos, against which our existence acquired dimensions of tragic and ironic parody. But are knowledge and lucidity sufficient comforts?

After this, what could *Presença* and neo-realism contribute to Portuguese society and literature? *Presença*'s key merit consisted in its efficient contribution to the acceptance and propagation of the works of the 1915 modernists. It also disseminated modern French and European art of the period. Despite the influence of Proust, Gide and Dostoyevsky, of psychoanalysis and of French criticism—beyond that of the Portuguese modernists—no author connected with *Presença* produced works comparable in significance to those of Pessoa, Sá-Carneiro and the other modernists. That is why Eduardo

Lourenço has quite rightly considered the journal *Presença* to be a clear step backward when compared with *Orpheu*.

Among the writers associated with *Presença*, the critic and novelist, João Gaspar Simões, left behind a vast amount of literary criticism—some, if not all of it (on Eça, Pessoa and the history of the novel), influential—thereby accomplishing an educational task that should not be belittled. He had received an anglo-saxon education, and this made him a favorite target for young structuralist critics in Portugal (mostly academics, imbued with ideas originating in France) in the 1960s and 1970s. José Régio—the creator of a fascinating literary voice—wrote novels, short stories, poems, plays and critical essays. His writings reveal a personality tortured by moral problems and gifted with a clear vocation for intellectual militancy. He helps the reader to understand a certain type of Portuguese provincial mentality and its limitations, for although he adopted a sincere attitude of protest, Régio never violated the boundaries and limits of the system he questioned.

Miguel Torga, the epitome of the solitary humanist, who split with the *Presença* group at an early stage, was a proud and intransigent enemy of Salazarism. Torga was the author of an influential collection of short stories, and was also a poet. His poems depict a vivid landscape: the human reality of the poor and the isolated world of the provinces. His fictional autobiographical works, *A Criação do Mundo* and the *Diários*, is also the work of a great writer capable of a simultaneously austere, intimate, pained, picturesque and moralistic tone.

Branquinho da Fonseca was a talented short story writer, as is especially clear from his masterpiece, *O Barão* (1942). Adolfo Casais Monteiro, who went into exile in Brazil, was to become one of Portugal's best literary critics. He was also the author of one of the most important collections of poetry published by *Presença*.

This period produced other important authors whose work was not directly related to *Presença*'s objectives or plans, but who nevertheless offer us an important view of Portuguese society—particularly its limitations and ills. Examples include Ferreira de Castro

(1898-1959), José Rodrigues Miguéis (1901-1980), Irene Lisboa (1892-1958), Domingos Monteiro (1903-1980) and Vitorino Nemésio (1901-1978).

Ferreira de Castro was self-educated and led a difficult and adventurous life in Brazil. He gained international renown with his novel *A Selva* (1930). With the publication of *Emigrantes* (1928), he developed a new form of realism: critical realism. Ferreira de Castro later published other works of fiction of a typically neo-realist nature, preoccupied chiefly with the social question, a concern dealt with to perfection in *A Lã e a Neve* (1947).

José Rodrigues Miguéis, who lived in exile in New York for many years, was one of the most erudite, refined and cosmopolitan fiction writers of his generation. He also belonged to the group of authors who heralded the beginning of neo-realism. His work reveals a great variety of interests, as well as a delight in experimentation with new techniques and narrative genres that make him original and difficult to classify. *Páscoa Feliz* (1932) reveals an important Dostoyevskian influence. *Léah* (1958), a collection of stories and novellas, inaugurates the mature phase of his career, which included such works as *Uma Aventura Inquietante* and *Um Homem Sorri à Morte com Meia Cara* (both 1959), *Escola do Paraíso* (1960) and *O Milagre Segundo Salomé* (1975).

Irene Lisboa (1892-1958) wrote both poetry and prose of great sensibility. Her use of male pseudonyms reveals her acute awareness of the difficulties of being a woman of letters. This writer modestly portrayed the anxieties and joys of common daily life. Her work—which lies somewhere between fiction and autobiography—portrays the difficult situation for women in the society of the time, through vignettes of urban or provincial life. *Solidão* (1939) and *Voltar Atrás Para Quê* (1956) are among her most significant works. Domingos Monteiro was best known for his short stories: *Enfermaria, Prisão e Casa Mortuária*, (1943).

University professor Vitorino Nemésio (1901-1978) was an outstanding figure in Portuguese literature of the time, producing poetry, novels (*Mau Tempo no Canal*, 1944) and critical essays. The fact that he never allied himself with any of the dominant aesthetic trends of his day makes his work particularly original.

After *Presença*, the literary movement that was to influence Portuguese literature for many decades to come was neo-realism. The neo-realists embraced the social concerns that had been dear to the realist and naturalist novelists of the nineteenth century. Influenced by Marxism, however, they considered the humanism of the writers of that period insufficient and believed that only a socialist revolution could correct the vices of economic liberalism and resolve the social question. It should be noted that *Presença* had opposed the "objective" claims of realism and naturalism, and had struggled to assert the value of a "subjective" art. The quarrel between the *presencistas* and the neo-realists, however, should not be taken too seriously. Essentially, the *presencistas* accused the neo-realists of ignoring aesthetic values, and the neo-realists accused the *presencistas* of defending art for art's sake. The neo-realists stated that they intended to synthesize all the aesthetic currents of the past, but that they could not understand an art disconnected from the problems and realities of its time.

Neo-realism was influenced by American and Brazilian writers of the era, and developed in two phases. Critics consider the first phase, between 1938 and 1950, to be more concerned with propaganda and doctrine, and less aesthetically sophisticated than the second. The second phase, which developed after 1950, includes works of a variety of tendencies and characteristics. It reached aesthetic maturity but never ceased to emphasize the determining impact of social mechanisms on individual lives. The neo-realists' worst enemy was liberalism, with Salazarism in second place. The novels of Carlos de Oliveira, for example, clearly show that the object of criticism was the social structure itself and not those wielding power at the time.

The first neo-realist author to achieve public recognition was Alves Redol (1911-1969). His novel *Gaibéus* (1939) is the work that, according to the critics, "officially" inaugurated neo-realism as a movement. The text and its preface added fuel to the debate between neo-realists and *presencistas* by declaring that *Gaibéus* had no pretensions towards being a work of art. In his later novels, Redol, who enjoyed great prestige during his lifetime, continued to narrate the stories of the poor and humble, and to describe social conflicts just as they occurred in various regions of the country.

Apart from Redol, the most important neo-realist authors were Soeiro Pereira Gomes (1909-1949), Fernando Namora (1919-1989), Manuel da Fonseca (1911-1993), Carlos de Oliveira (1921-1981) and José Cardoso Pires (1925-1999). Mário Dionísio (1916-1990), also a painter and art critic, and later Alexandre Pinheiro Torres (1923-1999), were prominent literary critics and theorists of neo-realism, as well as poets and novelists. The collection *O Novo Cancioneiro* also showcased poets of great sensibility and talent, such as Álvaro Feijó (1916-1941) and Políbio Gomes dos Santos (1911-1959). At the fringes of the movement, but similarly preoccupied with social problems and politically aware, were Augusto Abelaira (1926-2003)—one of the best Portuguese novelists of the period—Marmelo e Silva (1913-1991), Urbano Tavares Rodrigues (born 1923) and Jorge de Sena (1919-1978)—the prolific author of a vast collection of poetry, fiction and critical works. Two other important figures of the time who were not explicitly linked to neo-realism are Vergílio Ferreira (1916-1996), a novelist and essayist with philosophical tendencies, and the novelist Agustina Bessa Luís (born 1929).

Soeiro Pereira Gomes wrote the novels *Esteiros* (1941) and *Engrenagem* (1951). The latter portrays the class conflict inside a factory, with an epic talent similar to that of the Russian filmmaker, Sergei Eisenstein. Manuel da Fonseca is a talented poet, novelist and short story writer. The Alentejo region inspired him to write great works of poetry, such as *Cerro Maior* (1943) and *Seara do Vento* (1958). Fernando Namora was a poet and novelist, the author of numerous very successful works, including *Fogo na Noite Escura* (1943), *Casa da Malta* (1945), *O Fogo e as Cinzas* (1953) *Retalhos da Vida de um Médico* (two volumes, 1958 and 1963), and *O Trigo e o Joio* (1959).

It was Carlos de Oliveira though who reached a maturity in his work that made him probably the most important neo-realist writer. His poems, collected in *Trabalho Poético*, reveal a refined style and a remarkable austerity and gravity. Oliveira was also one of the writers whose work most disturbed the *presencistas*; they recognized his talent in dealing with social issues without ignoring conflicts of conscience and matters of temperament. Oliveira's novels, *Casa na Duna* (1943), *Alcateia* (1944), *Pequenos Burgueses* (1948) and *Uma Abelha na Chuva* (1953), clearly illustrate the two phases of neo-realism. They also show how Portuguese literature developed over this period, given that the author extensively reworked the first versions of his novels as his understanding of narrative technique and style developed. *Finisterra, Paisagem e Povoamento* (1978), his masterpiece, seems to express the impossibility of maintaining belief in the revolution. At the same time, it poses essential questions for neo-realists and humanists (neo-realism hoped to become the new humanism): the questions of private property, of law, of the possibility of knowledge, and of art. Two novels published in 1979, Augusto Abelaira's *Sem Tecto Entre Ruínas*, and Vergílio Ferreira's *Signo Sinal*, also reveal in their pessimism that the Revolution dreamt of by the neo-realists was a myth or utopia resulting from an over-simplification of reality.[6]

Very early in his career, José Cardoso Pires showed great stylistic sophistication. His short stories show the influence of American novelists; for example, the re-edited collections *Jogos do Azar* (1963), *O Anjo Ancorado* (1958) and *Hóspedes de Job* (1963). *O Delfim* (1968) is perhaps his most important work in the period leading up to the 1974 Revolution. After the revolution, the novels *Balada da Praia dos Cães* (1982) and *Alexandra Alpha* (1987) are understandably more direct and at ease with their criticism of social and political structures. In *A Cartilha do Marialva* (1960), Pires, whose skepticism was a constant feature of his work, created a sarcastic caricature of Portuguese machismo.

Augusto Abelaira is one of the most fascinating novelists of this generation. His preoccupation with the social question never prevents him from showing a particular sensitivity to the problems of individual fulfillment (through love, marriage, art). His characters come mostly from the urban middle classes and are often intellectuals. Abelaira reveals the contradictions and sense of guilt of this class. The inability to love, a poetic vision of the revolution, a somewhat obsessive attention to mental battles; and the refusal to simplify are the marks of his originality. *A Cidade das Flores* (1959), *Enseada Amena* (1966) and *Bolor* (1968) are among his most successful novels.

Urbano Tavares Rodrigues, the author of *Bastardos do Sol* (1959) and *Insubmissos* (1961), is another writer on the margins of the neorealist movement. He has produced a vast array of fictional works that balance criticism of the values and the hypocritical behavior of bourgeois society with episodes in which personal fulfillment through love is the main theme.

Vergílio Ferreira (1916-1996) is one of the most important Portuguese novelists to write in the second half of the twentieth century. *Para Sempre* (1983), *Até ao Fim* (1987) and *Em Nome da Terra* (1990), are outstanding examples of his extensive *oeuvre*. Ferreira began his career as a confirmed neo-realist, but started to question socio-economic explanations for individual problems from *Mudança* (1969) onwards. He preferred to create characters and plots that could reveal—in a somewhat artificial way—the complexity of existential malaise. It was only later, in novels such as *Aparição* (1959), *Alegria Breve* (1965) and *Rápida a Sombra* (1974) that he became one of the most interesting contemporary Portuguese novelists. The novels of Vergílio Ferreira can best be understood when taking into account his work as an essayist, and his preoccupation with aesthetic and philosophical issues (for instance, the volumes of *Espaço do Invisível*). Ferreira also produced a number of works that were deliberately provocative and polemic, such as his diary, *Conta Corrente* (several volumes from 1980 onwards).

The novelist Agustina Bessa Luís (born 1929) is another important figure who has produced a vast body of work in which fiction alternates with novelistic biography. She gained great renown with *A Sibila* (1954), a novel bordering on the neo-realist style. Her politically conservative (on the surface, at least) vision of the individual and society is far from optimistic, and the various forms of competition and social struggle (between the sexes, or between people from different social backgrounds and with different education) take the place of the class struggle grounded in neo-realist works.

Also on the fringes of neo-realism, although certainly a left-wing intellectual, is the noteworthy figure of Jorge de Sena. He was a talented poet, novelist, short story writer, critic and playwright. He began his career as an engineer but became a university professor of literature in Brazil and the United States. His *Sinais de Fogo* (1979) was one of the most significant Portuguese novels of its era. He is the author of several volumes of short stories, including *Andanças do Demónio* (1960), *Novas Andanças do Demónio* (1966), *O Físico Prodigioso* (1977) and of several volumes of poetry, from *Perseguição* (1942) to *Sobre Esta Praia* (1977). Hope and the search for sincerity and truth in human relationships mark his writing. At the same time he praises physical love, the body and desire. He sees art as a superior form of intelligence and individual fulfillment. He had an elitist and mythical view of the writer as an "exceptional" figure standing apart from the common masses. *Arte da Música* (1968), and the poems in which Sena "interprets" well-known paintings, illustrate the mythical attraction that art always held for him.

Marmelo e Silva (1911-1991) shared with Jorge de Sena a desire for sincerity and truth in human relations that led him to attack sexual taboos. However, his work has a discreet warmth and humanism that sheds light upon an opening up of ideas, and shows which ideas were considered most meaningful at the time. His most important works were the provocative novels, *Sedução* (1938) and *O Adolescente Agrilhoado* (1958).

The dispute between the *presencistas,* who defended a literature of the self, the "I," and the neo-realists, who defended a literature of the "We," the "Us," emerged from a difficult conflict between equally legitimate tendencies. That conflict was already apparent in Cesário Verde's poetry, which shows the poet divided between the desire to abandon himself to instinct, impulses, feelings, and "states of the soul," on the one hand, and the need to submit to the austere discipline of "virile" realism on the other. António Nobre and Mário de

Sá-Carneiro also felt this conflict. In a sense, even the work of Fernando Pessoa is a manifestation of the conflict between the values of the Self (one's impulses, anxieties and "states of soul") and the values of society (those imposed by the dominant world vision and political order). In fact, this conflict was already apparent within romanticism. It was expressed in the difference between romanticism and symbolism, on the one hand, and between nineteenth-century realism and naturalism, on the other. It is not surprising that Portuguese literature should have continued to attempt a synthesis of two apparently contradictory tendencies that were always difficult to resolve: namely, respect for individual impulses and the need to consider the order on which society is based.

The social preoccupations of the neo-realists (together with the guilty conscience that pushes revolutionary reform, attentive to the situation of the exploited and humiliated) dominated Portuguese literature from the mid-1930s to the beginning of the 1980s. At their most advanced stage, the neo-realists—while never forgetting social and economic structures—avoided creating crude social stereotypes, and instead made their characters clearly individual people. In some cases—the novels of Carlos de Oliveira, for example—the tendency to emphasize a Marxist explanation of life (whereby human life is linked to the conditions of production) superseded the tendency to account for the profound and original subjectivity of individuals. In Oliveira's poetry, however, one does not find commonplaces or the traces of the most topical Marxist ideology. Instead, care and compassion for others take the form of eternal humanism and permit a profound meditation on reality.

In other cases, the capacity to describe the inner lives and impulses of individuals attained—even in the novel—great sophistication, while retaining a "guilty conscience" or remorse for the social situation. The works of Augusto Abelaira and Jorge de Sena provide excellent examples of this tendency. The work of Agustina Bessa Luís, although apparently dominated by the author's desire to escape the neo-realist preoccupations with social issues, is, by contrast, a good example of the incapacity to give form to conscience, passion and individual fate without taking in consideration the social and economic context, and the constant harshness of competition and struggle that make up our existence.

Oliveira's *Finisterra* (1978), Ferreira's *Signo Sinal* and Abelaira's *Sem Tecto Entre Ruínas* (both 1979) seem to mark the end of neo-realism in the form of a movement based on the belief in revolution as its goal and an extraordinary event that would solve social and individual problems. This does not mean, however, that neo-realist tendencies disappeared altogether. In the wake of nineteenth century realism, neo-realism placed great emphasis on socio-economic, political and social structures as factors conditioning the situation of individuals and their capacity for fulfillment. Now, the tendency was to express these conflicts by grounding individual consciousness (based on imagination, myths, fantasies, desires, hopes and frustrations) and through human relationships that were not directly linked to the struggle for economic survival. The social question obviously remained a thorny one, but revolutionary solutions ceased to appear as a possible or even adequate path by which to resolve them. From the 1970s on, a new pessimism emerged that was born out of this new sense of awareness. It was accompanied by some cynicism, but it also allowed for the emergence of a new, vaguely defined, hope.

Portugal Reborn after the April Revolution of 1974

The work of Almeida Faria (born 1943) illustrates the apparently eternal and irresolvable conflict between the need for individual fulfillment and the inability to escape history. Faria's debut, *Rumor Branco* (1962), is an experimental narrative influenced by existentialism, that seemed to oppose neo-realism and, following in the footsteps of Vergílio Ferreira, definitively contributed to the introduction of a new tone and style into Portuguese literature. In 1965, Faria published *A Paixão*, probably his best novel. The social question emerges with force and surprising violence in this Faulknerian work, squarely placing this novel at the edge of neo-realism in thematic terms. The main merit of *A Paixão*, however, lies in its perfect fusion of *presencista* and existentialist ideals typical of the literature of the Self with neo-realist themes expressive of a literature of the "Us."

Faria's later novels (*Cortes*, 1978; *Lusitânia*, 1980; *Cavaleiro Andante*, 1983; *O Conquistador*, 1990) confirm his disillusionment with the revolution of 1974, which he considers a disappointing failure. He thus reinforces the vision found in the novels of Carlos de Oliveira, Vergílio Ferreira and Augusto Abelaira. The technocrats in power seemed to have found a way to satisfy their ambitions and to believe, not without a measure of provincialism, in the construction of a modern "European" Portugal. The most important novelists of the late 1970s and 1980s, on the other hand, carried on with the ideals of the "Carnation Revolution" and continued to express their disenchantment with Portuguese social, economic and political reality.

António Lobo Antunes (born 1942) published *Os Cus de Judas* in 1979. It presents an acerbic view of the colonial wars and of Portugal during that time. At the same time, he expresses the impossibility of the protagonist's readapting to Portuguese society (or even to the values of western civilization) after his wartime experiences in Africa. In later novels, such as *Memória de Elefante* (1979), *Fado Alexandrino* (1983), *Auto dos Danados* (1985), *Naus* (1988) and *Tratado das Paixões da Alma* (1990), to mention just a few of his works, Lobo Antunes continues to question the political, mental and economic structures of Portuguese society. One of his merits is his ability to weave together literary language and normal speech: he is not afraid to use swearwords. His agile style emerges as a form of protest and an expression of disdain for the hypocrisy and the apparent order of a bourgeois society falling into the hands of technocrats lacking in culture, ideals or scruples. It is worth mentioning Luís Pacheco (born 1926) in this context: his irreverent and literary works provocatively present him as a writer on the margins of society (for example: *Exercícios de Estilo* (1971); *Literatura Comestível* (1972); and *Textos Malditos* (1977), among others).

A poet and dramatist, but primarily a novelist, José Saramago (born 1922) became the most notable figure in the Portuguese literary world after he was awarded the Noble Prize for Literature in 1998. The Academy in Stockholm honored an author who is enormously successful both in Portugal and abroad, thanks to the extensive translation of his works. He is a virtuoso of style, who sets out reflections upon, and variations on the real or imagined history of Portugal (at times within his work, one can hear the echo of the medieval historical chronicles of Fernão Lopes). One of his first works, *Manual de Pintura e Caligrafia* (1977), is written in sober, straightforward prose, with no concessions to the traditional rhetoric of the novel. This shows the influence of the French *nouveau roman* on Saramago, but gives no clues as to how his writing was to develop in later works. *Levantado do Chão* (1980) is a beautifully written and constructed work, which appeared on the literary scene as a kind of "perfect neo-realist novel," the one no neo-realist had been able to write. *Memorial do Convento* (1982) changed everything and began a period of great popular success for Saramago, who seems to have found a way to please all types of audience. Afterwards came more success in Portugal and abroad with novels in which Saramago continued, with indisputable talent, to focus upon myths and the real or imagined history of his country and his countrymen: *O Ano da Morte de Ricardo Reis* (1984); *A Jangada de Pedra* (1986); *História do Cerco de Lisboa* (1989); *O Evangelho Segundo Jesus Cristo* (1991); *Ensaio sobre a Cegueira* (1995); *Todos os Nomes* (1997). We might also mention Saramago's diaries, several volumes of which have been published since 1994, under the title *Cadernos de Lanzarote*.

As noted above, after the somewhat unsuccessful revolution of 1974, José Cardoso Pires published works of fiction that met with great success. In them, Pires draws sarcastic caricatures of social vices and creates mediocre characters without any scruples. He presents a critique of contemporary society and of the failure of the April Revolution. The revolution (not exactly the one the neo-realists had dreamed of) had in the end been prepared and carried out under the leadership of the "April Captains" and by generals who, tired after long years of war in the colonies, rebelled against those in power.[7]

The Portuguese revolution is, however, just one among the many revolutions of this century that were more or less unsuccessful. Once they had realized that the social question could not easily be resolved, and that technocratic and liberal capitalism, as well as economic laws, interfered tragically with the life of the individual, the top Portuguese writers of the last quarter of the twentieth century produced works dominated by the great dilemmas of the Self and its inability to adapt to reality.

Having lost faith in utopian revolution, and having been forced to confront the harshness of reality—be it as participants, spectators or witnesses—contemporary novelists in Portugal have come increasingly closer to the thematic tendency already expressed by Vergílio Ferreira. The problematic relationships of the Self with reality and with the idea of fate have been the dominant perspective adopted by contemporary novelists in their presentation and description of existence. Dissatisfaction with the existing social order has not reduced. Instead, as exemplified by the protagonist of Ferreira's *Signo Sinal*, and the main character of Augusto Abelaira's *Sem Tecto Entre Ruínas*, the temptation to resolve the question of individual fulfillment in a selfish way—without the external support of social reform or utopian revolutions—has become paramount.

Other important writers to include in this account are: Mário Henrique Leiria (1923-1980); the playwright, Luís de Sttau Monteiro (1926-1993); António Alçada Baptista (born 1927); Nuno Bragança (1929-1985); Helder Macedo (born 1935); Álvaro Guerra (1936-2002); Américo Guerreiro de Sousa (born 1942); Paulo Castilho (born 1944); João Aguiar (born 1944); Mário de Carvalho (born 1944); João de Melo (born 1949); Manuel de Silva Ramos (born 1947); and Alface (born 1949).

Before we continue, we ought to mention Eduardo Lourenço (born 1923), who has written a huge number of highly original essays. He is best known for his considerations on the Portuguese national identity and its heritage of myth, set out in works such as *O Labirinto da Saudade—Psicanálise Mítica do Destino Português* (1987),

Nós e a Europa ou as Duas Razões (1988) or *O Esplendor do Caos*
(1998). Lourenço is also, and principally, one of Portugal's best literary critics, having published studies such as *Poesia e Metafísica* (1983),
Fernando Rei da Nossa Baviera (1986), *O Canto do Signo, Existência e
Literatura* (1957-1993, 1994). He works on the fringes of the academic world and efficiently manages to combine the cultures of literature, history and philosophy in his writing.

The tendency to emphasize individual reality and explore the
preoccupations of the Self and its darkest desires has always dominated poetic works. At times lyricism can be counteracted with vig-
orous, ironic or sarcastic social critique, which is what occurs in the
works of Alexandre O'Neill (1924-1986), Mário Cesariny (born
1923), and Jorge de Sena. All these writers are linked, to a greater or
lesser extent, with the Portuguese surrealist movement, started in
1947 by Mário Cesariny de Vasconcelos. António Maria Lisboa
(1928-1953), António Pedro (1909-1966), Alfredo Margarido (born
1925), Luís Pacheco and Mário Henrique Leiria are other names
closely associated with Portuguese surrealism. Despite the tendency
toward irony, sarcasm and parody, which can already be found among
the earliest forms of Portuguese literature, such as the *Cantigas de
Escárnio e Maldizer*, contemporary Portuguese poetry has more often
taken the form of subjective lyricism.

Two main tendencies have prevailed in contemporary Portuguese
poetry. The first, following on from the *Parnassians* and inspired by
Mallarmé, privileges the word and believes in the power of experimentation. It sees the poem as an object with an autonomous existence, capable of escaping the relationship with reality and thereby
creating an autonomous universe. The second tendency emphasizes
narration and the sentence, and focuses on the difficult relationship
of the individual (and language) with reality. This poetry of the word
on the one hand, and of the sentence on the other, is expressed in
various combinations of styles and forms, but each tendency can
only be imagined theoretically in its "pure," distinct state.

Great poetry does not exist if it does not show evidence of the
awareness or experience of the tragic condition of humanity. Even

so, the number of contemporary Portuguese poets of note is too long to include here. Apart from the poets already referred to, it is important to mention Ruy Belo (1933-1978), Eugénio de Andrade (born 1923), Sophia de Mello Breyner (born 1919), António Ramos Rosa (born 1924), Herberto Helder (born 1930), and Nuno Júdice (born 1949)—not only for the intrinsic value of their work, but also because they can be considered representative of key tendencies in contemporary Portuguese poetry.

Ruy Belo published a vast body of work before his premature death. In his poetry, lyricism co-exists with a disillusioned vision and a recurring bitterness in the face of reality. But the poet's mission is probably to indicate why, in times of want and misery, hope should be maintained in order to survive. Perhaps poetry is always the product of a tragic awareness of impossibility: namely, that of making desire and reality coincide. Poets console us because they find a way to take control of fate, despite lack, insufficiency, frustration and, at times, unhappiness. Ruy Belo's work seems to confirm this vision of poet's mission and the function of poetry. His last works are long poems in which he ironically plays with the more external formal aspects of poetry (rhyme and an ostensibly literary vocabulary and syntax), thereby questioning the traditional conception of poetry. Belo's exuberant and apparently chaotic style, which also owes a great deal to the poetry of Fernando Pessoa, can be seen as symptomatic of the impossibility of finding stability in the world, of imposing order on a reality that is complex, contradictory and excessively rich (at least in promises). Love for reality is so vehement in his poetry, furthermore, that the disorder through which it is represented makes the outer world emerge primarily as a sign of passion; the same passion that made Alberto Caeiro impose a rigid anti-sentimentalist discipline on himself. It is also as if, unlike Cesário Verde, Ruy Belo were openly manifesting the impossibility of submitting to the rigor of realism (the rigor imposed by a liberal society founded on production) and were establishing a final, rebellious and anarchistic rule of all the senses. It is perhaps for this reason that Belo's work bears obvious similarities to that of not only Fernando Pessoa, but also Mário de Sá-Carneiro.

In contrast to Ruy Belo, Eugénio de Andrade expresses a respect (in some senses still in the tradition of symbolism) for a formally exalted concept of poetic language and form. For Andrade, the word and the line are equally important, and his poetry is constructed along the aspiration to classical sobriety. The expression of common feelings, however—the capturing of moments of revelation, the identification and glorification of brief and discreet instants of plenitude—give Andrade's poetry a reassuring modernity and freshness, despite the note of classicism and a certain solemnity of tone.

A laconic poet when compared with Álvaro de Campos, Sena and Belo, Andrade does not rebelliously challenge the order of the world. At most he bemoans it, but always finds a way to reconcile himself with reality and with his fate. In this sense, his poetry contrasts strongly with that of Fernando Pessoa, who never ceased to question the meaning of existence and of words. Eugénio de Andrade is an anti-*Pascoaes* of sorts, aware of the limits of language and of the human tendency to expect the impossible. The value of his work lies in this capacity to reinvent reality without denying it. Sometimes bordering on the conventional, Andrade always escapes banality; using common words, but giving them symbolic meaning and enriching them through an alchemic process fuelled by his intimate knowledge of language. In this, he is similar to Camilo Pessanha.

António Ramos Rosa represents yet another trend in contemporary Portuguese poetry. Conscious of the high value of poetry (about which he has also published theoretical and critical essays that it is hard to consider in isolation from his own work), and aspiring to create the poem-object in the tradition of Mallarmé, Ramos Rosa believes that words can speak the unspeakable. He uses an elaborate syntax, avoids similarities with colloquial language and privileges the value of the word in itself. His poetry thus confers a mythical value upon elements such as *stone*, *horse* and *river*, for example. It is as though the solemnity of the poem, and the privileged moment of religious or divine interaction it establishes with reality, give the words it contains an aura of power and extraordinary meaning, causing the reader to forget that each word is only a sign standing in for the object it names.

Words also have a mythical power to name the unnamable for both Andrade and Herberto Helder. They have the power to give daily objects and experiences a "sacred" value. In Andrade's poetry, however, the word is in some way rescued and returned to daily life, making it interact with the new qualities it has been given. In the poetry of Helder, words acquire a mythical power to suggest or give form to the unnamable—that for which no name exists. Helder's syntax, however, is not an abnormal "narrative" syntax. Thanks to an alchemic process that attributes to words meanings dictated by their context, Herberto Helder succeeds in creating a vision or suggestion of the unnamable—of aspects or qualities of ours for which we do not have "words."

For Helder, words, whatever the meaning accorded to them in dictionaries or by common knowledge, can always acquire or be given new, original and complex meanings that are difficult to clarify. The creative activity of the poet expresses a profound disdain for the ruling linguistic order. The bastion of knowledge passed down unquestioningly is rebelliously and openly attacked. Helder reveals an overwhelming ambition to create an individual and original language and, in this way, to oppose order. His attitude also reveals something that can be seen as an expression of the highest mission of the poet: to contest—to deny that which already exists—or to question the relationship between words and what exists, to suggest new relationships and discover new meanings. In sum: to reinvent or discover reality by apparently transfiguring it.

Although this ambition merits appreciation and respect, and although it provides the reader with a fascinating experience, it must be said that Helder only partially achieves his objectives. His vocabulary, syntax and referential universe can gradually and eventually be deciphered as the reader becomes more familiar with his allusions and his style. Behind the new meanings given to words, we find recognizable concepts or a vague image of those concepts, albeit with less certainty and more confusion than is usually the case. Once we understand the rules of his game, the coherence of the world and of language is reconstructed.

Helder's poetry is that of proud rebellion against the law and of rhetoric against the gods. But despite the overweening pride it ostentatiously affects, this poetry also reveals the difficulty of being, the inability to achieve a status approaching that of divinity, the modesty and emptiness of a hesitant Self that exalts itself only because it fears that it will disappear, that its existence is uncertain. Are these poems illusory experiments in which human vanity is made to confront its own limits? A certain, initially disguised, despair infuses poems that are, on the surface, mildly ironic. The poetry of Herberto Helder ends up by confessing an ontological malaise which the poems of Fernando Pessoa and Mário de Sá-Carneiro had already proclaimed by alternative means. Herberto Helder is more than just a fascinating poet: he is also the author of *Os Passos em Volta* (1963). This volume of short stories is one of the best works of fiction in Portuguese literature because of its original style and its ability to speak of an inner life, of urban life, of exile and of the frustration of modern man.

In their rigorous and refined style and the classicism apparent in explicit literary references, the poems of Sophia de Mello Breyner are similar to those of Eugénio de Andrade. Breyner's poems are symbolist and *Parnassian* in their transformation of reality, in the way they create a "poetic reality" and in the poet's admiration of the nobility of poetry. Her poetry brings us face to face both with high-flown sentiments and the solemnity of feeling, even when the poem begins by dealing with an ordinary experience. This kind of literature is deliberately "literary:" "poetic feeling" is expressed in contrast to the "banality" of everyday life.

It is difficult to determine just how much contemporary Portuguese poetry owes to Pessoa and Sá-Carneiro. Pessoa wrote in all kinds of different styles, as if it had fallen to him to instruct the minor poets of his time and those of the future in all the different ways in which to write and speak about the world. Despite this strong influence, poets such as António Ramos Rosa, Eugénio de Andrade, Carlos de Oliveira, and even Sophia de Mello Breyner, seem to belong to another, more classical, tradition. What they owe to Portuguese modernism (by which I mean *Orpheu*—the only real modernist movement to take place in Portugal in the twentieth century—and particularly one of Pessoa's most important heteronyms, Ricardo Reis) is more difficult to identify.

The classicism that infuses the poetic voice of these authors in any case contrasts with the tendency towards the dispersion or disintegration of poetic discourse that is apparent in the work of Ruy Belo, Herberto Helder and Jorge de Sena. All of these poets can be considered heirs or disciples of Álvaro de Campos and, in part, of Alberto Caeiro, rather than Ricardo Reis. Jorge de Sena was one of the first people granted access to the box of manuscripts that was discovered after Fernando Pessoa's death. This contact with the modernist poet undoubtedly influenced Sena's work—in form, if not in depth.

A number of younger poets fit into these two traditions: the "poetry of the word;" and the "poetry of the sentence." Nuno Júdice could be described as the most interesting of them: his work combines rigor with a capacity for reflection similar to that of Andrade, Breyner and Oliveira, and an originality and ability to transform reality reminiscent of Helder. Júdice is a self-styled creator of myths, making him very similar to Helder in poetic attitude. He repeatedly reflects on the essence and technique of poetic writing. Whether he is meditating on poetry, on the act of writing or the Self, with its desires, ghosts and hallucinations, Júdice always reveals the same creative energy and a capacity to give reality a seductive mystery that makes it poetic. Reality is invested with symbolic values, and poetry shows that it can be exciting. The Self, in spite of the temptations to lose oneself fatally in its mythical labyrinth, always recovers a sense of its place in the world. Given this permanent lucidity, a sustained pragmatic contact with reality—whatever the seduction of mystery—the poetry of Nuno Júdice is very original, yet it maintains clear links with other poets.

Other less representative poets and poetic tendencies also deserve to be mentioned here. Certain neo-classical tendencies can be identified in the work of Vasco Graça Moura (born 1942)—acclaimed translator of Dante and other great European authors—and Luís Filipe Castro Mendes (born 1950). Fernando Echevarría (born 1929), and António Franco Alexandre (born 1944)—a poet whose work starts to impose itself as one of the most interesting and important to appear in recent years—stand out for the "philosophical" tone of their poetry, which is characterized by reflection and sobriety. Along the lines of neo-realism—but now stripped of its virulence— Manuel Alegre (born 1937) writes poetry that celebrates the conventional and popular commonplace beliefs of the Portuguese left. By contrast, Sophia de Mello Breyner's poetry is a way of celebrating the privileged moments of individual experience (and occasionally the traditional idea of the homeland and the countries of ancient culture) with educated and aristocratic solemnity.

The list of other significant contemporary poets should include, among others: Fernando Guimarães (born 1928), Alberto de Lacerda (born 1928), António Osório (born 1933), Pedro Támen (born 1934), Pedro Alvim (born 1935), Fernando Assis Pacheco (1937-1995), Alberto Pimenta (born 1937), Gastão Cruz (born 1941), João Miguel Fernandes Jorge (born 1943), Joaquim Manuel Magalhães (born 1945), Luís Miguel Nava (1957-1995), Paulo Teixeira and Fernando Pinto do Amaral.

The Significance of Literature Written by Women

This panoramic view of Portuguese literature would be seriously lacking if it failed to note the growing importance of work by women, work that have a style and sensitivity all of its own. The publication in 1972 of *Novas Cartas Portuguesas*, by Maria Isabel Barreno (born 1938), Maria Teresa Horta (born 1937) and Maria Velho da Costa (born 1938) had a great impact in Portugal and abroad. The book caused a scandal and became a symbol of the desire for sexual liberation of Portuguese women.

Serious concerns about the status and situation of women had already been manifested at the beginning of the twentieth century.

The works of Florbela Espanca (1894-1930) and Irene Lisboa, over different periods of time, staked a claim for women and paved the way for more women writers. Thanks to an initially favorable international context and to the "Carnation Revolution," that tradition—which already had some roots in the years preceding the First Republic—was able to develop further. Indeed, since then it has never stopped developing. Today, the number of contemporary women writers of significance in Portugal is notable, and this phenomenon cannot be considered in isolation from the changes in views on moral, emotional and sexual education—changes that owe much to the feminist struggle for equality of rights.

The list of women fiction writers most frequently cited in addition to those mentioned above, includes: Ilse Losa (born 1913); Patrícia Joyce (born 1913); Marta de Lima (born 1914); Maria Judite de Carvalho (1921-2001); Isabel da Nóbrega (born 1925); Fernanda Botelho (born 1926); Luísa Dacosta (born 1927); Ester de Lemos (born 1929); Olga Gonçalves (born 1929); Maria Gabriela Llansol (born 1931); Maria Ondina Braga (1932-2003); Teolinda Gersão (born 1940); Yvette Centeno (born 1940); Lídia Jorge (born 1946); Eduarda Dionísio (born 1946); Hélia Correia (born 1949); and Luísa Costa Gomes, to name but a few.

As far as poetry is concerned, the list of the most significant women writers include: Luísa Neto Jorge (1929-1989); Ana Hatherly (born 1929); Maria Teresa Horta (born 1937); Fiama Hasse Pais Brandão (born 1938); and, more recently, Ana Luísa Amaral, Maria do Rosário Pedreira and Adília Lopes. We also ought to mention Maria de Lourdes Belchior Pontes (1923-1998) for writing poetry with religious connotations.

Gender-based literary studies have also been developing in Portugal—to such an extent that literature by women has started to receive the recognition and attention that prejudice often denied it in the past. The small world of contemporary Portuguese literary studies has never escaped the logic of either power relations or of personal relationships. The future, should it take an interest in us, will ensure that the dead are put in their rightful place.

II | Portuguese Art in the Twentieth Century

João Pinharanda

In 1913, an international exhibition was held in New York that may be considered the first to introduce modern art to the United States. Organized by the Association of American Painters and Sculptors, the predictably scandalous Armory Show spread the news about European modernism. Amadeo de Souza Cardoso (1887–1918), a Portuguese painter resident in the French capital, was among the 300 artists whose works were exhibited. His eight paintings were displayed along with those of the French artists Georges Braque, Henri Matisse, Marcel Duchamp, Theodore Gleizes, Paul Cézanne, Paul Gauguin, Pierre-Auguste Renoir and Georges Seurat. Three of his paintings were sold to the collector, A. I. Eddy, who reproduced them in a famous book published in 1914, entitled *Cubists and Post-Impressionism*. On Eddy's death, the paintings were donated to the Art Institute of Chicago. In the same year, following Delaunay's suggestion, Souza-Cardozo participated in the First Autumn Salon of Der Sturm gallery in Berlin.

Souza-Cardoso introduced modernism to Portugal. His works were among the most original and brilliant in Europe during the 1910s. It is strange, therefore, that international art history hardly refers to his work. It is even stranger that his work did not give rise to a sustained artistic movement in Portugal. The continuing ignorance of his work at both the national and international levels can be considered symptomatic of cultural and artistic development in Portugal. It is part of a social structure and "mentality" that was already evident in the nineteenth century and that has shaped the course of twentieth century Portuguese art.

Portuguese cultural reality was influenced by the almost permanent state of political and social instability that reigned up to the 1930s, and also by a profound dependence on France. Initiated during the eighteenth century, this dependence lasted until the last quarter of the twentieth and affected all cultural groups. A concomitant reaction against this situation of dependence, however, gave rise to a dual mode of thinking: "identity" versus "cosmopolitanism," or "isolation" versus "internationalization." This dichotomy in turn led to the emergence of viewpoints, or even ideologies, that were not so much articulated as set in opposition to each other.

In Portugal, literature, particularly poetry and the novel, received more public and official recognition, and enjoyed higher status than the visual arts. Given the resistant nature of the factors shaping and reproducing patterns of taste, new cultural models arose only with the greatest difficulty. Naturalistic tastes thus remained dominant until the middle of the twentieth century. Modern art museums did not exist, and the lack of specialized information, critical discussion or in-depth debate on contemporary artistic realities was apparent. This conservative climate also consolidated traditional thinking in education, helping to limit the dissemination of international modern art in Portugal and the export of Portuguese art abroad. At the same time, Portugal had no public capable of supporting contemporary art; its national elites lacked cultural sophistication and taste. A *mecenas* culture—in which banks, foundations and the like supported the arts—did not emerge. It was virtually impossible to create a national art market, to establish pricing and trading criteria or to launch international artistic careers.

Artists worked against the current, isolated by the ultra-conservative environment. Vanguard radicals were repeatedly forced to "sell out" as previously anti-establishment artists became part of the establishment. Thus, new tastes were delayed from taking root, and prevailing tastes survived for abnormally long periods.

Conservatism permeated decision-making at all levels of Portuguese society; it penetrated political and cultural attitudes and shaped public opinion as well as the art market. Until the 1930s, it was almost impossible to crack the wall of naturalist taste. Indeed, only in the 1940s did that wall begin to crack, and from then on, only very gradually and slowly.

A dictatorial and interventionist state, excessively active in defining artistic matters, consolidated this situation. This is particularly important in a society that had a very limited capacity for individual initiative. Later, during the 1960s and 1970s, the self-imposed absence of the state led to the intervention of a private entity, the Calouste Gulbenkian Foundation (FCG—*Fundação Calouste Gulbenkian*) in the art world. The FCG changed artistic policy, but it was only in the 1980s and 1990s that a more pluralistic environment emerged.

The weakness of innovative artistic currents was also apparent in their fragile or distorted social echo. The production of art was not linked to a critical discourse with a capacity to establish a dialogue between art and the public. Artists themselves were unable to elaborate a theory of art to complement their work. Leading artists were not sufficiently committed on either an ethical or a poetic level. Finally, a historical awareness of art was conspicuously lacking; it was often produced in ignorance of, or isolation from, international trends.

From Symbolism to Modernism

Amadeo Souza-Cardoso was part of a cultural movement, led by the so-called Futurist Generation, that was decisive for the advent of the modern age in Portugal. The movement emerged at a time when the national cultural climate was at a very low ebb. The establishment of the republic in 1910 did not overcome the defeatism that the financial, economic, social and political crises of the nineteenth century had produced. The impact of the colonial and financial crises, along with the decline of the legitimacy of the monarchy, had been profound. A series of intellectuals and politicians committed suicide, among them Mouzinho de Albuquerque, a hero of the African campaigns; Soares dos Reis, the symbolist sculptor; Antero de Quental, a poet and founder of the Socialist Party; and Manuel Laranjeira, a writer and close friend of Souza-Cardoso. These men became the examples and symbols of that crisis. Their deaths led Miguel Unamuno to speak of the Portuguese as "a suicidal people."

Naturalism flourished in the arts (and would continue in favor for another 50 years). This style centered on José Malhoa (born 1855), a painter who died in 1933. A symbolism of French origins (rather than British or German) also existed, and was more in touch with the age. This current, however, was very weak and at times only implicit, even in the works of its greatest exponents, António Carneiro (1872-1930), Soares dos Reis (1847-1889) and Columbano (1857-1929).

Souza-Cardoso, and other artists of his generation, turned the tide against this intellectual climate. Their movement was centered in Lisbon, but its ideological driving force was Italian futurism. The aim of the movement was to give the Portuguese arts a sense of Europe. Literature initially predominated; the rest of the arts were affected only later. The movement's leading figures were literary men, such as Fernando Pessoa, a poet who initially wrote in the journal, *Águia*, and Mário Sá-Carneiro, who committed suicide in 1916. Other members had both literary and artistic careers, such as Almada Negreiros (1894-1970). Finally, there were artists who worked solely with the visual arts, such as Souza-Cardoso and another painter, Guilherme Santa-Rita (1889-1918). The magazine, *Orpheu,* united them, albeit only briefly (for only two issues were published), in 1915. They included important illustrations by Souza-Cardoso and Santa-Rita, however. The latter's works were practically the only examples of cubist-futurist work in Portugal, an opus the artist's family destroyed after his death.

With the exception of Pessoa, who had a British cultural background, Paris was the mecca for these artists, and it was there that

Souza-Cardoso's career began in 1906. The son of a well-to-do rural family from the north of Portugal, Souza-Cardoso went to Paris to study architecture, began to work as a caricaturist, and later abandoned his studies to dedicate himself entirely to painting. His social position allowed him to escape the fate of state pensioner, and the obligation to submit his works to the approval of conservative Portuguese teachers.

In Paris, Souza-Cardoso met Amadeo Modigliani and became his close friend. From that relationship arose a joint exhibition held in Souza Cardoso's luxurious studio in 1911. During this period, the two artists developed similar themes, painting stylized and decorative female figures rooted in Oriental, African and archaic art. In Modigliani's case, this period led to the definition of a style; but in Souza-Cardoso's case, it was merely one stage in a vertiginous artistic career.

In his search for a personal style, his work expressed all the artistic references of the period. In 1912, Souza-Cardoso published an album called *XX Dessins*, which was favorably reviewed by the poet Guillaume Apollinaire, a friend of the cubists. It was probably as a result of the notoriety this achieved that Souza-Cardoso was chosen to participate in the Armory Show. From a symbolist-inspired stylization of form and space, he went on to develop a quasi-cubist deconstruction of reality. From 1919 on, he painted abstract and chromatic landscapes that were heavily influenced by Robert Delaunay's studies of light. He subsequently experimented with expressionism, a style he never abandoned. Souza-Cardoso thus accumulated a variety of materials and artistic references, among them futurism, synthetic cubism and Dada. These influences were not eclectic; they coincided with the European avant-garde of the time, even though they were produced in relative isolation.

World War I took Souza-Cardoso back to Portugal, where he lived until his death on the eve of his planned return to Paris. During this period, he received the exiled Sonia and Robert Delaunay in Vila do Conde, a bourgeois beach resort in the north of Portugal. They associated with Negreiros and Eduardo Viana, briefly galvanizing the narrow Portuguese art world, as well as providing new inspiration for the work of both these painters.

By then, Souza-Cardoso had already established an autonomous style. He successfully combined a depiction of Portuguese popular images with a universal language portraying the modern, mechanical world. His work was formal, both in its use of color and its themes—a rare achievement in Portuguese art. He held two exhibitions in Portugal in 1916, one in Lisbon and the other in Oporto. Both caused great scandal. His personal character, however, turned him into a giant of national modernism. An art prize was established in his name that was awarded by the state from 1935 on; yet his work remained largely unknown in his own country until the 1950s.

A Balanced Modernism and Some Marginal Artists

The efforts of the war years faded quickly in the absence of a revolution in taste. Europe entered the so-called postwar phase of *retour à l'ordre*. The provocative voices and images of the surrealists and their First Manifesto of 1924 had only a delayed impact in this context. They gained ground later, in the 1930s, on the eve of the social and cultural disasters caused by World War II.

From a historical point of view, the 1920s and 1930s in Portugal were decades of profound crisis, just as they were for the Western world as a whole. They were characterized by a search for stabilizing political and economic solutions. In the end, a predominantly conservative society opted for a military, authoritarian remedy. The coup of 28 May 1926 led to a prolonged one-party, corporatist dictatorship with a parliamentary facade, similar to other European fascist regimes.

The international isolation and censorship imposed by Prime Minister António de Oliveira Salazar naturally affected the cultural world. Still, this period should not be interpreted in a linear or simplistic fashion. António Ferro, a journalist, member of the *Orpheu* group and an admirer of Mussolini, became Salazar's cultural ideologue. He persuaded the dictator to encourage modern artists' cooperation in the creation of a choreography—an image—for the

Estado Novo (New State), following the Italian model, which linked fascism and futurism. Through the *Secretariado de Propaganda Nacional* (SPN—National Propaganda Secretariat, later renamed the *Secretariado Nacional de Informação*, SNI—National Information Secretariat), Ferro established incentives, such as competitions, prizes, subsidies and public commissions for decorative work, posters, set designs and clothing, which the artists of the 1910s and 1920s produced. His protégés developed a "balanced modernism," and gained national prominence. Independent of their work and life in both aesthetic and political terms, these artists remained active until the 1960s and 1970s, establishing an artistic continuity that later evolved into a new academic and conservative market taste.

The leading lights of the 1920s and 1930s in Portugal were artists who successfully captured the formal values of the European avant-garde through a formal and chromatic synthesis. The best works of these years were graphic images that appeared on magazine covers, in publicity campaigns and on posters, as well as in the decoration of Portuguese pavilions at international exhibitions and fairs. The situation was so aesthetically fragile, however, that modernism in Portugal refers to something altogether different from its Western European meaning. It was assimilationist, superficial, eclectic, mundane and cosmopolitan, an interpretation of the break with the 1910s. Portuguese modernism, moreover, was almost completely ignorant of subsequent artistic developments, such as expressionism, surrealism and geometric abstraction. It predominated in a climate of almost total artistic consensus until the 1940s.

One of the most important representatives of this period was Almada Negreiros, a poet who wrote in *Orpheu,* and a caricaturist during the 1910s. Negreiros lived in Madrid and Paris during the 1920s without ever connecting with the local avant-garde. He continually questioned the aim and mission of art in Portugal, and he transplanted the call for immediate action characteristic of the futurist age into the symbolic realm, establishing himself as a theoretician and prophet. He gave greatest importance to the plastic arts, following Picasso's "neo-classicism." His greatest works, both of which owe much to his excellence as a sketch artist, are the murals that appear on buildings along two of Lisbon's docks, *Alcântara* (completed in 1945) and *Rocha* (1948).

The most interesting aspect of this period of "normalization," "academization" and assimilation of modernism, however, is the emergence of various marginal artists at the time. Their careers generally faded very quickly; like Souza-Cardozo, most of them became national myths, albeit less powerful ones. Most of them, furthermore, had emigrated and were disconnected from the national art world. On returning home, they remained fundamentally removed from the national scene. Most of them died young, either committing suicide or going mad.

Mário Eloy (1900-1951), for example, was schooled in Germany. He returned to Lisbon in 1932, an expressionist influenced by George Grosz and Otto Dix. His paintings and drawings expressed the violence of a radical solitude. His subsequent internment in a psychiatric hospital gave his work added meaning. Another example is Domingos Alvarez (1906-1942). This artist developed an expressionism characterized by great economy of means, both formal and chromatic, and deformed space and figures. The strangeness of his themes permitted him to develop an oniric and surreal naïve language. Alvarez died early from tuberculosis. Another artist of note, Júlio (1902-1969), was closer to the second German expressionist movement and to surrealism, and painted bold canvases of social critique. He was inconsistent, however, later developing a more figurative and lyrical style.

Of this group, only António Pedro (1909-1966) gained international fame in Paris. Like Souza-Cardoso, his economic and family situation made him independent. He was one of the vanguard of his time, and he signed the Dimensionist Manifesto of 1935, along with Duchamp, Wassily Kandinsky, Francis Picabia, Juan Arp, Joan Miró, Alexander Calder and others. This was a document that promoted cross-pollination among all creative forms.

Maria Helena Vieira da Silva (1908-1992), a member of the Second School of Paris, and her Hungarian husband, Arpad Szenes

(1899-1986), were the only other artists linking the Portuguese and international artistic worlds. The couple lived in Paris in the 1920s, but owned a studio in Lisbon and frequently stayed in Portugal throughout the 1930s. They established a relationship with the national literary and artistic community, although they remained peripheral as taste-makers and political outsiders. During this period, their work was a stylistic cross between expressionism and surrealism. They developed post-cubist analyses of space and post-impressionist studies of light. When the dictatorship refused to naturalize Szenes, the couple opted for French citizenship and cut ties with Portugal until the re-establishment of democracy in 1974.

The relationships she established in Portugal, however, earned Vieira da Silva a place in the gallery of famous artists who became myths. Her work never had true repercussions in Portuguese art, however. Her aesthetic influence came late and weakly. In the 1970s, Portuguese art collectors finally took an interest in her work, and thereby popularized it. This in turn had political repercussions, which culminated in her renaturalization after the revolution of 1974 and also led to the establishment of a foundation in her name in Lisbon in 1994.

The Three Paths

Following the Spanish Civil War and World War II, a new climate emerged that changed socio-political, cultural and artistic realities in Portugal, and produced a diversified, but coherent, artistic reality that lasted until the 1960s. The Exhibition of the Portuguese World, organized by the government in 1940 for the country's domestic and international glorification, displayed work by most of the country's contemporary artists, presenting a climactic synthesis of Portuguese modernism. António Ferro's selection of participants provoked violent reactions among the naturalists, a school still dominant in art institutions such as the Escola de Belas-Artes and the Sociedade Nacional de Belas-Artes (SNBA). The exhibition thus brought to light the divisions among the regime's social bases of support.

A first surrealist exhibition of the works of António Pedro and António Dacosta (1914-1990) took place the same year. It bore witness to a nascent artistic development that unfortunately did not take root. Pedro left for London, where he became a BBC announcer; Dacosta participated in official competitions and received the Amadeo Souza-Cardoso Prize in 1942.

The emergence of socially and politically committed neo-realist art further diversified art production. Neo-realist literary works were published in the journal, *Vértice*, which was inaugurated in 1940, and emerged with the novels of Alves Redol. The school gained notoriety with the General Arts Exhibition held in Lisbon between 1945 and 1956. This exhibition was an alternative to official art salons and to abstract and surrealist artwork. It was aesthetically and ideologically based on social realism. The examples of the Mexican muralists and the Brazilian painter Candido Portinari, however, predominated over Soviet models.

Geometric abstraction first emerged in Oporto with the Independent Exhibitions of 1943, another sign of artistic renewal. Fernando Lanhas (born 1923) was its leading light. The artistic pluralism of the 1940s was evident in the re-awakening of surrealism in 1947 with the return of António Pedro, the continuing presence of Dacosta, the emergence of many young men who had originated in neo-realism, and a series of exhibitions in 1949, 1950 and 1952. The artists of this decade rapidly divided into irreconcilable factions, which sustained a long dispute. One of the factions, directed by Pedro, included the critic José Augusto França, who eventually became a prominent critic and historian of the surrealist movement and of Portuguese art. The other faction, which was socially, historiographically and museologically marginalized, was more literary. Mário Cesariny (born 1933), one of the greatest poets of the century, became the aesthetic and ethical point of reference. From the 1950s on, Cesariny's art was based on abstract solutions and was notably free of stylistic constraints.

A debate developed between the proponents of neo-realism, surrealism and abstraction. Júlio Pomar (born 1936), António Dacosta and Lanhas are the key representatives of these tendencies. Pomar emigrated to Paris in the 1960s. Breaking away from the neo-realist formula, he developed freedom of gesture, color and theme, as well as an erotic subjectivism that drew him to Ingres and Matisse in the 1970s, to national and archaic cultural myths in the 1980s and, finally, to classic and baroque traditions in the 1990s.

Dacosta also lived in Paris from the 1940s onwards, becoming a magnet for other artists, just as Vieira da Silva had been. He abandoned painting until the end of the 1970s, although he maintained close relations with the Portuguese art world through Portuguese and Brazilian journals. His "return" to painting, however, confirmed the unparalleled quality of his surrealist canvases. An understanding of his work is indispensable for an understanding of Portuguese art in the 1980s. "Return to painting," moreover, is a doubly appropriate term in this case; it also means a return to childhood. Dacosta depicted images based on the simple memories of a childhood spent in the Azores, or human and cultural archetypes in a melancholy style that contemplates life and death.

Lanhas never abandoned his native city, Oporto. In 1944, despite the lack of access to international art imposed by the war, Lanhas painted the first Portuguese abstract paintings. He was not prolific, and nor did he undergo a clear evolution. His geometrism was based on simple lines and neutral colors. He painted free, zig-zagging or centralized structures. Background and form coexisted in his works alongside profoundly poetic graphic games. His work always reflected his interests in paleontology, architecture, archeology and astronomy.

The artworks and aesthetic options of the 1950s developed in a social and political climate dominated by a state whose right-wing, dictatorial nature had been further consolidated through participation in NATO's fight against communism. The state soon lost the cultural initiative, however. Salazar ceased to rely on the support of artists; the artists, in turn, became more radical. In 1950, António Ferro was removed from the SNI. Sculpture was the only medium that remained firmly under government control.

Art deco styles, renewed during the 1930s by Canto da Maya and Leopoldo de Almeida, were surpassed by a formal modernist archaism based on a historical exploration of the overseas empire and the nation's heroes. It was in the field of sculpture that a break with the past occurred through the emergence of abstract and surrealist experimentation, albeit within the restricted circle of independent exhibitions. Jorge Vieira (1922-1998), schooled in the United Kingdom during the 1950s under the influence of Reg Butler and Henry Moore, depicted abstract associations and surrealist themes. In his works, human and animal forms mingle, expressing a disturbing humor and irony. Vieira worked mostly in private spaces, on a small scale and with terracotta, although he also used iron.

Photography also emerged in this period as an autonomous artistic discipline. It had an intense social content, and was driven by a desire to register reality. Vitor Palla, Costa Martins and Sena da Silva were photography's leading exponents; Fernando Lemos (born 1926) practiced photography as a complement to his surrealist painting.

The Pluralist Decade

The diversity of work flowering in the 1940s and 1950s led to the emergence of a new artistic climate in the 1960s. From 1960 on, the range of artists, tendencies, activities and agents increased. The links between the national and international art worlds deepened, producing a profound alteration in national thinking. The capacity to absorb international art innovations, along with the speed of that absorption, increased during the period of pop art and dissident *nouveau realisme* and *arte povera*.

New types of initiatives emerged. First, individual initiatives were promoted by the massive emigration of artists to Europe from 1957-58 onwards. Second, socio-professional initiatives were galvanized by the conquest of the SNBA in the 1960s by the new generation of artists. Third, commercial initiatives arose with the inauguration of new art galleries in Lisbon, such as the Galeria de Março, the Pórtico and the Diário de Notícias, and later the Alvarez gallery in Oporto. Finally, private institutional initiatives were undertaken, led by the FCG and its international art grants scheme. Naturalist taste was finally surpassed as a new generation of artists, art agents, critics and institutional officials in the 1940s and 1950s channeled its new style through the FCG and the SNBA until the 1980s.

Emigration was decisive until the mid-1970s. It was initially an expression of aesthetic, ethical and political rebellion, and an escape from the colonial war, rather than a search for training. Later, however, it was supported by grants from the FCG, which did not submit its artists to the narrow criteria of academic evaluation. For the first time, Paris ceased to be the only mecca, although Europe remained dominant. The United Kingdom became a new destination, with London gaining importance from the 1970s onwards.

Generally speaking, works were influenced by international pop art trends. In Portugal, however, they were a creative response to the legacy of expressionism and surrealism. These styles also led surrealists to embrace non-geometric art. Most of the big names of the decade were influenced by anglo-saxon canons but also by French, Italian, and Spanish painters of the 1950s, and even by US gesturalism. Italian *arte povera*, on the other hand, was not an important influence.

Joaquim Rodrigo (1912-1997) sought to mix formal and chromatic compositional values with the primitivism of Luanda (Angola) and aboriginal art. He developed contemporary themes, which were sometimes political, almost always cultural, and even more often personal. He followed the rules of how to "paint right" with great precision. His paintings are akin to memory maps; their narrative quality and the formal archaism of the figures they depict, as well as their intimate nature, led to their rediscovery in the 1980s.

Paula Rego (born 1935), who has worked in London since the 1950s, holds a mythical place in the history of national art similar to that of Vieira da Silva: she embodies the capacity of Portuguese artists to gain international recognition. Although Rego is married to an British painter and has adopted British citizenship, she regularly exhibits her work in Portugal, and draws her inspiration mainly from childhood memories and popular culture. In the 1960s, she worked on explicitly political themes; subsequently, the depiction of a personal and intimate narrative delirium deepened, expressed through universal social and cultural archetypes.

Rego's painting has always conveyed an expressionist sensibility, and thus it lends continuity to the most marginal current in Portuguese art. In 1961, the display of Rego's and Rodrigo's paintings in the Second Exhibition of Plastic Arts at the FCG broke with the aesthetic currents of the 1950s, introducing a narrative structure that destroyed the linearity of an illustrationist discourse. Rego became very important in national artistic life in the 1980s, when her work began to gain international recognition. She is currently part of a group of British figurative painters who have followed Francis Bacon and Lucien Freud, but her art is distinctive in that it constructs a feminine vision of the world.

Other artists who were influenced by the British art scene are João Cutileiro (born 1947) and Bartolomeo Cid (today one of the most important engravers in the world) based at the Slade School of Art in London. Others include Ângelo de Sousa, Alberto Carneiro (born 1937) and Eduardo Batarda (born 1943). Batarda set up one of the most erudite, virulent and humorous galleries of Portuguese art between the 1960s and the 1980s. António Sena (born 1941) first explored pop art themes and later produced works reminiscent of the American, Cy Twombly. Yet another example is João Vieira (born 1934). In the 1970s, he participated in the first "happenings" ever to take place in Portugal. Sá Nogueira, Areal, Cesariny and even younger artists, such as Rui Leitão (1949-1976), are also worthy of note. Leitão's career was dramatically short, but he undertook an extraordinary reinterpretation of pop art.

Cutileiro was the most prolific sculptor of the 1960s, and went on to become the master of the new stone sculptors of the 1980s. He is an emblematic artist who uses industrial machinery to produce images of fragmentation. His most important piece of sculpture is a statue of King Sebastian (1973), which is now located in Lagos. In it, he challenges official canons of representation. His obsessive productivity is at times decorative and centered on the female figure.

The KWY Group, founded in Paris (it ironically used letters that do not exist in the Portuguese alphabet), included Lourdes Castro (born 1930), René Bertholo (born 1935), Costa Pinheiro (born 1932), João Vieira Escada (1934-1980) and two other (non-Portuguese) immigrants, Ian Voss and Christo. This group formulated solutions in the international context of neo-figurativism, and edited a serigraph journal featuring important European artists of the time. They dealt with the object or its absence, the mechanization of the world, the deconstruction of myths and the visual value of words or letters. Another Paris-based artist, Jorge Martins (born 1934), has recently undertaken publicly commissioned work for the Washington DC Metro. His narrative style pursues a study of light and of irony through constant reference to US and French cinema. Manuel Baptista (born 1936), yet another artist of this period, experiments with texture, monochromatic painting and the shaped canvas.

This new generation of emigrants eventually returned to Portugal, becoming either isolated or regionally integrated. They lived abroad and returned, moreover, without ever taking root in the local market and gaining critical attention. Those who remained abroad forsook sales in Portugal that was permitted by a growing art market. The III Gallery in Lisbon (founded in 1964), along with the alternative, Bucholz, were the decisive markets in this period.

Other artists integrated with the international art scene. António Palolo (1946-2000) became a phenomenon in the art market of the 1960s. He created syntheses of pop and psychedelic culture, both alien to erudite Portuguese culture. He also worked on shaped canvases and in the minimalist style. António Charrua (born 1945) was influenced by Robert Rauschenberg. Nikias Skapinakis (born 1931) worked at the end of the 1960s on graphic or so-called pop figuration, using mythological as well as everyday themes. Noronha da Costa (born 1942), working with light and representation, created Germanic, romantic and even cinematographic paintings later in his career.

A watershed in the national art scene was reached with the emergence of a specific group of artists: António Areal (1934-

1974), Álvaro Lapa (born 1939) and Joaquim Bravo (1935-1990). All three came from a literary and surrealist background, a recurrent situation in Portugal. All became aesthetic and ethical reference points, and had a decisive impact on the contradictory generations of 1980 and 1990.

Areal exerted an important tutelary influence during the 1960s and 1970s; he was one of the few Portuguese artists with a capacity for written aesthetic reflection. He initially developed informalist French and Pollockian paintings, later returning to the figurative style typical of the post-Rego and Rodrigo period. He focused on assemblage, derivation and fantastic and surrealist formulas. Later he evolved from the exploration of concepts (a series of painted empty boxes in 1969) to a critical study of the figure in the history of art (*The Ideal Collector*, 1973).

Lapa's radicalism ran even deeper. The austerity and strangeness of his media, as well as his fascination with the work of Robert Motherwell and William Burroughs, gesturalism, the cut-up and Zen led him to studies that had a decisive impact on Portuguese painting. Lapa studied the artistic method, the landscape and the portrait; he also studied expressive visual and written techniques, fusing them in the narrative and oneiric space of the canvas. Finally, he studied the relationship between art and the viewer.

Bravo gained critical acclaim only in the 1980s. His values were more immediately visual, although still marked by literary culture. The word, as expressed in the titles within his paintings, is always present. In Bravo's work, gesture, color and form strive to coincide; the canvas becomes a space for the presentation of synthetic and serialized gestures, which create archetypal or free forms. Bravo created a circle of intellectuals in Lagos, in the south of Portugal, bringing together various emerging artists, such as Cabrita Reis, Paulo Feliciano and Xana, who became influential from the 1980s on.

Alberto Carneiro, a sculptor working in Oporto, has sustained a uniquely permanent capacity for renewal. Carneiro produced the first "land art:" or, as he would have it, ecological art, in Portugal. His work explores nature and the body—his own. His materials include exotic woods and objects from nature or popular rural culture. Also critical to his work are the photographs he takes of his own movements in a particular landscape. He reflects critically on the creative process and the market.

Another group from the 1960s, the Quatro Vintes, also emerged in Oporto: from a school that had been very active since the 1940s. The Lisbon school at this time was stagnant, lacking dynamic professors. The Oporto group had an important impact in market terms, but was not aesthetically influential. A key figure of this group was Ângelo de Souza (born 1938). He produced powerful formal syntheses based on a simplification of reality, and was highly influenced by the Swiss painter Paul Klee. His syntheses are not oneiric, however, and they must be understood in light of their chromatic elements. His favorite medium was drawing, although his painting deepened abstract values in a study of color, light and space, similar to the monochromatic, minimalist paintings of Robert Mangold. Jorge Pinheiro (born 1931) and Armando Alves, other members of the Quatro Vintes, produced shaped sculptures in painted metal, as well as three-dimensional shaped canvases. In chronological and inventive terms, Pinheiro must be considered one of the most interesting examples of a European derivation of "serialism," of the shaped canvas and of minimalism. Since the 1990s, he has also been one of the most important cultivators of symbolic and metaphysical figurative art.

With the rise of Marcello Caetano in 1968, a process of liberalization began. It provoked a rapid economic transformation with the opening of the market to foreign investment, the acceleration of Portuguese integration into Europe and investment in the secondary and tertiary economic sectors. An inflationary financial cycle led to an artificial euphoria, with serious consequences for the future of an art market that had never really taken root. In sum, the 1960s were perhaps one of the most prolific decades, and certainly one of the most important in the course of the century. The majority of the artists of that period are still alive and fully active today. They have become recognized names among the general public, art institutions and critics.

The Emergence of Alternatives
and an International Conscience

The political transformations of the mid-1970s brought about a break with Portugal's historical and cultural past. The military coup of April 1974 rapidly degenerated into social revolution in the midst of a world economic crisis. The coup significantly altered artistic realities in Portugal. All national, social and cultural forces began to concentrate on social and political issues. Such was the force of this trend that a new form of artistic *dirigisme* emerged, based on "culture at the service of the people." During the revolutionary period from 1976 through 1977, the artificially sustained art market collapsed. Very few galleries survived, and there was no prospect of immediate recovery. At the same time, the state was preoccupied with the urgent questions of democratic consolidation and the elimination of the dictatorial legacy; it proved incapable of establishing coherent cultural policies.

In 1977, when art was thought of as a collective enterprise or as a field for avant-garde experimentation and subjective affirmation, an important exhibition, *Alternativa Zero*, was held in Lisbon. Ernesto Sousa, a critic closely linked with neo-realism, coordinated it. He had studied popular and erudite art, as well as cinema and literature. Sousa's opinions were always heterodox, polemical and radical. The aim of the show was to exhibit diverse conceptualist and minimalist art, as well as the performing and video arts. Video art, a diffuse, post-pop medium, was ill defined in Portugal; it was neither institutionally embraced nor highly regarded by the public. Significantly, despite its success, it closed a cycle in Portugal's artistic life.

In 1978, the international biennial of Vila Nova de Cerveira in the north of Portugal was established. It became one of the most important exhibitions held in the nation; the 1985 installment consecrated the artists of the 1980s. That it was not held in Lisbon indicates the desire in the art world to create the conditions for cultural decentralization, an objective still to be achieved today. The Vila Nova biennial also aimed to gather, albeit without very precise criteria, a vast range of artists, both famous and unknown, at a time when the art market was inoperative. Another shift in the political climate in the 1980s, however, put an end to the project.

Other attempts to create alternatives and open new centers were made, generally by schools or by members of the performing arts, but they lacked continuity. Initiatives were undertaken in localities such as Caldas da Rainha, Torres Vedras, Almada, Oporto and Coimbra (with the opening of the Centro de Artes Plásticas). Artists such as Julião Sarmento, Leonel Moura (born 1949), Cerveira Pinto (born 1942), Fernando Calhau (1948-2002) and José Barrias (born 1946)—all disciples of Ernesto Sousa—managed to keep up with world artistic developments in a steady timely, and culturally profound fashion. They overcame existing information, communication and circulation blocks, gaining access to foreign journals through emigration to new art centers, such as in the Netherlands (where a large community established itself), or simply through easier travel to the United States, Germany or Italy.

The careers consolidated in these years of crisis were those of Ângelo, Lapa, Carneiro, Cutileiro, Sena, Martins, Baptista, Guimarães, Batarda and Helena Almeida (born 1934). These artists flourished in personal and critical terms, but had little impact on the market. They renewed the studies of the 1960s and the emphasis on the (im)possibility of representation. Almeida undertook series of different activities, including photography, drawing, painting and collage. She became the photographic subject of her own work, and created a series of "lived-in" paintings using elements of traditional art. She created three-dimensional lines through a "horse-mane" effect, colored them with isolated brushstrokes; she dramatized her figures in space. Almeida also established one of the most solid feminine discourses in Portuguese art.

Utopias of Success

In the 1980s, the social, economic, financial and political crises of the previous years were overcome. In artistic terms, a new period of creativity began, and new artists gained national and international fame.

The social and cultural atmosphere of the 1980s was complex. National developments paralleled international realities through the new and irreversible democratic circulation of information. Disenchantment with revolutionary political participation was replaced by deepening individualistic cultural values, by a "fury to live" reminiscent of the liberalization of the 1960s, which Portugal had only timidly experienced. Political stabilization and the benefits of membership in the European Community promoted the development of the entrepreneurial and financial sectors, which began to channel profits into formerly unproductive areas.

Investment in the arts became a means to reinforce an often recently acquired social and political status. It was a process that paralleled the "yuppie" culture in other countries. The art galleries became part of this dynamic. They opened in unprecedented numbers, even if only in the traditional areas of Lisbon and Oporto. Art was sold at inflated prices.

The Quadrum Gallery in Lisbon (1973) represented artists of the 1960s and 1970s, as well as new artists of the 1980s. It did not play a leading market role, however. In 1975, the Módulo Gallery in Lisbon and Oporto staked their bets on the more "difficult" artists of the 1970s and the new names of the 1980s; it also failed in market terms. The Cómicos (now Luis Serpa) Gallery was established in Lisbon in 1984. It represented artists of the transitional period between the 1970s and 1980s and many international artists of *arte povera*, as well as conceptual artists and photographers. Finally, we have the EMI-Valentim de Carvalho Gallery (Lisbon, 1985-1995) that reestablished the artists of the 1960s and 1970s in the market. The III Gallery also recovered its position of the 1960s, now as a center exhibiting consecrated artists of the 1940s and 1950s, such as Pomar, Dacosta and Rego.

The re-emergence of traditional artists with the rise of modern art auctions was accompanied by the emergence of dozens of new artists, with many of them beginning their professional careers while still at art school. They cultivated an irreverent attitude toward the canons of previous generations, and they rapidly gained visibility in a press responding to a public hungry for new lifestyles. This specialized press, *au courant* with contemporary change, did not flourish, however, and the establishment reacted negatively to these changes. Certain newspapers, however, such as the weekly, *Expresso,* and the cultural weekly, *JL,* gathered an unusual amount of information on artistic activities.

A new generation of art critics had a more or less complicit relationship with new artists; Alexandre Pomar, Alexandre Melo and the author of this chapter are examples. A new phase of critical debate was inaugurated, although it never projected deeply enough to involve the art world as a whole because of a lack of articulation between the different interest groups and an absence of artists' associations.

Similarly, art institutions were not renewed, either in administrative terms or in an understanding of new realities. The modern generation, that had gained positions of power in these institutions during the 1950s and 1960s, retained those positions in the 1980s. The SNBA, the Associação Internacional de Críticos de Arte (AICA-Portuguese Section), and the art departments of the FCG and its art magazine, *Colóquio Artes,* systematically reacted against change. Only later, and in an isolated fashion, did they accept and participate in the new developments.

Attempts were made to establish alternative exhibition centers and artists' associations, such as the Cooperativa Diferença (connected with Ernesto de Sousa) and Arco (established in 1973), both in Lisbon; along with these were journals, such as *Arte Opinião,* also based in Lisbon. One of the SNBA's exhibition centers (open only to members) held important, career-launching, exhibitions.

It was through an event in 1983, called *After Modernism,* involving the classic arts-architecture, fashion, dance, music and debate, that a break with the past occurred. *After Modernism* was organized by the SNBA, and promoted by artists who had been associated with *Alternativa Zero.* The event brought together artists with a variety of backgrounds. Indeed, it was this event that simultaneously launched and popularized concepts of, and debates on, post-modernism in Portugal. References to the "trans-vanguard," "bad painting," new expressionism and the "return to painting" proliferated.

The establishment of a proper national museum of modern and contemporary art, however, did not occur. After 25 April 1974, two official proposals for the creation of a museum, had emerged. One suggested using the Gallery of Modern Art in Lisbon, which later burned down; the other recommended the Contemporary Art Center in Oporto, where the few exhibitions of contemporary art had been held. In 1984, a private museum, annexed to the headquarters and historical museum of the FCG, was inaugurated. Unfortunately, the policy of the Centro de Arte Moderna for its first ten years was suspicious of contemporary art. The museum can be credited, nevertheless, with holding the first historical review of national modern art, exhibiting the works of Amadeo, Almada, António Pedro, Areal and Menez, among others. It was only in 1988 that the plan for the creation of a national museum of modern art was finalized in Oporto. The Oporto museum has held numerous exhibitions of recent artwork, both national and international. The establishment of the planned Serralves Foundation, involving the construction of a building by Siza Vieira, and its cultural policy is still to come.

The state's inability to elaborate a national art policy affected other areas. Participation in the Venice Biennale was abandoned in 1986 and taken up again only in 1995—a significant gap in time. The absence of the state placed the cultural initiative in the hands of the FCG, which organized the São Paulo *Bienale*. Indeed, until very recently, the FCG was the *de facto* ministry of culture. It should be noted nevertheless, that despite the incoherence of state policies, a department of the Ministry of Culture, the Direcção Geral de Acção Cultural, supported the few important initiatives of this period. Artists such as Fernando Calhau (until his death in 2002), Julião Sarmento, Cerveira Pinto and João Vieira worked in this department and its successors.

Participation in international art fairs was initiated with the Arco fair in Madrid. These fairs created the best opportunities to promote the international visibility of Portuguese art. Although the Quadrum and the Módulo galleries had been important in this regard since the 1970s, it was the Arco fair of 1984 that led to the internationalization of both the market and art criticism. The FIAT fair in Paris, as well as exhibitions in Zurich, Cologne, Los Angeles, London and Tokyo, were also important venues throughout the decade. The galleries themselves were very weak, even during the golden age of the market. They needed state and private support from the FCG and the Luso-American Development Foundation (FLAD) to bear the costs of exhibiting at these fairs.

In the 1980s, an anti-conceptualist reaction, the affirmation of a thematic subjectivity and an absolute individualism, as well as the almost exclusive practice of traditional disciplines, predominated. Nevertheless, post-conceptualism and subjectivism blended during this decade; the cause was the avalanche of international historical information received by Belas Artes students and the conceptual references of the transitional artists of the 1970s and 1980s—Leonel Moura, Cerveira Pinto and Sarmento. Apart from the gallery owner, Luis Serpa, all these artists were linked to the organization of the *After Modernism* exhibition.

At the beginning of their careers, artists consolidated in groups. These groups, however, did not generate programmatic and aesthetic unity; rather, they permitted unity of action and a unified provocative affirmation. From them emerged a tendency toward "deconstruction-construction," an explicit desire to deconstruct historical systems of representation and to reorganize them in a discursive, neo-romantic and demiurgic fashion. The exhibition, *Archipelago*, organized by the SNBA in 1986, brought together artists such as Cabrita Reis (born 1956), Pedro Calapez (born 1953), José Pedro Croft (born 1957) and Rui Sanches (born 1955), who gained international recognition in the 1990s.

Among the artists who emerged immediately after that, the visual dominated over the verbal. Their work was eclectic, textured, chromatic, spatial and decorative; alien to any literary language; and a register of absolutely private sensibilities. As a group, these artists had no

specific designation; among them were Ana Vidigal and Pedro
Casqueiro (born 1959). Other artists recovered literary values and
developed a satirical or purely playful deconstruction of references and
themes: the *homeostéticos* included artists such as Pedro Portugal (born
1963), Pedro Proença (born 1962) and Xana (born 1959). They were
ironic playful, and derisory; they explored language games.
Pedro Calapez depicted isolated everyday objects on a large scale.
Later he developed "uninhabited paintings," based on architectural
constructions or landscapes and the abrupt citation characteristic of
pre-Renaissance art of the mannerist style. Pedro Casqueiro's particular style distanced him from the abstract and the figurative alike,
creating a visual transcription of life experiences; speed and the
unexpected nature of artistic situations dominated his work. Pedro
Portugal produced ironic and playful works reminiscent of the great
masters of international modernist and Portuguese painting. He
portrayed a more circumstantial vision of national reality, reordering
each work into great puzzles that demand deciphering. Finally,
Pedro Proença, a great sketch artist, depicted literary or erudite figures that invaded surfaces organized like architectural structures,
using the complex ornamentation of baroque images to make erudite and satirical references.

It is also important to note some autonomous careers, which,
although lacking in public and commercial visibility, expressed a
strong capacity for invention. The painter, Ilda David (born 1955),
and the sculptor, Manuel Rosa (born 1953), are cases in point. They
worked on concepts of time and myth. The sculptor, Fernanda Fragateiro (born 1962), derided constructivist values and explored the
conflicts between nature, architecture, habitation and culture.

Artists from Oporto were less important during this period than
they had been in the 1960s and 1970s. They worked in relative critical and market isolation, broken only after the 1985 Bienal de
Cerveira, the activity at the Roma e Pavia Gallery (today the Pedro
Oliveira Gallery), the establishment of the Nasoni/Atlântica Gallery
in 1986, and the National Modern Art Museum project in 1988.
The Espaço Lusitano Gallery, which opened in 1982, and the *Os*

Novos Primitivos exhibition of 1984, commissioned by Bernando Pinto de Almeida, also linked these artists to the 1980s. Most of them came from the performing arts; examples include Gerardo Burmester (born 1955), whose work initially revisited German romanticism and gradually developed a demiurgic expression. Albuquerque Mendes (born 1955), on the other hand, used a multiplicity of styles, including a disarticulated, Dadaist narrative style. Pedro Tudela (born 1962) deployed themes and means that were truculent and typical of this decade.

Public and creative re-launching of sculpture was important in this period. This trend was reinforced by the most important artist of the decade, João Cutileiro, with whom António Campos Rosado (born 1955), Pedro Rosado and Manuel Rosa worked. Cutileiro's teaching produced a break with tradition because he worked stone mechanically rather than manually. His work, representing the body and its symbolic spatial sense, also represented a break with the foregoing conceptual trend.

Another sculptor, José Pedro Croft, reworked the symbolic sculptural forms of prehistory, ancient Egypt and the romantic period, which he piled up and fragmented. His work evolved toward the study of archaic, basic forms, using first stone, then plaster and later, painted bronze. He balanced contradictory volumes and objects, such as solid geometric forms, with everyday objects, exploring the complex ambiguities of mirror games.

After studying in the United Kingdom and the United States, Rui Sanches became a leading artist of the 1980s. He was influenced by classicism and rationalism, by the French classicists Poussin and David, as well as by constructivism. He developed three-dimensional structures that comment on and upset thematic and formal references with the use of fragile materials, such as chipboard or wood agglomerates; or white paint over noble materials, such as bronze. His work reflects on the state of art; it is formally contained and conceptually weighty.

A younger artist, Rui Chafes (born 1966), showed rare and strong Germanic roots; he expressed a spirit of radical romanticism centered on the body and its ghosts, and he created closed atmospheres using prostheses or torture objects. He also worked with untreated iron, either painted black or chromed, to accentuate the emptiness of artistic objects in relation to ideas. Xana's work lay between painting and sculpture, and represented purely visual values. He painted in strong colors, presenting bulky, ephemeral architectural structures and purely playful or decorative installations, which also comment on urban and domestic realities.

Drawing also developed during this period, in practical, critical, and commercial terms, and was exhibited in specialized galleries and exhibitions. The works of Bravo, Calapez and Sarmento at the beginning of the 1980s, as well as Sanches, Chafes and Gaetan, are particularly important. Gaetan (born 1954) made his face the near-exclusive motif of his work, and developed a notable series of self-portraits that use a variety of forms and techniques.

From the mid-1980s on, photography developed, adopting the values of the plastic arts. The nomadic vision of Paulo Nozolino (born 1956) centered on the history of photography. The inner journey of Jorge Molder (born 1959) was more akin to the work of other photographers who accentuate the plastic languages, such as Blaufuks, Valente Alves, Augusto Alves da Silva and Luis Campos. In the 1990s, Molder has used a large format and his own face and studio as models and background.

A shift in emigration destinations and motivations during this period, along with grants to study in Britain and the United States, benefited artists such as Rui Sanches. António and Pedro Campos Rosado, Manuel Botelho, João Penalva and Graça Pereira Coutinho all went to London; Manuel Castro Caldas, Martim Avilez, Paulo Feliciano, Miguel Angelo Rocha and Pedro Sousa Vieira studied in New York. Institutional grant support from the FLAD and the Ernesto Sousa Foundation reinforced this trend. In terms of international success, Chafes, Sanches, Croft and Proença are important; they participated in the Venice Biennale of 1980. Calapez is also notable in this regard, as are José de Guimarães, Julião Sarmento and Cabrita Reis, who moved within stronger, albeit more disparate, circles.

José de Guimarães (born 1949) crossed African art themes with Western art. From the 1970s on, his work followed the work of Allan Davie and pop art. He is the best known of the group that studied abroad, for his art has been shown in Japan, Belgium and Italy. He is also the least avant-garde. Julião Sarmento is the very embodiment of tenacity in building a US and European fame. He has used the body as his theme since the 1970s. Sarmento is one of the most interesting of the post-conceptualists, invoking images of film culture, photography, American erotica and police fiction, and an attitude of permanent voyeurism toward the female figure, sex, violence and pleasure.

Cabrita Reis evolved from painter to sculptor and, later, to maker of installation art. His work established a strong constructive framework, which was then refined and monumentalized. He depicted powerful symbols and metaphors with poor, light-colored materials, including communicating structures such as chipboard, plaster, cloth, glass and electrical or plumbing materials; elements of an arcane memory in a Mediterranean climate.

The international careers of these artists reflect the radical lack of synchronicity at home between official art promotion policies and individual artists. Michael Biberstein (born 1946), a Swiss-American artist residing in Portugal since the 1980s, and completely part of the Portuguese art world, adds an element of internationalism to the national scene. The difference between the "romantic" landscapes painted in Portugal and those painted in Switzerland is obvious; the thinking that accompanies these paintings has been decisive for national artistic life. Finally, the works of Dacosta, Rego, Rodrigo, Ângelo, Carneiro, Lapa, Bravo and Batarda were re-launched in the 1980s.

The Present

Since the 1980s, latent crisis has once again become explicit through national and international political, economic and social changes: the breakdown of the Soviet Union, the fall of the Berlin Wall, the civil strife in Bosnia, the Gulf War, the spread of AIDS and the rampant hunger and genocide in Africa.

The artwork developed in this context has been characterized by a return to values rejected in the 1980s, which have been approached from a new perspective. The pomp and festivity of the 1980s are still disdained, and a reflection on the relationship between the creator, the work, the viewer and the market, as well as critical consecration, has developed. The collapse of the market has facilitated this anti-market vision. In addition, there is a desire to overcome the political utopias of the conceptualists of the 1970s.

International thinking and internationally oriented art center on the notion of the final stage of capitalism, the "spectacle society." They also re-evaluate feminist discourse, exploring the body in mutation, AIDS, nationalism and war, along with communication technologies and the recovery of non-visual artistic languages. In Portugal, however, the debate is incomplete, as though the evolution of Portuguese society itself did not permit a natural relationship with these phenomena. This trend is akin to what has occurred in relation to pop and conceptual art. On the one hand, some artists of the 1970s and 1980s have incorporated these elements into their work. On the other hand, radical and intense power games continue to develop over the control of the few and fragile cultural institutions in existence.

This struggle divides the artists of the 1980s generation. Cerveira Pinto, who writes in the weekly, O Independente, and Leonel Moura have set out on a separate course. In the 1980s, Moura altered his conceptualist career with an intense and militant "return to painting" based on primitive and strongly textured paintings. He has gone on to use ready-made images from other media, such as photography, or images of other artists with iconographic value nationally (the fado singer, Amália, King Sebastian or the poet, Pessoa) or internationally (Kant or Wittgenstein), over which he superimposes key words such as "Portugal", "Yes" and "Europe". Other artists have tried to develop a new understanding of their own work through post-conceptualism, language and irony games, constructivist references or a philosophical discourse.

At the same time new names emerge, who use their work as a true instrument for ideological rupture; one example is João Paulo

Feliciano (born 1963). Feliciano evolved from the metaphorical use of objects and recycled materials toward the construction of works based on a critical discourse that pokes fun at the relationship between art and money, art and society, and the inner creative process. His relationship with rock music as a band leader is essential to his work. A group linked to the Zero Gallery, which opened in Algés in 1990 (closing soon after), and to the review *ArtStrike*, includes Paulo Mendes (who became an important organizer of collective exhibitions) and Rui Serra. New artists in Oporto, such as André Magalhães, Fernando José Pereira and Cristina Mateus, use installation art, video and even painting to comment on society. Other independent careers of importance are those of Miguel Ângelo Rocha, Miguel Soares and Francisco Tropa.

The crisis of the 1990s has not provoked the disaster of the 1970s, which proves that the art world in Portugal has gained strength. Interest in art has not declined; on the contrary, new private schools have opened and new publications have emerged. Galleries going bankrupt have been few and far between. Some galleries emerged after the earlier crisis and have maintained their leadership position. Such is the case of the Alda Cortez and Graça Fonseca galleries, both of which opened in Lisbon in 1989. These galleries are in some ways, moreover, mouthpieces for the artists.

A declining art trade, nevertheless, has led to the dispersion of initiatives through a variety of alternative centers, be they in the capital or the provinces. These centers take advantage of buildings that might be available, ranging from ruins to structures recovered by private institutions or municipalities. Examples are the Sala do Veado in the Museum of Natural History; the Mitra and Galveias galleries in Lisbon; the Alfândega in Oporto; the reactivated Center for Plastic Arts in Coimbra; other facilities in Beja, Lagos and Faro and, more recently, Vila Velha de Ródão and Almada (with an art center that is dedicated to design).

On the other hand, more regular alternative events have also begun, such as Arte Pública in Lisbon (1991-94) and the Jornadas de Arte Contemporânea in Oporto (1993-95). The government and the large financial organizations have taken advantage of the break-down of private initiative to rethink their connection with and use of art in a more strategic way, as a means to rework their image. International events that have helped secure those links include *Europália* in Belgium (1992) and Lisbon, Cultural Capital in Lisbon (1994); the return to the Venice Biennale since 1995 (with Sarmento, Molder, João Penalva and Cabrita Reis in 2003); the reorganization of some museum spaces in Lisbon, such as the Museu do Chiado (whose director subverted the eighteenth century nature of the museum by introducing a more international vanguardist style); the continuation (although within low budgets) of the Centro Cultural de Belém's activities (1994-), which has incorporated exhibitions of design, photography and retrospectives of both national and international artists; the creation of a new cultural center, Culturgest, belonging to the largest public bank, the Caixa Geral de Depósitos, which expanded by opening a center in Oporto in 2002; the organization and consolidation of a collection by the FLAD presenting a coherent vision of the 1970s and 1980s in Portugal; the emergence of a large private collection, the Berardo, devoted exclusively to postwar international art and now, with a public museum close to Lisbon—the Sintra Museum of Modern Art-Berardo Collection—providing a new stimulus for internal creativity (with the launch in 2000 of the EDP prizes for painting, design and new and established artists). There is now a proliferation of exhibition space (the Zé dos Bois Gallery in Lisbon; Lugar-Comum in Oeiras; Maus Hábitos in Oporto, and many more), of multi-thematic and multi-disciplinary exhibition groups; the substitution of the decadence of intervention of general publications in the area of criticism by new publications, which are often ephemeral and marginal, that are associated with the universities or with groups of young artists and publishers (e.g. *Mimésis*)—publications that cover themes such as socio-politics, artistic urban-architectonics and design, or the collected publications on national or international authors.

This is the recent record of Portuguese art in which the financial crisis that was inherited from the recent socialist governments (1995-

2002), and which has been used by the present right-wing coalition government to justify a series of swingeing budget cuts in the areas of science, education and culture (the Ministry of Culture's budget has been cut by 6 per cent), and which are now jeopardizing, irreversibly, the previous government's acquisition policy. With the prospect of the IAC being transformed into a more generic institute, the expansion and consolidation of the support given to Portuguese artists on the international stage, the enhancement of decentralizing initiatives (for example, the proposed art centers in Aveiro and Tavira) and the acquisition of works of art for the national collections are now under threat.

Throughout the last one hundred years, a very strong current of individual artistic values has characterized Portuguese art. Yet Portugal has come to the end of the century without witnessing any change in the negative factors that have historically conditioned the nation's cultural and artistic life: the absence of an autonomous civil society and the art world's dependence on official protection, which, in turn, demonstrates artists' continuing difficulty in achieving national and international prominence.

It seems that Portugal has arrived at a turning point. The global re-evaluation of relations between identity and cultural cosmopolitanism, and the revitalization of the cultural agents in Portuguese society, are both taking place. It is a turning point of expansion and recognition. In this context, the specific characteristics of Portuguese art, and the atomized character of its creators, may gain an international dimension. In other words, the individual nature of Portuguese art production may eventually be integrated into the world's various art networks.

Notes

NOTES TO CHAPTER 1

1 A. C. Pinto and X. M. Nuñes, "Portugal and Spain," in R. Eatwell (ed.), *European political culture: conflict or convergence?* (London: Routledge, 1997), 172-92.

2 N. S. Teixeira, *O ultimatum inglês: política externa e política interna no Portugal de 1890* (Lisbon: Alfa, 1990).

3 H. Martins, "Portugal," in M. S. Archer and S. Giner (eds.), *Contemporary Europe: class, status and power* (London: Weidenfeld and Nicolson, 1971), 63.

4 P. Lains, *L'économie portugaise au XIXe siècle: croissance économique et commerce extérieur 1851-1913* (Paris: L'Harmatan, 1999); K. Schwartzman, *The social origins of democratic collapse: the First Portuguese Republic in the global economy* (Lawrence, KS: University Press of Kansas, 1989).

5 J. Reis, *O atraso económico português numa perspectiva histórica* (Lisbon: Imprensa Nacional, 1993).

6 This is an estimate, as the 1930 census transferred a large part of the primary sector to the tertiary sector.

7 P. T. de Almeida, *Eleições e caciquismo no Portugal oitocentista (1868-1890)* (Lisbon: DIFEL, 1991).

8 N. P. Mouzelis, *Politics in the semi-periphery: early parliamentarism and late industrialization in the Balkans and Latin America* (New York, NY: St. Martin's Press, 1986).

9 D. L. Wheeler, *Republican Portugal: a political history, 1910-1926* (Madison, WI: University of Wisconsin Press, 1978), 32-47.

10 H. Martins, "The breakdown of the Portuguese democratic republic," paper prepared for the VII World Congress of Sociology, Varna (1970), 6.

11 For an overview of the First Republic as a 'revolutionary' regime, see R. Ramos, *A segunda fundação*, volume 6 of J. Mattoso (ed.), *História de Portugal* (Lisbon: Estampa, 2002).

12 M. Dogan, "Romania, 1919-1938," in M. Weiner and E. Ozbudum (eds.), *Competitive elections and developing studies* (Durham, MA: Duke University Press, 1987), 369-89. According to Dogan's 'ideal type,' a 'mimic democracy' is 'a political system that imitates Western competitive democracy' and is 'likely to appear in societies with low degrees of urbanization and

industrialization,' with a strong 'landed gentry' and 'an immense majority of the population' being rural.

13 F. F. Lopes, *Poder político e caciquismo na Primeira República* (Lisbon: Estampa, 1994), 76.

14 Martins, "Breakdown," 8.

15 Ibid., 6.

16 Ibid.

17 M. F. Mónica, *O movimento socialista em Portugal (1875-1934)* (Lisbon: IED, 1985).

18 Schwartzman, *Social origins.*

19 Ibid., 132.

20 Ibid., 125.

21 V. P. Valente, "Revoluções: a 'República Velha'? (ensaio de interpretação política)," *Análise Social*, 115 (27) (1992), 7-63.

22 N. S. Teixeira, *O poder e a guerra: objectivos nacionais e estratégias políticas em Portugal, 1914-18* (Lisbon: Estampa, 1996).

23 F. R. de Meneses, *União Sagrada e Sidonismo: Portugal em guerra, 1916-1918* (Lisbon: Cosmos, 2000).

24 N. S. Teixeira, "A fome e a saudade: os prisoneiros portugueses na grande guerra," *Penélope*, 8 (1992), 91-114.

25 M. A. Samara, *Verdes e vermelhos: Portugal e a guerra no ano de Sidónio Pais* (Lisbon: Editorial Notícias, 2003).

26 For an excellent local study, see M. Baiôa, *Elites políticas em Évora: da I República à Ditadura Militar (1925-1926)* (Lisbon: Cosmos, 2000).

27 It is worth mentioning that the Communist Party, born of a split from anarcho-syndicalism, and very 'working class' based in terms of its first elites, played a very insignificant role in the final crisis of the Republic.

28 Schwartzman, *Social origins*, 184.

29 A. C. Pinto, "Portugal: crisis and early authoritarian takeover," in D. Berg-Schlosser and J. Mitchell (eds.), *The conditions of democracy in Europe, 1919-1939* (London: Macmillan, 2000).

30 J. M. Ferreira, *O comportamento político dos militares: forças armadas e regimes políticos em Portugal no século XX* (Lisbon: Estampa, 1992).

31 Wheeler, *Republican Portugal*, 193.

32 Ibid., 181.

33 Ibid., 185.

34 A. C. Pinto, *The Blueshirts: Portuguese fascism in interwar Europe* (New York, NY: SSM-Columbia University Press, 2000).

35 H. Martins, "Portugal," in S. Woolf (ed.), *European fascism* (New York, NY: Random House, 1969).

36 J. P. Rebelo, *Pela dedução à monarquia* (Lisbon: Gama, 1945), 74.

37 J. J. Linz and A. Stepan (eds.), *The breakdown of democratic regimes* (Baltimore, MA: Johns Hopkins University Press, 1978), 82; M. Tarchi, "The role of fascist (and similar) movements," in D. Berg-Schlosser and J. Mitchell (eds.), *Authoritarianism and democracy in Europe, 1919-39: comparative analyses* (London: Macmillan, 2002).

38 Ibid.

39 M. Blinkhorn (ed.), *Fascists and conservatives: the radical right and the establishment in twentieth-century Europe* (London: Routledge, 1990), 13.

40 J. J. Linz, "Political space and fascism as a late-comer," in S. U. Larsen et al. (eds.), *Who were the fascists? Social roots of European fascism* (Bergen: Universitäts Forlaget, 1980), 153-89.

41 Ibid., 164.

42 L. Farinha, *O Reviralho: revoltas republicanas contra a Ditadura e o Estado Novo, 1926-1940* (Lisbon: Estampa, 1998).

43 M. Braga da Cruz, *O partido e o estado no salazarismo* (Lisbon: Presença, 1988).

44 J. P. Pereira, *Álvaro Cunhal: uma biografia política*, vol. 1 (Lisbon: Temas e Debates, 2000).

45 A. C. Pinto, *Salazar's dictatorship and European fascism: problems of interpretation* (New York, NY: SSM-Columbia University Press, 1995).

46 A. C. Pinto (ed.), *Os presidentes da República Portuguesa* (Lisbon: Temas e Debates, 2000).

47 T. Faria, *Debaixo de fogo: Salazar e as forças armadas, 1933-1947* (Lisbon: Cosmos, 2001).

48 Ferreira, *O comportamento*, 175-202.

49 Carrilho, *Forças armadas*, 422.

50 F. Nogueira, *Salazar*, 6 vols. (Coimbra: Atlântida, 1977-85).

51 For the 1930s, see A. O. Salazar, *Discursos e notas políticas*, vol. 1 (Coimbra: Coimbra Editora, 1935).

52 J. J. Linz, "Totalitarian and authoritarian regimes," in F. Greenstein and N. Polsby (eds.), *Handbook of political science*, vol. 3 (Reading, MA: Addison-Wesley, 1975).

53 J. L. Gómez Navarro, *El regimen de Primo de Rivera* (Madrid: Cátedra, 1991).

54 S. G. Payne, *A history of fascism* (Madison, WI: University of Wisconsin Press, 1996).

55 R. Chueca, *El fascismo en los comienzos del régimen de Franco: un estudio sobre la FET-JONS* (Madrid: CES, 1983), 166; S. G. Payne, *Fascism in Spain, 1923-1977* (Madison, WI: University of Wisconsin Press, 1999).

56 Circular from the Minister of the Interior to the presidents of the UN District Commissions (29 December 1931), Folder 452, Box 5, Arquivo Geral do Ministério do Interior (AGMI)/Arquivo Nacional da Torre do Tombo (ANTT).

57 AOS/CO/PC-4, Arquivo Oliveira Salazar (AOS)/ANTT.

58 Cf. Braga da Cruz, *O partido*, 140.

59 P. T. de Almeida and A. C. Pinto, "Portuguese ministers, 1851-1999: social background and paths to power," in P. T. de Almeida, A. C. Pinto and N. Bermeo (eds.), *Who governs southern Europe? Regime change and ministerial recruitment, 1850-2000* (London: Frank Cass, 2003).

60 P. C. Schmitter, *Do autoritarismo à democracia* (Lisbon: Instituto de Ciências Sociais, 1999).

61 P. J. Williamson, *Corporatism in perspective: an introductory guide to corporatist theory* (London: Sage, 1989).

62 F. Patriarca, *A política social do salazarismo* (Lisbon: Imprensa Nacional, 1995).

63 J. C. Valente, *Estado Novo e alegria no trabalho: uma história política da FNAT (1935-1958)* (Lisbon: Colibri, 1999).

64 F. Rosas, *O Estado Novo nos anos trinta* (Lisbon: Estampa, 1986).

65 A. C. Pinto and N. A. Ribeiro, *A Acção Escolar Vanguarda (1933-1936)* (Lisbon: História Crítica, 1980).

66 L. N. Rodrigues, *A Legião Portuguesa* (Lisbon: Estampa, 1996).

67 S. Kuin, "A Mocidade Portuguesa nos anos trinta: anteprojectos e instauração de uma organização paramilitar de juventude," *Análise Social*, 122 (28) (1993), 155-88.

68 Rodrigues, *Legião*, 10.

69 A Portela, *Salazarismo e artes plásticas* (Lisbon: Bertrand, 1982); J. R. do Ó, "Salazarismo e cultura," in J. Serrão and A. H. Oliveira Marques (eds.), *Nova história de Portugal*, vol. 12 of F. Rosas (co-ord.), *Portugal e o Estado Novo* (Lisbon: Presença, 1992), 381-454; J. R. de Ó, *Os anos de Ferro: o dispositivo cultural durante a 'Política do Espírito'* (Lisbon: Estampa, 1999).

70 See chapter 2 for a detailed description of the reinvention of tradition. See chapter 11 for more on Ferro's recruitment of artists.

71 Salazar, *Discursos*, 259.

72 Cf. A. Caldeira, "Heróis e vilões na mitologia salazarista," *Penélope*, 15 (1995), 121-39.

73 For more on the women's organizations, see A. Cova and A. C. Pinto, "Women under Salazar's dictatorship," *Portuguese Journal of Social Science*, 1 (2) (2002), 129-46.

74 M. Braga da Cruz, "As relações entre o estado e a igreja," in Serrão and Oliveira Marques, *Nova história*, 211.

75 Ibid.

76 M. I. Rezola, "Breve panorama da situação da igreja católica em Portugal, 1930-1960," in Serrão and Oliveira Marques, *Nova história*, 238.

77 J. Barreto, *Religião e sociedade: dois ensaios* (Lisbon: Instituto de Ciências Sociais, 2002), 157-60.

78 Cf. J. Medina, *Salazar em França* (Lisbon: Bertrand, 1977), 50.

79 A. C. Pinto, "Elites, single parties and political decision-making in fascist-era dictatorships," *Contemporary European History*, 11 (3) (2002), 429-54.

80 S. G. Payne, "Authoritarianism in the smaller states of southern Europe," in H. E. Chehabi and A. Stepan (eds.), *Politics, society and democracy: comparative studies. Essays in honor of Juan J. Linz* (Boulder, CO: Westview Press, 1995).

81 N. S. Teixeira, *From neutrality to alignment: Portugal in the foundation of the Atlantic Pact* (Florence: European University Institute Working Paper HEC 9/91, 1991).

82 G. Clarence-Smith, *The Third Portuguese Empire, 1825-1975: a study in economic imperialism* (Manchester: Manchester University Press, 1985), 194-5; P. Lains, "Causas do colonialismo português em África, 1822-1975," *Análise Social*, 146-147 (33) (1998), 488-93.

83 Clarence-Smith, *Portuguese Empire*, 196.

84 Ibid., 193.

85 D. Corkill, *The Portuguese economy since 1947* (Edinburgh: Edinburgh University Press, 1993), 16.

86 J. M. Maravall, *Regimes, politics and markets: democratization and economic change in southern and eastern Europe* (Oxford: Oxford University Press, 1997).

87 See chapter 6.

88 J. P. Cann, *Counterinsurgency in Africa: the Portuguese way of war, 1961-1974* (Westport, VA: Greenwood Press, 1997).

89 A. J. Telo, "Portugal, 1958-1974: a sociedade em mudança," in H. de la Torre Gómez (ed.), *Portugal y España en el cambio político (1958-1978)* (Mérida: Universidad Nacional de Educación a Distancia, 1989), 88.

90 K. Maxwell, *The making of Portuguese democracy* (Cambridge: Cambridge University Press, 1995); A. C. Pinto, *O fim do Império Português: a cena internacional, a guerra colonial e a descolonização, 1961-1975* (Lisbon: Horizonte, 2001).

NOTES TO CHAPTER 2

1 While there is an extensive bibliography on the formation of Portugal's national consciousness, the existence of which is not in question, we are questioning the forms in which it has manifested itself.

2 J. Mattoso, *Identificação de um país: ensaio sobre as origens de Portugal, 1096-1325*, vol. 2 (Lisbon: Estampa, 1985), 211. The author has recently expanded on his reflections on this particular theme in J. Mattoso, *A identidade nacional* (Lisbon: Gradiva, 1998).

3 J. Revel, *A invenção da sociedade* (Lisbon: Difel, 1990), 192.

4 F. Bethencourt, *História das inquisições: Portugal, Espanha e Itália* (Lisbon: Círculo de Leitores, 1995).

5 A. C. Silva and A. M. Hespanha, "A identidade portuguesa," in J. Mattoso (ed.) *História de Portugal: o antigo regime (1620-1807)* (Lisbon: Estampa, 1994). See also F. Bethencourt, "Sociogénese do sentimento nacional," in F. Bethencourt and D. R. Curto (eds.) *A memória da nação: colóquio do Gabinete de Estudos de Simbologia realizado na Fundação Calouste Gulbenkian, 7-9 outubro, 1987* (Lisbon: Sá da Costa, 1991).

6 See K. Maxwell, *Pombal: paradox of the Enlightenment* (Cambridge: Cambridge University Press, 1995).

7 See J. M. Sobral, "A formação das nações e o nacionalismo: os paradigmas explicativos e o caso português," *Análise Social*, 37 (165) (2003), 1109, and, especially, J. M. Sobral, "Nações e o nacionalismo: algumas teorias recentes sobre a sua génese e persistência na Europa Ocidental e o caso português," *Inforgeo*, 11 (1996), 13-41.

8 Contrary to what happened in Spain, the anti-liberal conservative forces dominated this movement.

9 V. Alexandre, *Os sentidos do império: questão nacional e questão colonial na crise do antigo regime português* (Oporto: Afrontamento, 1993).

10 M. A. Lousada, "Nacionalismo e contra-revolução em Portugal: o episódio miguelista," *Luso-Brazilian Review*, 29 (1992), 63-70.

11 See M. de F. Bonifácio, *Seis estudos sobre o liberalismo português* (Lisbon: Estampa, 1991). On the pretext of policing slave trafficking, Britain continuously oversaw Portugal's African territories, see V. Alexandre, "Portugal e a abolição do tráfego de escravos (1834-1851)," *Análise Social*, 26 (111) (1991), 293-333.

12 R. Ramos, "A segunda fundação (1890-1926)," in J. Mattoso (ed.), *História de Portugal*, vol. 4 (Lisbon: Estampa, 1994), 30-8.

13 Ibid., 65.

14 L. R. Torgal, "A restauração nas ideologias e na historia," in *História e ideologia* (Coimbra: Livraria Minerva, 1989), 43.

15 Ramos, "A segunda fundação"; R. Ramos, "A formação da *intelligentsia* portuguesa (1860-1880)," *Análise Social*, 27 (116-17) (1992), 483-528.

16 N. S. Teixeira, *O ultimatum inglês: política externa e política interna no Portugal de 1890* (Lisbon: Alfa, 1990).

17 See A. Cabral, *Notas oitocentistas* (Lisbon: Portugália, 1973).

18 T. Braga, *Os centenários como síntese afectiva nas sociedades modernas* (Oporto: A. J. da Silva Teixeira, 1884), 227.

19 Cf. Ramos, "A segunda fundação," 65.

20 Ibid., 5-20.

21 See J. Leal, *Etnografia Portuguesa (1870-1970): cultura popular e identidade nacional* (Lisbon: Dom Quixote, 2000).

22 See J. Reis, *O atraso económico português, 1850-1930* (Lisbon: ICS/INCM, 1993), 227-53.

23 P. T. de Almeida, *Eleições e caciquismo no Portugal oitocentista (1868-1890)* (Lisbon: Difel, 1991).

24 See F. Catroga, *O republicanismo em Portugal: da formação ao 5 de Outubro de 1910*, 2nd ed. (Lisbon: Notícias, 2000).

25 N. S. Teixeira, *O poder e a guerra, 1914-1918* (Lisbon: Estampa, 1996).

26 S. C. Matos, *História, mitologia, imaginário nacional: a história no curso dos liceus (1885-1939)* (Lisbon: Horizonte, 1990).

27 N. S. Teixeira, "Do azul e branco ao verde rubro: a simbólica da bandeira nacional," in Bethencourt and Curto, *A memória da nação*, 335.

28 Ibid., 337.

29 A. C. Pinto, *Salazar's dictatorship and European fascism: problems of interpretation* (New York, NY: SSM-Columbia University Press, 1995).

30 F. M. da Costa, "Imaginário histórico, imaginário político," *Nação e Defesa*, 46 (April-June 1988), 11.

31 On this topic, see R. W. Sousa, *The rediscoverers: major writers in the Portuguese literature of national regeneration* (University Park, PA: Pennsylvania State University Press, 1981).

32 V. Alexandre, *Velho Brasil, novas Áfricas: Portugal e o Império, 1808-1975* (Oporto: Afrontamento, 2000).

33 A. Vakil, "Representations of the 'Discoveries' and the imaginary of the nation in Portuguese Integralism," *Portuguese Studies*, II (1995), 133-167.

34 D. de Melo, *Salazarismo e cultura Popular, 1933-1958* (Lisbon: Instituto de Ciências Sociais, 2001).

35 J. P. de Brito, "O Estado Novo e a aldeia mais portuguesa de Portugal," in *O fascismo em Portugal* (Lisbon: A Regra do Jogo, 1992), 508; see also Melo, *Salazarismo e cultura popular*.

36 M. F. Mónica, *Educação e sociedade no Portugal de Salazar* (Lisbon: Presença, 1978), 303.

37 J. R. do Ó, "Modernidade e tradição: algumas reflexões em torno da Exposição do Mundo Português," in *O Estado Novo: das origens ao fim da autarcia, 1926-1956* (Lisbon: Fragmentos, 1987), 177-85.

38 A. J. Telo, "Portugal, 1958-1974: sociedade em mudança," in H. de la Torre Gomez (ed.), *Portugal y Espana en el cambio politico (1958-1978)* (Mérida: Universidad National de Educación a Distancia, 1989), 74.

39 Urban is defined here as population centers with more than 10,000 inhabitants.

40 See K. Maxwell, *The making of Portuguese democracy* (Cambridge: Cambridge University Press, 1995); S. Lloyd-Jones and A. C. Pinto (eds.), *The last empire: thirty years of Portuguese decolonization* (Bristol: Intellect, 2003).

41 See A. C. Pinto and N. S. Teixeira (eds.), *Southern Europe and the making of the European Union* (New York, NY: SSM-Columbia University Press, 2002).

42 A. C. Pinto and X. M. Nuñes, "Portugal and Spain," in R. Eatwell (ed.), *European political cultures: conflict or convergence?* (London: Routledge, 1997), 172-92.

43 A. C. Pinto, "The radical right in contemporary Portugal," in L. Cheles (ed.), *The far right in Western Europe* (London and New York: Longman, 1995), 108-28.

44 See A. C. Pinto and N. S. Teixeira, "From Africa to Europe: Portugal and European Integration," in Pinto and Teixeira, *Southern Europe*, 38.

45 M. Bacalhau, *Atitudes, opiniões e comportamentos políticos dos Portugueses: 1973-1993* (Lisbon: FLAD, 1994), 255.

46 Ibid., 257.

47 V. Pérez-Dias, *The return of civil society: the emergence of democratic Spain* (Cambrige MA: Harvard University Press, 1993), 3.

48 A. C. Pinto and M. C. Lobo, "Forging a positive but instrumental view: Portuguese attitudes towards the EU, 1986-2002," in A. Dulphy and C. Maginand (eds.), *Public opinion and Europe: national identity in European perspective* (Paris: Peter Lang, 2003).

NOTES TO CHAPTER 3

1 E. da Costa, *Estudo sobre a administração civil das nossas possessões africanas* (Lisbon: Imprensa Nacional, 1903), 8-13, 37-39, and 57-86.

2 R. Pélissier, *História das campanhas de Angola* (Lisbon: Estampa, 1986), vol. 1, 294; vol. 2, 79.

3 M. Newitt, *Portugal in Africa: the last hundred years* (London: C. Hurst, 1981), 61.

4 R. Pélissier, *História de Moçambique* (Lisbon: Estampa, 1987), vol. 1, 205-7; vol. 2, 278-83.

5 Pélissier, *História das campanhas de Angola*, vol. 1, 233-35; vol. 2, 234-50; Pélissier, *História de Moçambique*, vol. 1, 211-2.

6 N. de Matos, *A província de Angola* (Oporto: Maranus, 1926), 15, 262.

7 See Decree Law 77 (9 December 1921).

8 Matos, *A província*, 117.

9 Ibid., 42.

10 Decree Laws 40 and 41 (3 August 1921).

11 Matos, *A província*, 305-11.

12 For the latter two acts, see Decree Laws 23.228 and 23.229 (15 November 1933).

13 Organic Charter of the Portuguese Colonial Empire (*Carta orgánica*), articles 227 and 228.

14 Decree Law 27.552 (5 March 1937), cf. J. P. Leite, *La formation de l'économie coloniale au Mozambique* (Paris: École des Hautes Etudes en Sciences Sociales, 1989), 192.

15 G. Clarence-Smith, *The Third Portuguese Empire, 1825-1975* (Manchester: Manchester University Press, 1985), Appendix 3, Figures 1 and 2.

16 Ibid., 150-51; Appendix 3; F. Rosas, *O Estado Novo nos anos trinta, 1928-1938* (Lisbon: Estampa, 1986), 141-2.

17 Rosas, *O Estado Novo*, 158-9.

18 Ibid., 143.

19 F. R. Salgado, *A evolução do comércio especial ultramarino* (Lisbon: AGC, 1939), Map 44.

20 L. Vail and L. White, *Capitalism and colonialism in Mozambique* (London: Heinemann, 1980), 272.

21 F. Rosas, *Portugal entre a paz e a guerra, 1939-1945* (Lisbon: Estampa, 1990), 239.

22 Ibid., 265-7

23 F. Rosas, *O Estado Novo (1926-1974)*, vol. 7 of J. Mattoso (ed.), *História de Portugal* (Lisbon: Círculo de Leitores, 1994), 489.

24 P. Leite, *Formation de l'économie coloniale*, 298.

25 E. Rocha, "Portugal, anos 60: crescimento económico e relações com as colónias," *Análise Social*, 13 (51) (1977), 593-617.

26 Measures taken by Marcelo Caetano compiled in *Providências legislativas* (Lisbon: AGC, 1945).

27 G. Freire, *Masters and the slaves*, (New York, NY: Alfred A. Knopf, 1946).

28 Decree Law 43.896 (9 June 1961).

29 Decree Law 43.730 (12 June 1961); Law 2.119 (24 June 1963).

NOTES TO CHAPTER 4

1 M. Caetano, *Portugal e a internacionalização dos problemas africanos: história duma batalha—da liberdade dos mares às Nações Unidas* (Lisbon: Bertrand, 1971); V. Alexandre, *Origens do colonialismo português moderno, 1822-1891* (Lisbon: Sá da Costa, 1979); N. S. Teixeira, "Colónias e colonialismo português na cena internacional," in F. Bethencourt and K. Chauduri (eds.), *História da expansão portuguesa: do Brasil para África*, volume 4 (Lisbon: Círculo de Leitores, 1998).

2 N. S. Teixeira, *O Ultimatum inglês: política externa e política interna no Portugal de 1890* (Lisbon: Alfa, 1990); V. Alexandre, chapter 2.

3 G. M. Guevara, *As relações lusa-alemãs antes da Primeira Guerra Mundial: a questão da concessão dos sanatórios da Ilha da Madeira* (Lisbon: Colibri, 1997); A. J. Telo, *Os Açores e o controlo do Atlântico, 1898-1948* (Oporto: Asa, 1993).

4 R. Langhorne, "Anglo-German negotiation concerning the future of the Portuguese Colonies," *The Historical Journal*, 2 (1973), 361-87; J. Willequet, "Anglo-German rivalry in Belgian and Portuguese Africa," in P. Gifford and Wm. Roger Louis (eds.), *Britain and Germany in Africa: imperial rivalry and colonial rule* (London: Yale University Press, 1967), 245-73.

5 F. Costa, *Portugal e a Guerra Anglo-Boer: política externa e opinião pública (1899-1902)* (Lisbon: Cosmos, 1998).

6 J. D. Vincent-Smith, *As relações políticas luso-britânicas (1910-1916)* (Lisbon: Horizonte, 1975); J. Derou, *Les relations franco-portugaises à l'époque de la première République parlementaire libérale, 5 octobre 1910-28 mai 1926* (Paris: Publications de la Sorbonne, 1986).

7 H. de la Torre Gómez, *Conspiração contra Portugal (1910-1912): as relações políticas entre Portugal e Espanha* (Lisbon: Horizonte, 1978).

8 F. Martins (ed.), *Portugal na Grande Guerra*, 2 vols. (Lisbon: Atica, 1934 and 1935).

9 H. de la Torre Gómez, *Antagonismo y fractura peninsular: España-Portugal 1910-1919* (Madrid: Espasa-Calpe, 1983); H. de la Torre Gómez, *Do perigo espanhol à amizade peninsular: Portugal-Espanha, 1919-1930* (Lisbon: Estampa, 1985); J. M. Ferreira, "Revisão histórica da participação de Portugal na Primeira Guerra," in J. M. Ferreira (ed.), *Portugal em transe: notas de política internacional e política de defesa* (Aveiro: Pandora, 1985).

10 N. S. Teixeira, *L'entrée du Portugal dans la Grande Guerre: objectifs nationaux et stratégies politiques* (Paris: Economica/ISC, 1998).

11 J. M. Ferreira, *Portugal na Conferência da Paz: Paris 1919* (Lisbon: Quetzal, 1992).

12 F. Rosas, *O salazarismo e a Aliança luso-britânica: estudos sobre a política externa do Estado Novo nos anos 30 a 40* (Lisbon: Fragmentos, 1988).

13 C. Oliveira, *Portugal y la segunda Republica Española, 1931-1936* (Madrid: Ediciones Cultura Hispanica, Instituto de Cooperación Iberoamericano, 1987); H. de la Torre Gómez, *La relacion peninsular en la antecámara de la guerra civil de España 1931-1936* (Merida: Universidad Nacional de Educación a Distancia, 1987).

14 I. Delgado, *Portugal e a guerra civil de Espanha* (Mem-Martins: Europa-América, 1980); C. Oliveira, *Salazar e a Guerra Civil de Espanha* (Lisbon: O Jornal, 1987).

15 M. Carrilho et al., *Portugal na Segunda Guerra Mundial: contributos para uma reavaliação* (Lisbon: Dom Quixote, 1989); F. Rosas, *Portugal entre a paz e a guerra: estudo do impacte da II Guerra Mundial na economia e na sociedade portuguesa (1939-1945)* (Lisbon: Estampa, 1990); A. J. Telo, *Portugal na segunda guerra, 1941-45*, 2 vols, (Lisbon: Vega, 1991); G. Stone, *The oldest ally: Britain and the Portuguese connection, 1936-1941* (London: Boydell 1994).

16 H. Janeiro, *Salazar e Pétain: as relações luso-francesas durante a Segunda Guerra Mundial, 1940-1944* (Lisbon: Cosmos, 1998).

17 F. Rolo, *Portugal e o plano Marshall: da rejeição à solicitação de ajuda financeira norte-americana, 1947-1952* (Lisbon: Estampa, 1994).

18 N. S. Teixeira, *From neutrality to alignment: Portugal in the foundation of the Atlantic pact* (Florence: European University Institute, 1991); A. J. Telo, *Portugal e NATO: o reencontro da tradição atlântica* (Lisbon: Cosmos, 1996).

19 A. E. D. Silva, "O litígio entre Portugal e a ONU 1960-1974," *Análise Social*, 30 (130) (1995), 5-50; F. Martins, "A política externa do Estado Novo: o Ultramar e a ONU 1955-1968," *Penélope*, 18 (1998), 189-206.

20 F. Antunes, *Kennedy e Salazar: o leão e a raposa* (Lisbon: Publisher, 1991); F. Antunes, *Nixon e Caetano* (Lisbon: Difusão Cultural, 1991); D. F. do Amaral, *A tentativa falhada de acordo Portugal-Estados Unidos sobre o futuro do Ultramar Português* (Coimbra: Coimbra Editora, 1994); L. N. Rodrigues, *Salazar-Kennedy: a crise de uma aliança* (Lisbon: Editorial Notícias, 2002).

21 A. C. Pinto and N. S. Teixeira (eds.), *Portugal e a unificação Europeia—Penélope*, 18 (1998); J. M. Ferreira, "Os regimes políticos em Portugal e a organização internacional da Europa," *Política Internacional*, 11 (1995), 5-39.

22 J. Sánchez Cervelló, El último imperio occidental: la descolonización portuguesa (1974-1975) (Mérida: UNED, Centro Regional de Extremadura, 1998); N. MacQueen, The decolonization of Portuguese Africa (London: Longman, 1997); C. Oliveira, Portugal, dos quatro cantos do mundo à Europa: a descolonização (1974-1976) (Lisbon: Cosmos, 1996).

23 J. M. Ferreira, "Portugal," in C. Zorgbibe (ed.), Dicionário de política internacional (Lisbon: Dom Quixote, 1990); A. J. Telo, "As relações internacionais da transição," in J. M. Brandão de Brito, "Do marcelismo ao fim do Império," in J. M. Brandão de Brito (ed.), Revolução e democracia (Lisbon: Notícias, 1999).

24 N. S. Teixeira, "Portugal e a NATO: 1949-1999," Nação e Defesa, 89 (1999), 15-41.

25 A. C. Pinto and N. S. Teixeira (eds.), Southern Europe and the making of the European Union (New York, NY: SSM-Columbia University Press, 2002); S. B. MacDonald, European destiny, Atlantic transformations: Portuguese foreign policy under the Second Republic, 1974-1992 (London: Transaction, 1993); J. M. Ferreira, "Political costs and benefits for Portugal arising from membership of the European Community," in J. da Silva Lopes (ed.), Portugal and EC membership evaluated (London: St. Martin's Press, 1993); J. Gama, "A adesão de Portugal às Comunidades Europeias," Política Internacional, 10 (1994/95), 5-19.

26 A. Barreto, "Portugal: democracy through Europe," in J. J. Anderson (ed.), Regional integration and democracy (New York, NY and Oxford: Rowman & Littlefield, 1999), 95-122; A. C. Pinto and N. S. Teixeira, "From Africa to Europe: Portugal and European integration," in A. C. Pinto and N. S. Teixeira (eds.), Southern Europe and the making of the European Union, 3-40.

NOTES TO CHAPTER 5

1 For an overview of convergence patterns, see A. Maddison, Monitoring the world economy, 1820-1992 (Paris: OECD, 1995); A. Maddison, The world economy: a millennial perspective (Paris: OECD, 2001); and P. Lains, "Catching-up to the European core: Portuguese economic growth, 1910-1990," Instituto de Ciências Sociais Working Papers 1-03 (2003). For the nineteenth century, see P. Lains, "Southern European economic backwardness revisited: open economy forces in Portugal and the Balkans, 1870-1913," Scandinavian Economic History Review, 50 (2002), 24-43.

2 A. Marques, Política económica e desenvolvimento em Portugal (1926-1959) (Lisbon: Horizonte, 1988), 23-6. See also F. Rosas, Salazarismo e fomento económico, 1928-1948: o primado do político na história económica do Estado Novo (Lisbon: Editorial Notícias, 2000), chapter 2. An alternative interpretation is provided in P. Lains, "New wine in old bottles: output and productivity trends in Portuguese agriculture, 1850-1950," European Review of Economic History, 7 (2003), 43-72.

3 See N. A. Leitão, "Portugal's European integration policy, 1947-1972," Journal of European Integration History, 7 (2001), 25-35.

4 F. P. de Moura, Por onde vai a economia portuguesa? (Lisbon: Seara Nova, 1973).

5 For example, see the proceedings of the conference on Desenvolvimento económico português no espaço europeu: determinantes e políticas (Lisbon: Banco de Portugal, 2002).

6 M. C. Lobo, "Portugal na Europa: uma leitura política da convergência económica," in A. Barreto (ed.), A situação social em Portugal, 1960-1999 (Lisbon: Imprensa de Ciências Sociais, 2000).

7 J. da S. Lopes, A economia portuguesa desde 1960 (Lisbon: Gradiva, 1996), 17, 23.

8 The United Kingdom, France, Germany (West Germany to 1991), Belgium, the Netherlands Italy, Sweden, Denmark and Norway.

9 In order to define growth cycles, growth rates are computed between peak years as a proxy for growth along a log-linear trend. It is not possible, however, to employ such procedure when comparing different sets of series because peak years may not coincide. Alternatively, we use the European phases of development defined by Maddison, *Monitoring*; and Maddison, *The world economy*.

10 P. Lains, *Os progressos do atraso: uma história económica de Portugal, 1842-1992* (Lisbon: Imprensa de Ciências Sociais, 2003), chapter 7.

11 For the income per capita series, see Lains, *Os progressos*, statistical appendix.

12 Maddison, *Monitoring*.

13 We consider *absolute* rates of convergence, which do not take into account differences in growth potential or in steady state growth rates and which are contemplated by estimates of *conditional* convergence, as defined by R. Barro and X. Sala-i-Maritn, *Economic growth* (New York, NY: McGraw-Hill, 1995).

14 See C. Ó Gráda and K. O'Rourke, "Irish economic growth, 1945-1988," in N. Crafts and G. Toniolo (eds.), *Economic growth in Europe since 1945* (Cambridge: Cambridge University Press, 1996).

15 Lains, "Catching-up."

16 See Maddison, *Monitoring*, 40-9. See also E. E. Denison, *Why growth rates differ: post-war experiences in nine Western countries* (Washington DC: The Brookings Institute, 1967); S. Dowrick and D.-T. Nguyen, "OECD comparative economic growth, 1950-1985: catch-up and convergence," *American Economic Review*, 79 (1989), 1010-30; and Crafts and Toniolo, *Economic growth*.

17 See L. Prados de la Escosura and J. G. Sanz, "Growth and macroeconomic performance in Spain, 1939-1993," in Crafts and Toniolo, *Economic growth*, 359.

18 Lains, "Catching-up."

19 Ibid.

20 See A. Teixeira, *Capital humano e capacidade de inovação: contributos para o estudo do crescimento económico português, 1960-1991* (Lisbon: Conselho Económico e Social, 1999) and L. Amaral, *How a country catches up: explaining economic growth in Portugal in the post-war period*, unpublished Ph.D. thesis (Florence: European University Institute, 2002).

21 V. Nehru and A. Dhareshwar, *New estimates of total factor productivity growth for developing and industrial countries*, World Bank Policy Research Working Papers 1313 (1994). See also J. Temple, "The new growth evidence," *Journal of Economic Literature*, 37 (1999), 120.

22 See A. Mateus, *Economia portuguesa: crescimento no contexto internacional (1910-1998)* (Lisbon: Verbo, 1998); Lopes, *A economia portuguesa*; and Amaral, *How a country*.

23 Van Ark and Crafts, *Quantititive aspects*, 5-6.

24 See Mateus, *Economia portuguesa*.

25 B. van Ark, "Convergence and divergence in the European periphery: productivity in eastern and southern Europe in retrospect," in van Ark and Crafts, *Quantitative aspects*, 298.

26 O. Afonso, *Contributo do comércio externo para o crescimento económico português, 1960-1993* (Lisbon: Conselho Económico e Social, 1999), 59-64.

27 Ibid., 74-82.

28 R. Levine and D. Renelt, "A sensitivity analysis of cross-country growth regressions," *American Economic Review*, 82 (1992), 942-63.

29 Crafts and Toniolo, *Economic growth*, Table 1.11.

30 Lains, "Catching-up."

31 Empirical tests on the export-led growth model have generally refuted a direct causality link between exports and growth. See A. Aguiar and O. Figueiredo, "Abertura e convergência da economia portuguesa, 1870-1990," *Estudos de Economia*, 19 (1999), 209-32.

32 The ratio is defined as the average of exports and imports over GDP, from Lopes, *A economia portuguesa*, Figure 4.1.

33 A. P. Barbosa et al., *O impacto do euro na economia portuguesa* (Lisbon: Dom Quixote, 1999), 149.

34 Mendes, "The development of the Portuguese economy," 16-21. The European Union effect is measured through the impact of structural funds alone.

35 Lains, *Os progressos*, chapter 6.

36 Agricultural labor productivity growth during 1973-90 is associated with the 2.8 per cent annual decline in the agricultural labor force. Both the decline in labor force and the increase in labor productivity were below rates for most Western European countries. See Lains, *Os progressos*, chapter 6, and B. van Ark and N. Crafts, "Sectoral growth accounting and structural change in post-war Europe," in van Ark and Crafts, *Quantitative aspects*, 84-164.

37 The decline in total factor productivity in the services sector after 1973 was due to the decline in labor productivity, which is related to the sharp increase in the rate of growth of employment in the sector. That increase is related, on the one hand, to the incorporation of immigrant workers from the colonies, and to the post-1975 employment protection legislation.

38 Lains, *Os progressos*, chapter 6.

39 Lopes, *A economia portuguesa*. See also M. Centeno, "Poupança pública *versus* poupança privada: que relação de longo prazo?," *Boletim Económico*, 1 (1) (1995), 67-72; and Mateus, *Economia portuguesa*, 194-8.

40 Lopes, *A economia portuguesa*, 87-8. See also J. B. Macedo, C. Corado and M. L. Porto, *The timing and sequencing of trade liberalization policies: Portugal, 1948-1986*, Universidade Nova de Lisboa: Faculdade de Economia Working Papers, 114 (1988); and J. Confraria, "Portugal: industrialization and backwardness," in J. Foreman-Peck and G. Federico (eds.), *European industrial policy: the twentieth century experience* (Oxford: Oxford University Press, 1999), 268-94.

41 Neves, *The Portuguese economy*, 72-3.

42 Lains, *Os progressos*, chapter 6. See also van Ark, "Sectoral growth," and S. Broadberry, "How did the United States and Germany overtake Britain? A sectoral analysis of comparative productivity levels, 1870-1990," *Journal of Economic History*, 58 (1998), 375-407.

43 L. P. Lopes, "Manufacturing productivity in Portugal in a comparative perspective," *Notas Económicas*, 4 (1994), 57-76.

44 Lains, "Catching-up."

NOTES TO CHAPTER 6

1 The following discussion draws heavily on four publications by M. I. B. Baganha: "Portuguese emigration: current characteristics and trends," Portuguese Report to COST A2

conference *Migration: Europe's integration and the labor force* (Leuven, 1991); "As correntes emigratórias portuguesas no século XX e o seu impacto na economia nacional," *Análise Social*, 39 (128) (1994), 959-80; "Principais características e tendências da emigração portuguesa," in *Estruturas sociais e desenvolvimento: actas do II Congresso Português de Sociologia* (Lisbon: Fragmentos, 1994), 819-35; "The market, the state, and the migrants: Portuguese emigration under the corporatist Regime," Paper presented to the ESF Conference *Migration and Development* (Crete, 1994).

2 Office Nationale d'Immigration (ONI) for the given years, in M. L. M. Antunes, "A emigração portuguesa desde 1950: dados e comentários," *Cadernos GIS*, 7, 73 (Lisbon: GIS, 1973), 109.

3 See L. M. Seruya, "Determinantes e características da emigração portuguesa, 1960-1979," in H.-M. Stahl et al., *Perspectivas da emigração portuguesa para a CEE, 1980-1990* (Lisbon: Moraes/IED, 1982), 37-64; M. M. Kritz, C. B. Keely and S. M. Tomasi (eds.), *Global trends in migration: theory and research on international population movement*, 3rd edition (Staten Island, NY: Center for Migration Studies, 1983); W. R. Bohning, *Studies in international labor migration* (London: Macmillan, 1984); J. P. Branco, *A estrutura da comunidade portuguesa em França* (Oporto: Secretaria de Estado das Comunidades Portuguesas/Centro de Estudos, 1986).

4 In the early 1980s, for example, the portion of unskilled workers was 45 per cent among the Portuguese immigrant labor force in France, similar to other foreign groups, but much higher than among natives. The share of unskilled laborers in the French active population was 29 per cent. See Branco, *A estrutura*, 70-71.

5 F. G. Cassolo Ribeiro, *Emigração portuguesa: aspectos relevantes relativos às políticas adoptadas no domínio da emigração portuguesa, desde a última guerra mundial. Contribuição para o seu estudo* (Oporto: Secretaria de Estado das Comunidades Portuguesas/Centro de Estudos, 1986), 41-42.

6 "Proposta de lei sobre política de emigração," in *Actas da Câmara Corporativa*, 142 (23 February 1973). See also Ribeiro, *Emigração portuguesa*, 95-110.

7 The figure does not include the 105,000 special legalisations performed by the Emigration Bureau between 1963 and 1969. See Antunes, "A emigração portuguesa," 13-15.

8 The estimate includes 975,000 arrivals to France and 212,000 arrivals to Germany, respectively.

9 Some 777,000 arrivals to France and Germany are not accounted for in the Portuguese official statistics. More specifically, comparing the French and Portuguese sources indicates that for the period 1960-69, 48 per cent of emigration to France went unregistered by Portuguese sources, and 81 per cent for 1970-79. For Germany, the Portuguese migratory flow is unregistered by 27 per cent for 1962-69 and by 42 per cent in 1970-79 (see Table 6.6). Previous works considered only illegal emigration to France. The totals are therefore different from the ones presented in this chapter. See, for example, J. C. F. de Almeida, "A emigração portuguesa para a França: alguns aspectos quantitativos," *Análise Social*, 2 (7-8) (1964), 599-622; M. L. M. Antunes, "Migrações, mobilidade social e identidade cultural: factos e hipóteses sobre o caso português," *Análise Social*, 17 (65) (1981), 17-37; Stahl, *Perspectivas da emigração*.

10 The last annual *Boletim* available from the *Secretaria de Estado das Comunidades Portuguesas* is for 1988.

11 Although important, the movement to Germany never attained the same intensity. Still, between 1970 and 1974 it represented 19 per cent of the global total.

12 See W. S. Bernard, "History of US immigration policy," in R. Easterlin et al., *Immigration* (Cambridge, MA: Harvard University Press, 1982), 103.

13 Office Nationale d'Immigration, quoted by Seruya, "Determinantes e características," 52; and OECD, *SOPEMI Reports* 1985, 1988, and 1990 (Paris: OECD).

14 C. Brettell, *Men who migrate, women who wait: population and history in a Portuguese parish* (Princeton, NY: Princeton University Press, 1986).

15 Ibid., 68.

16 The most relevant works are M. Silva et al., *Retorno, emigração e desenvolvimento regional em Portugal* (Lisbon: Instituto de Estudos para o Desenvolvimento, 1984); E. S. Ferreira, *Reintegração dos emigrantes portugueses: integração na CEE e desenvolvimento económico* (Lisbon: CEDEP/AE ISE, 1984); A. Paiva, *Portugal e a Europa: o fim de um ciclo migratório* (Lisbon: IED-CEDEP, 1985); M. Poinard, "Emigrantes portugueses: o regresso," *Análise Social*, 19 (75) (1983), 29-56.

17 After the mid-1980s, the information available points to a decrease in the level of returns. At the end of the decade, returns were between 25,000 and 26,000.

18 Poinard's study, "Emigrantes portugueses," based on 3,792 documents and files on Portuguese processes for aided return presented to French authorities in 1978, gives a slightly different portrait of the migrants returning from France. The mean duration of the stay in France was 9.5 years.

19 Employment was quite different in France and Germany. In France, 49 per cent of the returnees worked in construction and 25 per cent in manufacturing; in Germany, 13 per cent worked in construction and 60 per cent in manufacturing.

20 The most frequent reasons for return were missing the family and native land and concern with the children's education, 35 per cent; and health, retirement and labor accidents, 26 per cent.

21 See SECP, *Boletim anual* (1988), 83. For returns see Silva, *Retorno, emigração e desenvolvimento*, 49-52; Stahl, *Perspectivas da emigração*, 17.

22 A. M. Pereira, "Trade-off between emigration and remittances in the Portuguese economy," FE-UNL Working Paper, 129 (1989).

23 A. S. Nunes, "Portugal: sociedade dualista em evolução," *Análise Social*, 2 (7-8) (1964), 407-62; C. Almeida and A. Barreto, *Capitalismo e emigração em Portugal*, 3rd edition (Lisbon: Prelo, 1976); J. Serrão, *A emigração portuguesa: sondagem histórica*, 3rd edition (Lisbon: Horizonte, 1977);V. M. Godinho, *A estrutura da antiga sociedade portuguesa* (Lisbon: Arcádia, 1978).

24 E. S. Ferreira, *Origens e formas da emigração* (Lisbon: Iniciativas, 1976); J. P. Barosa and P. T. Pereira, "Economic integration and labor flows: the European Single Act and its consequences," FE-UNL Working Paper, 123 (1988); Pereira, "Trade-off between emigration and remittances," 1989.

25 Barosa and Pereira, "Economic integration and labor flows," 8.

26 Stahl, *Perspectivas da emigração*; I. J. Secombe and R. J. Lawless, "Some new trends in Mediterranean labor migration: the Middle East connection," *International Migration*, 23 (1) (1985), 123-48; Barosa and Pereira, "Economic integration and labor flows."

27 Barosa and Pereira, "Economic integration and labor flows," 13.

28 A. Paiva, *Portugal e a Europa: o fim de um ciclo migratório* (Lisbon: IED-CEDEP, 1985).

29 See the publications by Baganha cited in note 1. See also M. I. B. Baganha and J. Peixoto, "Trends in the '90s: the Portuguese migratory experience," in M. I. B. Baganha (ed.), *Immigration in Southern Europe* (Oeiras: Celta, 1997), 15-40.

Notes to Chapter 7

1 Most statistical data referred to in this article is taken from the following studies: A. Barreto, *A situação social em Portugal, 1960-1995*, vol. 1 (Lisbon: Imprensa de Ciências Sociais, 1996), and A. Barreto, *A situação social em Portugal, 1960-1999*, vol. 2 (Lisbon: Imprensa de Ciências Sociais, 2000). Two other sources referred to are the *Anuários estatísticos* and *Portugal social*, both Lisbon: Instituto Nacional de Estatística, various years; and the database *New cronos* from EUROSTAT (Luxembourg: Statistical Division of the European Union, various years).

2 Many historical events have had a decisive influence on social change, such as the revolution of 1974. But one must not lose sight of the inverse relationship: the foundation of the democratic state and the adoption of liberal politics owe much to economic growth, to the pressure from the middle classes and to social changes originating in the 1960s.

3 United Kingdom, Switzerland, Austria, Sweden, Norway, Denmark and Portugal. Finland and Iceland joined later. In 1973, the United Kingdom and Denmark (along with Ireland), left EFTA to join the Common Market (European Economic Community).

4 According to a study by EFTA, Portuguese industrial product grew by almost 80 per cent between 1960 and 1965, thanks to the effects of this new international framework; while exports to EFTA increased more than 140 per cent. In the same period, the increase of total Portuguese exports was only 76 per cent. See EFTA, *The effects of EFTA on the economies of member states* (Geneva: EFTA, 1969). See also V. X. Pintado, *Structure and growth of the Portuguese economy*, 2nd edition (Lisbon: Imprensa de Ciências Sociais, 2002).

5 Despite this opening up of the economy, the Portuguese government decided to keep certain sectors, companies and goods under special protection. This protection was the aim of Annex G of the Stockholm Convention, which created EFTA, and was put into effect in the first half of 1960.

6 According to official reports of the time in the agricultural regions of the south, namely the Alentejo, the Algarve and the Ribatejo, the average number of paid rural workdays varied between 140 and 160 days per year (*c.*1960).

7 See Barreto, *A situação social em Portugal, 1960-1995*.

8 The MPLA (*Movimento Popular de Libertação de Angola*—Popular Movement for the Liberation of Angola) began guerrilla operations in the city of Luanda in February 1961. In March, it was the turn of the UPA (*União dos Povos de Angola*—Union of Angolan People) to carry out several terrorist actions in various regions, especially against farm owners and their workers.

9 This figure represented more than 2 per cent of the total population of the country, a level that no other European country or the United States has attained in any colonial or overseas conflict since the World War II—including the Vietnam War.

10 The remaining Portuguese colonies became independent states in 1974 and 1975 (East Timor being a special case: having declared independence in 1975, it was annexed by Indonesia. Timor finally obtained its independence in 2002, thanks to UN intervention).

11 After 40 years of absolute power, Marcelo Caetano replaced Salazar who had suffered post-operative complications. Salazar died in 1970. Caetano was one of the principal leaders of the regime.

12 The various phases can be distinguished in what was a very complex process: the military coup on 25 April 1974; a political and social revolution between 1974 and 1975; a democratic counter-revolution between the end of 1975 and 1976 (this was the year in which a democratic constitution was approved; legislative, presidential and municipal elections took place, and the first democratic government was appointed); a period of democratic 'normalization,' between 1976 and 1982, until the revision of the constitution (from which were removed several revolutionary clauses and military tutelage over the regime) and the approval of new laws regarding the armed forces. The more political aspects of the whole process will not be dealt with here, but the experience had profound social and cultural effects.

13 The dragging on of the colonial war, with no prospects of a political solution, was the determining factor for the initiative and action by the military on 25 April 1974. In a country that lived under a dictatorship, there was no alternative action possible but a military coup, which would inevitably end by causing the downfall of the regime.

14 For several reasons, including the after effects of the war and decolonization, relations between Portugal and the newly independent states remain erratic and very fragile almost 30 years on.

15 Exports to the colonies made under the protectionist regime came to represent almost one-quarter of Portugal's external trade. Some basic commodities, such as oilseed, coffee, sugar, sisal, cotton, diamonds, oil and some other minerals had played a very important role in the Portuguese balance of trade.

16 See A. Barreto, *Anatomia de uma revolução: a reforma agrária no Alentejo, 1974/76* (Lisbon: Europa-América, 1986). In total, around 1.2 million hectares were occupied and placed in the hands of 'collective production units:' around 14 per cent of the area of the country, or one-quarter of useable agricultural land.

17 See A. P. Barbosa (ed.), *O impacto do euro na economia portuguesa* (Lisbon: Dom Quixote, 1999). See also "As implicações sociais do euro," in A. Barreto, *Tempo de incerteza* (Lisbon: Relógio d'Água, 2002).

18 According to a certain cultural and historiographical tradition, Portugal has known other periods of democracy, such as, for example, some decades in the nineteenth century (the period of the constitutional monarchy) and the 'First Republic' (1910-26). It can be said that, during these periods, there were moments in which fundamental liberties were practiced and more or less guaranteed, and in which a parliamentary institution existed and met (incidentally, it was dissolved several times). However, electoral capacity was reduced for the lower ends of the population (women, the destitute, the unemployed and the illiterate were almost always denied rights of suffrage). The parliament depended more on the government and on the monarchy than the other way around, and the principal political parties behaved almost like a dictatorship.

19 The fact, unusual in the Western world, that the constitution has been revised 5 times in 25 years does not negate this concordance: rather it confirms it. Effectively, two-thirds of votes are needed to approve a revision. What this means is that it was possible to find such a majority as many times as were deemed necessary by the two most important political parties, PSD (Social Democratic Party) and PS (Socialist Party).

7 Bruneau et al., *Democracy*, 40.

8 M. de F. A. Mendes and J. Miguéis, *Lei eleitoral da Assembleia da República* (Lisbon: Edição do Autor, 2002), 26-30.

9 See J. Montabés and C. Ortega, "Candidate selection in two rigid list systems: Spain and Portugal," paper prepared for presentation at the European Consortium for Political Research Joint Sessions, Mannheim (1999).

10 For a comparison of the Portuguese case with other consolidated Western democracies, see Freire, "Elecciones." For eastern Europe, see S. Birch, "Electoral systems and party systems in Europe, east and west," paper prepared for presentation at the first conference of the European Consortium for Political Research, Canterbury, 6-8 September (2001). In Portugal, the reduction in the size of parliament between the 1987 and 1991 elections—reducing average district magnitude from 11.4 to 10.5 deputies—has increased the effective threshold of representation from 6.2 per cent to 6.8 per cent.

11 Disproportionality is the difference between party seat shares and their share of the vote, and it is measured here by the Gallagher least squares index. See M. Gallagher, "Proportionality, disproportionality and electoral systems," *Electoral Studies*, 10 (1991), 33-51.

12 A. Lijphart, *Patterns of democracy: government forms and performance in 36 countries* (New Haven, CT: Yale University Press, 1999), 159-65. Using Loosemore and Hanby's index of disproportionality, Lopes and Freire place Norway below the Portuguese case in terms of average disproportionality between 1945 and 1997.

13 See, for example, M. Gallagher and M. Marsh, *Candidate selection in comparative perspective: the secret garden of politics* (London: Sage, 1988); J. M. Carey and M. S. Shugart, "Incentives to cultivate a personal vote: a rank ordering of electoral formulas," *Electoral Studies*, 14 (1995), 417-39; and P. Norris, "Legislative recruitment," in L. LeDuc, R. G. Niemi and P. Norris, P. (eds.), *Comparing democracies: elections and voting in global perspective* (London: Sage, 1996), 184-215.

14 See, for example, Braga da Cruz, *Instituições políticas*, 189-200; and A. Freire, *Recrutamento parlamentar: os deputados portugueses da Constituinte à VIII Legislatura* (Lisbon: STAPE, 2001), 45-53.

15 W. C. Opello, "Portugal's parliament: an organizational analysis of legislative performance," *Legislative Studies Quarterly*, 11 (1986), 297; Braga da Cruz, *Instituições políticas*, 199-200; Montabés and Ortega, "Candidate selection;" C. Leston-Bandeira, *Da legislação à legitimação: o papel do parlamento português* (Lisbon: Instituto de Ciências Sociais, 2002), 146-50.

16 For surveys of the debates see, among others, Braga da Cruz, *Instituições políticas*, 269-96; M. Braga da Cruz, "A revisão falhada do sistema eleitoral," *Análise Social*, 35 (154-155) (2000), 45-54; Freire, *Recrutamento*, 30-44.

17 As Lijphart puts it: 'Portugal is the only example of a clear trend toward fewer parties' in his sample of 36 consolidated democracies. See Lijphart, *Patterns*, 76.

18 R. Gunther and J. R. Montero, "The anchors of partisanship: a comparative analysis of voting behavior in four southern European democracies," in Diamandouros and Gunther, *Parties, politics*, 86-92.

19 See, among many: M. Bacalhau, "Mobilidade e transferência de voto através das sondagens," in M. B. Coelho (ed.), *Portugal: o sistema político e constitucional* (Lisbon: Instituto de Ciências Sociais, 1989), 247-50; J. Magone, "Party system change in southern Europe," in P. Pennings and J.-E. Lane (eds.), *Comparing party system change* (London: Routledge, 1998), 228-30.

20 M. C. Lobo, "The role of political parties in Portuguese democratic consolidation," *Party Politics*, 7 (2001), 650-1. See also M. C. Lobo, "A evolução do sistema partidário português à luz

de mudanças económicas e políticas (1976-1991)," *Análise Social,* 31 (139) (1996), 1099; and H. Bahro, "A influência de Max Weber na Constituição de Weimar e o semipresidencialismo português como sistema político de transição," *Análise Social,* 31 (138) (1996), 777-802.

21 F. F. Lopes and A. Freire, *Partidos políticos e sistemas eleitorais* (Oeiras: Celta, 2002), 182.

22 See I. van Biezen, "Building party organizations and the relevance of past models: the Communist and Socialist parties in Spain and Portugal," *West European Politics,* 21 (1998), 32-62; Lopes and Freire, *Partidos,* 52-5.

23 Cruz, *Instituições,* 310-17; J. Aguiar, "Partidos, eleições, dinâmica política (1975-1991)," *Análise Social,* 29 (125-126) (1994), 171-236; Gunther and Montero, "The anchors," 142-3; A. Freire, *Mudança eleitoral em Portugal: clivagens, economia e voto em eleições legislativas, 1983-1999* (Oeiras: Celta, 2001), 61-108; A. Freire, "Realinhamentos eleitorais, 1983-1999: estruturas sociais, economia e voto partidário," *Análise Social,* 37 (162) (2002), 143-6.

24 R. Gunther, "A democracia portuguesa em perspectiva comparada," *Análise Social,* 37 (162) (2002), 118-19.

25 J. Gaspar and N. Vitorino, *As eleições de 25 de Abril: geografia e imagem dos partidos* (Lisbon: Horizonte, 1976), 260-1; J. Gaspar and I. André, "Portugal—geografia eleitoral: 1975 e 1987," in Coelho, *Portugal,* 268-73.

26 Lobo, "A evolução," 1100-106.

27 L. de Winter, "The role of parliament in government formation and resignation," in H. Döring (ed.), *Parliaments and majority rule in Western Europe* (Frankfurt and New York, NY: Campus and St. Martin's Press, 1995), 115-51.

28 C. Leston-Bandeira, "Relationship between parliament and government in Portugal: an expression of the maturation of the political system," in P. Norton (ed.), *Parliaments and governments in Western Europe* (London: Frank Cass, 1998), 142-66.

29 Bruneau et al, "Democracy," 21.

30 Leston-Bandeira, "Relationship between parliament," 144.

31 In Portugal, executive control over the parliamentary agenda has been reinforced by the curtailment in 1988 of the special agenda-setting rights granted to opposition deputies, regardless of the size of their parliamentary party. See H. Döring, "Time as scarce resource: government control of the agenda," in Döring, *Parliaments,* 223-34; Leston-Bandeira, "Relationship between parliament," 154; Leston-Bandeira, *Da legislação,* 93-100.

32 See I. Mattson and K. Strøm, "Parliamentary committees," in Döring, *Parliaments,* 248-307; G. B. Powell, *Elections as instruments of democracy: majoritarian and proportional visions* (New Haven, CT: Yale University Press, 2000), 31-4.

33 A. Freire et al., *O parlamento português: uma reforma necessária* (Lisbon: Instituto de Ciências Sociais, 2002), 46.

34 See E. Damgaard, "How parties control committee members," in Döring, *Parliaments,* 315-21; J. M. Colomer, "Spain and Portugal," in J. M. Colomer (ed.), *Political institutions in Europe* (London: Routledge, 1998), 189-90.

35 See M. C. Lobo, "El incremento del poder del Primer Ministro en Portugal desde 1976," in Barreto, Gómez and Magalhães, *Portugal,* 175-205.

36 For a discussion of the similar French example, see G. Tsebelis, "Veto players and institutional analysis," *Governance,* 13 (2000), 441-74.

37 A. de Araújo, "El Presidente de la República en la evolución del sistema político de Portugal," in Barreto, Gómez and Magalhães, *Portugal*, 83-112.

38 Ibid., 92-4.

39 M. Duverger, "A new political system model: semi-presidential government," *European Journal of Political Research*, 8 (1980), 165-187; A. Lijphart, "Introduction," in A. Lijphart (ed.), *Parliamentary versus presidential government* (Oxford: Oxford University Press, 1992), 20-1.

40 P. C. Magalhães, "As armas dos fracos: o veto político e a litigância constitucional do Presidente da República," in *A reforma do estado em Portugal: problemas e perspectivas* (Lisbon: Bizâncio, 2001); E. Serrano, *As presidências abertas de Mário Soares* (Coimbra: Minerva, 2002).

41 M. C. Lobo, "Portugal na Europa, 1960.1996: uma leitura de convergência económica," in A. Barreto (ed.), *A situação social em Portugal 1960-1999*, vol. 2, *Indicadores sociais em Portugal e na União Europeia* (Lisbon: Instituto de Ciências Sociais, 2000), 632-41.

42 A. Freire and M. C. Lobo, 'Economia, ideologia e voto: Europa do Sul, 1985-2000', paper presented at the Fulbright Brainstrom Conference on Elections and Democracy, Lisbon (February 2002).

43 L. Morlino and J. Ramón Montero, "Legitimacy and democracy in southern Europe," in R. Gunther, P. N. Diamandouros and H.-J. Puhle, *The politics of democratic consolidation: southern Europe in comparative perspective* (Baltimore, MD: Johns Hopkins University Press, 1995); J. Ramón Montero, R. Gunther and M. Torcal, "Actitudes hacia la democracia en España: legitimidad, descontento y desfacción," *Revista Española de Investigaciones Sociológicas*, 83 (1998), 13-14.

44 Lijphart, *Patterns*, 275-87.

45 A. Freire and P. C. Magalhães, *A abstenção eleitoral em Portugal* (Lisbon: Instituto de Ciências Sociais, 2002), 43-54.

46 A. Freire, "Desempenho da democracia, representação e reforma política: o caso português em perspectiva comparada," paper presented at the conference *Portugal: Historia, Política, Sociedad, Universidad Complutense de Madrid* (UCM), Campus de Somosaguas, Madrid (November 2002).

47 A. Freire, P. C. Magalhães and A. Espírito Santo, "Political culture in Portugal," paper presented at the *Asia-Europe Survey Conference, Institute of Oriental Culture*, University of Tokyo (November 2002).

48 See, for example, H.-D. Klingemann, "Mapping political support in the 1990s," in P. Norris (ed.), *Critical citizens* (Oxford: Oxford University Press, 1999); R. J. Dalton, *Citizen politics: public opinion and political parties in advanced industrial democracies* (New York, NY: Chatham House, 2002); P. Norris, *Democratic phoenix: reinventing political activism* (Cambridge: Cambridge University Press, 2002).

NOTES TO CHAPTER 9

1 The author would like to thank European Parliament civil servants António Sobrinho and Nuno Carvalho for their kind assistance obtaining data for this Chapter.

2 See M. Bacalhau, *Atitudes, opiniões e comportamento eleitoral dos Portugueses* (Lisbon: FLAD, 1993); M. Bacalhau, "The image, identity and benefits of the EC," in J. S. Lopes, *Portugal and EC membership evaluated* (London: Pinter, 1993); J. Magone, "Attitudes of southern European citizens towards integration: before and after accession, 1974-2000," in A. C.

Pinto and N. S. Teixeira (eds.), *Southern Europe and the making of the European Union* (New York, NY: SSM—Columbia University Press, 2002); M. C. Lobo, "Portuguese attitudes towards the EU: social and political perspectives," *South European Society & Politics*, 8 (1) (2003); and A. C. Pinto and M. C. Lobo, "Forging a positive but instrumental view: Portuguese attitudes towards the EU, 1986-2002," in A. Dulphy and C. Maginand (eds.), *Public opinion and Europe: national identity in European perspective* (Paris: Peter Lang, 2003).

3   See L. F. Salgado Matos, "O sistema político português e a Comunidade Europeia," *Análise Social*, 28 (118-119) (1992), 773-87; and M. Bacalhau, "Portugal: an ephemeral election," in C. Eijk and M. Franklin (eds.), *Choosing Europe? The European electorate and national politics in the face of union* (Ann Arbor, MI: University of Michigan Press, 1996).

4   The Portuguese electorate has been asked to elect Members of the European Parliament on four occasions: 1987, 1989, 1994 and 1999. On the first occasion, the Portuguese MEPs were chosen in the mid-term of the European Parliamentary session, and their mandates ceased when the Europe-wide elections were convened. Since then, July elections have taken place almost simultaneously across Europe, as well as in Portugal, every five years.

5   This project, lead by Mark Franklin, Herman Schmitt, and Cees van der Eijk, involved, among other things, the fielding of three post-election surveys in 1989, 1994 and 1999. These surveys were organized slightly differently: the 1989 and 1994 post-election surveys were included in the regular *Eurobarometer* series. Then, the questions that directly related to the election were collected and a new database was compiled that became the "post-election study" in each case. In 1999, the survey was undertaken on its own, without being included in a *Eurobarometer* survey. The first two election surveys included a sample of 956 and 1000 cases, respectively, in Portugal were face-to-face and undertaken among the population aged 15 or over who were selected via multi-stage national probability samples and national stratified quota samples. In 1999, only 500 valid questionnaires were fielded by telephone. Respondents were Portuguese or citizens of EU-countries living in Portugal (able to speak the country's language), aged 18 years and over, and a random multi-stage process was adopted. This sample variation poses some problems in terms of what relationships can be tested statistically. In relation to the questions on the campaign, it was slightly discouraging to see that many interesting questions were asked only on one occasion, thus not allowing for a comparison between elections: which is our objective here.

6   N. Nugent, *The government and politics of the European Union* (London: Macmillan, 1995); D. Dinan, *Ever closer union? An introduction to the European Community* (London: Macmillan, 1999); D. Earnshaw and D. Judge, "From co-operation to co-decision: the European Parliament's path to legislative power," in J. Richardson (ed.), *European Union: politics and policy-making* (London: Routledge, 1996); and S. Hix, *The political system of the EU*, in http://personal.lse.ac.uk/HIX/Working Papers/01-Introduction.pdf

7   Ibid.

8   K. Reif and H. Schmitt, "Nine second-order elections: a conceptual framework for the analysis of European election results," *European Journal of Political Research*, 8 (1980), 3-44.

9   M. Marsh and M. Franklin, "The foundations: unanswered questions from the study of European elections," in Eijk and Franklin, *Choosing Europe?*, 12

10 In 1987 and 1989, it employed the same system to elect 24 members.

11 Law 14/87, article 2 (29 April 1987).

12 Directive 93/109/CE (6 December), published in *Official Journal of the European Communities*, L368 (31 December 1994).

13 There is incompatibility between being a Member of the European Parliament, and a member of government, or a member of the national parliament. See Law 14/87, article 6 (29 April 1987).

14 http://www.europarl.eu.int/

15 A. Blais and L. Massicote, "Electoral systems," in L. LeDuc, R. Niemi and P. Norris (eds.), *Comparing democracies* (London: Sage, 1996), 56.

16 G. Pridham, "The international context of democratic consolidation," in R. Gunther, P. Diamandorous and H.-J. Puhle (eds.), *The politics of democratic consolidation* (Baltimore: Johns Hopkins University Press, 1995), 180.

17 See B. Alvarez-Miranda, "A las puertas de la comunidad: consenso y disenso en el sur de Europa," *Working Paper* (Madrid: Juan March Institute, 1995), 8. The PS was perhaps the party that most championed accession to the EU as the main Portuguese national objective. See also M. C. Lobo and P. Magalhães, "From Third Wave to Third Way: the Portuguese Socialists and European integration," *Journal of Southern Europe and the Balkans*, 3 (1) (2001).

18 Alvarez-Miranda, "A las puertas de la comunidad," 8; A. Bosco, "Four actors in search of a role: the southern European Communist parties," in N. Diamandorous and R. Gunther, *Parties, politics and democracy in the new southern Europe* (Baltimore, CT: Johns Hopkins University Press, 1995), 337.

19 Lobo, "Portuguese attitudes towards the EU".

20 The PRD had attached itself to the Gaullist parliamentary group, whilst the PSD entered the liberal group (ELDR) in the European Parliament

21 D. B. Goldey, "The Portuguese elections of 1987 and 1991, and the Presidential election of 1991," *Electoral Studies*, 11 (2) (1992), 171-76.

22 *Expresso* (17 July 1987).

23 Partido Comunista Português, *Portugal e a CEE hoje: contribuições para o XII Congresso do PCP* (Lisbon: Avante!, 1988).

24 See Bacalhau, *Atitudes, opiniões e comportamento eleitoral*; Bacalhau, "The image, identity and benefits of the EC"; O. Niedermayer, "Trends and contrasts," in O. Niedermayer and R. Sinnot (eds.), *Public opinion and internationalized governance* (Oxford: Oxford University Press, 1995); Lobo, "Portuguese attitudes towards the EU."

25 Niedermayer, "Trends and contrasts," 62.

26 See the panel surveys published in *Expresso* between January and July 1989.

27 Lobo, "Portuguese attitudes towards the EU."

28 M. Franklin, M. Marsh and L. McLaren, "Uncorking the bottle: popular opposition to European unification in the wake of Maastricht," *JCMS*, 32 (4) (1994), 101-17.

29 D. Corkill, *The Portuguese economy since 1974* (Edinburgh: Edinburgh University Press, 1994).

30 S. Hix, "Parties at the European level," in P. Webb et al., *Political parties in advanced industrial democracies* (Oxford: Oxford University Press, 2002).

31 L. Pires, *Na hora europeia: dez ensaios sobre a Europa* (Lisbon: Grupo Parlamentar do Partido Popular Europeu, 1987).

32 Partido Comunista Português, *Resolução política do XIV Congresso do PCP: democracia e socialismo, o futuro de Portugal* (Lisbon: Avante!, 1992), 37.

33 Lobo and Magalhães, "From Third Wave to Third Way."

34 Público (4 June 1999).

35 Lobo, "Portuguese attitudes towards the EU."

36 Expresso (23 May 1987).

37 C. Hanley and C. Ysmal, "Le parti populaire européen et la recomposition des droites européenes," in Le vote des Quinze (Paris: PUF, 2000).

38 C. van der Eijk and M. Franklin, "Studying the elections of 1989 and 1994," in Eijk and Franklin, Choosing Europe?, 48-9.

39 Marsh and Franklin, "The foundations," 18.

40 A. Freire and P. Magalhães, A abstenção eleitoral em Portugal (Lisbon: Instituto de Ciências Sociais, 2002), 3.

41 Unfortunately, despite many efforts, it was impossible to obtain the data for residents over 18 years of age and with Portuguese nationality for the years in question; therefore we do not present the real versus official rates of participation in Portugal.

42 Freire and Magalhães, A abstenção eleitoral.

43 Due to space limitations, a table comparing abstention in elections to the European Parliament and the Portuguese parliament will not be presented. To summarize, abstentions in national legislative elections have increased from 27.4 per cent in 1987 to 38.2 per cent in 1999; whilst abstentions in elections to the European Parliament have risen from 27.6 per cent to 60.1 per cent in the same period. All figures are from official sources. See STAPE at http://www.stape.pt/

44 Voting is mandatory in three EU member-states: Belgium, Greece and Luxembourg.

45 P. Delwit, "Participation électorale et scrutin européen: une légitimité minimale," in Le vote des Quinze (Paris: PUF, 2000), 297.

46 See footnote 13.

47 Bacalhau has performed a similar analysis for the 1989 election, and by Franklin et al. for the 1994 election; however, in this chapter my analysis includes slightly different variables that are fewer in number in order to avoid multicollinearity. Also, the previous authors only showed the r2 contribution of the aggregated block of variables, whilst I show the added value of each of the variables within each block. For instance, it is possible to discern that within the "socio-demographic" block, only age is significant, and also understand how the importance of these independent variables change over time. In addition, I have also added the independent t-samples test for 1999. See Marsh and Franklin, "The foundations," 49.

48 Freire and Magalhães, A abstenção eleitoral; J. M. L. Viegas and S. Faria, "A abstenção nas legislativas de 2002," paper presented to the conference Portugal at the Polls: I, Lisbon: FLAD (27-28 February 2003).

49 The reasons for this conclusion derive, to an extent, from the study's methodology: the study does not compare the incumbent's vote in the European Parliamentary elections to the vote in the previous national legislative elections to see if, in fact, they were punished: rather, it compares it to the declared voting intention had there been a national legislative election on the day of the survey. This method was not followed because it seems that there is a strong incentive to be coherent and choose the same party on both questions (voting intention for national legislative elections and voter recall for European Parliamentary elections). Thus, in the Portuguese, only 33.6 per cent declared that they would vote for the incumbant governing party had there been a national legislative election on that day, while 33.7

per cent stated that they had voted PSD in the previous European election. The study concludes that in 1989 the government party was not punished. If we take the actual election result in 1987 (50 per cent of valid votes) as our baseline, then the 1989 European election result was clearly a punishment of the incumbeant; this seems more realistic than putative vote intentions, where the respondent's wish for seeming rational may outweigh his desire for stating his intentions truthfully. In fact, the PSD went on to repeat the 1987 election result in 1991.

50 E. Oppenhuis, C. van der Eijk and M. Franklin, "The party context: outcomes," in Eijk and Franklin, *Choosing Europe?*, 295-303.

51 M. C. Lobo, "A evolução do sistema partidário português à luz de mudanças económicas e políticas, (1976-1991)," *Análise Social*, 31 (139) (1996), 1085-115.

52 A. Freire and M. C. Lobo, "Election report: the legislative elections of 2002," *West European Politics*, 4 (2002).

53 Oppenhuis, Eijk and Franklin, "The party context."

54 Eijk and Franklin, *Choosing Europe?*

55 A. Barreto, "Portugal: democracy through Europe," in J. J. Anderson (ed.), *Democracy and regional integration* (Oxford: Rowman and Littlefield, 1999).

NOTES TO CHAPTER 10

1 The link between literary discourse and everyday speech is an important characteristic of modernism. While everyday spoken language makes itself part of literature, expelling the more 'solemn' types of discourse, it seems that literary texts have also increased their capacity to provide the reader with a more complete, more perfect vision of real life and experience. Nevertheless, instead of speaking of progress, it might be more appropriate to state that Portuguese literature evolved, like all literary history, along two different paths. The first might be called 'popular' or mass literature, illustrated by the Galaico-Portuguese, *Cantigas de Escárnio*, and especially the *Cantigas de Maldizer*, and to which Gil Vicente's dramatic works belong—albeit recuperating the learned language that they parody. The second might be considered 'learned,' aspiring, as it does through its language and style, to rise above the banality and chaos (apparent or actual) of the day to day discourses of real life and sometimes ending up simply being pretentious.

2 On this matter, see my article "Formas de 'corrente de consciência' em algumas narrativas do século XIX: os exemplos precursores de Alexandre Herculano e Almeida Garrett," *Arquivos do Centro Cultural Português*, Vol. XXXII (Lisbon and Paris: Fundação Calouste Gulbenkian, 1993), 195-234.

3 To consider, as some critics have, that the story of the girl and the nightingales is the only fictional and the best-written part of the work, is to flagrantly ignore the text as a coherent whole and devalue Garrett's courage to experiment. On the other hand, Fernão Mendes Pinto's *Peregrinação* was already in many ways similar to Garrett's, largely due a spontaneous style close to that of practical everyday language, as well as for its ambiguous nature (is it fiction? Autobiography? Today we know that autobiography is in itself a kind of fiction). Unlike Fernão Mendes Pinto, Camões, in *Os Lusíadas*, conformed successfully to the 'literary model' of the epic poem, but within it we can glimpse the beginnings of the future realism of prose fiction.

4 A. J. Saraiva and O. Lopes, *História da literatura portuguesa*, 16th edition (Oporto: Porto Editora, 1992), 1004.

5 Ibid., 1027.

6 See J. C. dos Santos, "Augusto Abelaira e Vergílio Ferreira: plenitudes breves e absolutos adiados," *Arquivos do Centro Cultural Português*, Paris, 19 (1983), 4, 13, 68. See also J. C. dos Santos, "Tendances du roman contemporain au Portugal: du neo-realisme a l'actualité," *L'Enseignement et l'expansion de la littérature portugaise en France* (Paris: Fondation Calouste Gulbenkian, 1986), 197-239.

7 See my article, "Belles lettres, revolutionary promise and reality," in R. Herr (ed.), *The new Portugal: democracy and Europe, international and area studies* (Berkeley, CA: University of California at Berkeley, 1992), 163-180.

NOTES TO CHAPTER II

1 J. A. França, *A arte em Portugal no século XX* (Lisbon: Bertrand, 1974).

2 J. A. França, *A pintura surrealista em Portugal* (Lisbon: Artis, 1966).

3 J. A. França, *A pintura abstracta portuguesa* (Lisbon: Artis, 1960).

4 R. M. Gonçalves, *100 pintores portugueses do século XX* (Lisbon: Alfa, 1986).

5 R. M. Gonçalves, *Pintura e escultura em Portugal* (Lisbon: Instituto de Cultura, 1984).

6 A. Melo and J. Pinharanda, *A arte portuguesa contemporânea* (Lisbon: Perspectivas, 1986).

7 P. Pereira (ed.), *Arte portuguesa* (Lisbon: Círculo dos Leitores, 1995).

8 M. C. de Vasconcelos, *A intervenção surrealista em Portugal* (Lisbon: Artis, 1966).

Contributors

VALENTIM ALEXANDRE is a Senior Fellow at Lisbon University's Social Science Institute. He holds a Ph.D. from the New University of Lisbon. His current interest is Portuguese colonialism during the nineteenth and twentieth centuries. He has written *Os sentidos do império: questão nacional e questão colonial na crise do antigo regime português* (1993); *Velho Brasil, novas Africas: Portugal e o império, 1808-1975* (2000); and is the co-editor of *O império africano, 1825-1890* (1998).

MARIA IOANNIS B. BAGANHA is a Professor at the University of Coimbra's Faculty of Economics. She holds a Ph.D. from the University of Pennsylvania and her research interests are the economic and social dimensions of emigration. She is the author of numerous articles on this topic as well as *Portuguese emigration to the United States, 1820-1930* (1990); *Immigration in Southern Europe* (1997).

ANTÓNIO BARRETO is a Senior Fellow at Lisbon University's Institute of Social Science and Professor of Sociology at the New University of Lisbon's Law Faculty. He holds a Ph.D. from the University of Geneva. He was Portugal's minister of agriculture from 1976-78. His main research interests are social change and administrative reform in Portugal. He has written several books, including: *Anatomia de uma revolução* (1987); *A situação social em Portugal* (2 volumes— 1996 and 2000); and *Tempo de incerteza* (2002).

PEDRO LAINS is a Senior Fellow at Lisbon University's Institute of Social Science and Professor of History at the University of Évora. He holds a Ph.D. from the European University Institute, Florence. He has been a Visiting Professor at Madrid's Carlos III University and Brown University. His main research interests are the economic history of Portugal, Europe and Portuguese Africa. He recently published *L'economie portugaise au XIXe siècle* (1999) and *Os progressos do atraso: uma nova história económica de Portugal* (2003).

MARINA COSTA LOBO is a Junior Fellow at Lisbon University's Institute of Social Science. She holds a Ph.D. from the University of Oxford. Her main research interests are political parties, electoral behavior, and the European Union. She is the author of many articles on these topics and of the book, *Governar em democracia* (2003) and co-author of *O parlamento português: uma reforma necessária* (2002).

PEDRO MAGALHÃES is a Junior Fellow at Lisbon University's Institute of Social Science and Professor of Politics at the Portuguese Catholic University. He holds a Ph.D. from the Ohio State University. His main research interests are judicial politics, electoral behavior and democratization. He co-authored *A abstenção eleitoral em Portugal* (2002); *O parlamento português: uma reforma necessária* (2002); and co-edited, *Portugal: democracia y política* (2003).

NUNO G. MONTEIRO is a Senior Fellow at Lisbon University's Institute of Social Science and Professor of History at ISCTE, Lisbon. He holds a Ph.D. from the New University of Lisbon. His main research interests are the social history of eighteenth- and nineteenth-century Portugal. He is the author of several articles, as well the books *O crepúsculo dos grandes, 1750-1832* (1997); *Elites e poderes: entre o antigo regime e a revolução liberal* (2003).

JOÃO PINHARANDA is a lecturer of modern art at IADE, Lisbon, and an art critic for the daily newspaper, *Público*. He holds a Masters in art history from the New University of Lisbon, and has written extensively on Portuguese contemporary art. He is co-author of *Arte portuguesa contemporânea* (1986), and *Alguns corpos: imagens da arte portuguesa entre 1950 e 1990* (1998).

ANTÓNIO COSTA PINTO is a Senior Fellow at Lisbon University's Institute of Social Science and Professor of Modern European History and Politics at ISCTE, Lisbon. He holds a Ph.D. from the European University Institute, Florence. He has been a Visiting Professor at Stanford University (1993), and a Senior Visiting Fellow at Princeton University (1996) and at the University of California, Berkeley (2000). He is the author of *The Blue Shirts* (2000), and recently co-edited *Southern Europe and the making of the European Union* (2002); *Who governs Southern Europe? Regime change and ministerial recruitment* (2003); *The last empire: thirty years of Portuguese decolonization* (2003).

JOÃO CAMILO DOS SANTOS is a Professor of Portuguese and Brazilian Literature at the University of California-Santa Barbara, where he is the Director of the Center of Portuguese Literature and of the Journal *Santa Barbara Portuguese Studies*. He holds a *Doctorat D'État* from the University of Rennes, France. He has published numerous articles and books, including *Carlos de Oliveira et le Roman* (1987); *Os malefícios da literatura, do amor e da civilização: ensaios sobre Camilo Castelo Branco* (1992); *Nunca mais se apagam as imagens* (1996); *A ambição sublime* (2002).

NUNO SEVERIANO TEIXEIRA is a Professor of International Relations and Director of the Portuguese Institute of International Relations at the New University of Lisbon. He holds a Ph. D. from the European University Institute, Florence. He has been a Visiting Professor at Georgetown University and, from 2000 to 2002, was Portugal's minister of home affairs. He has published extensively on Portuguese foreign policy and on military history, including: *L'entrée du Portugal dans la Grande Guerre: objectifs nationaux et stratégies politiques* (1998). He recently co-edited *Southern Europe and the making of the European Union* (2002).

Index

Abelaira, Augusto: 247-55
Acção Escolar Vanguarda (AEV).
    See SCHOOL ACTION VANGUARD
Action Française: 9
Additional Protocol:
    Iberian Pact (1940), 104;
    European Association Agreement
    (1972), 115
Africa:
    African nationalism, 81;
    Anglo-Portuguese Treaty (1891), 88;
    Berlin Conference (1885), 64, 87;
    British Ultimatum (1890), 52, 64, 87;
    Brito Camacho, 69;
    Cold War, 81;
    colonial wars, 58, 80-1, 115;
    colonialism, 10-14, 55-8, 63-6, 70-111,
        141;
    decolonization, 80, 111-5;
    economy and trade, 44, 63, 75-6, 83;
    liberation movements, 82, 110;
    Luso-South African Convention
        (1909), 69;
    migration, 58, 154-61;
    Organic Statute for Portuguese
        Catholic Missions, 71;
    Países Africanos de Língua Oficial
        Portuguesa (PALOP), 116;
    Paiva Couceiro, 9;
    Portuguese military presence, 64;

    post-colonial relationship with
        Portugal, 60, 116;
    'Scramble' for, 52-4, 70, 83-91;
    World War I, 10, 66, 98-9;
    World War II, 104
Afro-Asian and Non-Aligned Move-
    ment: 109
After Modernism: 285-7
Águia: 236, 268
Aguiar, João: 255
Air Transported Brigade: 115
Albania: 114
Albuquerque, Mendes: 289
Albuquerque, Mouzinho de: 65, 268
Alegre, Manuel: 262
Alexandre, António Franco: 262
Alface: 255
Alfonso XIII: 88-96
Algeciras Conference: 90
Almada: 283, 293
Almeida, António José de: 14
Almeida, Bernardo Pinto de: 289
Almeida, Helena: 283
Almeida, Leopoldo de: 276
Alvarez, Domingos: 272
Alves, Valente: 290
Amadeo Souza-Cardoso Prize: 274
Amaral, Ana Luísa: 263
Amaral, Fernando Pinto do: 262
Andrade, Eugénio de: 257-61

Andrade, Freire de: 65
Anglo-German Agreements
  (1912/1913): 97
Anglo-Portuguese Alliance: 10, 29, 92-4
Anglo-Portuguese Treaties
  (1642/1661): 92
Anglo-Portuguese Treaty (1810): 86
Angola: 2, 138,
  Bakongo Revolt (1913-15), 65;
  British Ultimatum (1890), 2, 52, 64, 87;
  colonial war, 77-82, 110-1, 160;
  Congo Insurrection (1961), 80;
  economy and trade, 67-77;
  extent, 64;
  League of Nations, 67;
  Luanda (primitivism in art), 277;
  Luanda Uprising (1961), 80;
  migration, 68, 76, 160-1;
  Norton de Matos, 67-8;
  Ovimbundo Revolt (1902), 65-6;
  Political, Civil and Criminal Statute
  (1926), 71
Anticlericalism: 8-9
Antunes, António Lobo: 253
Antunes, Ernesto Melo: 113
Apollinaire, Guillaume: 269
Arbitration Treaty.
  See TREATY OF WINDSOR
Areal, António: 278-80, 286
Armed forces: 3, 9-10, 17-29, 82, 103,
  113-7, 160-77
Armed Forces Movement (MFA): 133
Arp, Juan: 272
Arte Povera: 276-7, 284
Arte Pública: 293
ArtStrike: 293
Assis, Machado de: 232
Associação Internacional de Críticos
  de Arte (AICA): 285
Association of American Painters and
  Sculptors: 265
Athena: 240
Australia: 185
Austria: 31-3, 42, 169, 186

Azores: 61, 105-7, 115, 188;
  Lajes Agreements, 81, 90, 95, 105-7, 115

Bacon, Francis: 278
Bakongo Revolt.
  See ANGOLA
Baptista, António Alçada: 255
Baptista, Manuel: 379, 283
Barreno, Maria Isabel: 262
Barrias, José: 283
Batarda, Eduardo: 278, 283, 291
Beja: 186, 293
Belgium: 30, 100, 164, 186, 291;
  Europália, 294
Belo, Ruy: 257-8, 261
Berlin Conference (1885): 64, 86-7
Berlin Treaty: 88
Bertholo, René: 279
Biberstein, Michael: 291
Blaufuks: 290
Bloco de Esquerda (Left Bloc).
  See POLITICAL PARTIES
Boer War: 89
Bolama Bay.
  See GUINEA-BISSAU
Botelho, Fernanda: 263
Botelho, Manuel: 290
Braga: 21, 166
Braga, Maria Ondina: 263
Braga, Teófilo: 53
Bragança, Nuno: 255
Brandão, Fiama Hasse Pais: 263
Brandão, Raul: 237-8
Braque, Georges: 265
Bravo, Joaquim: 280, 290-1
Brazil: 30, 51, 63, 67, 100-1, 110;
  independence, 1, 51, 63;
  Juscelino Kubitchek, 109;
  migration, 139, 144-7, 160, 164;
  recognizes First Republic, 94;
  remittances, 50, 124
Breyner, Sophia de Mello: 257-62
Britain.
  See UNITED KINGDOM

British Ultimatum (1890): 1, 52-5, 86-93.
See also PINK MAP
Burmester, Gerardo: 289
Burroughs, William: 280
Butler, Reg: 276

Cabeçadas, Mendes: 21
Caeiro, Alberto: 241-2, 257, 261
Caetano, Marcello: 22, 43-5, 82, 161,
170, 281
Calapez, Pedro: 287-90
Caldas da Rainha: 283
Caldas, Manuel Castro: 290
Calder, Alexander: 272
Calhau, Fernando: 283, 286
Calouste Gulbenkian Foundation
(FCG): 267, 277-8, 286-7;
Colóquio Artes, 285
Camacho, Manuel Brito: 14, 69
Camões, Luís: 53, 228-43
Campos, Álvaro de: 241, 258, 261
Campos, António: 290
Campos, Luís: 290
Canada: 107, 144, 146, 160
Cape Verde: 64, 75
Carbonária.
See FIRST REPUBLIC
Cardoso, Amadeo de Souza: 265-72
Carlos I: 88-93
Carmona, Óscar: 25-8
Carnation Revolution (1974): 46, 59,
82, 113-5, 142, 154, 161-2, 170-84,
193, 248-5, 263, 273, 282-4
Carneiro, Alberto: 278-83, 291
Carneiro, António: 268
Cartagena Agreement (1907): 92-6
Carvalho, Maria Judite de: 263
Carvalho, Mário de: 255
Casas do Povo.
See NEW STATE
Casqueiro, Pedro, 288
Castelo Branco, Camilo: 228-32, 237
Castilho, Paulo: 255
Castro, Ferreira de: 244-5

Castro, Lourdes: 279
Catholic Center Party (PCC).
See POLITICAL PARTIES
Catholic Church: 9-12, 24-41, 56
Cavaco Silva, Aníbal: 214
Centauro: 240
Centeno, Yvette: 263
Centro Cultural de Belém: 294
Centro Democrático Social (CDS).
See POLITICAL PARTIES
Cerejeira, Manuel: 30
Cerveira Bienal (1985): 288
Cesariny de Vasconcelos, Mário: 256,
274, 278
Cézanne, Paul: 265
Chafes, Rui: 289-90
Charrua, António: 279
China: 64, 114
Christian Democracy Academic Cen-
ter (CADC): 30
Christo: 279
Cid, Bartolomeu: 278
CINCIBERLAND.
See NORTH ATLANTIC TREATY ORGA-
NIZATION (NATO)
Coimbra: 166, 283, 293;
University of, 11, 29-30
Coimbra, Leonardo: 236
Cold War: 43-6, 81: 90, 106-8
Colonial Act (1930): 71-9
Colonial Empire and the Overseas
Administrative Reform Act: 72
Colonial Pact: 73-6
Colonial war: 1, 44, 58, 77-81, 160-7,
277
Columbano: 268
Communist Party (PCP).
See POLITICAL PARTIES
Concordat (1940): 41
Confederação Geral do Trabalho (CGT).
See GENERAL LABOUR CONFEDERATION
Congo: 64;
Angolan, 80;
Belgian, 74, 80

Congress of Vienna (1815): 86
Constitution:
   (1911), 4, 12-4;
   (1933), 25-7, 32-3, 40, 141;
   revision (1951), 76-9;
   revision (1971), 82;
   (1976), 61, 142, 162, 181
Constructivism: 289
Contemporânea: 240
Corporatism: 33-4
Correia, Hélia: 263
Cortesão, Jaime: 236-7
Costa Gomes, Luísa: 263
Costa, Afonso: 14
Costa, Eduardo da: 65
Costa, Maria Velho da: 262
Costa, Noronha da: 279
Couceiro, Paiva: 9
Coutinho, Graça Pereira: 290
Critical-realism: 245
Croft, José Pedro: 387-90
Cruz, Gastão: 262
Cubism: 265-73;
   Cubism and Post-Impressionism (1914),
   265
Culturgest: 294
Cunha Leal, Francisco da: 17
Cutileiro, João: 289

Dacosta, António: 263, 274-5, 284, 291
Dada: 269, 289
David, Ilda: 288
Davie, Allan: 291
De Gaulle, Charles: 112
Decolonization: 43-6, 57-60, 82-8, 106-
   14, 164
332 Contemporary Portugal
Delaunay, Robert: 265, 269
Delgado, Humberto: 29, 44
Democracy: 117, 172;
   concerns, 201;
   consolidation, 46, 59, 114-6;
   Europe, 114, 183;
   institutionalization, 46, 178-80;

'mimic', 4;
nationalism, 21;
opposition, 25;
organic, 43;
overthrow, 23;
Salazar's rejection of, 30, 108;
support for, 201;
transition, 45, 55-9, 112-4, 273
Democratic Left: 15
Democratic Party.
   See POLITICAL PARTIES
'Democratization, decolonization,
   development': 113
Dimensionist Manifesto (1935): 272
Dinis, Júlio: 228-34
Dionísio, Eduarda: 263
Dionísio, Mário: 247
Diu.
   See INDIA
Dix, Otto: 272
Doppo Lavoro: 32
Duarte, Afonso: 236
Duchamp, Marcel: 265

Eanes, Ramalho: 192
East Timor: 57, 64, 71, 104
EC.
   See UUROPEAN COMMUNITY
Echevarría, Fernando: 262
Economic development: 2, 99, 194, 225;
   causal factors, 122;
   colonial war, 44;
   colonies, 76, 83;
   Europe, 166, 201;
   fascism, 23;
   industrialization, 142;
   migration, 142;
   phases, 124
Economic intervention: 35, 73
Eddy, A. I.: 265
Education: 161, 182, 197, 202;
   art, 266;
   curriculum, 52, 77;
   demographics, 181;

during New State, 39-42;
efficiency, 172;
employment demographics, 165-6;
expansion, 55, 171-2;
expenditure, 39-44, 173, 295;
higher education, 171;
illiteracy, 171;
private education, 172;
reform, 121-8;
Roman Catholic, 40;
standards, 128;
system, 166-71
EdwardVII: 88
EEC.
    See EUROPEAN ECONOMIC COMMUNITY
EECC.
    See EUROPEAN ECONOMIC COOPERA-
    TION COUNCIL
EFTA.
    See EUROPEAN FREE TRADE ASSOCIATION
Eh Real!: 240
Eisenhower, Dwight: 109
Eisenstein, Segei: 247
Elections: 212;
    abstention, 211-21;
    demanded by the United Kingdom,
        95;
    European Parliament, 203-26;
    'first order', 205, 217;
    incumbency, 221-2;
    polarization, 206-15;
    political parties, 188, 220-4;
    role of president, 199;
    'second-order', 204-6, 220-5;
    system, 183-206;
    voting behavior, 188-222
Elites:
    attitudes, 3-4, 20, 39-42, 50-72, 112;
    contemporary art, 266;
    New State, 38-56
Elizabeth II: 109
Eloy, Mário: 272
Emigration: 142;
    demographics, 46, 54-61, 69, 139-76,
        161-4, 182;
    economics, 45, 142, 153, 162;
    Junta da Emigração, 141;
    'migratory cycle', 155;
    Secretaria de Estado de Emigração,
        143
Empire: 1, 4, 30, 54, 63-6, 77, 82-8, 181;
    'Scramble' for Africa, 64, 70, 83, 91;
    Colonial Act (1930), 71-2;
    crisis of legitimacy, 78-83;
    decolonization, 45-6, 60, 78, 161;
    in Portuguese art, 276;
    symbolism, 2, 56-9, 70-6, 83
Employment:
    agricultural, 160, 169, 175;
    and Europe, 154, 169, 194, 207;
    black economy, 180;
    contracts, 168;
    industrial, 169;
    self-employment, 175;
    services, 169;
    structural changes, 154, 167-9;
    unemployment, 154;
    women, 168-9
EMU.
    See EUROPEAN MONETARY UNION
Enes, António: 65
Entente Cordiale: 89-96
Escada, João Vieira: 279
Escola das Belas Artes: 273, 287
Espanca, Florbela: 238, 263
Estado Novo.
    See NEW STATE
Estatuto do Trabalho Nacional (ETN).
    See NATIONAL LABOR STATUTE
EU.
    See EUROPEAN UNION
Europe:
    decline of Great Powers, 106;
    defense, 107, 210;
    economy, 119-36;
    integration, 112-20, 162, 208;
    Marshall Plan, 112, 140;
    migration, 140-50, 155, 164-9;

reconstruction, 106, 112, 140;
relations with, 102, 106, 111-7
European art: 243, 279
European Common Market: 159
European Community (EC): 59-62,
   116-8, 203-8, 284
European Council: 115
European Economic Community
   (EEC): 59, 77, 112, 132-40, 162
European Economic Cooperation
   Council (EECC): 112
European Election Studies: 203, 211
European Free Trade Association
   (EFTA): 58, 77, 112-7, 121, 132-3,
   159-62
European Monetary Union (EMU):
   209-10
European Parliament: 203-26
European Peoples' Party (EPP).
   See POLITICAL PARTIES
European Socialists (ES).
   See POLITICAL PARTIES
European Union (EU): 46, 61, 116-21,
   132-5, 162, 168-73, 176-82, 203-20,
   225-6
Évora: 166, 186
Exhibitions:
   After Modernism (1983), 285;
   Alternativa Zero (1977), 282;
   Archipelago (1986), 287;
   Armory Show (1913), 265;
   Exhibition of the Portuguese World
      (1940), 57, 72, 273;
   General Arts Exhibition, 274;
   Independent Exhibitions, 274;
   Novos Primitivos (1984), 289;
   Second Exhibition of Plastic Arts
      (1961), 278
Exílio: 240
Expressionism: 235, 269-78, 286

Faria, Almeida: 252-3
Faro: 166, 293
Fascism:

and authoritarianism, 41;
and the Church, 24;
clerico-fascism, 40;
and conservatism, 23;
dictatorships, 43;
emergence of, 19-23;
failure, 19;
and futurism, 38, 271;
and Integralism, 19;
Italian, 16;
and liberalism, 23;
Military Dictatorship, 25;
National-Syndicalism, 20;
New State, 26-42;
paramilitary organization, 43;
youth, 22
Feijó, Álvaro: 247
Feliciano, Paulo: 280, 290-3
Ferreira, Vergílio: 247-55
Ferro, António: 19, 36-8, 270-5
Finland: 186
First Manifesto.
   See SURREALISM
First Republic:
   bienio rosso, 22-4;
   Carbonária, 4;
   coups d'état, 3-9, 13, 17-22, 55, 70;
   fascism, 19-23;
   political instability, 7-15;
   political system, 3-7, 185;
   regime question, 3-32;
   World War I, 7-11, 103
Fonseca, Branquinho da: 244
Fonseca, Manuel da: 247
Fragateiro, Fernanda: 288
França, José Augusto: 274
France: 47-9, 185, 196-9;
   Algeciras Conference (1905), 90;
   Anglo-German Agreement (1912), 97;
   cultural influence, 244, 264-6, 279;
   First Portuguese Republic, 93-4;
   invasion of Portugal, 50, 86;
   migration, 45, 139-64;
   President Loubet, 88;

President MacMahon, 87;
Vichy, 33-7, 105;
World War I, 14, 94-5
Franco, Francisco: 31-2, 40, 103-10;
relations with Salazar, 30, 42, 103-4;
Spanish Civil War, 43, 103
Franco-German Agreement (1911): 96
Franco-Portuguese Convention (1886):
87
Franco-Spanish Agreement (1912): 96
Freyre, Gilberto: 79
Fundação Calouste Gulbenkian (FCG).
See CALOUSTE GULBENKIAN FOUNDA-
TION
Futurism: 19, 38, 268-71;
Futurist Generation, 267

Gaetan: 290
Galleries:
Alda Cortez, 293;
Alvares, 276;
Bois, 294;
Cómicos, 284;
Cooperativa Diferença, 285;
Der Sturm, 265;
Espaço Lusitano, 288;
Graça Fonseca, 293;
III, 279, 284;
Lisbon Modern Art, 286;
Luís Serpa, 284;
Módulo, 284;
Nasoni/Atlântica, 288;
Pedro Oliveira, 288;
Quadrum, 284;
Roma e Pavia, 288;
Valentim de Carvalho, 284;
Zero, 293
Garrett, Almeida: 51, 228-34, 243
Gaugin, Paul: 265
General Labour Confederation (CGT):
15
Generation of 1870: 52, 234
Geometric abstraction: 271-4
German-Soviet Pact: 38

Germany: 54, 97-100, 186, 272;
Africa, 70, 91-8;
Algeciras Conference (1905), 90;
Berlin Conference (1885), 87;
Berlin Treaty, 88;
Haldane Mission, 97;
migration, 139, 144-8, 164;
Nazis, 26, 104;
Partition Agreement (1898), 91;
rapprochement with Portugal, 81-7;
relations with the United Kingdom,
10, 89-97;
Wilhelm II, 88;
World War I, 11;
World War II, 103-5
Gersão, Teolinda: 263
Gleizes, Theodore: 265
Goa.
See INDIA
Gomes da Costa, Manuel: 21
Gomes, Manuel Teixeira: 237
Gomes, Soeiro Pereira: 247
Gonçalves, Olga: 263
Gonçalves, Vasco: 113
Gramido Convention (1847): 86
Grant, Ulysses S., 87
Great Britain.
See UNITED KINGDOM
Greece: 42, 119, 124-5, 169-77, 187, 196
Grosz, George: 272
Guarda Nacional Republicana (GNR).
See NATIONAL REPUBLICAN GUARD
Guimarães: 56
Guimarães, Fernando: 262, 283
Guimarães, José de: 290-1
Guinea-Bissau:
Bolama Bay, 87;
colonial war, 77-82, 111, 160;
economy, 75-7;
extent, 64;
Gulf of Guinea, 69;
independence, 114;
World War I, 66
Guterres, António: 196, 210

Hague Summit (1969): 112
Haldane Mission (1912): 97
Hammarskjold, Dag: 109
Hatherly, Ana: 263
Helder, Herberto: 257-61
Herculano, Alexandre: 51, 228-34
Homeostéticos: 288
Horta, Maria Teresa: 262-3
Humanism: 244-51
Hungary: 31, 42

Iberia: 45, 108-9, 117
Iberian Pact (1939): 103-8
Iberianism: 49-52, 92-3
IBERLAND.
   See NORTH ATLANTIC TREATY ORGA-
   NIZATION (NATO)
Ícaro: 240
Iceland: 187
Independent Army Division: 115
Independent Mixed Brigade: 115
India: 63, 110;
   Damão, Diu and Goa, 64, 78, 110-11,
      161;
   Jawaharlal Nehru, 110
Indian Union:
   See INDIA
Indonesia: 109
Industrial revolution: 82
Industrialization: 2-3, 21, 119, 136, 167, 181
Integralism: 9;
   armed forces, 17-21;
   coups, 19-22;
   fascism, 19;
   literature, 236;
   Marcello Caetano, 22;
   politics, 16-24;
   'second-generation', 22
International Labor Organization
   (ILO): 71
Ireland: 125, 169, 176, 196, 209
Israel: 45, 186
Italy: 283, 291;

Carta del Lavoro, 34;
   colonialism, 70;
   Fascism, 24-6
Japan: 185
Jorge, João Miguel Fernandes: 262
Jorge, Lídia: 263
Jorge, Luísa Neto: 263
Joyce, Patrícia: 263
Júdice, Nuno: 257, 261
Júlio: 272

Kandinsky, Wassily: 272
Klee, Paul: 281
Kubitchek, Juscelino: 109
KWY Group: 279

Labor, Ministry of: 154
Lacerda, Alberto de: 262
Lagos: 278, 280, 293
Lajes.
   See AZORES
Lanhas, Fernando: 274-5
Lapa, Álvaro: 280, 283, 291
Laranjeiro, Manuel: 268
Law of Separation of Church and State
   (1911): 95
League of Nations: 67;
   colonialism, 67, 72, 100;
   Executive Committee, 100;
   Financial Commission, 101;
   Native Labor Code (1928), 71;
   Permanent Commission of
      Mandates, 100;
   Portugal, 100-1
Left Bloc.
   See POLITICAL PARTIES
Legião Portuguesa (LP).
   See PORTUGUESE LEGION
Legitimacy:
   First Republic, 21, 99;
   colonialism, 57;
   constitutional monarchy, 267;
   Europe, 225;
   national institutions, 225

Leiria, Mário Henrique: 255-6
Leitão, Rui: 278
Lemos, Ester de: 263
Lemos, Fernando: 276
Liberalism: 52, 230-1;
  alternatives to, 22-4;
  communism and socialism, 21;
  cultural resonance, 51, 228-34;
  ideology, 1-4, 20, 51-5, 86, 229-35,
    246, 255;
  Integralism, 20-1;
  liberal elites, 39;
  neo-realism, 246;
  New State and Salazarism, 25-30,
    40-1, 56;
  overthrow, 22-6, 42;
  politics, 3-9, 51-5, 231-6, 257;
  regime, 5, 19-30, 51-4, 230, 240;
  rejection of, 23
Liberal professions: 35, 175
Liberal Revolution (1820-1834): 48,
    229, 235-6
Liberalization: 44-5, 284;
  economic, 60-78, 160;
  political, 161, 281
Lima, Marta de: 263
Linz, Juan J.: 22, 31
Lisboa, António Maria: 256
Lisboa, Irene: 245, 263
Lisbon: 3;
  coups and riots, 11-13;
  Cultural Capital of Europe (1994), 294;
  exhibitions, 57, 274, 293;
  galleries, 268, 276-9, 284, 293-4;
  industry, 142;
  migration, 148, 166;
  murals, 272;
  museums, 293-4;
  visit of British fleet (1900), 89
Lisbon National Library Group: 236
Lisbon-London-Madrid triangle: 101-2
Literature and art:
  existentialist, 252;
  feminist, 262-3, 292;

modernist, 228-42;
  neo-realist, 243-51;
  progressivist, 228;
  realist, 250;
  surrealist, 256;
  visual arts, 266
Lithuania: 42
Llansol, Maria Gabriela: 263
London: 277-8, 287
London Commission for Non-Inter-
    vention in the Spanish Civil War: 103
Lopes, Adília: 263
Lose, Ilse: 263
Loubet, Emile François: 88-9
Lourenço Marques.
  See MOZAMBIQUE
Lourenço, Eduardo: 244, 255-6
Luanda.
  See ANGOLA
Luís, Agustina Bessa: 247-51
Lusitanian Nationalism: 19
Lusitanismo.
  See INTEGRALISM
Luso-American Development Founda-
    tion (FLAD): 287, 290, 294
Luso-Brazilian Community: 109
Luso-German Convention (1886): 87
Luso-Spanish Treaty of Friendship and
    Non-Agression (1939) (Iberian
    Pact): 103-8
Lusotropicalismo.
  See FREYRE, GILBERTO
Luxembourg: 139, 164, 169, 186

Maastricht Treaty: 204-11
Macao: 64, 101, 104, 238
Macedo, Helder: 225
MacMahon, Duc de Magenta: 87
Madeira: 61, 90, 147, 188
Magalhães, André: 293
Magalhães, Joaquim Manuel: 262
Malhoa, José: 268
Mallarmé: 256
Mangold, Robert: 281

Manuel II: 49
Mapa Cor-de-rosa,
    See PINK MAP
Margarido, Alfredo: 256
Marshall Plan: 106, 112, 140
Martins, Costa: 276
Martins, Jorge: 279
Massis, Henry: 41
Mateus, Cristina: 293
Matisse, Henri: 265
Matos, Norton de: 68-70
Maya, Canto da: 276
Melo, Alexandre: 285
Melo, João de: 255
Mendes, Luís Filipe Castro: 262
Mendes, Paulo: 293
MFA.
    See ARMED FORCES MOVEMENT
Miguéis, José Rodrigues: 245
Military coup:
    (1915), 7;
    (1925), 19;
    (1926), 17-22, 70;
    (1961), 80;
    (1974), 46, 59, 82, 113-5, 142, 161,
        178-84, 248-55, 263
Military Dictatorship: 17-30
Miró, Joan: 272
Mocidade Portuguesa (MP).
    See PORTUGUESE YOUTH
Modernism:
    in literature, 228-61;
    in visual arts, 265-86;
    Orpheu, 239, 261
Modigliani, Amadeu: 269
Molder, Jorge: 290, 294
Moniz, Botelho: 111
Monteiro, Adolfo Casais: 244
Monteiro, Domingos: 245
Monteiro, Manuel: 209
Moore, Sir Henry: 276
Moreira, Adriano: 208
Motherwell, Robert: 280
Moura, Leonel: 283, 287, 292

Moura, Vasco Graça: 262
Movement for the Defense of the
    Colonies: 70
Movimento das Forças Armadas (MFA).
    See ARMED FORCES MOVEMENT
Mozambique: 101;
    British Ultimatum (1890), 2, 52, 64, 87;
    Colonial Act (1930), 72;
    colonial war, 77-82, 111, 160;
    Delagoa Bay, 69;
    economy and development, 69-77;
    extent, 64;
    Great Powers, 67-70;
    Kingdom of Gaza Campaign (1895),
        65-6;
    Lourenço Marques Bay dispute, 87;
    Lourenço Marques Railway, 69, 92;
    migration, 76, 160-1;
    Mozambique Company, 69;
    Niassa Company, 69;
    Political, Civil and Criminal Statute
        (1926), 71;
    World War I, 66
Munch, Eduard: 235
Museu do Chiado: 294
Museum of Modern Art (Sintra): 294
Museum of Natural History: 293

Nacionalismo Lusitano (NL).
    See LUSITANIAN NATIONALISM
Namora, Fernando: 247
National Assembly: 29-33
National Foundation for Joy at Work
    (FNAT): 35
National Health Service: 171
National Information Secretariat
    (SNI): 43, 271-5
National Institute of Labor and Welfare
    (INPT): 34
National Labor Statute (ETN) (1933): 34
National Modern Art Museum: 288
National Propaganda Secretariat
    (SPN): 38-43, 56, 271
National Republican Guard (GNR): 14-8

National Syndicalism: 20-2, 36-7
Nationalism: 51-2, 61, 292;
  African, 81;
  anti-British, 2-4, 51-4, 93;
  anti-French, 50;
  cultural, 51;
  economic, 44;
  imperial, 2, 52-9, 83-8;
  New State, 29, 55-7;
  political, 48-54;
  radical, 12;
  reactionary, 20
Nationalist Party.
  See POLITICAL PARTIES
Native Labor Code (1928): 71-4
NATO.
  See NORTH ATLANTIC TREATY ORGA-
  NIZATION
Nava, Luís Muguel: 262
Negreiros, Almada: 239, 268-72, 286
Nehru, Jawaharlal: 110
Nemésio, Vitorino: 245
Neo-colonialism: 207
Neo-Garretism: 236
Neo-realism: 235-54, 262, 274-5, 282
Neo-romanticism: 287
Nepal: 109
Netherlands: 142, 164, 169, 186
New State: 10, 27-8, 271;
  1933 Constitution, 25-6, 32;
  armed forces, 28; arts, 271;
  Casas do Povo, 35;
  Catholic Action, 40-1;
  grémios, 35;
  National Labor Statute (ETN), 34;
  National Union, 31-3;
  nationalism, 55;
  political system, 10-26-33
Niassa Company.
  See MOZAMBIQUE
Nobre, António: 229, 235-41, 250
Nóbrega, Isabel da: 263
North Atlantic Treaty Organization
  (NATO) (1949): 106-9, 112-6:

anticommunism, 275;
  CINCIBERLAND, 115;
  colonial wars, 110-5;
  IBERLAND, 115;
  Portugal, 43, 107-9, 118;
  Spain, 117-8;
  United Kingdom, 108
Norway: 106-7
Nozolino, Paulo: 290
Nuno Álvares Crusade: 16

O Independente: 292
O'Neill, Alexandre: 256
OECD.
  See ORGANIZATION FOR ECONOMIC
  COOPERATION AND DEVELOPMENT
Oil crises (1973-1974): 141, 155, 164
Oliveira, Carlos de: 246-53, 261
Oporto: 5, 270-2, 283-94;
  cultural centers, 286, 293-4;
  exhibitions, 274;
  Jornadas de Arte Contemporânea, 293;
  Monarchy of the North, 12-7;
  the Oporto Group, 281
Organic Bases of the Colonial Admin-
  istration (1926): 70
Organic Charter of the Portuguese
  Colonial Empire: 72
Organic Overseas Law (1953): 79
Organic Statute for the Portuguese
  Catholic Missions in Africa (1926): 70
Organization for Economic Coopera-
  tion and Development (OECD):
  154, 201
Organizations of Economic Coordina-
  tion: 35
Ornelas, Aires de: 65
Orpheu: 233, 239, 244, 268-70
'Os Verdes' (Partido Ecologista) (PEV).
  See POLITICAL PARTIES
Osório, António: 262
Overseas Administrative Reform Act: 72
Ovimbundu.
  See ANGOLA

Pacheco, Luis: 253-6
Pais, Sidónio: 10, 31;
  1911 Constitution, 12;
  assassinated, 12;
  Catholic Center Party, 9;
  collapse of regime, 13;
  December 1917 coup, 8-12;
  Integralism, 21;
  legacy, 17;
  political system, 12-4;
  regime question, 24;
  Unionist Party, 11
Paises Africanos de Língua Oficial Portuguesa (PALOP): 116
Pakistan: 109
Palla, Vítor: 276
Paulo, António: 279
Parliament: 2-21, 27-33, 88, 162, 177-99, 270
Parnassians: 256
Partido Comunista Português (PCP) (Portuguese Communist Party).
  See POLITICAL PARTIES
Partido do Centro Católico (PCC) (Catholic Center Party).
  See POLITICAL PARTIES
Partido Popular (PP) (Popular Party).
  See POLITICAL PARTIES
Partido Popular Democrático (PPD) (Popular Democratic Party).
  See POLITICAL PARTIES
Partido Renovador Democrático (PRD) (Democratic Renewal Party).
  See POLITICAL PARTIES
Partido Social Democrata (PSD) (Social Democratic Party).
  See POLITICAL PARTIES
Partido Socialista (PS) (Socialist Party).
  See POLITICAL PARTIES
Patuleia civil war (1847): 86.
  See also GRAMIDO CONVENTION
Paul VI: 111

Pedreira, Maria do Rosário: 263
Pedro, Alvim: 262
Pedro, António: 256, 272-4, 286
Penalva, João: 290, 294
Peninsular Pact.
  See IBERIAN PACT
Pereira, Fernando José: 293
Pereira, Pedro Teotónio: 34
Peru: 109
Pessanha, Camilo: 235-41, 258
Pessoa, Fernando: 228, 236-44, 251, 257-61, 268, 292
Picabia, Francis: 272
Pimenta de Castro: 7
Pimenta, Alberto: 262
Pinheiro, Costa: 279
Pinheiro, Jorge: 281
Pink Map: 2, 52, 64, 87-8
Pinto, Cerveira: 283-92
Pintor, Santa Rita: 239
Pious XII: 41
Pires, José Cardoso: 247-8, 254
Pires, Lucas: 214, 223
Poland: 31, 42, 103
Political parties:
  Catholic Center Party (PCC), 9, 24, 30;
  Communist Party (PCP), 14, 26, 59, 183, 190-3, 202, 207-14, 223;
  Democratic Party, 4-24;
  Democratic Renewal Party (PRD), 192, 207-8, 213-4;
  Democratic Unity Coalition (CDU), 214, 223;
  European Democratic Alliance (EDA), 209;
  European Peoples' Party (EPP), 207-9, 215;
  European Socialists (ES), 207, 215;
  Evolutionist Party, 5-14;
  Left Bloc, 202;
  Liberal Party, 14;
  Lusitanian Nationalism (NL), 19;
  National Republican Party (PNR), 12, 31;

National Union (UN), 25-40, 184-6;
Nationalist Party, 17;
Popular Democratic Party (PPD),
190;
Popular Party (PP), 190, 200-2, 209-14, 222-3;
Republican Party (PRP), 3-6, 93;
Sidónio Pais Center Party, 19;
Social Democratic Center (CDS),
191, 196, 200-2, 207-14, 222-5;
Social Democratic Party (PSD), 190-202, 207-22;
Socialist Party (PS), 7, 190-215, 221-2;
The Greens (PEV), 223;
Union of Economic Interests (UIE), 15
Unionist Party, 5-14
Political system:
colonial, 79;
democratic, 162, 202;
European, 204;
First Republic, 7-24, 54-5;
in literature, 231;
'mimic' democracy, 4;
New State, 10, 29-42
Pomar, Alexandre: 285
Pomar, Júlio: 274-5, 284
Pontes, Maria de Lourdes Belchior: 263
Portalegre: 186
Portinari, Cândido: 274
Portugal and the Future.
See SPÍNOLA, ANTÓNIO DE
Portugal Futurista: 240
Portugal, Pedro: 288
Portugal: 26;
anticlericalism, 9, 95;
authoritarianism, 34, 55-7, 102;
Church, 9, 40-1, 177;
colonialism, 1, 44-113; 160-1;
culture, 51, 159;
decolonization, 58-60, 110-4, 161;
democracy, 46, 59-60, 177-83, 255;
economy, 44-5, 60, 69-92, 121-37,
152-76;
education, 128, 171-7;

foreign policy, 2, 55, 85-101, 109, 117;
migration, 45, 139-64;
modernism, 228-43, 261, 271-3, 291;
nationalism and national identity, 2,
39, 47-63, 83, 255, 268;
NATO, 115-8;
politics, 4, 52, 59, 70, 183-225;
relations with Brazil, 110;
relations with Europe, 60, 116-7,
203-12, 225, 281;
relations with France, 96-8;
relations with Germany, 86-98;
relations with Spain, 96, 100-10;
relations with the United Kingdom,
10, 29, 86-110;
relations with the United States,
106-11;
World War I, 10-11, 54, 98-100;
World War II, 103-5
Portuguese Economic Space: 77-82
Portuguese Expeditionary Corps
(CEP): 10
Portuguese Legion (LP): 36-43
Portuguese Youth (MP): 32-40
Presença: 239-46
Preto, Rolão: 19, 24, 34-6
Primo de Rivera, Miguel: 16, 31
Proença, Pedro: 288-90
Proença, Raul: 237

Quadros, Jânio: 111
Quadruple Alliance: 86
Quatro Vintes: 281
Queirós, Eça de: 228-44
Quental, Antero de: 228-38, 268

Rauschenberg, Robert: 279
Realism: 234-57
Reconstituintes: 15
'Red Legion': 15
Redol, Alves: 246-7, 274
Regime question: 9-24, 94
Régio, José: 244
Rego, Paula: 277-91

Reis, Cabrita: 280, 287-94
Reis, Ricardo: 241, 261, 268
Reis, Soares dos: 268
Renascença Portuguesa: 236
Renoir, Pierre-Auguste: 265
Revista Portuguesa: 240
Rhodes, Cecil: 66
Ribeiro, Aquilino: 237
Ribeiro, Bernardim: 238
Rocha.
    See NEGREIROS, ALMADA
Rocha, Miguel Ângelo: 290-3
Rodrigo, Joaquim: 277-80, 291
Rodrigues, Urbano Tavares: 247-9
Romania: 4, 165
Romanticism: 232-7, 251, 289
Rosa, António Ramos: 257-60
Rosa, Manuel: 288-9
Rosada, António Campos: 289
Rosado, Pedro: 289-90
Ross, Edward: 70
Russia: 165

Sá-Carneiro, Mário de: 228-30, 236,
    239-43, 251, 257-60, 268
Salazar, António de Oliveira: 9, 24-9,
    55, 270;
    anticommunism 36;
    armed forces, 28;
    background, 29;
    career, 22-30, 101;
    colonial war, 44-57, 159;
    colonialism, 71-3, 102-11;
    coups, 29, 44, 80;
    decolonization, 110;
    economy, 124, 159;
    fascism, 36;
    First Republic, 106-9;
    foreign policy, 102-12;
    Marcello Caetano, 22, 43, 82, 161;
    Marshall Plan, 106;
    National Union (UN), 32-3;
    politics, 24-41, 56, 101-5;
    relations with Spain, 30-6, 102-3;
    relations with the United Kingdom,
        29;
    World War II, 29, 43, 103-5
Salazarism: 244-6;
    anticommunism, 43;
    armed forces, 28;
    Church, 40;
    coups, 111;
    fascistization, 36;
    ideology, 26-9, 39-42, 57;
    longevity, 42, 55;
    origins, 24;
    political elite, 33;
    political system, 33, 55
Sampaio, Jorge: 200
Sanches, Rui: 287-90
Santa-Rita, Guilherme: 268
Santos Costa: 29
Santos, Maria: 214
Santos, Pobílio Gomes dos: 247
São Tomé and Príncipe: 64, 75
Saramago, José: 253-4
Sarmento, Julião: 283-94
Sartori, Giovanni: 31
Saudosismo: 236
School Action Vanguard (AEV): 36
Seara Nova: 236
Second Exhibition of Plastic Arts: 278
Second School of Paris: 272
Second Treaty of Windsor (1904): 89
Secretariado de Propaganda Nacional (SPN).
    See NATIONAL PROPAGANDA SECRE-
    TARIAT
Secretariado Nacional de Informação (SNI).
    See NATIONAL INFORMATION SECRE-
    TARIAT
Selassie, Haile: 190
Sena Sugar Estate: 69
Sena, António de: 278, 283
Sena, Jorge de: 247-56, 261
Senegal: 64
Sérgio, António: 236-7
Serpa, Luís: 287
Serra, Rui: 293

Seurat, Georges: 265
Silva Ramos, Manuel de: 255
Silva, Augusto Alves da: 290
Silva, Maria Helena Vieira da: 272-5
Silva, Marmelo e: 247-50
Silva, Sena da: 276
Simões, João Gaspar: 244
Single European Act (SEA): 116, 204
Skapinakis, Nikias: 279
Slade School of Art: 278
Soares, Bernardo: 241
Soares, Mário: 200
Soares, Miguel: 293
Social Darwinism: 65
Socialist Party (PS).
    See POLITICAL PARTIES
Sociedade Nacional de Belas Artes
    (SNBA): 273-7, 285-7
Sousa, Américo Guerreiro de: 255
Sousa, Ângelo: 278
Sousa, Ernesto: 282-5
Sousa Ernesto Foundation: 290
South Africa: 69-70, 100, 160, 239
Soviet Union: 43, 104-8, 114, 291
Spain: 47, 85, 169-87;
    Alfonso XIII, 88, 96;
    authoritarianism, 33, 102;
    Civil War, 26-37, 101-3, 273;
    democratization, 60, 117;
    economy, 45, 119, 124-7;
    Europe, 60, 117-8;
    General Franco, 30, 105;
    Iberian Pact, 103-5;
    Iberianism, 49, 63, 93-102;
    League of Nations, 100;
    NATO, 108-9, 117;
    Miguel Primo de Rivera, 16, 31;
    relations with France, 96;
    relations with India, 110;
    relations with Portugal, 60, 89-99;
    relations with the United Kingdom,
        92-8;
    Second Republic, 26, 36, 102;
    strategic importance, 108;

UN, 109;
World War II, 104-8
Spínola, António de: 113
Sttau Monteiro, Luís de: 255
Sudoeste: 240
Suffrage: 4-5, 12-4, 20, 27, 82, 162
Sukarno: 109
Surrealism: 256, 271-80;
    First Manifesto (1924): 270
Sweden: 186
Symbolism: 36, 235, 251-8, 265-8

Támen, Pedro: 262
Teixeira, Paulo: 262
Thailand: 109
The 'Three Marias': 262
Timor.
    See EAST TIMOR
Torga, Miguel: 237, 244
Torres Vedras: 283
Torres, Alexandre Pinheiro: 247
Treaty of Accession (1985): 116
Treaty of Amsterdam (1999): 204
Treaty of Brussels (1948): 107
Treaty of Rome (1957): 112
Treaty of Versailles (1919): 99
Treaty of Windsor (1904): 89, 92
Tribunal of the Holy Offices of the
    Inquisition: 49
Tropa, Francisco: 293
Tudela, Pedro: 289
Twombly, Cy: 278

Ukraine: 165
Unamuno, Miguel: 268
Union of Economic Interests (UIE).
    See POLITICAL PARTIES
Unionist Party.
    See POLITICAL PARTIES
United Kingdom: 47, 106, 196;
    Algeciras Conference (1905), 90;
    Anglo-Portuguese Alliance, 29, 94-8;
    Anglo-Portuguese Treaty (1810), 86;
    Berlin Conference (1885), 86-8;

British Ultimatum (1890), 1-2, 52, 86-7;
Cartagena Agreement (1907), 92;
Congress of Vienna (1815), 86;
Edward VII, 88-90;
EFTA, 112;
Elizabeth II, 109;
Treaty of Rome (1957), 112, 208;
NATO, 108;
Partition Agreement (1898), 91;
Portugal's colonial wars, 93-104, 111;
relations with France, 94-5;
relations with Germany, 10, 89-97;
relations with Portugal, 1, 10, 43, 50-4, 86-110;
relations with Spain, 89-93;
Second Anglo-Portuguese Treaty (1891), 88;
Secret Declaration (1899), 90;
Treaty of Windsor (1904), 90;
World War I, 10;
World War II, 98
United Nations (UN): 43, 109-11
United States: 107;
Lajes Agreements, 81-90, 106, 115;
migration, 139-47, 160;
NATO, 106-12;
Portugal's colonial wars, 81-111;
President Eisenhower, 109;
President Grant, 87;
relations with Portugal, 94, 108-11;
Treaty of Brussels (1948), 107
Urbanization: 2, 20, 58-61, 166
Urban-rural divide: 9, 22

Vatican.
See CATHOLIC CHURCH
Venice Biennale: 286, 290, 294
Verde, Cesário: 228-42, 250, 257
Verlaine, Paul: 238
Vértice: 274
Viana, Eduardo: 269
Vidigal, Ana: 288
Vieira, João: 278, 286

Vieira, Jorge: 276
Vieira, Pedro Sousa: 290
Vila Nova de Cerveira Biennial: 282
Vila Velha de Ródão, 293
Viseu: 166
Voss, Ian: 279

Western European Union (WEU): 117-8
Wilhelm II: 88
Women:
earnings, 176;
economy, 165-7;
education, 165;
employment, 165-8;
literature, 262-3;
social status, 28, 229, 245
World War I: 7, 10, 269;
economic effects, 76, 119-23;
Germany, 97;
Portugal's involvement, 10-13, 54, 97-9;
Portuguese colonies, 78;
United Kingdom, 10, 97
World War II: 273;
economic effects, 75, 119-24;
migration, 139-45;
Portuguese neutrality, 28-9, 43, 104-5

Xana: 280, 288-90
Xavier, Caldas: 65
XX Dessins: 269

Yugoslavia: 119, 165

Zambezi Campaign (1869): 64
Zambezi River: 69